PAUL & the GNOSTICS

PAUL & the GNOSTICS

Walter Schmithals

Translated by
John E. Steely

Nashville ABINGDON PRESS New York

PAUL AND THE GNOSTICS

Originally published as *Paulus und die Gnostiker.*

Copyright © 1972 by Abingdon Press
Translation from the German language with the approval
of Herbert Reich Evangelischer Verlag, Hamburg. Copyright © 1965, Herbert Reich Evangelischer Verlag, Hamburg.

ISBN: 0-687-30492-x

Library of Congress Catalog Card Number: 70-175130

SET UP, PRINTED, AND BOUND BY THE
PARTHENON PRESS, AT NASHVILLE,
TENNESSEE, UNITED STATES OF AMERICA

To the Memory of
my Father
(died Sept. 20, 1958)
1 Peter 1:13 Blessed be the God and Father of
our Lord Jesus Christ! By his great
mercy we have been born ~~again~~ anew
to a living hope through the resurrection
and   of Jesus Christ from the dead.

my Mother
(died Sept. 1, 1961)
Psalm 31:16
Let thy face shine on thy servant;
save me in thy steadfast love!

46051

Translator's Preface

The stimulus provided for New Testament studies by the work of Professor Schmithals is well known. It is a pleasure to have a part in bringing that work within the reach of a wider audience. The task has been made easier by the author's own generous encouragement and by his helpful response to inquiries. The changes and additions which he has supplied for this translation make it a revised edition which, therefore, will not correspond at every point with the German edition of 1965.

The Southeastern Seminary Alumni Fund provided help with the costs of preparing the typescript for publication. A special word of thanks must go to Mrs. Norma Owens Hash for her diligent and skillful work in typing the work from a handwritten copy, and to my family for their unfailing help and interest in this undertaking.

John E. Steely
Wake Forest, North Carolina

Foreword

The estimate of the relations between parties in primitive Christianity still stands today under the impact of the studies of F. C. Baur.

The essays presented here, in continuation of my work on *Die Gnosis in Korinth* (FRLANT 66 [1969, 3rd ed.]; cited in the following as Vol. 1; English translation as *Gnosticism in Corinth,* trans. John E. Steely, Abingdon Press, 1971), run counter to the dominant trend in modern study and go back to F. C. Baur to the extent that they, like Baur, are able to perceive only *one* decisive contrast in primitive Christianity. On the other hand, they represent a radical break with Baur's thesis, which likewise is still influential today, that this was the contrast between Pauline and Judaistic Christianity.

The first four essays concern themselves with Paul's opponents in various communities that had been established by him. The fifth essay makes use in a comprehensive way of the insights gained therein as well as in *Die Gnosis in Korinth* for introductory questions relating to the Corpus Paulinum.

Insofar as the essays have already appeared earlier in print, they have been revised, in parts significantly.

The present study finds its continuation in my work on *Paulus und Jakobus* (FRLANT 85 [1963]; English translation as *Paul and James,* trans. Dorothea M. Barton, SBT 46 [1965]; cited in the following as Vol. 3).

My thanks must be expressed above all to the Theological Faculty of the Philipps-Universität of Marburg, who accepted the present essays together with the above-mentioned work on *Paul and James* as *Habilitationsschrift.*

Contents

I

The Heretics in Galatia[1]

I

At first glance, at least, it appears to be a rather foolish and, even more, an unpromising undertaking, with the wealth which is afforded us in this book, to occupy ourselves with the heretics in Galatia. There are few problems in the realm of New Testament introduction in which the scholars of all eras are so unanimously and indisputably of *one* mind as here.

The heretics in Galatia are Judaizers, that is, Christians who demand the observance of the Jewish law on a greater or lesser scale, but in any case including circumcision: thus they are Christians in whose opinion membership in the eschatological community of the Messiah who has appeared in Jesus depends upon membership in the national cultic union, constituted through the rite of circumcision, of the ancient people of the covenant. This thesis is the presupposition of the exegesis of the Galatian epistle in the commentaries, not its conclusion; and it can be such a presupposition because no one would deny it.[2] Paul's battle against circumcision apparently so little admits of another interpretation that, so far as I know, no one has yet attempted to dispute the appearance of Judaizers in Galatia.

---

[1] The following essay is a greatly expanded version of a *Promotionsvorlesung* which was delivered on May 12, 1955, before the Theological Faculty of the University of Marburg. First published in ZNW 47 (1956) : 25-67. The present version has been revised.

[2] W. Bousset, in *Die Schriften des Neuen Testaments*, II (1908, 2nd ed.) : 29, e.g., begins his remarks on "the occasion and aim of the epistle" thus: "Judaistic opponents of Paul had invaded the Galatian communities," and he continues: "Paul treats these people with the greatest scorn." Thus it apparently is unnecessary to justify the assertion of the judaizing opposition to Paul or to defend it against other theses.

Hence in an investigation of Paul's Galatian opponents it seems to be possible only to concern oneself with the question of the "more or less" in their observance of the law—and with the question as to their origin, and thus with fitting this Galatian movement into the phenomena of primitive Christianity known to us in general.

The first question—how far does the Galatian legalism go?— is answered by the introductions to the New Testament and in the commentaries with a simple compilation of Paul's polemical statements which are relevant and instructive for the question, and this then leaves to the imagination of the exegetes a great deal of room which naturally is difficult to control.

The second question is more difficult. Who stands back of this movement? It appears to me that the attempts to identify the "pillars" in Jerusalem—that is, James, Peter, and John; or one of these; or others from their circle; but in any case participants with Paul in the so-called apostolic council—either as the immediate or indirect sponsors of the anti-Pauline missionaries in Galatia, or even as these missionaries themselves, are slowly disappearing,[3] and for good reason (see below, pp. 21-24). But then there would come into question, from among the known phenomena of early Christianity, only those "stealthily introduced false brethren" whom Paul mentions in Gal. 2:4 [4]—if indeed they were Christians at all! Then such sayings as Matt. 10:5-6, 23; 5:17 ff. (possibly also Matt. 8:5-10 par.; Mark 7:24-30 par.) : "I am sent only to the lost sheep of the house of Israel" [5] would be native to their circle.

Of course I regard it as more likely that the "false brethren" in Jerusalem were Jews who had not yet been baptized in the name of Jesus.[6]

But if there was not among the Jewish Christians a radical group that went beyond James, it becomes difficult to answer the question

---

[3] With some exceptions, E. Stauffer (*New Testament Theology*, trans. John Marsh [1955], p. 38) sees "James' supporters" at work in Galatia. H. Schlier ([1], p. 172) leaves the question open. H. J. Schoeps ([2], p. 68) presumes that messengers from James were creating agitation in Galatia (more hesitantly on pp. 261-62) ; otherwise in [1], pp. 69 ff.

[4] One may hardly put Acts 15:5, 24, alongside this; cf. Vol. 3, pp. 38 ff.

[5] See Vol. 3, pp. 109 ff.

[6] See *ibid.*

as to who is responsible for the agitation in Galatia. To be sure, if one decides for that reason nevertheless to presuppose such a radical group,[7] there arises another difficulty that is no less considerable. Is it conceivable that these people, who obviously in principle rejected a Gentile mission, yet now conduct such an extensive and methodical Gentile mission as is presupposed by their appearance even in Galatia alone, to say nothing of other places? This obviously is inconceivable. A worldwide judaizing Gentile mission is a contradiction in itself. The conjecture that in the Judaizers in Galatia we have to do with some Jewish Christians from Judea who happened to be passing through, which is asserted, e.g., by W. Foerster (*Apophoreta*, BZNW 30 [1964]: 137) and R. McL. Wilson (*Studia Evangelica* IV [1968]: 360), appears to me, in view of the impact of the appearance of these people, to be makeshift explanation.

When one has once recognized this fundamental difficulty—which thus consists in the fact that we are supposed to encounter in Galatia judaizing missionaries who were still far more radical than James on a systematic missionary tour in the Gentile world—then one will not be disinclined at least to leaf through a small study on our theme by Wilhelm Lütgert, which the Halle professor published in 1919 under the title *Gesetz und Geist* (Law and Spirit). Lütgert's kind of study certainly does not always do justice to all the demands of scholarship. Nevertheless the work deserves more than merely a place in the bibliographies of our commentaries. That is to say, Lütgert has pointed to a number of Paul's polemical statements which, he alleges, cannot be understood as directed against Judaizers. From this he concludes that in the community in Galatia there had been formed, probably as a reaction against the Judaistic agitation, an ultra-Pauline, pneumatic

---

[7] "There was a strong group in early Christianity which regarded circumcision and submission to the law as the indispensable presupposition of any genuine Christian profession. These men, originally led by some former Pharisees (Acts 15:5), thus also stood in opposition to James and Peter. Their hatred, however, was directed against Paul" (H. W. Beyer in NTD 8 [1955, 7th ed.]: 2). One may hardly appeal to the book of Acts; moreover, it can hardly be proved that the group thus characterized was a *strong* group in the primitive Christian era. In principle, however, Beyer may be right when he reckons with a group in early Christianity which was more radical than James; the only question is: since when was there such a group? (cf. Vol. 3, pp. 108 ff.).

and even libertine group, against which Paul also protested.[8]

Here I can refrain from a refutation of this untenable thesis of the double battlefront of the Galatian epistle,[9] especially since to my knowledge it has evoked no significant response.[10] But it would be wrong for us to assume that therewith we were already relieved of the trouble of re-examining the exposition of the passages in which Lütgert regards an anti-judaizing battlefront to be ruled out. This is all the less permissible since H. Schlier sees, in a passage which had already attracted Lütgert's attention,[11] the necessity of modifying the traditional Judaizer theory in a distinctive manner. There[12] he speaks suddenly of the "so-called Judaizers," who do not stem from the rabbinical tendency of Judaism but are said to be native to the apocryphal, indeed to Gnostic, Judaism.[13]

---

[8] Here he stands in the line of succession of W. M. L. de Wette (*Kurzgefasstes exegetisches Handbuch zum Neuen Testament* [1845, 2nd ed.], pp. 74 ff.) and his pupils (cf. Lütgert, [1], p. 16). A. H. Francke (*Die galatischen Gegner des Paulus*, ThStKr [1882], pp. 133 ff.) also argues for a tendency in Galatia which is marked by discernible Hellenistic influences. Similarly on occasion also J. B. Lightfoot, *Saint Paul's Epistle to the Galatians* (1896, 10th ed.), p. 208, probably following de Wette.

[9] Cf. notes 15 and 109.

[10] Lütgert's book was discussed by Pott in ThLZ (1919), cols. 267-68, and by K. Deissner in *Die Theologie der Gegenwart*, XIV (1920): 205-11. In 1929, in a supplement to the *Harvard Theological Studies*, J. H. Ropes repeated Lütgert's thesis, since the latter's work had "received too little attention in the disturbed period immediately following the War and seems generally to have escaped notice since that time" (*The Singular Problem of the Epistle to the Galatians*, HThSt XIV [1929] : 2). His independent repetition of Lütgert's work is clearer and more lucid than Lütgert's essay itself; the latter's obvious errors and exaggerations are corrected, though it is true that nothing essentially new is brought forward. Of course Ropes also fails to produce among the exegetes any more agreement for Lütgert's thesis than it had previously gained. Cf. Charles H. Talbert in *Nov. Test.* 9 (1967): 27-28.

[11] Lütgert, [1], pp. 67 ff.

[12] Schlier, [1], pp. 136, 144. Unfortunately Schlier does not go into any of Lütgert's other critical notes.

[13] Similarly now G. Stählin also thinks (RGG [3rd ed.], II: 1188): "Thus one will have to reckon with a sectarian Jewish Christian movement which was gnostically colored, but still in the main was legalistically oriented." The weakness of such an interpretation lies in the necessary foregoing of any fitting of such a movement into the special developments in primitive Christianity otherwise known to us. This holds true also with respect to K. Wegenast, *Das Verständnis der Tradition bei Paulus und in den Deuteropaulinen* (WMANT 8 [1962]: 36 ff.) ; cf. below, p. 42. Following Schlier, B. Reicke [1] thinks that the "Gnostic character of the false teaching" in Galatia is to be recognized in many an indication. Of course he lets these very Gnostics at the same time be Judaizers, which is still less conceivable than the double battlefront held by Lütgert. H. Conzelmann

This is, however, a remarkable and consequential affirmation: For Judaizers are—this is in fact precisely what this concept intends to say—representatives of the *Pharisaic-legalist* Christianity, not Christians of Hellenistic or Gnostic (people used to say "Essene" [14]) stamp. Hence it is utterly inconsistent when Schlier in his commentary, altogether in an appropriation of the general tradition, speaks of *Judaizers* as the heretics in Galatia, although at one passage he must explain that they were *not* Judaizers, but only *so-called* Judaizers. (On the latest edition of Schlier's commentary on Galatians, cf. p. 16, n. 13; pp. 42-43.)

If one considers these difficulties—that is to say, Schlier's inconsistency, Lütgert's objections to a single battlefront in the Galatian epistle, and our fundamental reservations about a Judaistic world mission at all—then it appears to me nevertheless justified, if not necessary, once again to pose the question about the heretics in Galatia.

In so doing I make two presuppositions for our investigation. I presuppose, *first,* that the battle line in the Galatian epistle is a single one. So long as Paul himself does not explicitly indicate that he is engaged in a polemic against different groups, one must have serious reasons for the assertion of a double heresy in Galatia, an assertion which at best could stand at the end of an investigation and hardly ever has been entirely satisfactory.[15]

---

also recently asserts correctly that the Gnostic movement "had already left its traces in Galatia" (*Der Brief an die Kolosser*, NTD 8 [1962, 9th ed.]: 147), and in the new edition of his commentary ([1] 1962, 12th ed.), H. Schlier consistently eliminates the labeling of the opponents as Judaizers.

[14] This is done again now, to be sure with a reference to the intensifying of the Torah in the desert sects, by H. Kosmala (*Hebräer, Essener, Christen* [1959]), when on p. 11 he calls the Galatian false teachers "believers only in the old Essene sense."

[15] Hence Lütgert has rightly found little acceptance for his thesis, just as was the case before him with A. H. Francke (pp. 133 ff.), who has a first anti-Pauline movement in Galatia issue from native Jewish Christians with a strong Hellenistic touch, and a second from Judaizers from Jerusalem (for criticism, cf. A. Hilgenfeld, ZwTh 1883, pp. 333 ff.), and after him with J. H. Ropes (see n. 10). The assertion of a twofold battlefront, which for the Corinthian epistles still in fact is widespread, is for the most part a transitional solution between a no longer tenable, or at least doubted, older thesis and a newer view which is not yet fully recognized or is not yet able to prevail. It is characteristic that Lütgert cannot cite a single passage in which Paul *expressis verbis* addresses himself to a second group of heretics in the community. But so long as there are to be found differences only *in substance* in the apostle's polemic, it is the task of the investigator

Further, I presuppose that Paul was only meagerly informed about goings-on in Galatia. If he had received an official embassy or a detailed epistle, he could not have failed to make any mention of this at all. He apparently knows only some reproaches or demands and aspects of the heretics' conduct, without seeming to know anything exact about their source and hence about their general bearing. He shows himself to be best informed in the paraenetic passages, and thus on those questions which one is most likely to become acquainted with through hearsay. (On this, cf. now the significant and correct methodological reflections in H. Schlier, [1], [1962, 12th ed.], p. 19.)

Of course it is frequently assumed (for example, by R. A. Lipsius) that already on his second visit in Galatia Paul had personally debated with his opponents, who were already at that time active there. But even the fact of a second visit of Paul to Galatia after an initial visit is anything but assured. Appeal is made to Gal. 4:13: οἴδατε δὲ ὅτι δι' ἀσθένειαν τῆς σαρκὸς εὐηγγελισάμην ὑμῖν τὸ πρότερον, and τὸ πρότερον here is understood in the sense of the classical Greek as "the first time" as contrasted with a second time. But "πρότερος has surrendered the meaning of 'the first of two' to πρῶτος and now means only 'earlier'" (Blass-Debrunner, § 62). Cf., e.g., Gen. 13:3; 28:19; I Tim. 1:13; John 6:62; 9:8; 7:50 (variant reading), where a second visit of Nicodemus to Jesus is not in mind, and Job 42:5, where the enlargement with reference to "a second time" is forbidden. Accordingly Gal. 4:13 may be understood to mean ". . . that I proclaimed the gospel to you *at that time."*

Acts 18:21 ff. cannot be placed in opposition to this. The difficulties of this passage and the doubts about the trip to Jerusalem apparently portrayed there are well known. It is true that in a way the decision about a second visit of Paul in Galatia depends on the question whether Galatians is addressed to the inhabitants of the *country* of Galatia or the *province* bearing that name. We cannot broach this much-discussed and extensively treated problem here.[16]

But even assuming that a second visit had taken place, a debate of Paul with his later opponents is to be documented from Galatians for this visit only by contrivance. Indeed, ὡς προειρήκαμεν (Gal. 1:9) will hardly refer back to vs. 8 (thus Luther and most of the earlier exegetes; cf. II Cor. 7:3), but must have reference to a visit of Paul

---

to explore the question: Against what *one* movement could the apparently differing motifs of the polemic be directed?

[16] See the introductions and commentaries.

in Galatia; but a solemn warning against another gospel of Gentile, Jewish, or Christian kind is obvious also and precisely for the founding visit (cf. Gal. 5:21). The same holds true for Gal. 5:3, if the πάλιν does not refer back to ideas from Gal. 3, for example 3:10. If Paul had actually had a debate already during a second visit with the opponents who are combated in the Galatian epistle, more evidence of this than two uncertain traces would have to be visible in the discussion now repeated in writing. It is evident that Paul is completely surprised at the apostasy of the Galatians; his agitation and his whole line of argument fit poorly with the assumption that on the basis of his personal experiences in Galatia he would have had to reckon on such a development. (Thus, correctly, K. v. Hofmann, A. Jülicher, T. Zahn; *contra* H. Schlier, F. Sieffert, R. A. Lipsius.)

Moreover, the ἐτρέχετε καλῶς (Gal. 5:7) obviously applies not only to the time down to his second visit, but down to the present, in which he hears for the first time that this course is being hindered. The question, τίς ὑμᾶς ἐνέκοψεν (Gal. 5:7), would be out of place even as a rhetorical question if Paul had already become personally acquainted with his opponents in Galatia.

II

The above-mentioned charges or demands of his Galatian opponents which had come to Paul's ears, however, are what especially interest us. Indeed we do not need long to search for them. At the very beginning of the first sentence of the Galatian epistle the defensive polemic is present in full strength: Paul, an apostle, not from men nor through a man, but through Jesus Christ . . . . The accusation is clear: Paul is said to have received his apostolate, not immediately from God, as befits an apostle, but from or through men.

The same accusation also appears in another form in the first two chapters of the epistle, which belong together: Paul is said to have received his *gospel* from men: "For you are to know, brethren, that the gospel preached by me is not according to man; for I have neither received it nor learned it from a man, but through the revelation of Jesus Christ" (Gal. 1:11-12). Thus for the schismatic Christians in Galatia, purity of the gospel and the nonmediated character of the apostolate are inseparable from one another,[17] a conception which will be significant for determining the nature of these Christians, a conception however which Paul shares with them. For Paul does not say that one can receive his apostolate also from men and demand unconditional obedience for a gospel proclaimed with such apostolic authority. He rather says: naturally the apostle must be called by God if he is to proclaim the gospel with apostolic authority. But I am in fact called by him.[18] *I too* have not received my gospel from men but—*like* the opponents—through a revelation of Jesus Christ (Gal. 1:12). It pleased the One who separated me from my mother's womb and called me by his grace to reveal his Son in me[19] (Gal. 1:15-16). Then I was active as an apostle for more than fifteen years before I came into contact with those who, in Jerusalem,[20] were apostles before me, a contact so close that I might very well have received my gospel from them (Gal. 1:16–2:1).[21] In this meeting and later I preserved the inde-

---

[17] In Gal. 2:7 ff., εὐαγγέλιον and ἀποστολή alternate with the same sense: the *gospel* is entrusted to Paul independently, for the *apostolate* has been bestowed on him independently alongside Peter. Hence the old dispute about whether in 1:13 ff. Paul is defending his teaching or his apostolic office is idle (cf. F. Sieffert, *Der Brief an die Galater* in Meyer's *Kommentar,* VII [1899, 9th. ed.]: 57 n.).

[18] Gal. 1:6-9 shows how highly Paul esteems his apostolic authority. He places his mission above himself and above any angel from heaven (ἡμεῖς ἢ ἄγγελος ἐξ οὐρανοῦ, (Gal. 1:8). Thus it is not something human, indeed not even something superhuman and angelic. It is divine, for Paul himself has received it directly from God (Gal. 1:1, 12). Therefore any other message, whether it come from other men, from Paul himself, or from a heavenly being, deserves the ἀνάθεμα.

[19] "εὐδόκησεν . . . ἀποκαλύψαι τὸν υἱὸν αὐτοῦ ἐν ἐμοί," i.e., "it pleased him to call me to be an *apostle*," as I Cor. 9:1 shows. ἐν ἐμοί stands for the simple dative; cf. P. Stuhlmacher, *Das paulinische Evangelium*, I, *Vorgeschichte* (1968) : 82, n. 1.

[20] The charge against Paul was not necessarily one of specific dependency on the Jerusalem authorities. Possibly it concerned dependence on men in general. Of course Paul assumes as self-evident that only the apostles in Jerusalem can come into question as the ones from whom he has received his apostolate. Therefore the proof that he is independent of them means the proof of the independence of his apostolate absolutely. When Paul therein assumes as obvious that the charge against him has to do with dependence on *Jerusalem*, although he could just as easily at least have learned his gospel from any Christian (Lütgert, [1], p. 44), this apparently shows that the δοκοῦντες in Jerusalem claimed some kind of legitimate overall leadership of the church, to which of course Paul is not willing to bow.

[21] *Before* his call such a contact would have been out of the question. Gal. 1: 13-14, where Paul emphatically refers to his hostility toward the Christians, probably is meant to be understood thus. "How should any kind of contact with the apostolic tradition have exerted a positive influence—this question even here is to be taken in Paul's sense—on a Jew who is engaged in such constant active hatred against the messianic people of God, the church?" (H. Schlier, [1], p. 22).

After his call Paul did not apply to men at all (Gal. 1:16*b*), not even to the

pendence of my gospel (or apostolate; Gal. 2:7-8; see n. 17) throughout. Titus did not have to be circumcised in Jerusalem (Gal. 2:3); for the sake of the truth of my gospel [22] (! Gal. 2:14) I vigorously withstood Peter and even thereby demonstrated my independence (Gal. 2:11 ff.); and the "pillars" in Jerusalem finally confirmed to me by a handshake that the gospel among the heathen was entrusted to me by God just as independently as Peter was called to be an apostle to the Jews (Gal. 2:7 ff.).[23]

Thus Paul can prove that the assertion that he had received his gospel or his apostolate from men even historically simply cannot be true.[24]

All this is well known. But who it was who made such charges against Paul is still unknown. Some say, "the Judaizers in Jeru-

---

Jerusalem apostles, but sojourned in Arabia and Damascus (Gal. 1:17). Only after a three-year period of activity did he visit Jerusalem for the first time since his conversion. He wanted only to get acquainted with *Peter* (on ἱστορῆσαι, see H. Schlier, [1], p. 30), with whom he remained fourteen days (Gal. 1:18; cf. O. Bauernfeind, "Die Begegnung zwischen Paulus und Kephas, Gal. 1, 18-20," ZNW 47 [1956]: 268-76). He did not even see another apostle; he saw only James, whom however he apparently does not count among the apostles without reservation (cf. I Cor. 9:5; 15:7; H. Schlier, [1], p. 31; W. G. Kümmel in Lietzmann, *An die Korinther* [1949, 4th ed.], p. 40, line 28; W. Schmithals, *The Office of Apostle*, trans. J. E. Steely [1969], pp. 64-65). Then he again stayed so far from Jerusalem that he remained wholly unknown by face to the communities in Judea (Gal. 1:21-24). Only after another fourteen years did he once more make his way to Jerusalem (Gal. 2:1), and then it was κατὰ ἀποκάλυψιν, so that "his second journey occurred neither on his own initiative nor at the demand of the Jerusalem authorities" (H. Schlier, [1], p. 35).

[22] And this again means: in the authority of my independent call to be an apostle.

[23] The only obligation which Paul accepted, namely to remember the poor in Jerusalem (Gal. 2:10), proves precisely the utter independence of the Gentile Christian communities and their apostles from Jerusalem; for the collection, which he zealously undertook (Rom. 15:25 ff.; I Cor. 16:1; II Cor. 8-9), is for *Paul* a voluntary act of compassion (ηὐδόκησαν, Rom. 15:26; cf. II Cor. 8:14), even though those in Jerusalem may also have demanded it or understood it as an act of legal obligation (cf. K. Holl, *Gesammelte Aufsätze*, II [1928]: 59 ff.).

[24] Naturally Paul cannot in the same way historically adduce the *positive* proof that he actually has been called by God himself. This accounts for the great detail in his offering of the negative proof. The view, occasionally expressed, that Paul's opponents had pictured the encounters and agreements between Paul and the people in Jerusalem differently (W. Lütgert, [1], p. 43), so that Paul must correct them with his version, is not to be inferred from Paul's words. Only in Gal. 2:6b can there *possibly* be a hint that sometime someone has reported an arrangement like, for example, the so-called apostolic decree (Acts 15:20) as accepted by Paul. (What E. Stauffer writes on this, p. 37, n. 55, is, of course, pure fantasy.) But if this had happened also in Galatia with the knowledge of Paul, we would have to expect that he would have gone into the matter more specifically.

salem." But this is ruled out. *First,* no one in Jerusalem had such a view of the apostolate as we encounter in Galatia. For this point I do not propose to appeal to the argument that the leaders of the original congregation at that time did not yet hold the title of apostle at all, although I regard this thesis, not entirely new but recently discussed with some emphasis,[25] as thoroughly correct and proven. But further, anyone who still believes that the apostolate was native to the primitive community in Jerusalem or at least had become at home there in the meantime[26] cannot assert that in some circles of the primitive community people had bound the gospel to the apostolate in such a way as is the case in Galatia, so that the authenticity of the message was measured simply by the apostolate of the messenger. This is contradicted by all that we know of the primitive community.

It was just the other way around: The authenticity of the office of the messenger was measured by the correctness of the message, as is shown for example by the dispute about circumcision. Any different kind of legitimation of the messenger is not attested by anything for the early original community. Some have asserted that for the Jerusalem Christians, personal acquaintance with the *historical* Jesus was a criterion of the authorized apostle (Paul is "only a pupil of apostles, since he had no connection with Christ so long as the latter was active on earth," F. Sieffert, p. 17; he had "in fact not had personal association with the Messiah as had the earlier apostles, had not like them been personally called to be his disciple," R. A. Lipsius, in *Handcommentar zum NT,* II, 2: 8; the false teachers "will have pointed to the fact that Paul was not even an immediate disciple of Jesus," W. Bousset, p. 29; ". . . it is a significant question whether he rightly bears the name of apostle . . . . His right to it is contested because he had been familiar with neither the Jesus who lived upon

---

[25] Cf. Holger Mosbech, "Apostolos in the New Testament," *Studia Theologica* II (1949/50) : 166 ff.; K. Holl, *Gesammelte Aufsätze,* II: 55; *The Office of Apostle,* pp. 67 ff.

[26] In Gal. 1:17, 19, Paul already presupposes ἀπόστολοι in Jerusalem. Peter belongs among them in any case (cf. Gal. 2:8). We do not know who the others were. Paul never calls the "Twelve" apostles. They cannot be meant in Gal. 1:19, because it is hardly believable that during a fourteen-day stay in Jerusalem Paul could remain unknown to the restricted circle of the "Twelve," especially when it was said to have been their task, except for Peter (Gal. 2:8), to tarry in Jerusalem (Acts 1:4; 8:1). Thus in the ἀπόστολοι mentioned in Gal. 1:19 we apparently have to do with missionaries who were bound to Jerusalem, but like Paul were mostly on the road as "emissaries." Cf. *The Office of Apostle,* pp. 82 ff.

earth nor the members of his first community," O. Holtzmann, *Das Neue Testament* [1926], p. 477; ". . . They may have had association with the earthly Jesus-Messiah or they themselves or others base their recognition thereupon," H. Schlier, [1], p. 43; "What they once were and what Paul declares in Gal. 2:6 to be unimportant was their relationship to the earthly Jesus," E. Haenchen, ZThK 63 [1966]: 153). This is an apparently ineradicable assertion for which any convincing evidence in the New Testament is lacking.[27] James, the most important partner in the dialogue at the "Council" in Jerusalem, had not been a companion of the earthly Jesus at all, and possibly not even the twelve in their totality. A special teaching authority of the "Twelve" is already excluded by the fact that James, the later leader of the original community, does not belong to their number. But if people in Jerusalem had held an encounter with the *exalted* Christ to be constitutive for the legitimacy of the authoritative proclaimer of the gospel, one could not conceive of wishing to exclude Paul.

Second, either Paul must have lied when he asserted that the pillars in Jerusalem had solemnly recognized his apostolate, or these pillars, directly or through their envoys, in a most malicious and base fashion, had broken their promise, without Paul's knowing anything of it—for when he writes Gal. 1 and 2, at any rate, he still knows nothing of such behavior.[28] Both alternatives may be ruled out.[29]

But *third*—and this is the decisive point—it is inconceivable that the Jerusalem apostles in Galatia accuse Paul of being dependent *upon themselves* or, in case they were only representatives of the Jerusalem authorities, that *like themselves* he is dedependent upon the apostles in Jerusalem. Therewith one can indeed minimize his authority as an apostle, but certainly cannot reject his gospel. Such an assertion, however much it discredits Paul as an apostle, would rather be a commendation of his gospel. If some are bringing from Jerusalem another gospel than Paul had brought, because that of Paul is false, then they had to accuse Paul that with respect to this one true gospel he had re-

---

[27] Of course this assertion is an ancient one. It dominates Luke's historical work where it is even found *expressis verbis* (Acts 1:21). It supports the Lucan concept of tradition and the view of the apostolate which is bound up with it, and is shown precisely thereby to be a construction just as unhistorical as these other specifically Lucan conceptions.

[28] Cf. n. 151.

[29] Cf. A. H. Francke, p. 137.

mained independent in an inadmissible fashion, not that he was
dependent on it.[30]

This difficulty naturally has long been recognized.[31] Hence it
is explained: "Paul, they say, is no apostle but only a subordinate
fellow worker and assistant . . . . Thus where his gospel diverges
from the preaching of the genuine disciples of the Messiah, it is
not his authority but theirs that has to prevail" (R. A. Lipsius,
p. 8).

Similarly F. Sieffert, p. 57: ". . . that he (Paul) in fact had received
the content and commission of his proclamation from men, i.e.,
from Christians converted earlier and especially from the original
apostles, that is to say, insofar as this proclamation harmonizes at all
with the original apostles' teaching." T. Zahn, [1], I: 119: "They
must have represented it as though in the first period after his conversion Paul had occupied a wholly subordinate position, one dependent upon the earlier apostles. Over against that, the independence with which Paul operated in the territory of the Gentile
mission must then have appeared as an unjustified bit of arrogance,
and the sharp deviation from the life forms of the Jewish Christianity
of Palestine . . . as a falling away from original Christianity." W.
Bousset, p. 30: "Everything that is good in Paul's gospel he has, they
say, from them (the apostles in Jerusalem) ; what is his own is human
imagination." According to K. v. Hofmann, *Der Brief Pauli an die
Galater* (1872, 2nd ed., p. 227), the Judaizers have represented it in
such a way as though Paul "had actually acknowledged his subordina-
tion to the apostles, and only where he is seen in the midst of his
Gentile Christian following . . . did he appear with the pride of one
of equal standing as compared with the apostles of the mother congregation." Cf. further J. Jeremias in ZNW 49 (1958) : 153: ". . . the
Judaizers say: 'All that Paul knows of Jesus that is reliable he has
from Peter (vs. 12). What he has to say beyond this is his own
invention . . . .'" J. Roloff, *Apostolat-Verkündigung-Kirche* (1965),
p. 66: ". . . people probably were accusing him of having received his
gospel in Damascus or Antioch from a source that could not be

---

[30] "Consequently, by the current theory the Judaizers are represented as trying
to undermine Paul's work by declaring that he had accepted authority and received influence from the very group with which they themselves had substantial
sympathy. Dependence on such authorities, it would seem, ought rather to have
been a merit in their eyes than a source of discredit" (J. H. Ropes, *The Singular
Problem of the Epistle to the Galatians*) .

[31] Cf. W. Lütgert, [1], pp. 45 ff. But H. Schlier [1] appears curiously not to
have noticed it.

checked." D. Georgi, p. 36: "Paul had not been accused of dependence upon Jerusalem, but precisely of holding the tradition in contempt."

These quotations, which could be multiplied if one desired, are altogether variations on the *one* theme: they are efforts to explain how the Jerusalemites can *reproach* Paul for dependence upon themselves. But every one of these explanations runs aground on the very fact that the *charge* actually concerns *dependence,* and not a single word concerns *apostasy*.[32] But this means that one must completely abandon the fiction that behind the heretics in Galatia stands the authority of the leaders in Jerusalem.

It is of no avail to refer to those ultra-Jacobine Judaizers who perhaps were present,[33] who possibly did not acknowledge the agreement of the "apostolic council." [34] Then of course the reservation about the agreement having been broken would disappear.[35] But we do not encounter such a group in a worldwide Gentile mission. For it, moreover, the view of the apostolate which appears in Galatia is even more inconceivable[36] than for the "pillars." And finally, when they make against Paul the

---

[32] Hence it is a complete inversion of the facts of the matter when O. Holtzmann (p. 481) describes Paul's assertion in Gal. 1:20 as "sarcastic of course," "for the opponents made his slight [sic] contact with the primitive community a reproach against him." The assumption of judaizing opposition of course presupposes such sarcasm. Yet Paul's line of argument excludes it. The dilemma is to be solved only when one drops the assumption of the judaizing opposition. Like Holtzmann, D. Georgi (p. 36, n. 113) also disputes the apologetic character of Gal. 1:11–2:10 and calls the passage "aggressive-polemical," since people had accused Paul of "holding the tradition in contempt." As though Paul would have had to bother with all the historical apparatus in chaps. 1 and 2 in order to *confirm* this charge!

[33] See pp. 14-15.

[34] Thus F. Sieffert, pp. 18-19, against A. H. Francke, p. 137; further, E. Hirsch, ZNW 29 (1930): 193-94; H. J. Schoeps, [1], pp. 69 ff.

[35] Thus, correctly, J. Munck, *Paul and the Salvation of Mankind* (trans. Frank Clarke [1959]), p. 86: "Paul's argument would be spun out of thin air if the Jerusalemites for a long time had no longer recognized the argements of the "apostles' council." ". . . We meet no Jewish Christian emissaries in the Pauline churches, either before or after the meeting in Jerusalem" (p. 105; cf. pp. 109 ff.).

[36] How should such people have been able at all to publish such a standard for the legitimacy of an apostle as is set up in Galatia, a standard according to which the source of the apostolate automatically passes judgment on what is taught? For them it can no longer even be *supposed* that they appealed to a connection with the historical Jesus, for one could not boast of such acquaintance *against* the "Twelve." But the παρείσακτοι ψευδάδελφοι of Gal. 2:4 cannot possibly have belonged to the circle of the "Twelve."

weighty *accusation* that he is dependent on the so-called original apostles, they must have been not ultra-Jacobine but anti-Jacobine.[37] But that there were such anti-Jacobine Judaizers, who thus put Paul on the side of James and *thereby* make him out as a false teacher, is not attested by anything, and is rather ruled out by all that is attested.[38]

This, among other things, is to be raised as an objection against the unfortunately too little noted essay by W. Foerster, "Die δοκοῦντες in Gal. 2," ZNW 36 (1937): 286 ff., who rightly recognizes the impossibility of bringing Paul's opponents in Galatia into connection with the authorities in Jerusalem. He too sees that the false brethren of Gal. 2:4 are sharply opposed to Paul *and* to the so-called original apostles. They see "Paul as it were in the extended line of the original apostles" (p. 290). But that these false brethren are extreme Jewish Christians and as such attack Paul because of his dependence on the lax Jerusalem authorities, so that in response to their charges Paul must emphasize his independence of these "original apostles"—this, of course, I regard, for the reasons indicated, as not conceivable.

B. Weiss (*Lehrbuch der Einleitung in das NT* [1897, 3rd ed.], pp. 170-71) has the Judaizers coming from Jewish Christian communities which had already existed in Galatia before Paul. With this also at least the one difficulty about the breaking of the agreement of the apostolic council could be removed. Moreover, the judaizing mission among the Gentiles would become understandable. But we know nothing of such communities. And who would have established them in such an early period? Finally, Rom. 15:20 speaks decisively against this thesis which has nothing to document it.

W. Michaelis ("Judaistische Heidenchristen," ZNW 30 [1931]: 83) pleads for the view that the mission in Galatia issued from Gentile Christians who in a pre-Pauline period had been converted and had been circumcised before baptism. Now they are demanding later circumcision of the uncircumcised baptized people in Galatia. Therewith he takes up a thesis which E. Hirsch (in ZNW 29 [1930]: 192 ff.) attempted to establish, especially with Gal. 6:13 (and Gal. 5:12). Of course this explanation is older than Hirsch's essay. Hirsch himself refers to H. Lietzmann on Gal. 6:13; Michaelis, by way of supplement, to G. Hoennicke, *Das Judenchristentum im ersten und zweiten Jahrhundert* (Berlin, 1900), p. 118, n. 2; F. Sieffert, p. 354; W. M. L.

---

[37] This is seen quite correctly by H. W. Beyer in NTD 8 (1955, 7th ed.): 2.
[38] The more extreme Jewish Christianity is, the higher the position it accords to James (H. J. Schoeps, [2], pp. 122 ff.).

de Wette, *Das Neue Testament griechisch mit kurzem Kommentar* (Halle, 1885), II: 243-44, 283. But Hirsch has the merit of having made this thesis interesting. O. Holtzmann has already shown in ZNW 30 (1931): 76 ff., that the interpretation of περιτεμνόμενοι (Gal. 6:13) which Hirsch has made foundational and with which his thesis stands or falls is not necessary. Similarly H. Schlier, [1], p. 207. It is utterly unproven that because of Gal. 5:10, "whoever it may be," "old Gentile Christian friends of Paul . . . , who once, when he was still working out of Antioch, had worked with him in the evangelizing of Gentile Christians, now take a position against him for a circumcised Christianity from among the Gentiles." But even if one adopts this hypothesis, which of course is theoretically possible, the difficulties in asserting that Paul's opponents in Galatia are Judaizers do not diminish; that is to say, both Hirsch and Michaelis presuppose that the agitators come from Antioch and obviously have connections with their "authorities" in Jerusalem.

J. Munck, pp. 87 ff., again takes up Hirsch's thesis on Gal. 6:13; the "οἱ περιτεμνόμενοι" can only mean "those who have themselves circumcised," i.e., recently circumcised Gentile Christians; yet Munck does not succeed in refuting the arguments against the *necessity* of such an interpretation. It is true that he convincingly shows that there was never a countermission of judaizing missionaries from Jerusalem in the Pauline missionary territory (although not all the arguments which he adduces are compelling). But then when he attempts to explain the various elements of agitation against Paul, his suggestions become untenable and his exegeses unreliable. Thus Paul is said to be in complete agreement with the Jerusalemites on the question of righteousness by faith without the law. The actual judaizing interpretation—e.g., in Galatia—was rather first formed among the Gentile Christians who, in the absence of personal contact, misunderstood the Jerusalemites as Judaizers (up until then there had not been any such), then became like the misunderstood Jerusalemites (and therewith established the judaizing movement), but therein are rejected by Paul and the Jerusalemites. Such a misunderstanding is *rendered possible*, Munck asserts, by Paul's portrayal to the Galatians of a sympathetic picture of the whole of Jewish Christianity, and it *came about* because the Galatians, under the influence of the Old Testament, which knows only the Jews as the people of salvation, desired as Christians now also to become Jews. In view of the impossibility of deriving the judaizing tendency in Galatia from Jewish Christianity, to which the Gentile mission was foreign (this he very

27

properly points out), Munck would have had first to test the thesis as to whether they were actually *Judaizers* who were doing the agitating in Galatia, before he attempted such an imaginative reconstruction of the history of primitive Christianity.

J. H. Ropes (p. 45) thinks: "All that we need suppose is that certain gentile Christians had proved susceptible to the efforts of local synagogue Jews, and had tried to persuade the churches as a whole to accept Jewish Rites, including circumcision." This thesis lacks any exegetical basis; even psychologically it is not very credible, and it does not have any parallel, since Ropes's reference to the Ἰουδαισμός of the Ignatian epistles, in which it refers to the manner of conduct of a *Gnostic* Jewish Christianity, naturally is out of place. It is possible only under the unnecessary and unproven presupposition, held by Ropes, of a twofold opposition to Paul, since then the judaizing stream becomes relatively insignificant and the main thrust of Paul's polemic can be understood as directed against the "pneumatics." A. Fridrichsen, "Die Apologie des Paulus Gal. 1" (in *Paulus und die Urgemeinde* [1921], pp. 53-76), correctly sees the difficulty in the traditional explanation: ". . . If the agitators describe Paul as a pupil of the original apostles, they could not possibly in the same breath represent his gospel as error" (p. 54). In view of this fact, how does Fridrichsen explain Gal. 1? Now the Galatian preachers are Palestinian agitators of the circumcision party behind whom the legitimate Jerusalem church leadership stands. They charge against Paul that his law-free gospel to the Gentiles is not divine, but κατὰ ἄνθρωπον (hence Gal. 1:11). Therein "opposing Palestinian circles" are said to have been Paul's spiritual fathers. Thus it comes to a dispute between Paul and the Jerusalemites. In view of this dispute the agitators in Galatia accuse Paul: ". . . Called to account by the authorities in Jerusalem, he had not had the courage to remain true to his spiritual fathers, but conducted himself servilely and courted the favor of the great." According to Fridrichsen, in the face of this accusation Paul in Gal. 1-2 is supposed to have sought to prove the original character of his gospel and his steadfast behavior.

But it is nowhere shown that people were accusing Paul of dependence on opposing, hellenistically oriented circles in Palestine. And the charge of being a man-pleaser in Gal. 1:10 is by no means the key to the understanding of Gal. 1-2, but demands another explanation than the thesis of a submissive attitude of Paul toward the so-called original apostles; see pp. 56 ff.

Thus it does not work to try to bring the heretics in Galatia into a convincing and tenable connection with the Judaizers of Palestine.[39] But then who is opposing Paul with the basic argument that an apostle must have received his apostolic authority and therewith *automatically* his gospel directly from God or Christ, so that in Gal. 1:12 Paul counters by saying that *he too*— that is to say, as they assert of themselves—has received the gospel, not from men, but by means of an ἀποκάλυψις?

This argument is genuinely Gnostic. The Gnostic apostle is not identified by means of a chain of tradition, by the apostolic succession, but by direct pneumatic vocation. When Paul says, "Am I not an apostle? Have I not seen Jesus our Lord?" (I Cor. 9:1), this combination, which represents an *equation,* is in origin typically Gnostic.[40] The Gnostic apostle is called by God directly.[41] He then is shown to be such by means of the σημεῖα τοῦ ἀποστόλου (II Cor. 12:12), that is to say, ἐν σημείοις τε καὶ τέρασιν καὶ δυνάμεσιν (II Cor. 12:12; Rom. 15:19; Heb. 2:4), i.e., through the ecstatic attestation of the pneuma-self.[42]

---

[39] It will also be noted that in Gal. 1:6-9 Paul denounces the false gospel of the opponents, while in Gal. 2:1 ff. he testifies to the fellowship in the gospel with the Jerusalemites. Thus the Jerusalemites cannot possibly be the opponents who are being combated.

[40] In I Cor. 9:1-2 Paul is answering the charges of his Gnostic opponents that he is neither ἐλεύθερος nor ἀπόστολος. This is shown by vs. 3 as the decisive conclusion of the parenthetical comment of I Cor. 9:1-3. Cf. *The Office of Apostle*, p. 26; Vol. 1, pp. 218 ff.

[41] A vision of the celestial world and of the way to it, mediated by ὀπτασίαι and ἀποκαλύψεις, may have been the special precondition for the office of the Gnostic apostle. On this, one may compare I Cor. 9:1; 15:5-8; II Cor. 12:1; Gal. 1:12, 16 with the conclusion of the Coptic Gnostic gospel fragment, first published by A. Jakoby in 1900, in which Jesus speaks: ". . . (that therewith I) may reveal to you all my glory and show to you all your power and the secret of your apostleship. . . . Our eyes penetrated all places, we beheld the glory of his deity and all the glory ((of his lordship)). He clothed ((us)) ((with)) the power ((of our)) apostle((ship)). . . ." Cf. *The Office of Apostle*, pp. 198 ff.

[42] Here we have an apparently fixed formula of Gnostic origin which occurs also in I Thess. 1:5, shows through in I Cor. 2:4, and appears in transposed form in II Thess. 2:9. In view of its formula-like character, it is very difficult to say what it is intended to express in the passages in which it occurs in the church's literature. At any rate it has lost its original meaning in Paul, since he replaces the ecstatic demonstration of his apostolate with the reference to his zealous service and the success of his labors (Rom. 15:19-20; I Cor. 9:1 ff.; II Cor. 3:1 ff.; 5:11-15; 10:12-18), but in II Cor. 12:12 to the concrete demands of his Gnostic opponents for ecstatic demonstration of his apostolate answers only with the citation of the Gnostic formula. Since in view of I Cor. 14:18-19 and II Cor. 5:11-15 the Corinthian Gnostics will have been right in their assertion that Paul had withheld

The "apostolic tradition" is indeed nothing but an early, and early successful, attempt of the church which was in the anti-Gnostic battle and in the debate with Marcion to limit the apostles to the twelve disciples (+ Paul: Luke!) and to concede to them alone as Jesus' personal disciples the evangelical authority and the power to hand this on by the laying-on of hands (Pastoral Epistles!), in order thus to take away from the pneumatic apostolate the immediate authority which for Paul was still so self-evident. In connection with the monarchical episcopate the apostolic tradition then was developed into the apostolic succession.

This Gnostic understanding of the apostle can be studied nowhere better than in the Corinthian epistles, especially in II Corinthians,[43] and this in the demands which the Gnostic apostles in Corinth make upon Paul if they are to recognize him on an equal basis as an apostle,[44] as well as in the evidence with which Paul proves that he fulfills this demand.[45]

In Corinth, moreover, as in Galatia, the question about the *content* of the Pauline proclamation, and thus about the truth of his gospel, is to be decided by the question about

---

from the Corinthians the (gnostically understood) gift of the πνεῦμα, in II Cor. 12:12 Paul will most probably have been thinking, as in I Cor. 2:4 and especially in I Thess. 1:5 (cf. pp. 140-41), of the miraculous effects of the Word.

[43] In I Cor. Paul must already defend his apostolate against attacks from the opposition (I Cor. 9:3), yet, seen as a whole, he is still attacking constantly the opponents' teaching. Differently in II Cor., where in the polemical sections (II Cor. 2:14-7:4; 10-13) Paul is almost exclusively defending himself against attacks on his personal apostolic authority.

[44] These demands call for speaking in tongues (I Cor. 14) or for a demonstration of the Christ who is speaking in Paul (II Cor. 13:3); for his proclamation which has been issued only in contemptible words (II Cor. 10:10) conceals the gospel (II Cor. 4:3). The apostle has to preach *himself* as pneuma-self (II Cor. 4:5; 10:12), and therefore may not withhold his ecstasy from the community (II Cor. 5:11, 13), but must produce for it the proof of his apostolate by means of the ecstatic σημεῖα τοῦ ἀποστόλου. He must prove that the Pneuma-Christ is in him (II Cor. 13:5). According to II Cor. 12:1, in particular the demand for ecstatic *rapture* also appears to have been emphasized.

[45] Paul indeed sharply rejects the Gnostic norm for the legitimacy of the apostle: The apostle does not commend himself, but God commends him by blessing his preaching (II Cor. 10:13-18); hence he has to preach before the community, not to adduce his ecstasies (II Cor. 5:11-15), and would rather speak five words τῷ νοΐ than one thousand ἐν γλώσσῃ (I Cor. 14:19); therefore he tells only very reluctantly of his raptures, which for him indeed have nothing to do with his apostolate (II Cor. 12:1, 11). But even Paul allows no doubt to arise that the apostle must be called immediately by God and his opponents' demand, for a proof of qualification of the apostle for his office, is in principle justified (I Cor. 9:1 ff.; 15:7 ff.; II Cor. 5:11*b*). This shows the Gnostic heritage of his view of the apostolate.

his apostolate.[46] This too is just as typically and originally Gnostic as it is un-Jewish and therefore un-Judaistic.[47]

In this connection one may also refer to Gal. 6:6. Generally, the expositors rightly presume that the situation in Galatia gives Paul occasion to warn against forsaking fellowship with the teachers. Only thereby is the connection of Gal. 6:6 with the preceding and following statements given. The dispute over the understanding of "ἐν πᾶσιν ἀγαθοῖς" ("ethically good" or "earthly goods") hardly makes much sense, since even the earthly goods belong to the "good" and Paul apparently does not reflect at all on the kind of "good," but places the stress entirely on κοινωνείτω: obey your teachers (Heb. 13:7; 13:17; 13:24; I Thess. 5:12); do not forsake those who instruct you in the λόγος, i.e., in the "already relatively fixed doctrine" (H. Schlier, [1], p. 203)—so long in any case as it is not a fellowship in the evil (ἐν πᾶσιν ἀγαθοῖς).

Sufficient in itself was the assumption that some in Galatia were turning away from the old teachers because of the new "teaching." W. Lütgert ([1], p. 20) of course presumes moreover that the pneumatics, who hold in contempt the "officeholders," are misleading the community "to give expression to this contempt by forsaking the teachers." In view of this formulation one must indeed ask to what extent the ministry of the κατηχοῦντες was already understood as *office,* but this much is certainly correct, that the status of the teachers who repeated the traditional doctrine could just as little find favor in the eyes of the Gnostics as could an apostle who only handed

---

[46] The distinctive thing about the situation in Corinth is indeed that the Gnostics direct their attacks not against the *teaching* of Paul but against his *office.* People are willing to listen to what he says only if he first has proved by a preliminary σημεῖον that Christ actually is speaking in him (II Cor. 13:3), i.e., that he is a pneumatic person. If he can prove this and has thereby legitimized himself as an apostle, his "message" is demonstrated in its truth. For this message in fact does not consist of a collection of revealed or handed-down teachings, nor is it a word of God which calls to decision. It is rather the ecstatic demonstration that there is πνεῦμα and the call to others to awaken their sleeping Pneuma and therewith to find themselves again. The genuine Gnostic operates with his entire proclamation in the realm of being and of reality, and indeed of self-being, of his own reality. Gnosticism answers the question of what man *is.* Only one who shows that (according to Gnostic standards) he is not *nothing* (II Cor. 12:11) but possesses the Pneuma, can claim standing in the community.

[47] The Jewish prophet demands obedience for his word. He does not identify himself in advance. Only the fulfillment of his utterance attests the authenticity of the prophetic office (Jer. 28:9). Just so, according to Paul's understanding, the truth of the apostle's proclamation is not demonstrated by a prior testimony for his person. The preaching of the crucified Christ bears its truth in itself in such a way that, demanding obedience, it is confirmed precisely by the obedience (I Cor. 9:2a). In this Paul is altogether in agreement with the primitive community.

on a message received from men. Thus it is evident that the Gnostic apostles were agitating against these Galatian teachers, and that not primarily against their *teaching,* explaining their own teaching to be the correct one, but against the teachers as such, since for the Gnostics the authoritative thing for Christian existence was not the ὁδοὶ ἐν Χριστῷ which Paul taught πανταχοῦ ἐν πάσῃ ἐκκλησίᾳ (I Cor. 4:17), which were repeated in the tradition of the community (I Cor. 15:3) and which therefore were bound up with κατηχοῦντες; instead, the presence of the Pneuma, which was not received by the disciple from his teacher but could only be awakened in man by a *pneumatic* person, determined this existence. If some rejected Paul's apostolate because it lacked pneumatic immediacy, then any teacher could even less find acceptance from the Gnostic pneumatics. In view of this situation, as it correspondingly appears certainly in Heb. 13:7, 17, but probably also in I Thess. 5:12 [48] (cf. I Clem. 21.6), Paul's exhortation to maintain fellowship with the teachers in all good things is easily understandable.

Thus with the assumption of Gnostic opposition to Paul, any reason for excising Gal. 6:6 as a gloss disappears, though this occasionally is done because the situation in Galatia which is presupposed in this verse appears as unlikely. (O. Holtzmann, p. 503; Gal. 6:6 "is certainly an insertion.") H. Lietzmann's comment on Gal. 6:6 also becomes untenable: "But in any explanation, the specific occasion which prompted Paul to offer this admonition remains obscure to us: here again we lack the knowledge of happenings within the Galatian communities" (*An die Galater,* HNT 10 [1932, 3rd ed.]: *in loc.*).

Thus the first two chapters of Galatians and the verse just discussed are to be understood, particularly if Paul is setting himself against some kind of Christian Gnostics who—as in Corinth—wish to eliminate his influence by disputing his apostolate. But can the other controverted problems be fitted into this context? This is now the decisive question.

III

In view of the statement that the Galatian false teachers demand circumcision, this question appears to require a negative answer. In any case it was this matter of circumcision which

---

[48] Cf. pp. 167 ff.

heretofore has not allowed any doubt to arise that it was *Judaizers* in Galatia who brought the community into disorder. And yet here, in my judgment, doubt is altogether in place—a twofold doubt.

First: if the Judaizers in Galatia demand circumcision of the Gentile Christians, they place them under the Jewish law and demand of them its observance. But this obviously is so little the case in Galatia that, first of all, *Paul himself* must call the community's attention to this consequence, and he does this solemnly: "Therefore I testify once more to every man who is circumcised that he must keep the whole law" (Gal. 5:3). This the Galatians had apparently not been able to gather from the message proclaimed by the false teachers.[49] No wonder, since Paul finds that those who were circumcised *themselves* νόμον οὐ φυλάσσουσιν (Gal. 6:13),[50] and this obviously means a renunciation of the law in principle.[51] But then these false teachers can hardly have been

---

[49] Thus, *inter alia*, T. Zahn, according to whom "the alien Judaizers understood it to give them the appearance of a certain liberality" ([1], p. 119).

Naturally I do not deny that "in 5:3 Paul did not make known to the Galatians a new fact, but only wanted to remind them anew of a known fact which they had not sufficiently taken into consideration" (W. G. Kümmel, *Introduction to the New Testament*, pp. 195-96). Only I do not understand how *for this reason* the Galatian opponents are "in any case, . . . advocates of a Jewish legalism." Whether Paul for the first time or repeatedly impressed upon the Galatians that the adoption of circumcision for the Gentiles is simply the decision for the way of the righteousness of the law is quite unimportant for our question; for in either case one does not understand why Paul has to enlighten the Galatians on a state of affairs which is the *program* of the alleged Judaizers. For that the Galatian false teachers camouflaged their judaizing character, Kümmel first of all would not wish to assert, since according to his opinion "no one can deny that the Galatian intruders demanded the acceptance of the Law." Of course the verses adduced in favor of this statement—2:16; 3:21b; 4:21; 5:4—in my opinion say nothing of the sort: in these passages the opponents are not even being addressed. But precisely if the opponents actually were promoting circumcision as a sign of the chosen righteousness of the law, *Paul* did not need to enlighten the community *anew* about the connection between circumcision and law.

[50] "Concretely this (*scil.*, the teaching of the Judaizers) consisted in the demand for circumcision (5:2, 12), but apparently without its implying also the obligation to accept the law in its entirety (5:3)," writes H. J. Schoeps, [1], p. 72.

[51] This has already been noted frequently (F. Sieffert, p. 300; W. Lütgert, [1], pp. 101 ff.; H. Schlier, [1], p. 166; J. B. Lightfoot, p. 222). On the other hand, it is inserted into Paul's words in Gal. 6:13 when E. Hirsch (ZNW 29 [1930]: 194) first presupposes that among the Galatian opponents what was involved was Gentile Christians who were later circumcised (see p. 26), in order then to conclude from this: "It is obvious that Gentiles who let themselves be circumcised cannot keep the law just as do those who are born Jews. For there is much that pertains to the keeping of the law by way of knowledge and practice which is

Judaizers.[52] H. Schlier, A. Oepke, and others rightly comment on Gal. 4:21 ("you who wish to be under the law"), "they have *not* indeed (in spite of vs. 10) exactly put themselves under the law" (A. Oepke, p. 110), a fact which Paul states but does not explain and which, according to what has been said, cannot rightly be explained by a reference to a deficiency in zeal in the demanded fulfilling of the law, but is to be regarded as an expression of the basically relative validity of the law in Galatia.

More important is a second point. It had been decided in Jerusalem indeed that *Gentile* Christians did not need to be circumcised, and the way in which Paul tells of this makes it appear inconceivable that this decision had already been sabotaged at that time by the Jerusalemites.[53] But even in later times the question of circumcision played a surprisingly limited role in the discussion with the Jewish Christian groups,[54] and none of what H. J. Schoeps adduces in his *Theologie und Geschichte des Judenchristentums*[55] allows the conclusion that after the apostolic council there ever was a judaizing tendency which consistently demanded circumcision even of all Gentile Christians.[56] Rather,

---

acquired only by education from youth onward." What is involved in the defective fulfilling of the law of the Galatian heretics is not "bungling in Judaism" (*ibid.*) but a well-defined libertine tendency; this will become clear below.

[52] It is clear that Paul is making against the περιτεμνόμενοι a *moral* accusation out of their failure to fulfill the law. Hence they cannot have been serious Judaizers who, like all men, do not achieve the aim of their striving (Gal. 3:10 ff.), but only Jewish Christians who did not think of taking the law upon themselves. W. Lütgert, who sets this forth clearly (Paul "sets himself against a Pharisaic preaching of the law which then still does not actually take the law seriously," [1], p. 103), then to be sure neglects the decisive question of how a Judaism thus formed could develop, appear on the scene in Galatia, and vanish again without leaving a trace. With the statement, "This is the well-known Judaism with which John the Baptist and Jesus also had to do," all the less is gained for the identification of the early judaizing tendency, since one can hardly doubt the seriousness of the zeal for the law among the Pharisees with whom Jesus had to do.

[53] H. Lietzmann's judgment is incomprehensible to me: "It is clearly evident . . . from the Galatian epistle that the men in Jerusalem have continually violated the agreement of Gal. 2:9" (SBA 1936, pp. 406-7=*Kleine Schriften* I [1958]: 118).

[54] Cf. H. J. Schoeps, [1], p. 138.

[55] [1], pp. 135-43.

[56] If such a demand was perhaps again raised later by a group of Jewish Christians, it can only have had declamatory significance. But no great weight can be placed on what Augustine (Contra Faustum Manichaeum, XIX, 17) and Jerome (Comm. in Jes., on Isa. 1:12) remark on this. Other accounts have not come to my attention. On Justin's Dial. 47.3, cf. H. J. Schoeps, [1], p. 14; see also below, p. 222, n. 17; pp. 224-25.

in the post-apostolic era, the consciously Jewish Christian part of early Christianity, which held fast to circumcision, a practice never contested by Paul, outside Palestine could probably not maintain even to the end of the first century its independence over against Hellenistic and Gnostic Christianity.[57] It sank more and more into insignificance, was absorbed into syncretism,[58] and rightly soon appeared to the Great Church as a sect which, although it practiced circumcision, never thereby became dangerous to the church[59] and moreover never influenced it.

But this means that the Galatian mission and circumcision as a *judaizing* version would stand in utter isolation.[60] Any connection with the past would be severed by the apostolic council; any *continuation* into the future is lacking.[61]

The situation becomes quite different when we envisage an agitation by Jewish or Jewish-Christian Gnosticism. Jewish

---

[57] So far as these communities did not succumb to Gnosticism, they found themselves at the latest in the battle against Gnosticism in league with the Gentile Christian communities. Already in Corinth in Paul's time we can detect a common defensive front of "Paul's people" and "Apollos' people," i.e., the Gentile Christians, with the Jewish Christian "Peter's people" against the Gnostic "Christ's people." And even earlier Peter's original behavior in Antioch (Gal. 2:12a) testifies that in the Gentile world the Jewish Christians early joined forces with the Gentile Christians. Cf. also Vol. 3, pp. 113 ff.

[58] Cf. O. Cullmann, in *Neutestamentliche Studien für Rudolf Bultmann* (1954), p. 49. Even H. J. Schoeps, who so stoutly disputes any Gnostic influence on Jewish Christianity ([1]), must now at least admit some syncretistic influences for the later period (*Studia Theologica* VIII [1955]: 48-49).

[59] The sources which Schoeps utilizes in his studies are related almost without exception to groups in Coelesyria and Transjordan (cf. *Studia Theologica* VIII [1955]: 43), an indication that even in terms of territory the influence of heretical Jewish Christians can never have been significant.

[60] O. Holtzmann apparently senses this (ZNW 30 [1931]: 79): "In the meeting of Gal. 2:1-10 the Jerusalem leaders did not demand circumcision (2:3). Only after knowledge of the circumstances in the community in Antioch, after the dispute between Peter and Paul, and Paul's departure from Syria-Cilicia was circumcision declared to be necessary. But after the failure of the thrust into Galatia the Jerusalemites again took their distance from it." Of course this could explain a great deal. But unfortunately this account, which is not very believable either historically or psychologically, is a (necessary) construction on the basis of the assumption that the Judaizers from Jerusalem had appeared in Galatia; it is not a proof of this assumption.

[61] R. Bultmann has well observed this; according to him the appearance of Judaizers in the Pauline missionary territory, "as the Galatian epistle testifies and the Philippian epistle suggests," remained only an episode, the significance of which lies only in the fact that it forced Paul into the theological discussion to which we owe the Galatian epistle ([2], p. 108). Of course precisely this episodic event inescapably poses the question whether then those who were preaching circumcision in Galatia were actually Judaizers.

Christian Gnostics, whose home in any case was *not* Judea, naturally had no connection at all with the "apostolic council" and its agreements. But even in the later period *their* missionary work was indeed not limited in scope. Rather, Gnosticism seriously threatened the community that was growing up in the Hellenistic environment. And of it—and this is now the most important thing—the church fathers unanimously know to report that precisely in the early, the New Testament, the Pauline era, and precisely in Gentile territory, especially in Asia Minor, it had preached circumcision.[62] I can refrain from enumerating in detail the abundance of documentation for this to be found in Hippolytus, Tertullian, Epiphanius, Philastrius, and others.[63] It is most obvious to select the Jewish Christian Gnostic Cerinthus, particularly as described by Epiphanius, for comparison with the Galatian adversaries of Paul. In *all* the accounts of the church fathers we can detect how dangerous Cerinthus must have been to the beginning Gentile Christianity.[64] His appear-

---

[62] It is not surprising that the church fathers often represent the early Gnostics who approved of circumcision as half-Judaizers, at a time when people no longer knew much of the determinative Jewish components of early Gnosticism.

[63] Iren. I, 26.2 (Gnostic Ebionites): *circumciduntur ac perseverant in his consuetudinibus quae sunt secundum legem et iudaico charactere vitae.* Cf. Hipp. Phil. VII, 34.1-2; Tert. de praescr. haer. 33; Eus. CH III, 27; Epiph. Haer. XXX, 2. περιετμήθη, φασίν, ὁ Χριστός καὶ σὺ περιτμήθητι, Epiph. Haer. XXX, 26; cf. XXX, 28, 31, 33.

Hipp. Phil. IX, 14.1 (Elchasaites): οὗτος . . . φάσκων δεῖν περιτέμνεσθαι καὶ κατὰ νόμον ζῆν τοὺς πεπιστευκότας. Philastrius Haer. 36 (Cerinthus): *docet autem circumcidi et sabbatizare . . . dicens debere circumcidi homines.* Cf. Epiph. Haer. XXVIII, 1 ff. Cf. further Epiph. Haer. XIX, 5; Titus 1:10; Ps. Tert. adv. omn. haer. 3; art. "Dositheos" in RE; A. Hilgenfeld, *Die Ketzergeschichte des Urchristentums* (1884), pp. 411-46; J. P. Steffes, *Das Wesen des Gnostizismus und sein Verhältnis zum katholischen Dogma* (Paderborn, 1922), pp. 57-76; E. Lohse in ThWNT VII: 33-34.

[64] The later the tradition about Cerinthus, the more confused it is. But the very fact that along with Gnostic false teachings people later attributed to him every possible heresy shows how strongly he continued for a long time to live in the consciousness of the community as a dangerous rival of ecclesiastical Christianity. The report is said to come from Polycarp that the disciple John, when he encountered Cerinthus in a bathhouse in Ephesus, cried out, horrified, "Let us flee lest the bathhouse in which Cerinthus, the enemy of the truth, is, should collapse" (Iren. III, 3.4; cf. Eus. CH IV, 14.6; III, 28.6). According to Iren. III, 11.1 Cerinthus' error is said to be combated in the Gospel of John. Conversely, the people labeled ἄλογοι by Epiphanius make Cerinthus the author of the Johannine writings of the New Testament, which they regard as heretical (Epiph. Haer. LI, 3; Philastrius Haer. 60). At the latest from the end of the second century onward, Cerinthus also was regarded as the champion of heretical chiliasm (Eus. CH III, 28. 2, 4; VII, 25.2-3). Cf. B. Reicke, [1], pp. 283 ff.

ance in Asia Minor is historically incontestable. Asia is said to have been his homeland.[65] Epiphanius even reports[66] that his school flourished in Galatia. In any case he belongs to the early period,[67] to the beginnings of Christian Gnosticism, and without question connects typical Gnosticism[68] with a confession of Christ and with Jewish practices such as that of circumcision. One need not immediately assume that they were Cerinthians who appeared in Galatia,[69] but in no case can one at once attribute the false teachers, because of their circumcision, to the judaizing party.[70] This heretical feature fits at least just as well—following what has been said, even far better—at any rate in that time and place, with Jewish Christian Gnostics[71] who are conducting a mission in Paul's tracks.[72]

The reasons for circumcision within Gnosticism naturally are other than those within Judaism. Gnostic circumcision could never obligate one to keep the law in the Pharisaic sense, whatever may have been

---

[65] Epiph. Haer. XXVIII, 6; cf. Iren. I, 26.1: *et Cerinthus autem quidam in Asia . . . docuit.*

[66] Haer. XXVIII, 6.

[67] Tertullian already—or still—saw Gnostic Ebionites being opposed in the Galatian epistle (de praescr. haer. 33) and even Jerome was of the opinion that Paul *"frequenter percutit"* Cerinthus (Praef. in comm. super Matthaeum, t. VII, p. 4 Vallarsi=H. Lietzmann, *Kleine Texte*, 1, p. 10) .

[68] Cf. Eus. CH III, 28.

[69] On the other hand, there is nothing that would exclude such an assumption. Cf. now also H. Schlier, [1] (1962, 12th ed.) , pp. 23-24.

[70] E. Lohmeyer presumes that the Gnostic false teachers in Colossae also practice the rite of circumcision (*Der Brief an die Kolosser* [1953], pp. 6, 8, 108 ff.) , yet this cannot be inferred with certainty from Col. 2:11 (see below) .

[71] In this connection it is worthy of note that the early form of Christian Gnosticism must have been *Jewish* Christian Gnosticism. The proclamation of Jesus Christ can have gained admittance in the first period only in the sphere of Judaism. So, just as the Palestinian primitive community lives in close association with the apocalyptic theology of contemporary Judaism, the Judaistic communities stand in the line of continuity with rabbinical theology and the Hellenistic communities continue traditions of the Jewish synagogue, early Christian Gnosticism forms the continuation of pre-Christian Jewish Gnosticism. Hence it is only natural that Jewish features occur all the more frequently in Christian Gnosticism the earlier this Gnosticism is demonstrable. "Marcionite" tendencies on the other hand were remote from early Gnosticism. Above all the mythological motifs of primeval history and the accounts of the Mosaic period found in early Gnosticism, even beyond the Jewish and Christian territory, a lively interest; on this, cf. J. Jervell, *Imago Dei* (1960) , pp. 122 ff.; W. Schultz, *Dokumente der Gnosis* (1910) , p. IX; Vol. 1, pp. 71 ff. Only in isolated instances do people in Jewish Gnostic circles appear to have expressed a radical criticism of the law as Paul's argument in Gal. 3:6-29 presupposes it.

[72] See W. Bauer, [1], p. 89.

practiced in individual Gnostic groups by way of observance of the law. It never did so in Galatia, as was stated above—an important argument for the correctness of our thesis. But Gnosticism was highly adaptable. Precisely the cultic observances, which admittedly were especially stubbornly held, it made serviceable for itself, and in doing so it naturally had to reinterpret them. Thus, just as for example in the Gnostic supper the connection of the bread with the σάρξ of Christ could not be accepted and therefore the bread was interpreted in terms of the cosmic body of Christ,[73] so also circumcision underwent a Gnostic reinterpretation. Traces of this appear to me to have been preserved in Col. 2:9 ff. (cf. Eph. 2:11).[74] Within a section that heavily relies on Gnostic tradition,[75] there is mention of the "circumcision not made with hands," by means of which Christians are circumcised in the "putting off of the body of flesh, in the circumcision of Christ." A little later we read that the Christians were "dead in the uncircumcision of your flesh." Now if in the Christian amplification of the Gnostic model the foreskin or the entire body of flesh is equated with sin, and circumcision with baptism, it is unmistakably clear that in the model, which indeed is somewhat less than complete, the foreskin symbolized the body of flesh and thus the—really performed—act of circumcision portrayed the liberation of the pneuma-self from the prison of this body.[76] Only thus does the intricate symbolism of this passage become understandable.[77]

---

[73] This Gnostic tradition stands behind I Cor. 10:16b-17, when Paul also apparently understands σῶμα in parallel to αἷμα. Similarly, the eucharistic prayers of the Didache stem from this Gnostic stream of tradition (Did. 9.3-4). In these prayers the cup also is connected in a roundabout way, by way of the gnostically interpreted vine (of David; cf. Ps. 80:9-20), with the primal man rather than with the blood of Christ; in Gnosticism the primal man often appears as the vine. *One* bread also in Ign. Eph. 20.2.

[74] The interpretation of circumcision found here is unique. This makes interpretation of the passage difficult. But cf. also Od. Sol. 11.3 and Phil. 3:3.

[75] Cf. G. Bornkamm, *Das Ende des Gesetzes* (1952), p. 145, and the commentaries.

[76] Gnostic baptism had the same symbolic meaning, as is shown by the mythological tradition which Paul uses (cf. Iren. I, 23.5; I, 21.3) in Rom. 6:3 ff. (cf. Gal. 3:27). The conception, frequently occurring in Gnostic tradition and adopted into the Synoptic tradition, that the Pneuma came upon Jesus at his *baptism*, is also to be understood from the perspective that baptism symbolized the mortification of the old man and the liberation of the Pneuma. The Synoptic reports of Jesus' baptism naturally have obscured this Gnostic conception to a large extent.

[77] E. Lohmeyer (pp. 108 ff., 114) strives honestly with this passage. But since he sees Paul here waging a polemic against the Jewish custom of circumcision among the Colossian false teachers, and yet does not notice that the author of the Colossian epistle here in truth is expanding and reshaping the original pattern of a Gnostic hymn to Christ, his exposition, in spite of many a correct point

But for the Gnostic original there thus results a splendid and striking interpretation of circumcision which may well have been proposed in Galatia. Cf. also Saying 123 of the recently discovered Gospel of Philip (Leipoldt-Schenke, p. 62): "When Abraham rejoiced that he would see that which he was to see, he cut off the flesh of his foreskin, whereby he shows us that it is necessary to destroy the flesh of the members of the world." In this connection one may further compare the interpretation which is given in the Naassene Preaching (in Hipp. V, 7) to the mythological story that the mother of the gods mutilated Attis, her own lover: "For Attis was mutilated, that is to say of the earthly parts of the lower creation, and thus came to the eternal higher being." Cf. W. Bousset, *Kyrios Christos* (ET 1970), p. 190. The equation of private parts = demonic body, which underlies the interpretation of circumcision given, also occurs explicitly in the Coptic Gospel of Thomas, Saying 38, which was already known to us through Pap. Oxyr. 655 and through Clem. Alex. Strom. III. 13.92: one is to put off shame or tread under foot the garment of shame.

Of course Paul indicates in Gal. 6:12 a reason for the demand of circumcision made by the Galatian heretics: They propose by means of circumcision to relieve the community of persecution by the Jews (who tolerated circumcised Christians, as the existence of the primitive community in Jerusalem shows) or by the Gentiles (the Jewish religion of circumcision is *religio licita*). Only this is their intention (Gal. 6:12), for they themselves do not keep the law (Gal. 6:13*a*). The only thing that concerns them is to be able to "glory" in the circumcision performed on the Galatians (Gal. 6:13*b*; on the concept of "glorying" cf. in the same context Phil. 3:2-6; see pp. 88-89), which in the context must mean that they expect to use, in the face of potential persecutors, the accomplished circumcision as proof of their deserving of protection. This is first nothing more than a sarcastic accusation by Paul. Since for Paul circumcision can only have the meaning that the one circumcised places himself under the law (Gal. 5:3), but the circumcision party do *not* connect this demand with circumcision (Gal. 6:13),[78] he is at a loss about the sense and reason in the practice of circumcision in Galatia.

---

of insight, remains unsatisfying. Lohmeyer's thesis on Col. 2:11 is taken over by G. Bornkamm, *Das Ende des Gesetzes,* p. 147. It is possible that in 2:8 ff. the author of Colossians is waging a polemic against the custom of circumcision practiced in Colossae by Gnostics, by using the weapons of his opponents; cf. H. Conzelmann, p. 143.

[78] See pp. 33-34.

Of course it is not ruled out that Jewish Christian Gnostics held to circumcision also for the sake of toleration by the Jews, as the Jewish Christians in Jerusalem did.[79] Nevertheless it is noteworthy that a serious religious interest for Gnosticism precisely in the observance of circumcision is just as little evident as in other outward signs (cf. Iren. I, 21.4). At least the Gnostic interpretation of the Supper also created no little difficulty (flesh and blood!). Gnosticism appropriated to itself these ceremonies when it was expedient—and thus possibly for the sake of toleration—but could, on the other hand, wholly abstain from them. Among the Jewish Christian Gnostics against whom Philippians warns, circumcision still occurs (Phil. 3:2 ff.); in Corinth we hear nothing more about it, although Corinth certainly was reached by the same current of the Jewish Christian–Gnostic mission which a little earlier had moved through Asia Minor and Macedonia.

Thus it may well be that the Galatian false teachers to a considerable extent held to the practice of circumcision for tactical reasons; indeed, the thought of their personal security *alone* may—as Paul says in Gal. 6:12—in the meantime have supported their demand for circumcision, while the religious motivation of the demand for circumcision received only a more secondary significance. But the more this is the case, and thus the more Paul in Gal. 6:12-13 gives a genuine justification for the legalism of the Galatian heretics, the less are we dealing here with Judaizers for whom circumcision was the central expression of their religious conviction (cf. A. Oepke, p. 159).

Gal. 5:11 also argues for this: "But, brethren, if I am still preaching circumcision, why am I still being persecuted?" From this remark it must be concluded that some in Galatia were asserting that even his preaching included circumcision. Now one cannot seriously have set before the Galatians the misleading assertion that Paul demands circumcision of his communities. But Paul's remark becomes understandable if people in Galatia had pointed out that Paul also had been able for tactical reasons to affirm circumcision, since possibly he himself had performed it for Timothy (Acts 16:3; see Vol. 3, pp. 93 ff.), but in any case had conceded it for Jewish Christians (Gal. 2:1-10; see Vol. 3, pp. 38 ff.), and in other legal ceremonies also he could become "a Jew to the Jews" (I Cor. 9:20 ff.; cf. e.g., Acts 21:15-26, and on this, Vol. 3, pp. 85 ff.). Such reference to Paul's conduct, however, makes sense only if people in Galatia valued circumcision as

---

[79] Cf. Vol. 3, pp. 43 ff.; W. Marxsen, pp. 52 ff.

he did and did not regard it as the beginning of a way of salvation determined by the law.

Thus also it is not true that Paul had succumbed to a *misunderstanding* of the opponents' position when in Gal. 3–4 he wages a polemic explicitly against the way of the law as a way to salvation. Paul knows throughout that the Galatian heretics are demanding circumcision *without* being willing to keep the law (Gal. 6:13). Hence Paul himself must first make the community aware of the logical consequences which the adoption of circumcision brings with it. Paul's theological reflection in Gal. 3:1–5:12 on righteousness by works and righteousness by faith, for which Gal. 2:19-21 prepared the way, thus is not to be interpreted as though Paul is presupposing in these theological statements that some *in Galatia* consciously intended to go the way of pure law-righteousness. It is indeed characteristic that this middle section of the Galatian epistle, in contrast to all other sections, contains hardly any direct references to the situation in Galatia. This central part of Galatians rather gives witness that *for Paul* the adoption of circumcision can mean nothing other than an attempt to achieve righteousness without faith through works. Therefore the circumcision being practiced in Galatia *must* have the same meaning for the Galatians *coram Deo,* regardless of whether they themselves know it or not (Gal. 5:3), whether they concern themselves with the fulfillment of the law or—incomprehensibly— neglect it, in spite of circumcision (Gal. 6:13). Thus chaps. 3–4 do not interrupt the train of thought, but are intended to warn against the *consequences* which are given for the Galatians with their going over to the side of the opponents.

An exegesis of Gal. 3:1–5:12 would show that all the sections of this part of the epistle in which the situation in Galatia is not directly addressed (3:6-14; 3:15-18; 3:19–4:7; 4:21-31) contain current *topoi* of Paul's discussion with the *Jews* over the question of the law in which the general proof is brought forward that and why since Christ the law has lost its validity for Christians. None of these sections was conceived for the Galatian epistle. None of these sections therefore discloses any more for the situation in Galatia than the fact that people there in *some* way were holding to the law. None of these sections is supposed to say more in the context of the Pauline argument than this: For the believers, the law can claim *no sort* of validity any longer. If one observes this context in the history of tradition, one cannot adduce the traditional anti-synagogal pieces in Gal. 3:1–5:12 in favor of the theory that the false teachers in Galatia were Judaizers, as is done, e.g., by W. Foerster ("Abfassungszeit und Ziel des Galater-briefes," in *Apophoreta*, BZNW 30 [1964]: 139-40), H. Koester ("ΓΝΩΜΑΙ ΔΙΑΦΟΡΟΙ," HTR 58 [1965]: 307 ff.), D. Lührmann (*Das Offenbarungsverständnis bei Paulus und in paulinischen Gemeinden* [1965], pp. 67 ff.), D. Georgi (pp. 35-36), and others. Further, I cannot share E. Güttgemanns' reservations (pp. 184-85), that it will not do "simply to cut out Gal. 3:6–4:20 as having no reference to the situation in Galatia, since it involves the 'core' of the epistle"; for this core is precisely the core of *Pauline* theology and to this extent Pauline *interpretation* of the situation in Galatia. But those sections in which Paul expressly addresses the situation in Galatia (3:1-5; 4:8-11; 4:12-20; 5:1-12) allow us to see that people in Galatia obviously were not thinking of going the way of the righteousness of the law.

K. Wegenast, pp. 36 ff., agrees with my description of the opponents not as Judaizers but as Jewish Gnostics, but thinks that from Gal. 3–4 he can infer decisive information on the position of the opponents. As I have said, I cannot agree with this. Wegenast's sentence, "Paul's opponents by no means condemn the apostle because he, as they say, is dependent on the Jerusalem apostles—this is nowhere said—but because he demanded neither circumcision nor the keeping of the Jewish law by the communities" (p. 39, n. 3), turns the actual state of things upside down. For that in Gal. 1–2 Paul is *defending himself against the charge* that he is dependent on men is just as evident as the fact that he comes to speak on circumcision precisely not apologetically but *polemically*—against the practice of circumcision in Galatia—as then this theme also imperceptibly grows out of Gal. 2:15 ff., the *polemic* against Peter. Hence nowhere, even in Gal. 3–4 or in any other passage in the epistle, is it evident that Paul is defending himself against the charge that he does not bind his communities to the law; one could rather infer from 5:11 the opposite charge.

In the new twelfth edition of his commentary ([1], p. 19), H. Schlier writes: "In any case this is clear at one point: [the opponents] are demanding that in order to be saved the Galatian Gentile Christians let themselves be circumcised. This is clearly attested in Gal. 5:2-3, 6, 12; 6:12-13." Actually in not one of these passages is it even suggested that the Galatian false teachers are demanding circumcision *for the sake of salvation*. Quite the contrary: it is *Paul* who by means of repeated arguments through the entire epistle must first make clear to the Galatians the significance of the problem of the law *for salvation*.

In this sense E. Jüngel (*Paulus und Jesus* [1962], p. 32, n. 1) in principle rightly judges the handling of the problem of the law in the Galatian epistle. But cf. also H. Schlier himself in [1] (12th ed.), p. 24. Above all, the treatment of our problem by W. Marxsen, pp. 50 ff., is courageous, delightfully unconventional, and—except for some details—convincing. Unfortunately, because of technical reasons connected with printing it was not possible for me to consider his statements more thoroughly. Cf. further R. Bultmann, *Theologie des Neuen Testaments* (5th ed., 1965), p. 110, n. 1; E. Güttgemanns, p. 133, n. 42; pp. 179-80; 184-85; Charles H. Talbert, in *Nov. Test.* 9 (1967) : 26 ff.; K. Kertelge, *Rechtfertigung bei Paulus* (1967), pp. 196 ff.

IV

The fact that the Galatian heretics demand circumcision does not speak against but for the thesis that in them we have to do with Gnostics, Jewish or Jewish Christian. Indeed, this thesis becomes compelling and necessary if in other respects people did not actually think of placing the yoke of the law on the necks of the Galatians. In spite of what was said earlier, it could almost look as though this was being done after all. In any case, Paul once complains to the Galatians that they are observing "days, months, seasons, and years" (Gal. 4:10). This looks very much like the observance of Jewish festivals.

But it only has this appearance. In fact, it is precisely this passage that lets H. Schlier speak of only "so-called Judaizers." [80]

Of course it has generally been attempted—it logically had to be attempted—to connect the ἡμέραι, μῆνες, καιροί, and ἐνιαυτοί with sabbaths, fasts, and feast days, with special months or new-moon days, with festival seasons, hours of prayer, or something of the sort, and finally with sabbatical years, new year's feasts, and so on.[81] Up to the sabbatical and jubilee years (Exod. 23: 10 ff.; Lev. 25:1 ff.; Deut. 15:1 ff.; 31:10), of the actual observance of which in New Testament times no convincing report has been handed down to us,[82] such a connection certainly is theoretically possible.

---

[80] H. Schlier, [1], p. 136. Cf. also K. Kertelge, pp. 196 ff.

[81] Cf. H. Schlier, [1], p. 145, n. 1; W. Rordorf, *Sunday*, pp. 131 ff.

[82] Cf. H. Schlier, [1], p. 146.

One must, however, observe that here Paul is not at all formulating his argument *ad hoc* or enumerating the individual times which have been reported to him as now observed by the Galatians. Rather he is employing a current familiar list which was not widespread in Jewish orthodoxy but frequently occurs above all in the apocryphal and Gnostic or gnosticizing literature.[83] The most obvious passage for us to compare is naturally Col. 2:16,[84] "Let no man judge you . . . because of feasts, new moons and sabbaths." [85] This passage also shows the true background of such observance: "Let no one condemn you who (and now these practitioners are characterized) takes pleasure in humility[86] and angel worship, relies on visions, and is without reason puffed up in his earthly mind." [87] This description is clear, though not fully distinct in every respect. It concerns Gnostics, and their observance of definite times fits together with angel worship, i.e., with the fact that the demonic powers, which for Hellenism to a great extent and in particular for Gnosticism appear embodied in the stars, rule at definite times, and at these times threaten men.[88] "There are wicked stars of godlessness. Let this now be said to you God-fearers and disciples: beware of the powerful influence of the days of their rule. Begin no work on their days and baptize neither man nor woman in the

---

[83] Judith 8.6; Eth. Enoch 72.1; 75.3-4; 79.2; 80.6-7; 82.7 ff.; Jubil. 1.14; Damasc. 8.15; Sir. 33.7 ff.; Diogn. 4.5; Just. Dial. 8.4; Slav. Enoch 19.1 ff.; 43.2; Hipp. Phil. IX, 16.2; V, 9; Cic. de nat. deor. I, 36 (from Zeno) ; Lidzbarski, *Ginza* 136.7; 197.22; 313.5 ff.; E. Lohse in ThWNT VII: 33-34; E. S. Drower, *The Secret Adam* (1960) , p. 68.

[84] Cf. E. Lohmeyer, pp. 121 ff., n. 70; B. Reicke, *Studia Theologica* VI (1953) : 41, 51; G. Bornkamm, "Die Häresie des Kolosserbriefes," in *Das Ende des Gesetzes* (1952) , pp. 139-56.

[85] On σαββατίζειν in Gnosticism, cf. Logion 28 of the Coptic Gospel of Thomas. It corresponds to Pap. Oxyr. 1, lines 4-11=Hennecke-Schneemelcher-Wilson, I: 106. Cf. E. Lohse in ThWNT VII: 33-34.

[86] ταπεινοφροσύνη here and in vs. 23 cannot denote "humility" as obedient disposition, e.g. in the Pauline sense. B. Reicke (see n. 84) renders the word, with good justification, as "asceticism" (cf. M. Dibelius, *An die Kolosser*, HNT 12 [1927, 2nd ed.]: 26) . It fits thus into the context.

[87] Col. 2:18; the passage is admittedly difficult to translate. I follow Lohmeyer's translation, which appears to me to be apt.

[88] The formula certainly has been oriented in form to Gen. 1:14 ff.: Γενηθήτωσαν φωστῆρες . . . καὶ ἔστωσαν εἰς σημεῖα καὶ εἰς καιροὺς καὶ εἰς ἡμέρας καὶ εἰς ἐνιαυτοὺς . . . καὶ ἄρχειν τῆς ἡμέρας καὶ τῆς νυκτός. . . . This passage in Genesis however then will also have provided the exegetical basis for angel worship in gnosticizing Judaism. Hence it is no accident that this formula always occurs in the vicinity of Judaism.

days of their power, when the moon moves through them and journeys with them. Guard yourself against this day, until it has hastened on away from them . . . ." [89]

Such Gnostic speculations must also stand behind the Galatian observance of certain times.[90] Paul also is aware of this; for even if he does not speak of the service of ἄγγελοι, still he does speak in the same sense of service under those who by nature are not God or of the poor and beggarly στοιχεῖα, the world powers, to which the Galatians are returning.[91] This too has its parallel in that passage in Colossians. The Colossians are liberated from the στοιχεῖα τοῦ κόσμου, to which they are again subjecting themselves with their angel worship in the observance of feasts, new moons, and sabbaths.[92]

Therewith is indicated the tendency out of which we must understand Paul's remark that the Galatians are observing days, months, seasons, and years. No more than a tendency, to be sure. No details can be inferred from this widely used formula, which Paul probably used because he was not sufficiently informed on concrete particulars, and which he in no case wants to have un-

---

[89] A quotation from the book Elchasai preserved in Hipp. Phil. IX, 162 (ed. Wendland, p. 254, 21 ff.). Cf. J. M. Allegro, *Die Botschaft vom Toten Meer* (Fischer-Bücherei, 1957), p. 98. M. Weise, "Kultzeiten und kultischer Bundesschluss in der 'Ordensregel' vom Toten Meer" (Diss. Jena, 1955); see the author's own note in ThLZ 1957, cols. 386-87.

[90] This eliminates the reflection of O. Holtzmann (p. 495), which to be sure is somewhat peculiar anyway. "Nevertheless it is curious that the man who here is opposing the Jewish calendar of feasts himself—even in commerce with Gentile Christians—always reckoned time by the Jewish week and the Jewish days."

[91] Gal. 4:3, 8-9. Nowadays it may be acknowledged as proved that in the στοιχεῖα τοῦ κόσμου we have to do with personal angelic powers (cf. H. Schlier, [1], pp. 133 ff.). Of course the accusation of the *service* of angels is polemical. It was precisely the power of the demonic forces that the Galatian opponents wanted to escape. After all, the concept στοιχεῖα may well deserve to be understood as Pauline *interpretamentum* rather than as Galatian terminology. In any case, however, it would be inconceivable that Paul regards the observance of the *Jewish* feast days as the worship of pagan gods. Hence in 4:10 he cannot have in mind any judaizing behavior.

[92] The similarity of the terminology and of the argument in Gal. 4:8-10 and Col. 2:16-23 inexorably compels us to see the same opponents being combated in both passages. This holds true not only in case the Colossian epistle were written by Paul himself—then of course no more discussion of this question should even be allowed—but also under the assumption that Colossians is deutero-Pauline. If one wishes to see Judaizers combated in Gal. 4:8-10, one must therefore accept the assumption of the same false teachers for Colossae. Since this is impossible, there remains only the possibility of assuming for the Galatian epistle also an anti-Gnostic battle line.

derstood as focused in a particular way. However, the tendency into which we look with Paul is not Pharisaism or a judaizing tendency as Pharisaism's unloved offspring, but Gnosticism in one of its varieties.[93]

V

The Galatians come under their laws—essentially different laws from those of the Judaizers. They are the laws of the πνευματικοί, for whom not bodily discipline but ecstatic licentiousness is characteristic. But people in Galatia apparently were identifying themselves emphatically as πνευματικοί. W. Lütgert has already pointed this out.[94] In Gal. 6:1 Paul writes: "Brethren, if a man be discovered in some transgression, you pneumatic ones restore him in the spirit of meekness." The emphatic address, ὑμεῖς οἱ πνευματικοί, indicates that here Paul is adopting the emphasized self-assertion of the Galatians, or of some of them,[95] especially when one places Gal. 4:21 alongside it: "Tell me, οἱ ὑπὸ νόμον θέλοντες εἶναι, . . ." W. Lütgert concludes from this that Paul is addressing two different groups in the community in these two passages, because Judaistic circumcision and the pneumatic state are mutually exclusive.[96] Indeed! But Gnostic circumcision and the pneumatic state go together well.

Gal. 3:2 may also be understood from this perspective. "Now

---

[93] Even the strict observance of times among the Essenes (Jos. Bell. II, 8.9) and related groups (Damasc. 13) , among these the sanctification of the Sabbath, may be traced back less to Pharisaic than to gnosticizing influence, especially since speculations about angels (Jos. Bell. II, 8.7) and even veneration of the sun (Jos. Bell. II, 8.5) are not lacking there; cf. n. 89.

[94] [1], pp. 12-13.

[95] Thus, rightly, most modern exegetes. "ὑμεῖς οἱ πνευματικοί hardly means simply the 'community of Christians.' Here it rather has a somewhat sarcastic sound: 'you who pose as πνευματικοί'" (H. Lietzmann, HNT 10 [1932, 3rd ed.]: in loc.). Cf. Hipp. Phil. V, 9 (ed. Duncker-Schneidewin, 174, 21-22) : ἡμεῖς δ' ἐσμέν, φησίν, οἱ πνευματικοί (cf. V, 8 = 164, 70-71) .

[96] This also creates difficulties for other exegetes on Gal. 6:1. J. B. Lightfoot (p. 215) remarks on ὑμεῖς οἱ πνευματικοί: "St. Paul had once and again urged them to walk by the Spirit (V, 16, 25) . This explains the forms of address here: 'ye who have taken my lesson to heart, ye who would indeed be guided by the Spirit.'" But this interpretation bears on its face the stamp of difficulty all the more clearly since Lightfoot expresses himself explicitly against the conjecture that here Paul is turning "to the party of more liberal views, who had taken his side against the Judaizers." The ones addressed in Gal. 6:1 are unquestionably Christians who deliberately and with emphasis identify themselves as pneumatics (cf. Rom. 15:1: οἱ δύνατοι) .

I should like to know this of you: did you receive the Spirit by works of the law or by the preaching of faith?" This sentence then first takes on its full import if it inquires after the Galatians' emphatic assertion that they had (received) the Spirit. The "πνεῦμα λαμβάνειν," used absolutely and presumably stemming from the language of the mystery cults, occurs in Paul among other places also in II Cor. 11:4, and here in indubitable adoption of a Gnostic thesis. Just so in Gal. 3:5 Paul may be going into the Galatians' current assertion that they had the "Spirit" and "mighty deeds" were taking place among them. In any case in Gal. 3:5 we have to do with what are typical assertions for the Gnostic pneumatic, insofar as by "mighty deeds" are to be understood ecstatic productions of the Pneuma, in which the Gnostic message is manifested as a divine message itself. A comparison for example with II Cor. 12:11-12 (see Vol. 1, pp. 281-82) and I Thess. 1:5 (see below, pp. 136 ff.) makes it clear that in other places as well Paul had to debate with the claim and demand made by false teachers who had infiltrated the community to produce and to experience "mighty deeds." Cf. also n. 42 above.

The dialectic of Gal. 5:25, εἰ ζῶμεν πνεύματι, πνεύματι καὶ στοιχῶμεν, will also have its specific occasion in the Galatian assertion, meant in terms of being, that one "lives in the Spirit," an undisputed assertion,[97] which Paul however, in view of the *conduct* of the pneumatics, which was little Spirit-wrought, sees himself compelled to complete with a reference to the existential significance of such possession of the Spirit: then we also wish to walk by the Spirit.[98] The fundamental cleavage between "having the Spirit" and "walking in the Spirit" as it is found in Galatia is not possible in a Pauline community, since here the

---

[97] "Those who are addressed here live in the Spirit: this is a fact which is not only claimed by them, but is also conceded to them by Paul—but they must be admonished that if they live in the Spirit, they are also to walk in the Spirit" (W. Lütgert, [1], p. 19).

[98] According to the evidence of the passages cited, Paul perhaps had not become aware that the stressing of the pneumatic state was a part of the heretical program in Galatia. No wonder, for Paul naturally was of the persuasion that he himself had already brought the Pneuma to the Galatians (Gal. 3:2). The case is different in Corinth, where the community directs an inquiry to Paul "touching those who are pneumatics" (I Cor. 12:3) and Paul has comprehended that the Corinthians have received a πνεῦμα ἕτερον from the ψευδαπόστολοι (II Cor. 11:4).

possession of the Spirit is manifested precisely in conduct,[99] but indeed is possible in a Gnostic community in which the πνεῦμα is shown to be present in ecstatic experience, especially in speaking in tongues, quite independent from any "Christian conduct." [100]

Among the Gnostics, possession of the Pneuma and self-praise stand in constant connection.[101] Hence the apostle's definite admonition: "If anyone thinks himself to be something although he is nothing, he deceives himself" (Gal. 6:3) [102]. For instead of their "walking in the Spirit," Paul declares that the pneumatics in Galatia are κενόδοξοι, filled with unfounded desire for glory,[103] provoke one another with their pneumatic-ecstatic endowments (ἀλλήλους προκαλούμενοι) and therewith naturally also arouse envy among those whose spiritual gifts are less[104] (ἀλλήλοις φθονοῦντες, cf. I Cor. 12:4 ff.) : Gal. 5:26.

---

[99] Cf. Rom. 8:2 ff.; I Cor. 3:1 ff.; Gal. 5:17; 6:7 ff., et passim. One must not allow himself to be misled, by Paul's Gnostic terminology which often has even an animistic sound, to the misapprehension that for him also the Pneuma is a piece of divine substance.

[100] Gal. 5:16 then could also belong in this context: "Walk in the Spirit (scil., whom you in fact explicitly claim to possess) and you will not fulfill the lusts of the flesh."

[101] Cf., e.g., Iren. I, 13.6, where the disciples of Marcus are called perfect, "quasi nemo possit exaequari magnitudini agnitionis ipsorum, nec si Paulum aut Petrum dicas, vel alterum quendam apostolorum: sed plus omnibus se cognovisse et magnitudinem agnitionis illius, quae est inenarrabilis virtutis, solos ebibisse. Esse autem se in altitudine super omnem virtutem: quapropter et libere omnia agere, nullum in nullo timorem habentes. Propter enim redemptionem et incomprehensibiles et invisibiles fieri iudici." By virtue of his pneuma-self the Gnostic is of divine nature, and hence also of divine power and divine perfection. He is τέλειος (Corp. Herm. IV, 4; R. Reitzenstein, Die hellenistischen Mysterienreligionen [3rd ed.], pp. 338-39). Paul sets himself against this heightened self-consciousness also in the Corinthian pneumatics, who are "puffed up" and "boast" because they are "filled," "rich," and have already "become kings" (I Cor. 4:6 ff.; cf. I Cor. 4:10; 5:2; 8:1; II Cor. 12:1 ff., 20; Col. 2:18; Clem. Alex. Strom. IV, 23.149; IV, 6.40; Iren. I, 23.5; 25.3; II, 26.1), and in the "perfect" in Philippi, whom he challenges to see their perfection in their being able, like Paul, to say: "οὐχ ὅτι ἤδη ἔλαβον ἢ ἤδη τετελείωμαι, διώκω δέ . . ." (Phil. 3:12 ff.). Cf. also the anti-Gnostic polemic in Hermas Sim. IX, 22 and M. Dibelius in HNT in loc. Cf. below, pp. 96-97; 233-34; Vol. 1, pp. 61 ff.

[102] The Gnostics are "something" because they are Pneuma. Paul, who for them is only σάρξ (II Cor. 10:2), is therefore "nothing" (II Cor. 10:2; 12:11). Paul must turn this judgment around. Only the grace of God makes one who himself is nothing (II Cor. 3:5-6) into something (I Cor. 15:10).

[103] The concept καύχημα or καυχᾶσθαι applied to the opponents occurs in 6:4 and 6:13-14.

[104] ". . . did some here as in Corinth envy those provided with special gifts of the Spirit (6:1)?" (H. Lietzmann, HNT 10: in loc.).

Naturally it is difficult to fill these varied ambiguous expressions with a specific meaning. An understanding of them in detail can be gained only in terms of the total evaluation of the Galatian heresy. Of course under the presupposition of a judaizing false teaching one gets into difficulty with them. Even the fact that people were glorying in circumcision does not shed much light. But it is utterly inconceivable that some even envied others because of their circumcision (which one would have been able to have performed on himself at any time). Therefore Cramer, for example (*Kommentar zum Galaterbrief* [1890]), excises this verse. H. Schlier, F. Sieffert, and many others refrain from giving an explanation for it out of the concrete situation, which however is just as much demanded for Gal. 5:13–6:10 as for the other parts of the epistle. ("It is clear that something had occurred which alarmed him on this point," J. B. Lightfoot, p. 214, who then however does not clarify the expressions in Gal. 5:26 substantively and specifically.) Nevertheless Gnostic pneumatics are splendidly described by the characterization in Gal. 5:26. For them the glorying (which for Paul is "empty") is proper, because they "proclaim" themselves, i.e. their pneuma-self (II Cor. 4:5, 10:12).

προκαλεῖσθαι means to provoke or to challenge (cf. H. Schlier, [1], p. 198). The ecstatic demonstrations of the pneumatic challenge another to awaken the Pneuma which resides in him also. If this is done, it is reason for now finding his καύχημα εἰς τὸν ἕτερον (Gal. 6:4; cf. 6:13). If it does not succeed, then the ecstatic praxis is a provocation to envy. Envy among Christians (ἀλλήλοις φθονοῦντες) is in fact proper if a "ὑπερβολὴ τῶν ἀποκαλύψεων" (II Cor. 12:7), if speaking in tongues (I Cor. 14) and ecstasies (II Cor. 5:13) prove a special quality of Christian existence, as the Gnostics in contrast with Paul assert (II Cor. 5:11 ff., 12:11), a quality which naturally is not attainable for everyone.

But high estimation of the Pneuma always means for the Gnostic, for whom the Pneuma is indeed his own *self*, also rejection of the σάρξ as the prison of this pneuma-self. Therefore the man who is only σάρξ is nothing.[105] Paul, in the eyes of the Galatian heretics so little a pneumatic that indeed he must receive even his gospel from other men, is therefore as a mere "sarkic" to be held only in contempt. No wonder that he then bitterly complains that people once had received him "as an

---

[105] For "redemption extends only to the soul, the body cannot help decaying, as befits its nature" (Iren. I, 24.5). Cf. n. 102.

angel of God," indeed as "Christ Jesus" himself, although at that time he had proclaimed the gospel δι' ἀσθένειαν τῆς σαρκός,[106] that they would have "plucked out their eyes for him," *without* having succumbed to the temptation which lay "ἐν τῇ σαρκί μου," in the wretched flesh of the ill Paul, and without "spitting in his presence in contempt," in short, that *once* people took no offense at his flesh, but now because of this flesh[107] he has "become their enemy" (Gal. 4:12 ff.). "Where now is your blessing?" he asks in despair. "They make much of you, to no good purpose," these new apostles. "They want to separate you from me, so that you will make much of them." And this because of the weakness of my flesh! [108] And you are going along with that! What am I to say to this? "I should like to be with you now and to change my language; for I am puzzled about you."

It is superfluous to emphasize that in all this an anti-judaizing battlefront for Paul does not come into the picture at all. Even clearer is the Gnostic accusation: Paul indeed is only a "sarkic."

Since the accusation of bodily weakness on the part of Judaizers would be entirely unaccountable, the commentators all assume that

---

[106] The expression is disputed. The ancient expositors throughout understand it as "in weakness"; the Latins translate it as "per infirmitatem." Yet the grammar clearly argues for "on account of weakness of the flesh." (Thus almost all modern commentaries and grammars.) Thus Paul intends explicitly to affirm that he not only had preached to the Galatians in fleshly weakness, but that even the *occasion* of his preaching in Galatia was a sickness which kept him there against his will.

[107] Paul indeed asks, ὥστε ἐχθρὸς ὑμῶν γέγονα ἀληθεύων ὑμῖν, but naturally he does not mean with this question to give the reason offered by the Galatians for his now having become their enemy, but intends to point to the paradox of their relation to him: then you took no offense at my flesh in its weakness but received me as an angel of God; when you now no longer receive me, it is logical that my fleshly weakness cannot be the reason for such behavior. So do you account me as an enemy because I declare the truth to you? Precisely this argument of Paul shows that in truth people in Galatia were declaiming against Paul on account of the apostle's fleshly weakness.

[108] Naturally the Gnostics did not denounce Paul especially for the weakness of *his* flesh and demand of an apostle robust health or greater bodily strength. The charge was that Paul was only an ἄνθρωπος σαρκινός, a man of merely contemptible and weak fleshliness, not a pneumatic. Of course it is nothing less than obvious that Paul connected the accusation with his special bodily weakness. For his thought, basically Jewish, the contempt for corporeality as such had to appear inconceivable. Thus he indeed also understands the accusation of the Corinthian Gnostics, which was meant in a substantial sense, that he was a "sarkic," as meaning that they were accusing him of "fleshly conduct" (II Cor. 10:2-3), and their denial of the bodily resurrection makes these Gnostics appear to him as radical skeptics (I Cor. 15). Cf. Lidzbarski, *Ginza*, 42.13 ff.; Iren. V, 3.2.

Paul *on his own initiative* refers to the fact that during his founding
visit the Galatians were not offended at his weakness. Then the intention of the apostle's statements in Gal. 4:13-20 would be to point
the Galatians to their joyful acceptance of his person during the time
of his first preaching in Galatia, of which now no trace is any longer
to be seen. The reference to his lamentable physical condition during that first sojourn then would only have had the purpose of
praising the heartiness of this readiness of acceptance. But it is not
very clear how Paul could get the idea that his sickness would easily
have been able to do harm to the persuasive force of his message or
to teach him to hold himself in contempt rather than (as would
then be more likely) to feel sorry for himself. Apart from this, however, the important reference, placed at the climactic point of his
statements in Gal. 4:12 ff., to Paul's weakness on his founding visit
and the Galatians' positive reaction to it may indicate that Paul *himself* is concerned about this fact of the past, in order to stress the
Galatians' inconsistency when *today* they are offended at his weakness.
Finally, vs. 17 in fact also makes it clear that Paul had in mind the
ζῆλος of his opponents when he wrote the preceding verse, of those
opponents who are sowing enmity (vs. 16) between the Galatians
and Paul by teaching them to scorn Paul because of his "fleshliness."

One may now also compare the detailed treatment of Gal. 4:12-20
by E. Güttgemanns (pp. 170 ff.), which among other things, by
means of an instructive comparison with II Cor., comes to the conclusion that people were scorning Paul as apostle because he was not
emancipated from his "flesh." Of course Güttgemanns overshoots the
mark when he understands the weakness of the apostle as an epiphany
of the crucified Christ.

VI

The πνευματικοί are also ἐλεύθεροι, that is, people liberated from
the σάρξ and all moral regulations connected with it. Whether
Paul consciously is referring to the expressions of the Galatian
opponents, when in Gal. 5:1 and 5:13 he says, "for freedom
Christ has set you free," or, "for you are called to freedom," is
indeed not certain but still very probable. For in both cases
Paul must continue with the warning: "Stand fast now and do
not submit yourselves again to the yoke of bondage," or: "Only
do not use your freedom for an occasion to serve the flesh." In
both passages the stress unmistakably falls on the final clause,

so that Paul is not, in teaching about freedom, summoning to freedom, but is opposing the misuse of freedom. Above all the latter passage[109] gives the impression that Paul very likely knows that some in Galatia *with a reference to* ἐλευθερία were walking κατὰ σάρκα, so that he indeed grants that we Christians are free persons, but in view of his historical understanding of such Christian freedom demands quite a different way of proving ἐλευθερία from that of the Gnostics in their mythic-essentialist thought.

But be that as it may, it is sufficiently clear that people in Galatia were preaching circumcision but for the rest were thinking and living in libertine rather than legalistic fashion. Paul must take a stand emphatically and at length, even though not always very concretely,[110] against walking κατὰ σάρκα. Some passages have just been cited (Gal. 5:1, 13, 16), and 5:3 and 6:13 were mentioned earlier. Of course it is difficult to say to what extent the ἔργα τῆς σαρκός which Paul then enumerates in detail in 5:19 ff. have *concrete* reference to the situation in Galatia. Nevertheless the typically Gnostic manners of conduct[111] are placed at the beginning: πορνεία and ἀκαθαρσία on the one hand, ἀσέλγεια[112] and εἰδωλολατρία on the other hand. φαρμακεία = magic could have been a Gnostic term in Galatia or could describe the Galatian behavior as Paul understood it. Then follow no fewer than seven different expressions for controversies or divisions, in

---

[109] W. Lütgert places great weight on this passage for establishing his thesis of a twofold battlefront in Galatia. He can rightly point to the fact that traditional exposition of the section Gal. 5:13 ff. is full of contradictions ([1], p. 14). But Lütgert's explanation itself on Gal. 5:13 ff., which, in addition to W. M. L. de Wette (see Lütgert, [1], p. 16) and others, J. B. Lightfoot also had already held, collapses on the fact that Gal. 5:1 and 5:13 cannot be understood as directed against different pneumatics, as he wishes to do. *The same* preachers of freedom who stand in peril of a moral abuse of their freedom (Gal. 5:13) are putting on the bondage-yoke of circumcision (Gal. 5:1). K. v. Hofmann (pp. 171-72) wants to draw Gal. 5:13 to 5:1-12. This would make possible a unified anti-judaizing understanding of Gal. 5:1 and 5:13, but of course is exegetically untenable.

[110] It is otherwise in the Corinthian epistles, where Paul shows himself significantly better informed.

[111] Unchastity and participating in meals offered to idols; cf. Rev. 2:14, 20; Iren. I, 6.3.

[112] ἀσέλγεια means licentiousness quite generally, sensuality. It frequently is used specifically to denote sexual debauchery. In Rom. 13:13 and Gal. 5:19 as also in II Cor. 12:21, I should take it to mean excesses in the worship of idols, perhaps gluttony, possibly also sexual excesses. Cf. Vol. 1, p. 223.

such heaping up certainly with a view to the situation in Galatia.[113] Then mention is made of φθόνος = envy, which also appears in Gal. 5:26 and there has direct reference to the situation in Galatia.[114] Finally, μέθαι and κῶμοι at the end fit again with ἀσέλγεια and εἰδωλολατρία, the pagan meals sacrificed to idols,[115] in which in fact the Gnostics in Corinth also take part unhesitatingly with an explicit appeal to their freedom.[116] Over against this, then, in the enumeration of the "fruits of the Spirit" [117] there appears, in addition to the eight expressions for "peaceableness," [118] only ἐγκράτεια (continence, self-discipline) ;[119] for οἱ τοῦ Χριστοῦ [120] have crucified the flesh with its passions and appetites. Thus every one of these vices and virtues fits precisely into the situation which we have shown to exist in Galatia,[121] which does not hold true under the presupposition of a judaizing opposition to Paul.

Paul must also warn against error—and thus indeed the Gnostic conduct must appear to the Christian Paul, and in fact thus did the Gnostics think in principle[122] also—as though one

---

[113] On details, cf. S. Wibbing, *Die Tugend- und Lasterkataloge im Neuen Testament* (1959), pp. 95 ff.

[114] Cf. p. 48.

[115] In I Peter 4:3 also the κῶμοι occur together with εἰδωλολατρία.

[116] I Cor. 6:12-13; 8:1 ff.; 10:23 ff. B. Reicke ([1] pp. 248 ff.) thinks of the disorders during the observance of the Supper which are attested to us in Corinth by I Cor. 11:20 ff. This too is possible, but in the context of the catalog of vices is quite remote from both concepts.

[117] Gal. 5:22-23.

[118] Even πίστις is to be understood here in this sense (cf. H. Schlier, [1], p. 190).

[119] "Apparently this Hellenistic concept denotes for him the inner and outer conduct which is set in contrast to πορνεία, ἀκαθαρσία, ἀσέλγεια, and the μέθαι and κῶμοι (5:20-21)" (H. Schlier, [1], pp. 191-92).

[120] The Χριστοῦ εἶναι is the exclusive self-designation of the Corinthian Gnostics (I Cor. 1:12; II Cor. 10:7). That in Gal. 5:24 Paul is taking up the same-sounding designation of the Galatian Gnostics is of course unlikely, since this originally Gnostic-mythological formula is familiar to Paul himself for designation of the Christian status (Rom. 8:9; I Cor. 3:23; 15:23).

[121] If one places alongside Gal. 5:19 ff. the catalog of vices in Rom. 1:29 ff., for example, where Paul intends to charactize the totality of heathen sins, one will sense how purposefully Paul makes his formulation in his catalogs of vices in spite of his thoroughgoing use of traditional concepts and groups of concepts in detail.

[122] Cf. Iren. I, 6.2: "*Quemadmodum enim choicum impossibile est salutem percipere, sic iterum quod spiritale impossibile esse corruptelam percipere, licet in quibuscunque fuerint factis.*" The dualistic Gnostic anthropology with its ethical implications becomes clearest in the anti-Gnostic polemic in Hermas Sim. V, 7 (cf. Sim. VIII, 6.5; IX, 22): "Keep your flesh pure and unspotted, ἵνα τὸ

could sow to the flesh and yet from the πνεῦμα reap eternal life.[123] "Be not deceived, God is not mocked; for whatsoever a man soweth, that shall he also reap." [124] Only one who *sows* to the Spirit will also reap of the Spirit. How he *walks*, not what he *is*, is the decisive thing about a man.

Thus the mockery of God (μυκτηρίζειν) does not consist in that "God will not allow His will and grace to be treated with contempt through man's obeying and trusting his carnal and sinful nature and not God" (W. H. Preisker in TDNT IV: 796) —Paul never elsewhere describes this basic human disobedience as *mockery* of God—but in the fact some in Galatia were consciously stressing the possession of the divine Pneuma, for this reason held themselves to be perfect Christians and openly boasted of their piety (Gal. 5:26; 6:3), but at the same time were sowing to the σάρξ, and were doing that equally consciously and emphatically. It must appear to Paul as a mockery of God when a person walks according to the flesh *while appealing to the Spirit of God*. Such behavior of the Galatians, which makes God into a minister of sin, caricatures God. Only thus does the μυκτηρίζειν take on its concrete sense.

Approximately one-fourth of the Galatian epistle is directed more or less pointedly against the sarkic conduct of the Galatians,[125] and this in such a way that this polemic cannot be separated from the debate with the pneumatics, the circumcision

---

πνεῦμα τὸ κατοικοῦν ἐν αὐτῇ may give a good testimony for it, and your flesh may be justified. Do not let the opinion arise in you that your flesh is perishable, so that you abuse and stain it. For if you stain your flesh, you also stain τὸ πνεῦμα τὸ ἅγιον. . . . For the two belong together and cannot be stained separately." Cf. also the parable, in its present form certainly anti-libertine, of the blind man and the cripple in the Apocryphon of Ezekiel in Epiph. Haer. LXIV, 70.5 ff. (=Synhedrin 91a, b; Goldschmidt IX: 33-34).

[123] "They are deceiving themselves by believing that they can sow to the flesh and reap of the Spirit. That is the audacious assurance of the pneumatics which is reported here; they fancy that for them as the bearers of the Spirit the fruit of the Spirit, eternal life, is assured" (W. Lütgert, [1], p. 21).

[124] Gal. 6:7. Paul formulates the well-known and widely used proverb (H. Schlier, [1], p. 204) in such a way that the emphasis which he wishes to make is clearly to be heard: ὃ γὰρ ἐὰν σπείρῃ ἄνθρωπος, τοῦτο καὶ θερίσει.

[125] In view of this fact the insistence is hardly justified that Paul would have had to set himself much *more clearly* against libertine tendencies in Galatia if these tendencies actually had been present (G. Stählin in RGG [3rd ed.], II, col. 1188). Naturally Paul sets himself much *more concretely* against Gnostic libertinism, as also against other Gnostic views, for example in the Corinthian epistles —for the simple reason that later on he is better informed.

party, and so on. The two are interwoven. "All those who want εὐπροσωπῆσαι ἐν σαρκί would compel you to be circumcised" (Gal. 6:12). With this sentence Paul concludes the polemic against the sarkic behavior. This means, however, that in the εὐπροσωπῆσαι ἐν σαρκί, which possibly is intentionally ambiguous,[126] at least there is *also* the meaning: "Those who because of their fleshly conduct wish to be esteemed are requiring circumcision of you," naturally without being able therefore to think of "keeping the law themselves," as Paul continues (Gal. 6:13). But the Gnostics wish "to be esteemed because of their fleshly conduct." In the contempt for the flesh which is expressed therein lies their glory.[127]

That in all this Paul is not opposing Judaizers should be beyond discussion. The commentaries therefore throughout silently refrain from placing the corresponding utterances of Paul in connection with the concrete situation as it is supposed to exist in Galatia, although the concrete connection is always obvious and of course is even emphasized in all the passages which fit into the preconceived picture of the judaizing agitation. Anyone who poses the problem for himself then either remarks that in Gal. 5:13 ff. Paul is refuting *the charge of the Judaizers* that freedom from the law is a freedom to sin,[128] an assertion that turns upside down the facts of the case, for Paul himself in fact is making a charge, not defending himself, or one writes that these admonitions were aimed at those "who with the observance of outward ordinances were placing themselves under the Mosaic law, but in the proper fulfilling of the same by walking in the Spirit and in love were negligent, while they reproach the Pauline teaching with the consequence of moral lawlessness." Imagine: Judaizers who keep the cultic law, although Paul says they do not (Gal. 6:13), who moreover reproach Paul with moral libertinism but themselves seek their glory in fleshly conduct! [129]

---

[126] Cf. H. Schlier, [1], p. 207.

[127] Cf. the proud Gnostic catchword in Corinth, "πάντα μοι ἔξεστιν" (I Cor. 6:12; 10:23).

[128] Thus, besides many earlier writers, among others also H. Schlier [1] and H. Lietzmann, [3], *in loc.;* further W. Michaelis, [1], p. 189. But not even the slightest evidence for such an assertion is to be inferred from the text. "There is no defense here at all, but only an attack" (W. Lütgert, [1], p. 15).

[129] How could Paul warn Judaistic zealots for the law not to abuse their *freedom* εἰς ἀφορμὴν τῇ σαρκί (Gal. 5:13) !?

VII

One small point is yet to be noted. In Gal. 1:10 Paul writes: ἄρτι γὰρ ἀνθρώπους πείθω ἢ τὸν θεόν; ἢ ζητῶ ἀνθρώποις ἀρέσκειν. Unfortunately it can hardly be determined from the passage itself how the accusation against which Paul is defending himself here was meant by his opponents. Certainly "those whose charge he now takes up may have explained that he was persuading men, by which more was being said, namely that he was leading men astray" (H. Schlier, [1], p. 15). But with this statement the background of such an attack on Paul still is not disclosed.

Under the assumption of a Gnostic opposition one may, of course, adduce II Cor. 5:11 ff. as a precise parallel.[130] Here the charge against Paul is apparently that he only persuades men, or seeks to convince them, but withholds from them the ecstatic (II Cor. 5:13) φανέρωσις τοῦ πνεύματος (II Cor. 5:11; cf. I Cor. 12:7), a charge which runs through large sections of the Corinthian epistles and which Paul accepts, since ecstatic exhibitions do not edify the community (I Cor. 14:3, 12, 17), but the apostle is indeed constrained by the love of Christ to live for others (II Cor. 5:14-15). Paul reserves ecstasy for his personal relationship with God (I Cor. 14:2; II Cor. 5:11, 13). The same charge then is to be suspected behind Gal. 1:10, although it is not immediately clear how Paul understood it; for even what Paul says is difficult to understand.

It may hardly be possible to put the two questions in Gal. 1:10 entirely in parallel, for ἀνθρώπους πείθειν, "which does always include a converting or an intention to convert" (R. Bultmann in ThWNT VI, 2: 25) is not equivalent in meaning to ἀνθρώποις ἀρέσκειν. Thus the questions are, at least in some measure, different in content. So then the determination of Paul's meaning depends on whether one understands the first clause as a disjunctive interrogative clause (to persuade either man or God), or whether one sets ἢ τὸν θεόν in parallel to ἀνθρώπους. The latter is the only likely choice. The stress then lies on πείθω, and Paul is asking whether he now is *persuading* men. So the two clauses are *formally* coordinate, for the second question indeed asks whether

---

[130] Cf. R. Bultmann, [1], pp. 1 ff.; Vol. 1, pp. 187 ff.

he now is seeking to *please* men. In both cases the answer is "No!" The ἢ τὸν θεόν inserted into the first clause, which "one would prefer entirely to dispense with" (W. Bousset, p. 34), permits the disclaimer of *any* unbecoming πείθειν by Paul to become plainer: we are persuading no one at all! Still it is not *necessary* to assume that anyone had accused Paul of wishing to persuade even God (which of course would be easily understandable as a sneering charge of the Gnostics against the "unpneumatic" preaching of Paul). In the second clause the addition of ἢ τὸν θεόν was already ruled out because to *please* God was obviously Paul's will and of course a corresponding accusation of the opponents could not be present here.

Thus Paul had become aware of the charge of ἀνθρώπους πείθειν that had been raised against him. He must understand this πείθειν, which can mean "convince" (Acts 18:4; 19:8; 28:23) as well as "outtalk," "prevail upon," "lead astray," "corrupt" (Acts 14:19; 12:20; Matt. 27:20; 28:14; Herm. Sim. VIII, 6.5; cf. TDNT VI: 1 ff.), in the negative sense, and rightly rejects this charge of dishonesty.[131] The case is different in II Cor. 5:11 ff., where in the meantime he has become acquainted with the back-ground of this accusation: In contrast to the Gnostic pneumatics he is able *only* to convince or persuade. Now he naturally must affirm this charge, for to convince with the word in sobriety (σωφρονοῦμεν, II Cor. 5:13) is precisely his task and his aim.

In this connection it is interesting that the argument in Gal. 1:10 ff. occurs in the form of a chiasm:

(a) 10*a*   Am I now persuading men or even God?

(b) 10*b*   Or am I seeking to please men?

(b) 10*c*   If I still desired to please men, I should no longer be Christ's servant.

(a) 11 ff.   For you should know, brethren, that the gospel which is preached by me is not human in char-acter; for I too have not received it from men . . . .

---

[131] Cf. Acta Pet. c. Sim. 55 (ed. Lipsius-Bonnet, I, 203.1-2), where it is asserted of Simon: οὗτος διὰ τῆς τοῦ πατρὸς αὐτοῦ τοῦ διαβόλου παιδεύσεως πείθει τοὺς ἀνθρώπους.

It is clear that Paul understands the accusation (a), that he is *persuading* men, rightly in the sense of the complaint against his gospel, that it is human, not divine, and with a gospel that is only human one can only persuade.

In view of the formal parallelism of the two questions in Gal. 1:10, it is to be presumed that the second clause also refutes a polemical remark of his opponents. Of course what stands behind the assertion that Paul is seeking to please men is not to be decided from the Galatian passage itself and certainly was not known even to Paul. This charge occurs with the same words in I Thess. 2:4, apparently with the concrete background that Paul obtains the favor of the community with flattery in order to enrich himself with the collection.[132]

Likewise in II Cor. 3:1 and 5:12 Paul must defend himself against corresponding slanders, to which he alludes also in II Cor. 10:12 ff.; 12:11., *et passim*. These slanders can be connected with passages such as I Cor. 2:1 ff.; 4:16; 7:7; 9:1 ff.; 11:1; 14:18, and others. It seems likely that the *intention* of these charges was always the same: Paul wants to enrich himself in the gathering of the collection, which—as I Cor. 16:1 shows—had long been in preparation in Galatia.

But, however things may have been in that regard, the charge of πείθειν, which is demonstrated by II Cor. 5:11 ff. to be typically Gnostic and is rendered understandable by the same passage, allows us also to detect behind Gal. 1:10 the same Gnostic polemic. Thus also E. Güttgemanns, pp. 298 ff.

VIII

This concludes my argument. Much could have been presented in more detail, and there is much that could be added. But if what has been said in such brevity was understandable and was understood, then what is actually decisive for the evaluation of our theme is said and understood. Since I now in good conscience can give assurance that, so far as I know, I have omitted no passage that would count significantly for a judaizing opposition to Paul,[133] my personal conviction that the heretics in Galatia

---

[132] Cf. below, pp. 146 ff.
[133] On Gal. 3–4, see p. 41.

were Jewish Christian Gnostics should be acceptable.[134] I said at
the beginning that it is not known to me that the appearance of
Judaizers in Galatia had ever been disputed. Perhaps I am deceiving myself in this. But even if I were correct, the explanations offered here would not represent an epoch-making event in
the history of interpretation. It would be only a small step—even
though, as I think, a necessary and long overdue one—forward
on the long road that began when criticism set in with the younger
Tübingen School.

F. C. Baur, as is well known, taught the interpretation of early
Catholicism as a synthesis of Paulinism and the judaizing
tendency.[135] This thesis could be held only if a somewhat wide
distribution of anti-Pauline judaizing was assured.[136] The criticism
of the Tübingen School around Baur naturally did not let the
opportunity pass to attack or even to overthrow, among others,
this thesis of the significance of the Judaizers, which was the one
channel that opened into the synthesis of early Catholicism. The

---

[134] The picture of the Galatian heresy is to be filled out in details from the
Corinthian epistles. For this purpose I refer the reader to Vol. 1. The only de-
tectable difference in the picture of the Gnostic opponents in Galatia and those
in Corinth consists in the fact that circumcision was not practiced in Corinth.
This rules out a Judaistic heresy for Corinth, for to the Judaizers as to Judaism,
rejection of circumcision signifies self-abandonment. For Gnosticism, on the
other hand, circumcision is an unnecessary action with only symbolic significance,
which one could, for tactical external reasons, just as well maintain as abandon.
That the custom of circumcision among Jewish Christian Gnostics in the Syrian-
Palestinian territory was common and was still practiced in Galatia is just as
likely as the fact that it was given up as the progress of the Gnostic mission advanced toward the West. Thus the church's heresy fighters cannot in fact report of any of the later Gnostics that they practiced circumcision. Cf. Vol. 1,
pp. 118-19.

[135] One of the most shortsighted theses in this connection of the brilliant
F. C. Baur, which to be sure was very early abandoned by his pupils (C. Holsten),
was that Peter was the champion of the judaizing effort.

[136] Baur gives a comprehensive summary of the results of his research in his
Kirchengeschichte der ersten drei Jahrhunderte (1863, 3rd ed). For him the only
purely Judaistic writing in the New Testament is the Apocalypse, in whose letters
to the churches the "Pauline heresy" is said to be opposed. For the rest he relies
on the sources which are still under discussion today: the false teachers in
Galatia and Corinth; the Epistle to the Romans; the accounts in the book of
Acts; Papias and Hegesippus; the Pseudo-Clementine writings. These quite scanty
sources, hardly augmented even by his pupils, could therefore provide a basis for
Baur's construction of history only because its already previously established
structure demanded in primitive Christianity two antithetical phenomena of
equal weight. A. Jülicher (Einleitung in das Neue Testament [1906, 5th and 6th
eds.], p. 14) rightly identifies Baur's chief mistake: "He overestimates the significance of Judaistic elements in earliest Christianity."

success of this criticism is evident. Who is there today who still would seriously look for Judaizers in the New Testament epistles outside the Corpus Paulinum? [137] Even the heretics of the Pastoral Epistles, of the letters in the Apocalypse, of the Ignatian epistles, of I Clement,[138] as well as of the Colossian epistle, have long been recognized as—more or less Jewish Christian— Gnostics.[139]

Of that proud might of Judaism only some fragments have remained,[140] represented, if one disregards Palestine itself,[141] by

---

[137] Of course F. C. Baur himself did not do this. The Epistle of James served for him, as did the epistles of Peter and the Epistle to the Hebrews, as a product of the mediating tendency. This shows how successfully he strove for historical impartiality. The efforts to this day, to save the genuineness of James and thus an originally Judaistic document, want to be judged less by the standard of strict criticism than by that of historical and theological taste.

[138] Cf. W. Bauer, [1], pp. 95 ff. Unfortunately the author of I Clem. does not go into the situation in Corinth with the concreteness which is desirable for us. Still he apparently is opposing disrespect for office, controversies in the community, immodest arrogance against God and the brethren, denial of the resurrection, turning away from love, and abandonment of the forms of worship that had been handed down. If one does not wish to account for the weighty official communication of the Roman community, contrary to all likelihood, by unweighty reasons ("It was a matter of personal cliques, without any basis in principle," A. v. Harnack, *Einführung in die alte Kirchengeschichte* [1929], p. 92), then in view of the polemic mentioned above, the only thing that comes into consideration as the occasion for I Clement is a division created by Gnostics in the Corinthian community. The features being opposed are all found again in the Corinthian epistles or in Galatians.

[139] In the Pastoral Epistles as well as in Colossians, already Baur sees Gnostics being opposed. Hence he places these writings very late. It was primarily the battle against Gnosticism which, in Baur's opinion, brought the Judaists and Paulinists together (an observation which in a more modest measure and for the early post-apostolic period is correct). Baur had, it is true, a historically completely inappropriate picture of the beginnings of Gnosticism, but he was the best expert among his contemporaries on this religious phenomenon. In 1827 he took his doctor's degree with "De gnosticorum christianismo ideali," and in 1835 he wrote his work, *Die christliche Gnosis oder die christliche Religionsphilosophie in ihrer geschichtlichen Entwicklung.*

[140] Even the Epistle to the Romans has not been regarded for a long time now as an anti-Judaistic polemical writing, as Baur with others interpreted it. It is unnecessary *even* to assume that the Roman Christians "before their baptism submitted to circumcision and committed themselves to the law" (W. Michaelis, [1], p. 158), even though naturally there will have been circumcised Jews and former proselytes among them. Rom. 16, a letter of recommendation for Phoebe addressed to Ephesus, contains in vss. 17 ff. warnings not against Judaizers but against Gnostics; see below, pp. 219 ff.

[141] This must be done because we are concerned only with the question of how far the extremist Jewish Christians pursued the Gentile mission. The later, already more or less syncretistically permeated sources on which H. J. Schoeps [2] relies (patristic and rabbinical accounts; fragments of Jewish Christian

Paul's opponents in Galatia, Corinth, and Philippi,[142] and even these fragments are in part under heavy attack already. It appears to me to be only a question of time until the ancient and already widespread recognition generally prevails, that in Corinth neither Judaizers nor Judaizers *and* Gnostics,[143] but only Jewish Christian Gnostics are working against Paul.[144] In Phil. 3 also Jewish Christian Gnostics are being opposed.[145]

W. Lütgert rightly says: "Many times a hypothesis is carried only with difficulty because people do not pursue it consistently enough and do not sufficiently detach themselves from the prevailing view" ([1], p. 5). This point has special weight here because the anti-Pauline disturbances in Galatia, Corinth, and Philippi[146] apparently belong together, and therefore stand and fall together. The Galatian pillar of judaizing tendency however stood heretofore quite unshaken. But—"this too, already shaky, can collapse overnight," I am tempted to say in Uhland's words. It would be desirable for this collapse, which would effect the

---

gospels; Symmachus' translation of the Old Testament; the Ebionite source documents of the Pseudo-Clementines) "refer almost without exception to groups in Coelesyria or Transjordan which were assembled out of the descendants of the emigrated Jerusalem primitive community and probably still other communities which had left Palestine shortly before 70 and around 135" (H. J. Schoeps in *Studia Theologica* VIII: 43). These sources therefore to a great extent drop out as sources for the evaluation of the heretical mission in Galatia.

[142] It does not matter for our inquiry whether the community in Philippi like the communities in Corinth and Galatia already was having to deal with internal difficulties (thus, correctly, most interpreters), or whether Paul in Phil. 3:2 ff. is speaking preventively, as e.g. W. Michaelis ([1], p. 203), H. Appel (*Einleitung in das NT* [1922], p. 57) and others think.

[143] This peculiar hybrid hypothesis, which W. Lütgert rightly could not maintain for Galatia, still enjoys at present a widespread preference in connection with the Corinthian epistles. The Judaizers theory is no longer tenable for Corinth, and there is a widespread reluctance to recognize a Jewish Christian Gnosticism; so there arises that unsatisfactory compromise, in which all the signs of a solution devised to relieve one in a dilemma are already outwardly visible. Thus, for example, according to H. Windisch (*Der zweite Korintherbrief*, Meyer's *Kommentar*, VI [1924, 9th ed.]: 25-26) the solution of the problem of the Corinthian heresy is "to be found in the distinguishing of a pneumatic-Gnostic tendency which had already arisen in Corinth before I Cor. and an agitation by itinerant Jewish preachers which perhaps already had begun before I Cor. but only after I Cor. had taken a powerful upswing." But just as little in the Corinthian letters as in Galatians does Paul indicate by even a hint that he is of the opinion that he is fighting different adversaries.

[144] On this, I refer to Vol. 1.

[145] Cf. below, pp. 65 ff.

[146] Ephesus also might be mentioned here: Rom. 16:17 ff. (see below, pp. 219 ff.), as well as Thessalonica (see below, pp. 123 ff.).

other ruins also, to happen as soon as possible. Not that the way would then be open for revolutionary discoveries!

But the necessary clarity would come into the picture of the apostolic era at one point. That is to say, although not a word of Paul's could be cited to support this view, one previously had to begin nevertheless with the assumption that the agreements of the so-called apostolic council, according to which the mission territory was amicably and peacefully divided between τὰ ἔθνη and ἡ περιτομή, had been broken by the Jerusalemites. This has caused much confusion and created unnecessary difficulties. If the dogma of the judaizing agitation in Paul's Gentile mission territory is proved to be a false doctrine, one may believe Paul and trust the Jerusalemites that on both sides people had kept their word, and this would clear up many a point of confusion; but this is not the place to discuss it.[147]

It would also relieve many a tension in exegesis, because still today frequently, in good old traditional fashion, judaizing efforts are introduced where an *ex*egesis encounters only Jewish or Jewish Christian Gnosticism.

Finally, one then also would no longer need to contend about the question whether Christian Gnosticism is a *product* or a *manifestation* of primitive Christianity. It would then be demonstrated at least to be contemporary with Hellenistic Christianity. Of course here is the tender spot of our inquiry. The reluctance, which though unfounded is nevertheless understandable,[148] to admit Christian Gnosticism into the beginnings of Christianity is the strongest retarding factor, which even in the most impossible cases would rather recognize a judaizing tendency or a hybrid

---

[147] Cf. Vol. 3, *passim*.

[148] This reluctance is understandable because then one can no longer maintain the originality of many New Testament concepts, conceptions, and ideas, particularly also within the redeemer myth. It is unfounded because the truth of the New Testament kerygma no more depends upon the originality of its forms of expression than upon the singularity of a historical or mythical happening. Whoever thinks this has rendered any access to this truth more difficult. Surprising is the utter ease with which Catholic scholarship presupposes the presence of a well-defined Gnosticism in the pre-Christian period. Thus, for example, F. Sagnard (see *Theologische Rundschau* [1954], p. 323), J. P. Steffes (*Das Wesen des Gnostizismus* [1922], pp. 4 ff.), and others. The uncritical distinction in principle between the "naturalistic non-Christian religions" and the supernatural doctrinal structure of Catholicism is so firmly fixed that one apparently feels himself completely secure within his own dogmatic system.

product of mixing or of transition than a Christian Gnosticism.

It is not possible here to pursue in detail the problematic sketched so far. Nevertheless this much may be affirmed: One can arrive at the idea of regarding Gnosticism as a degenerate manifestation of Christianity only if he views it solely in its outward structure, in its myths, its language, its conceptual forms. An existential interpretation of Gnosticism, which perceives the fundamental opposition to Christianity of this independent religion with a well-defined understanding of the world and of self, forbids any such derivation. To be sure, this says nothing yet about the *time* when Gnosticism arose. But since the connections with Gnosticism of Paul's language and that of numerous other late Jewish and early Christian writings, among them also the new texts from the Dead Sea, are indisputable, but since according to what has just been said these connections cannot be explained by a reference to "preforms of Gnosticism" (that is already inconceivable because the myth forms the language for itself, never a language the myth; the Pauline language, for example, thus already presupposes the genuinely Gnostic myth, it does not create it) —Gnosticism must be pre-Pauline. Besides, Christian Gnostic systems like those of the Cainites, Sethians, Melchisedekians, and others continue an often still clearly recognizable system of pre-Christian Jewish Gnosticism.

Of course one may not even expect that documents of a "pure" pre-Christian Gnosticism will ever come to light, thus that a "pure" Gnostic sect ever existed. Indeed there also was never a "pure" Christianity, but only a Hellenistic Christianity, a Jewish Christianity, a gnosticizing Christianity, thus a Christianity which from time to time made use of the forms of existing manifestations of religion for the expression of its own religious understanding. Just so Gnosticism also existed only in the concrete forms of Jewish, Christian, and the manifold pagan Gnosticism (in association with Parseeism, Hellenism, the mystery cults, the Egyptian revelatory deities, and so on).[149] Therefore Christian Gnosticism is just as legitimate a form of this religious movement as, say, the Jewish Gnosticism of the pre-Christian era—as indeed also a gnosticizing Christianity no less than the Hellenistic one is a proper Christianity if it maintains the genuinely Christian understanding of existence.

Awareness of this fact of course must not lead one into the error of evaporating the religious phenomenon of Gnosticism, which was no less clearly defined than was Christianity, into a mere "Gnostic

---

[149] Cf. H. J. Schoeps, [3], pp. 39-40.

way of thinking," for which one then can look in *all* religious confessions, as H. S. Nyberg does ("Das Christentum als religionsgeschichtliches Problem," *Zeitschrift für Missionskunde*, 50 [1935]: 297 ff., esp. 301). Such a judgment does not consider the particularity of the Gnostic myth as the specific form of expression of such a "way of thinking." It is possible that the myth known to us and in its basic features constantly maintained in all Gnostic systems is only *one* form of expression of this so-called "Gnostic way of thinking." But the name "Gnosticism" should continue to be reserved for this concrete form of expression, and not for the comprehensive way of thinking.[150]

It was not my intention with these brief statements to convince the reader that Jewish Christian Gnostics were agitating against Paul in Galatia and to force upon him the consequences bound up with such conviction, some of which I have suggested. I am quite satisfied if a person concedes to me my conviction as not unfounded [151] and hence shares my opinion that the thesis that Paul's opponents in Galatia were Judaizers in the future may no longer be the presupposition of exegesis but, if at all held, must then be its conclusion.[152]

---

[150] Cf. Vol. 1, pp. 25 ff.

[151] It is evident that Paul does not classify his opponents in Galatia with any of the "Christian sects" known to him. He apparently had no opinion at all about their origin. Thus he certainly does not seek them among the participants in the so-called apostolic council. This is already ruled out by the absolutely neutral account of the actions taken in Jerusalem. Besides, against the charge that his gospel is false because he is dependent on men he could not possibly defend himself with the argument that he is independent of the *Jerusalem* authorities, as he in fact does, if he had regarded it as even remotely possible that the Jerusalemites *themselves* had raised this charge against him. For even for Paul it would have had to be paradoxical to assume that the Jerusalemites rejected the Pauline gospel on account of dependence on their own proclamation.

The mere fact that Paul does not seek his opponents in the circles which were gathered around Peter or James should rule out the notion that the Galatian heretics belonged to these circles.

[152] Nothing is gained here by slogans, especially not if they are false. L. Goppelt, e.g., charges me, in view of the present essay, with having replaced "the Pan-Judaism of the Tübingen School with an imaginary Pan-Gnosticism" (*Die Kirche in ihrer Geschichte*, IA, p. 55, n. 12). But of course I am not thinking of restricting the diverse world in which primitive Christianity made its appearance to the movements of Paulinism and Jewish Christian Gnosticism instead of to the insignificant contrast of Paulinism and Judaism, as Baur did. Where would I have given occasion for such a ridiculous assumption? The attempt offered here to discover the various historical backgrounds of the discussion in the Galatian epistle may be open to attack. But the catchword "Pan-Gnosticism" does not even meet, much less refute, the attempt.

II

The False Teachers of the Epistle to the Philippians[1]

I

In 1908 W. Lütgert published his study of the *Freiheitspredigt und Schwarmgeister in Korinth* ("The Preaching of Freedom and the Fanatics in Corinth").[2] Prompted by some remarks of Theodor Zahn,[3] he attempted to prove that Paul's opponents in Corinth were not Judaizers but Gnostic pneumatics, fanatics who had fallen away from the teaching of Paul. This thesis, indeed not a new one but never significantly proposed apart from the view formulated by F. C. Baur of the shape of early Christianity, itself demanded that it be tested on other sources of primitive Christianity. Thus there followed in 1909 the treatments of "The False Teachers of the Pastoral Epistles" (*Die Irrlehrer der Pastoralbriefe*)[4] and "The 'Perfect' in the Epistle to the Philippians and the Enthusiasts in Thessalonica" (*Die Vollkommenen im Philipperbrief und die Enthusiasten in Thessalonich*);[5] in 1911, under the title *Amt und Geist im Kampf* ("Office and Spirit in Conflict"),[6] studies of the "Schwarmgeister" ("fanatics," "enthusiasts") opposed in the Johannine epistles, I Clement, and the Ignatian epistles; in 1913 under the same aspect on the "Epistle to the Romans as a Historical Problem" (*Römerbrief als historisches Problem*);[7] and finally, in 1919, a "study of the

---

[1] First published in ZThK 54 (1957): 297-341, and revised for publication in the present form.
[2] BFTh XII (1908), 3. Heft.
[3] [1], II: 102-3.
[4] BFTh XIII (1909), 3. Heft.
[5] BFTh XIII (1909), 6. Heft.
[6] BFTh XV (1911), 4. and 5. Heft.
[7] BFTh XVII (1913), 2. Heft.

prehistory of the Galatian epistle" under the theme of "Law and Spirit" (*Gesetz und Geist*),[8] which posited gnosticizing false teachers for Galatia also.

In the introduction to this last and undoubtedly boldest work we find the noteworthy sentence: "Many times a hypothesis is carried only with difficulty because people do not pursue it consistently enough and do not sufficiently detach themselves from the prevailing view." Indeed, Lütgert's consistency, which did not halt even at the apparently so indisputably anti-Judaistic Galatian epistle, is admirable. Only through such consistency and thoroughness could his thesis, which in no individual case was entirely new, make an impact.

Of course even Lütgert still was not consistent enough. This caused him to gain very little unrestrained agreement. In the solution of the historical question which he propounded he stopped halfway. He succeeded in essence splendidly, even though for the most part not thoroughly enough, in characterizing the numerous similar false teachings; for—and this is the first inconsistency—to the so important question of the source of the early Christian "enthusiastic" heresy he did not succeed in giving a convincing answer. The Gnosticism which he knew was to him a product of the decay of Paulinism in the Hellenisic environment which emerged everywhere unmediated. He overlooked the indications, contained in his sources in abundance, of the fact that the "enthusiasm" was supported by an organized missionary movement.

Still more significant was another inconsistency. Lütgert did not succeed in entirely replacing the old thesis of the Judaizers with his new view of the situation. At least for the Galatian and Philippian letters he had to acknowledge a double battlefront for Paul: against the ultra-Paulinist fanatics and against the Judaizers from Jerusalem.

One cannot make of these inconsistencies an accusation against Lütgert. The picture which his times had of the pneumatics in early Christianity was quite imperfect. In the meantime we have come to possess a more adequate conception of the Gnostic current in the Judaism of the New Testament era and in early

---

[8] BFTh XXII (1919), 6. Heft.

Christianity. We know of the extra-Christian origin of Gnosticism, and we are acquainted with the strong Jewish touch which affected it at the time of the New Testament in the Syrian-Mesopotamian region. On the basis of this better knowledge I have attempted to draw a new picture of the heretics in Corinth.[9] Without yet knowing Lütgert's later works, I had the same experience as he had: In the other documents of primitive Christianity also, in which the prevailing opinion sees Judaizers being opposed, one must and can make the successful effort to deduce Gnostic opposition. In an essay on "The Heretics in Galatia," [10] I have attempted—on what is certainly the most difficult object—to produce evidence that in Galatia not Judaizers but only Jewish Christian Gnostics were active against Paul. Here now the corresponding evidence for the Philippian epistle is to be presented. A study of the Thessalonian epistles in similar perspective follows on pp. 123 ff. To interpret the Epistle to the Romans in this sense appears to me just as mistaken as F. C. Baur's attempt to expound it as an anti-Judaistic polemical document. Only in Rom. 16, a chapter addressed to Ephesus, we find in vss. 17-20 an anti-Gnostic polemic which justifies a brief investigation.[11] With the other writings of primitive Christianity adduced by Lütgert, already today no resistance that is to be taken seriously may any longer be raised against his assertion that they are debating with a (more or less Jewish Christian) Gnosticism.

II

Of course I must first beg the reader's indulgence, since we must apply ourselves to a literary-critical problem by way of introduction. The integrity of the Philippian epistle is not undisputed. To be sure the efforts to cut out non-Pauline insertions in Philippians[12] belong just as definitively to the past as does the contesting of the genuineness of the Philippian epistle at all.[13] However, that Philippians was assembled by an editor out of sev-

---

[9] See Vol. 1.

[10] See above, pp. 13 ff.

[11] See below, pp. 219 ff.

[12] Most recently by W. D. Völter in *Theol. Tijdschrift* (1892), pp. 10-44, 117-46.

[13] Thus first F. C. Baur, *Paulus* (1st ed.), pp. 450 ff. With special emphasis his pupil Holsten (JpTh [1875], pp. 425 ff.; [1876], pp. 58 ff., 282 ff.).

eral epistles of Paul is an assertion which even today still is occasionally held.

This thesis is an old one. It is already found in Stephan le Moyne.[14] In the nineteenth century it was not seldom advocated (Heinrichs, Paulus, Hausrath, Clemen,[15] and others). H. J. Holtzmann[16] was not wholly disinclined toward it. J. Weiss[17] held Phil. 3:2–4:1 to be a fragment of another genuine letter of Paul. R. Bultmann has followed him in his lectures. Of course no textbook of introduction and no commentary of the twentieth century has adopted as its own this literary-critical operation.[18] Indeed, there are introductions which do not even consider this question worth mentioning.[19]

To be sure, such an attitude may go too far. What H. J. Holtzmann wrote in 1886 [20] still has its validity today: "In 3:1 there is still a stone of stumbling that has not been taken away. . . . The murmuring of all the water of criticism at this passage makes us suspect that in fact a rock is hidden beneath the surface here." But more: "This 'most letter-like of all letters' is, in distinction from the actual epistles, written without strict context," [21] a judgment in which the exegetes are in agreement.[22] This lack of a context "is the faithful expression of the apostle's attitude at that time, which was moved by changing impressions." [23] "Perhaps the apostle's outlook itself at that time was changing in corresponding fashion from day to day," thinks H. J. Holtzmann;[24] ". . . here

---

[14] *Varia Sacra* (1685), II: 332 ff.

[15] C. Clemen, *Die Einheitlichkeit der paulinischen Briefe,* pp. 133 ff.; there also a survey of the literary-critical operations on Philippians since Stephan le Moyne.

[16] *Einleitung in das Neue Testament* (1886), p. 301.

[17] *Earliest Christianity,* p. 387. Cf. A. Schweitzer, *The Mysticism of Paul the Apostle,* p. 49, who holds Phil. 3:2–4:9 to be a fragment of an independent letter.

[18] J. H. Michael, *The Epistle of Paul to the Philippians* (The Moffatt New Testament Commentary [1946, 4th ed.], pp. XI-XII, forms an exception. He excises 3:1b-19 as an interpolation of a Pauline fragment, but regards it as impossible ever to account more precisely for the origin of this fragment. More recently F. W. Beare, *The Epistle to the Philippians* (1959), and others also affirm literary-critical operations on the Philippian epistle; cf. below, pp. 80-81.

[19] E.g., Knopf-Lietzmann-Weinel, *Einleitung in das Neue Testament* (1949, 5th ed.).

[20] *Einleitung,* p. 301.

[21] *Ibid.,* p. 300.

[22] T. Zahn ([1], I: 556) speaks of a "carelessness of the style."

[23] R. A. Lipsius, *Handcommentar,* p. 210.

[24] *Einleitung,* p. 300.

the very attitude of the apostle has changed during the writing; the hope of life and rejoicing in death alternate; . . . we become accustomed to making a psychological evaluation of attitudes of the imprisoned, sickly, lonely man," writes A. Jülicher.[25] Expressions of this kind may be multiplied at will.

But only with difficulty can the literary problem of the Philippian epistle be reinterpreted upon closer examination into a psychological one. The epistle begins in the strict form of most of Paul's writings with a heading (1:1-2) and a proem (1:3-11). Then Paul comes to the purpose of his letter: Γινώσκειν δὲ ὑμᾶς βούλομαι, ἀδελφοί, ὅτι τὰ κατ' ἐμὲ. . . . He then translates this intention into deed and in 1:12-26 tells of how things stand with him. Still more skillfully and more impressively than was the case in the proem, Paul lets the Philippians know, by involving them so personally in his fate, how deeply he feels himself bound to them.

Thus he has well prepared the apparently real concern of his epistle: the admonition to concord and worthy conduct within the community (1:27–2:18). It must have come to the ears of the apostle that in this respect things in Philippi were not all the best (1:27: ἀκούω τὰ περὶ ὑμῶν).[26] Already in the proem one must suspect this background behind the conventional forms of the wishes for the community (1:6, 9-11).[27] We learn nothing of the specific occasion of his solicitous admonitions; moreover, it cannot be said with certainty who are the ἀντικείμενοι (1:28) who are apparently leading astray the community in its unity of faith.[28]

---

[25] *Einleitung*, pp. 109-10.

[26] Cf. J. Müller-Bardorff, "Zur Frage der literarischen Einheit des Philipperbriefes," p. 591.

[27] R. A. Lipsius, p. 209.

[28] This is suggested by the context in which vss. 28-30 are embedded: exhortations to μία ψυχή, to κοινωνία πνεύματος, and to ταπεινοφροσύνη. G. Bornkamm ([3], p. 198) sees a reference made in 1:28-30 to Jews or pagans who are troubling the community. These verses may well be understood in this sense. But the constant exhortations to unanimity do not fit in well with this, and those to humility in 2:3 ff. even more awkwardly. As in I Thess. 3, the actual problem in Philippi also may lie in the threat to the community by false teachers. The whole tenor of both epistles or composites of epistles, in which θλίψεις of the community are only very briefly mentioned, argues for this. This judgment is confirmed in detail in the following interpretation of the relevant passages in Philippians. For this book it cannot be determined with certainty whether and how oppressions by Jews or Gentiles are bound up with the basic problem. If the adversaries of 1:28 are Jews or Gentiles who are threatening the Christians inde-

Paul himself is probably too little informed to be able to give more concrete admonition. As at the beginning of his correspondence with the Corinthians (I Cor. 11:18) ,[29] he has learned of the situation in Philippi only by hearsay (1:27). He may have known no more of the ἀντικείμενοι than we learn from his words. Certainly he had had no occasion previously for similar admonitions. This explains the careful psychological preparation of his admonitory words. He does not consider the situation very serious; otherwise he could not have certified of the community at the beginning of the epistle that ἄχρι τοῦ νῦν they stand in the fellowship of the gospel (1:5). Nevertheless his words are urgent and a testimony of sincere concern (1:27; 2:2 ff., 12, 16). Moreover, he deems it necessary to send Timotheus, his closest fellow worker, to Philippi as soon as the course of his own fate will have emerged (2:19-23) ,[30] and he hopes to be able himself to make a journey there later (2:24).

Therewith the central theme of the epistle is treated finally and the transition is made to the remarks, which belong at the close of the writing, about the future development of the relationship of writer and recipient. Epaphras, the envoy of the Philippians, is sent back to his home community with words of commendation. He is the bearer of the epistle. It emerges from 2:30 that he not only had brought the Philippians' gift to Paul, but also had been placed at the apostle's disposal by the Philippian community for personal service. That Paul releases him from this latter task precisely at this moment—and earlier than originally intended (2:28)—is indeed well explained by the Philippians' anxiety over Epaphras' life-endangering illness (2:25-30), but certainly may also have had the unnamed reason that

---

pendent of the false teachers—the comparison with Paul's troubles mentioned in vs. 30 argues *in favor* of this interpretation—then the threat from without obviously makes the internal unity especially important. Anyone who concludes from 1:28-30 that at the time of the epistle the community was under acute oppression from without, cannot therefore see therein the occasion of the epistle, not even of chaps. 1 and 2. The repeated exhortations to oneness of mind and to humility point, as will soon become even clearer, to the internal threat as the real danger to the community. Cf. now also W. Marxsen, *Introduction to the New Testament*, pp. 62-63.

[29] Vol. 1, pp. 90-91.

[30] The tension between 2:21 in this section and 1:14 on the other hand hardly justifies literary-critical surgery.

Paul wanted at once to have a man he trusted in the apparently threatened community, a man who could at least get him more exact reports on circumstances in Philippi. Hence the recommendation in 2:29!

"With this communication about Epaphroditus now the epistle seems to be at an end." [31] τὸ λοιπόν (3:1) leads into the concluding exhortations,[32] which for the most part are very brief.[33] The exhortation to joy in 3:1a repeats corresponding challenges in 1:25, 2:18, and 2:28-29; in the consciousness of this fact Paul adds 3:1b.[34] Now we expect "at the most only a couple of added admonitions of the kind that we actually find in the fourth chapter. With the τὸ λοιπόν the 'clausula epistolae' appears to begin." [35] But actually there follows an unusually sharp warning against Gnostic false teachers, whose teachings we shall explore further, and then still many other things follow. Such an epistolary style is—not only in Paul—unprecedented.[36]

May one psychologically justify the break after 3:1? In view of the clarity, the affectionate warmth, and the psychologically skillful construction of the epistle down to 3:1, in view of the sovereign concentration on the subject which distinguishes this part of the epistle, one cannot suddenly begin in 3:2 "making a psychological evaluation of attitudes of the imprisoned, sickly, lonely man." [37] Naturally everything can be explained in such a way, especially when one takes into account some sleepless nights,

---

[31] P. Ewald, *Der Brief des Paulus an die Philipper*, p. 161.

[32] "With τὸ λοιπόν the apostle comes to the conclusion," thus R. A. Lipsius, p. 233. "Presumably Paul intends here to come to a conclusion," M. Dibelius, [1], *in loc.* H. Grotius had already made this comment; cf. W. M. L. de Wette, *Lehrbuch der historisch-kritischen Einleitung*, 2. Theil, 5th ed. (1848), p. 296.

[33] Cf. below, pp. 129 ff.

[34] The numerous attempts to disturb this obvious connection and to tie 3:1b to the following are dictated by the effort to smooth over the break between 3:1 and 3:2 ff. Even if these attempts were more convincingly grounded than is the case, one could not decide in their favor.

[35] P. Ewald, p. 161.

[36] "It will always remain curious that precisely where the epistle seems tending to end . . . , it actually first finds its center" (H. J. Holtzmann, *Einleitung*, p. 301). E. Haupt, *Die Gefangenschaftsbriefe* (1897), "Einleitung," pp. 99-100, on the other hand refers to I Thess. 4:1, where Paul similarly begins with λοιπὸν οὖν. Similarly B. S. Mackay, "Further Thoughts on Philippians," NTS 7 (1961): 163-64, who also recalls II Thess. 3:1. Of course! But I Thess. 4:1 and II Thess. 3:1, precisely like Phil. 3:1, belong to the conclusions of epistles! Cf. pp. 133, 192.

[37] A. Jülicher, *Einleitung*, p. 110.

unexpected worries, spiritual depressions,[38] lapses in dictation, and sudden epileptic attacks. But such a procedure can make no claim to be scientific. It is out of the question that Paul, who down to 3:1 presents the model example of a clear and definite epistle, in the conclusion of the epistle, which "in rapid succession lays on the hearts of the readers various things which are not connected, . . . after the exhortation to a joyful frame of mind" presents "a warning with reference to the Judaizers, . . . only that this turns out for him . . . more elaborately." [39] How one can describe 3:2–4:1 as an elaborately constructed concluding remark is even more of a psychological problem.

It would be a different matter if Paul had explained this somehow. But this does not happen. The attempt to trace back the first appendix in 3:2 ff. to a belated stimulus from Timotheus[40] or to the arrival of new reports[41] or to new stirring experiences[42] of the apostle fails because of the lack of such explanation. In such cases every normal letter-writer accounts for and explains his unusual conduct. One might adduce from other epistolary literature a parallel to such abrupt changes in style! The problem yields only to a literary solution: in 3:2 there begins an editorial insertion into Paul's epistle.

Still another consideration also leads to this conclusion. The thread of the epistle which is interrupted in 3:1 is again taken up abruptly in 4:4. Verses 3:1 and 4:4 fit together so exactly that upon sober reflection one must come to the conclusion that a later hand has pulled the two verses apart. The concluding exhortations which are introduced with 3:1 find in 4:4-6 their immediate continuation and are ended with a benediction (4: 7),[43] which also usually forms the conclusion of the epistle. Anyone who finds a psychological explanation to shed light on the abandonment by Paul in 3:2 ff. so abruptly of the form and train of thought of his epistle still must fail if he proposes to explain that in 4:4 Paul again takes up the train of thought of his epistle

---

[38] Thus most recently M. Albertz, *Die Botschaft des Neuen Testaments,* I (1955) : 320.

[39] E. Haupt, *Der Brief an die Philipper,* p. 124.

[40] Thus P. Ewald, pp. 162-63.

[41] Thus J. B. Lightfoot, *Philippians* (1881) , pp. 69, 143.

[42] Thus W. Lueken, *Die Schriften des Neuen Testaments,* II: 383.

[43] Cf. below, pp. 129 ff.

and carries it through to the end, as though in the meantime nothing at all has happened, as though he has completely forgotten what he had set forth from 3:2 onward, as though he had just written 3:1. Only one who can make Paul psychologically comprehensible as the redactor of his own epistle can refrain from seeing here the hand of a strange redactor.

Yet a third reason argues for the view that 3:2–4:3 is an editorial insertion from another epistle of Paul. Up to the present time there is controversy over the question whether the adversaries opposed by Paul in 3:2 ff. are or were already active in Philippi, or whether Paul is warning about them preventively. Now it is at once clear that Paul sees the community threatened by the people from the circumcision. Otherwise the statements in 3:2 ff. would be incomprehensible. It is moreover clear that the Philippians must already have formed some kind of acquaintance with these false teachers. In any case, in 3:2 ff. Paul proceeds from the fact that the movement which he is opposing is known to the Philippians already. This section would be inconceivable as first information about a false teaching unknown to the Philippians. Now this acquaintance could have been communicated indirectly. This is asserted by the exegetes who relate 3:1b to what follows and from this deduce that Paul has already written, in an earlier letter which has been lost, the τὰ αὐτά which now follows in 3:2 ff.[44] But we have just rejected any such division of vs. 3:1. Besides, Paul's statements in 3:2 ff. presuppose an acquaintance on the part of the Philippians with the opposed false doctrine, an acquaintance which can hardly have come about other than directly. How foolish Paul's attempt to defend his authority (3:4 ff.) would be, if no one had attempted among the Philippians themselves to undermine this authority! The numerous allusions of the section 3:2 ff., which will engage our attention later, could be understandable only to a person who has not learned merely by utterances of a third person about the people and problems to which reference is made. Moreover, the vigorous and passionate tone of the discussion in 3:2 ff. is hardly understandable if Paul, even repeatedly, should tell of a movement which for the Philippians at first had only theoretical significance. Verses 3:17

---

[44] R. A. Lipsius, p. 234; E. Haupt, p. 125; P. Ewald, pp. 163-64.

and 4:1 are hardly even conceivable as warnings in advance. The same is true for 4:9, which belongs in this context (see below). Above all, 3:13 and 3:15 show that Paul so addresses his opponents, the τέλειοι, and sets himself at a distance from them that they must have been among the recipients of his epistle. In 3:15*b* a difference between members of the community in Philippi and Paul is directly addressed (see below). Verses 3:17-18 and 4:9 presuppose that in the community at Philippi, alongside those who walk according to the apostle's example, other Christians also set themselves up as examples, whom Paul describes as enemies of the cross of Christ. But all this means that the community in Philippi is immediately threatened by the false teachers against whom Paul warns in 3:2 ff.

If one now recalls the exhortations to unity in faith, to fellowship in the Spirit, to unanimity of thought, to holding fast the word of life, to purity in the perverse generation of this age, to a walk χωρὶς γογγυσμῶν καὶ διαλογισμῶν, exhortations to which the major part of the Philippian epistle which is interrupted after 3:1 is devoted (1:27–2:18), these exhortations can have no other reason than the dissension brought into the community by the false teachers. Indeed the statements in 3:2 ff. conclude with just such exhortations (4:1-3, 8-9; see below). But the so widely different attitudes to the problem such as are offered on the one hand by 1:27–2:18 and on the other hand by 3:2 ff. do not fit into *one* epistle. Paul could not so cautiously and so generally exhort them to maintain the unity of the faith, as he does in 1:27–2:18, if he had already had available to him the information which he uses in passionate agitation in 3:2 ff. What we have here is rather—in precise parallel to his correspondence with the Corinthians—two distinct attitudes on the same questions, wherein Paul shows himself at the time of his second writing very much better informed than in his first reference to the events in Philippi.[45] This advance in understanding too has its

---

[45] Perhaps a brief look at Phil. 1:12-18 can underscore this point. Paul tells the Philippians that his imprisonment has served the spread of the gospel (vs. 12); for in the first place Paul has thereby become widely known (vs. 13) as a prisoner of Christ (and thus Christ himself has become known), and in the second place the majority of the brethren have been encouraged, in trust in God, by Paul's imprisonment even more fearlessly to speak the word of God (vs. 14). Thus far the train of thought is clear in essence. Now in vss. 15-17, in the form

parallel in the correspondence with Corinth.[46]

The passage 3:2–4:3 is thus the corpus of an epistle (C) which Paul composed after the writing (B) which includes 1:1–3:1 and 4:4-7 and—possibly up to some concluding salutations—is preserved in its entirety. The editor has been obliged to omit the beginning of this epistle C. The conclusion, on the other hand—again in that case without some closing greetings—is preserved in 4:8-9. The personal remarks in 4:2-3 already show that Paul is nearing the end of his epistle. With τὸ λοιπόν in 4:8 the concluding exhortations of epistle C are introduced, just as in 3:1 those of epistle B, and closed with the benediction, as usual, in 4:9b. Thus the editor builds into the close of epistle B the corpus of

---

of a chiasm, two groups of preachers are spoken of. One group preaches out of envy and strife, and with the motivation of causing trouble for the imprisoned Paul; the others preach with goodwill and love and remember that Paul is in prison for the sake of the gospel.

How are these two groups related to the πλείονες mentioned in vs. 14? Since these πλείονες are introduced as those who proclaim the word of God without fear, and the unnamed remaining "few" thus were intimidated by Paul's imprisonment and were anxiously silent, then *both* groups mentioned in vss. 15-17 must belong to the πλείονες. Hence, according to vs. 18, Paul rejoices over the preaching of *both* groups.

But it is precisely because vs. 18 in its confident judgment points back to vs. 14 that vss. 15-17 are so remarkable. M. Dibelius ([1], *in loc.*) rightly considers them an excursus. But then it is likely that in vss. 15-17 Paul does not particularly wish to describe more precisely those many who (in Ephesus) have derived confidence from his bonds. It is true that he allows the topic of the excursus in vss. 15-17 to be given by vs. 14: he is speaking of those who preach boldly. But his gaze is not directed at the Ephesians. If this is the case, then we are rid of the difficulty which otherwise would lie in the fact that the same people who gain courage from Paul's bonds (vs. 14) seek to afflict the apostle in his imprisonment (vs. 17).

But where is his gaze directed? For it is not to be doubted that there is a concrete occasion for the excursus in vss. 15-17. Now no assumption is more likely than that Paul is referring to the circumstances in Philippi; for the Philippians in fact are to read the epistle. Thus in *Philippi* are those of whom Paul knows that they indeed preach Christ, but not ἁγνῶς, but rather out of envy and strife. He does not yet have more precise acquaintance with these preachers, and hence his judgment is in the last part still positive (vs. 18). Only in the next epistle does he call them dogs.

The Philippians may have understood this reference and hardly will have had the idea, in which exegetes down to the present have doggedly persisted, that in Phil. 1:15-17 we are being informed about conditions in Ephesus (or Rome or Caesarea). Only thus are the remarks in vss. 15-17 significant and pertinent; for as a reference to the situation in the place where Paul is imprisoned they must have been just as puzzling to the Philippians as they are for us.

[46] Cf. Vol. 1, pp. 101 ff. G. Friedrich (p. 107) also correctly sees emerging already in epistle B "the first indications" of the "Gnostic Jewish Christians" who are attacked in epistle C.

epistle C, whose closing words (4:8-9) he detaches and appends to the close of epistle B (4:4-7).[47]

---

[47] From this literary-critical result some questions which are of interest here may possibly be clarified:

a) A *crux* for the exegetes has always been the abrupt address γνήσιε σύζυγε (4:3) in the middle of a writing addressed to the community. By this must be meant someone whose identity could not be in doubt, so it is reasoned, and then people go on to suggest Paul's wife, the husband of one of the two women named in 4:2, Peter, Christ, a brother of Paul, the jail keeper at Philippi, Lydia, Silas, or even Epaphras, who as the scribe of the epistle by mistake inserted into it a remark of Paul which was meant for him personally. (On these identifications, see T. Zahn, [1], I: 537-38; P. Ewald, pp. 216-17; R. A. Lipsius, p. 242.) All this is fantasy. Therefore most exegetes have recourse to the view that here σύζυγος is a proper name, and Paul means by γνήσιε σύζυγε, "Syzygos, you who are a true 'yoke fellow,' i.e., who do honor to your name." But σύζυγος is nowhere attested as a proper name. Hence we can only take σύζυγος as an appellative, and Paul is thus addressing a "true companion." As explanation of this view which is impossible in the epistle in its present form there is offered the suggestion that the redactor has replaced a proper name with the σύζυγε because in the conflating of the epistles the name had to disappear. This way of working would correspond to his procedure in I Cor. 16:12 and II Cor. 12:18, where original proper names were replaced by the appellative ἀδελφοί (see the commentaries *in loc.* and Vol. 1, p. 110, n. 41). In this case the original name in 4:3 could be either that of Epaphras, who in fact at the time of epistle C was again in Philippi (but could Paul thus favor him as over against the leaders of the community?), or that of Timotheus (cf. Phil. 2:20; I Tim. 1:21; thus already D. Völter, *Theol. Tijdschrift* [1892], p. 124), who then would have begun his journey after Paul's release, as announced in 2:19, or, as is more likely, the journey mentioned in Acts 19:22 (see below, pp. 250 ff.). With reference to Timotheus it would also fit well that Paul expressly requests him to look after the two women in Philippi, just as the fact that Paul introduces these women to him. Either would be extraordinary with reference to a resident Philippian. The address of epistle C could then explicitly have named Timotheus along with the community and (or) the community's leaders.

Another explanation is also possible. The prescript of epistle C is not preserved for us. It could be that this epistle was addressed not to the community as a whole but to an individual person, presumably the leader of the community or the ἀπαρχή of Philippi. Then the address γνήσιε σύζυγε would not be surprising, but the exhortation to look after the women would be, as would the reference to their earlier activity in Philippi. In addition, it may be objected against this interpretation that in epistle C Paul is always addressing a number of ἀδελφοί. This objection leads us to another problem.

b) It has always been a conspicuous fact that in the introduction to Philippians, as distinguished from his other epistles to the various communities, Paul especially addresses the ἐπίσκοποι and διάκονοι. This is in fact remarkable and has given occasion to the excision of the σὺν ἐπισκόποις καὶ διακόνοις. This address would be at once understandable in a communication to a community leader, who is addressed with his bishops and deacons. Hence it should be asked whether the words σὺν ἐπισκόποις καὶ διακόνοις were not inserted into 1:1 from the prescript of epistle C. The editor allowed himself to perform a similar manipulation in the introduction to our II Corinthians, where the words σὺν τοῖς ἁγίοις πᾶσιν τοὺς οὖσιν ἐν ὅλῃ τῇ Ἀχαΐᾳ doubtless are inserted into the address, presumably from the salutation of the writing, preserved in II Cor. 9, which recommends the collection (see Vol. 1, p. 97, n. 27; p. 89, n. 13).

What now is the situation with respect to the closing section, 4:10-23? An attempt could be made to connect it with epistle B.[48] But epistle B has already come to a close in 3:1+4:4-7. That Paul afterward, without any explanation for his forgetfulness, expresses his thanks for the gift of the Philippians is just as unbelievable as such an instance of forgetfulness itself.[49] In addition, there is the fact that in 4:21-23 a third epistolary conclusion is preserved.[50] This leads to the conjecture that in 4:10-23 we have to do with part of a third epistle of Paul to Philippi. T. Zahn[51] has seen, quite correctly: "At first sight we might call 4:10-20 a doublet of 1:3-8." This means that this epistle probably is

---

If one regards it as improbable that there was among or alongside the ἐπίσκοποι καὶ διάκονοι an especially prominent community leader, one can combine the reflections under a) and b) in such a way that epistle C was directed to Timotheus and the leadership of the community in Philippi consisting of ἐπίσκοποι καὶ διάκονοι. This is not improbable and would explain the salutation in 1:1 as well as 4:3, and also the fact that in epistle C throughout Paul is addressing a number of addressees; naturally it remains only a supposition. Finally, anyone who holds the σὺν ἐπισκόποις καὶ διακόνοις in 1:1 to be an addition created by the editor himself then would have to regard epistle C as directed to Timotheus and the community in Philippi. For the addition, it might be considered whether it is not meant to give support to the struggle of the guardians of the tradition, namely the bishops and deacons, against the reaction of the Gnostic pneumatic at the time of the redactor.

c) The question often posed by the defenders of the literary unity of the Philippian epistle, as to what then prompted the redactor to his work, is indeed unimportant for the question as to the editing itself—the literary state of things alone is decisive for that—but of course is in itself justified.

If in epistle C we have a writing not addressed to the entire community, a reason for the redactional work could be seen in that fact. The hand of the redactor, who was also the editor of a first collection of Paul's epistles, is certainly to be credited with the catholicizing remark in the prescript of I Corinthians which introduced his collection: σὺν πᾶσιν τοῖς ἐπικαλουμένοις τὸ ὄνομα τοῦ κυρίου ἡμῶν Ἰησοῦ Χριστοῦ ἐν παντὶ τόπῳ, αὐτῶν καὶ ἡμῶν. Therewith he reveals to us a tendency of his work which is also shown in the expansion of the address of II Corinthians: the epistles of Paul are to be of binding force for the entire church. This requirement is least fulfilled by a writing directed to individual members of the community. It is therefore easily understandable when such a letter is furnished, by means of redactional conflation, with a comprehensive address. For more on this, see Vol. 1, pp. 88 ff.; below, pp. 270 ff. Cf. now also W. Marxsen, pp. 66 ff.

[48] This section cannot belong to epistle C since, at the time of writing epistle B, Paul already had in his possession (2:25) the collection for which he expresses thanks in 4:10 ff.; he therefore could not be expressing his thanks for the first time in the later epistle C.

[49] Cf. J. Müller-Bardorff, pp. 596 ff.

[50] Of course in 4:21-22 there also could be the concluding salutations of epistle B or C to be joined to 4:6 or 4:9a. But such rearrangement is unnecessary. Cf. now also W. Marxsen, p. 62.

[51] I: 564.

lacking only the prescript which had to be removed before 4:10. Therewith the character of the epistle preserved in 4:10-23 is evident: it involves a brief letter of thanks to Philippi, sent after the reception of the gift of the community there which was delivered by Epaphras. P. Ewald has already determined that such a writing must have existed.[52] For such a determination no very great ingenuity is required. Epistle B was in fact first written after Epaphras had delivered the collection (2:25) and had undertaken the ministry of the gospel representing the entire community at Philippi with Paul (2:30), meanwhile had fallen ill and then recovered enough to be able to undertake the journey to Philippi (2:25 ff.). Thus there must be at least an interval of some months between the reception of the collection and epistle B. That Paul has let this time elapse without thanks is all the more unbelievable[53] since in these months, as can be demonstrated, connections back and forth between Paul's place of residence and Philippi did exist (1:27; 2:26).

The passage 4:10 ff. now by no means gives the impression of being a second expression of thanks, repeated in epistle B; rather, in this section we have to do with the actual note of thanks, which however was not written only after a months-long delay and even then because of Paul's pure forgetfulness could barely be appended to one of his epistles—how could the certainly unfeigned sincerity of his thanks be harmonized with such indifference toward the gift?—but was composed and sent right away after the gift was received.[54] This first letter of the extant correspondence we call epistle A. That in 2:25 Paul could think of the gift from Philippi without expressing any thanks is now no longer so incomprehensible as it must appear under the as-

---

[52] P. Ewald, pp. 23-24.

[53] In spite of E. Haupt's remarkable attempt at explanation (p. 102): ". . . We know Paul's temperament which, when he was filled with anxiety, made him incapable of undertaking anything else, and which had a crippling effect upon him." This crippling anxiety is supposed to have been Epaphras' illness. Since, in view of II Cor. 11:28-29, with such a temperament Paul would have had to be at all times incapable of doing anything, one is somewhat amazed at his not exactly inconsiderable life's work.

[54] Epaphras certainly reported at once to the Philippians his arrival at Paul's side. Hence it is not even necessary to assume that in 4:21-22 the redactor has excised greetings from Epaphras.

sumption of the unity of the Philippian epistle. The Philippians indeed had long had in hand the note of thanks of 4:10-23 when Paul wrote epistle B with its 2:25.

Thus the course of events as we can reconstruct it on the basis of the correspondence preserved in our canonical Philippian epistle is as follows:

Paul receives—probably already in prison (4:14) [55]—a gift of money from the community at Philippi through their "apostle" (2:25) Epaphras (4:18). He sends his thanks in a brief note A, which presumably is preserved for us, in its entirety except for the prescript, in 4:10-23.[56] Later Epaphras, who remained behind to minister to Paul, falls ill (2:25-30), and the Philippians hear of this (2:26). Paul, on the other hand, hears that in the community at Philippi divisions are appearing and "adversaries" are at work (1:27 ff.). In anxiety over these conditions he writes epistle B, which, except perhaps for some closing salutations, is preserved for us in its entirety in 1:1–3:1 and 4:4-7. The exhortations in 1:27–2:18 form the major part of this epistle. Out of the same anxiety he will have sent Epaphras back to Philippi and planned Timotheus' early visit as well as his own (1:26; 2:19-30). Later, probably only a little later, he gains more precise information about the people who are provoking the difficulties in Philippi. Perhaps he recognizes in them acquaintances from the (concluded?) Galatian controversies or the Corinthian confusion.[57] At any rate he is able in a third writing C[58] (3:2–4:3+4:8-9) more concretely to repeat his admonitions,

---

[55] J. Müller-Bardorff, pp. 597-98, disagrees.

[56] Of course it is possible that some communications about Paul's views which were irreconcilable with what is said in 1:12 ff., or similar remarks, have been eliminated.

[57] I and II Thess. also probably fall in this period; see below, pp. 181 ff., 247 ff.

[58] Here I summarize the results of the literary-critical analysis:

Epistle A: 4:10-23
Epistle B: 1:1–3:1+4:4-7
Epistle C: 3:2–4:3+4:8-9

The unpedantic but skillful method of the editing, which avoids interference with the text, shows the same hand which was at work in the editing of the Corinthian epistles (see Vol. 1, pp. 100-101).

It is hazardous to support the literary-critical analysis of Philippians by referring to the fact that Polycarp, in his Phil. 3.2, speaks of Paul, ὃς καὶ ἀπὼν ὑμῖν ἔγραψεν ἐπιστολάς. The plural ἐπιστολάς could perhaps, if need be, be otherwise explained (see J. B. Lightfoot, *Saint Paul's Epistle to the Galatians*, pp. 140-41). But if our Philippians convincingly gives occasion for literary-

but at the same time also must do it more anxiously and urgently.[59] Our task now is to determine the theological stance

---

critical operations. on the other hand the remark of Polycarp is best explained by the view that he still possessed the individual epistles of Paul to Philippi or knew that the Philippian epistle circulating in the communities was the result of a redactional conflation.

[59] Now most recently Bruce D. Rahtjen ("The Three Letters of Paul to the Philippians," NTS 6 [1960]: 167-73) has taken a position for three epistles editorially reworked in our Philippian epistle. He gives a brief survey of the study, refers, among others, to Polycarp, and makes the division as follows:

(A) 4:10-20
(B) 1:1–2:30+4:21-23
(C) 3:1–4:9

This division coincides to a large extent with my analysis, with which Rahtjen apparently was not acquainted. It is true that Rahtjen assumes that the three epistles were composed in Rome; this hinders him in the correct historical interpretation of his individual epistles which have been recovered by literary studies.

F. W. Beare also has just recently offered a literary-critical analysis of the Philippian epistle which in essence is correct. He makes the following division:

(A) 4:10-20
(B) 1:1–3:1+4:2-9, 21-23
(C) 3:2–4:1

His justification for this operation of course is only very brief.

On the other hand, J. Müller-Bardorff writes in detail "Zur Frage der literarischen Einheit des Philipperbriefes." His analysis corresponds in essence to the one which I have given. Above all, he sees that 3:1 is continued in 4:4. He also correctly recognizes the presence of three epistolary conclusions, only he unnecessarily (see p. 71 above) excises 3:1b as a redactional gloss. Further, he places 4:1-3 after 2:16, thus in epistle B; consequently then he must also rearrange 2:17-18; he places these two verses after 1:26. This literary-critical operation appears to me in all its parts unnecessary and unfounded (see below, n. 194).

In addition, I cannot agree with J. Müller-Bardorff that Phil. A belongs to the first Corinthian sojourn of Paul, and thus to the so-called second missionary journey, while according to Müller-Bardorff Phil. B was written in an Ephesian imprisonment in the course of the third missionary journey, and Phil. C finally in connection with the last stay in Corinth. Phil. A and Phil. B, with their evident proximity to the same matter of the collection which is bound up with the name of Epaphras cannot be pulled so far apart. Müller-Bardorff indeed sees this difficulty, but he regards it as less of a problem than the fact that in Phil. 4:16 Paul mentions only a gift of the Philippians for Paul sent to *Thessalonica,* while in II Cor. 11:9 a gift of the Macedonians for Paul sent to *Corinth* is also mentioned. Since in Phil. 4:16 Paul would have had to mention this gift if he had already possessed it at the time of Phil. A, one must place Phil. A before the delivery of this gift, thus early in Paul's first sojourn at Corinth. But the fact that in Phil. 4:16 Paul does not speak of the gift of the "brethren coming from Macedonia" which is mentioned in II Cor. 11:9 simply shows that these Macedonian brethren did not come from Philippi (but from Thessalonica or from another of the Macedonian communities). On the time of the composition of the three epistles to Philippi, see also below, pp. 115-16, 249 ff.

The fact that Müller-Bardorff (1958), Beare (1959), and Rahtjen (1960), independent of one another and apparently also independent of my essay first published in 1957, which only Müller-Bardorff mentions in an addition to the

of these intruders. Our analysis has shown that epistle A yields nothing for this purpose. Epistle B offers hardly any concrete indications; besides, in epistle B, using the scanty reports which reached him (1:27), Paul was not protected from misunderstandings. Thus the major source for our investigation is epistle C.

proofs, have proposed a literary-critical analysis of the Philippian epistle which at the decisive points is in agreement among them and with my proposal, may raise the correctness of this analysis beyond all doubt.

B. S. Mackay, "Further Thoughts on Philippians," NTS 7 [1961]: 161 ff., discusses Rahtjen's essay and attempts to refute the arguments which according to Rahtjen render the integrity of Philippians doubtful. Now it is indubitably true that not all of Rahtjen's arguments are equally sound. Therefore they occasionally afford welcome points of beginning for criticism. On the whole, however, Mackay has not succeeded in making a convincing defense of the unity of the epistle.

Any attempt at a literary-critical analysis of the Philippian epistle is a hypothesis, as well in general as, even more, in detail. But the thesis of the literary unity of Philippians is no less a hypothesis. Anyone who concedes this can hardly prefer the latter hypothesis to the former, which *alone* solves the literary problems of the epistle without interpretative dislocations. I should affirm this *inter alia*, against W. G. Kümmel, *Introduction to the New Testament*, 1965, p. 235, but also in the face of the distinguished critical discussion of my literary-critical effort by W. Michaelis ([3], pp. 28 ff.) .

Most recently, G. Bornkamm ([3], pp. 192 ff.) has adopted precisely the analysis which I have proposed, also arranges the epistles in the order given above, rightly regards them as having been written from Ephesus and therefore belonging in close connection with the epistles to Corinth. He does not, however, express himself on the relationship of the adversaries in Corinth and those in Philippi to each other.

G. Friedrich, *Der Brief an die Philipper* (pp. 95, 115-16), also now holds Philippians to be a conflation of epistles: so far as I can see, the first German commentary in this century which surrenders the hypothesis of the literary unity of Philippians! Cf. now also W. Marxsen, pp. 61 ff.

Cf. also B. Rigaux, *Saint Paul et ses Lettres, Studia Neotestamentica* 2 (1962) : 157. J. Gnilka, [1], pp. 5 ff., considers a threefold division of Philippians as very well possible, but contents himself with a twofold division: A: 1:1–3:1a; 4:2-7, 10-23; B: 3:1b–4:1, 8-9.

Arguing for the literary unity of the epistle are C. O. Buchanan, in *Evang. Quart.* 36 (1964) : 157-66 (with composition in Rome), and Victor H. Furnish, in NTS 10 (1963) : 80-88. The latter grants that in 3:1a Paul begins the conclusion of the letter, but surmises that the apostle then, following a sudden inspiration, wrote down in 3:2 ff. what he had originally intended to give Epaphroditus and Timotheus as oral admonition, namely specific detailed paraenesis. 3:1b forms the transition to this detailed paraenesis and would be translated as follows: It is not burdensome to me to write down now the same admonitions which I am also sending to you orally, but it provides specific help for you. Furnish himself recognizes the hypothetical character of these conjectures and also knows that therewith he leaves the problem of 4:10-20 unsolved. T. E. Pollard ("The Integrity of Philippians," NTS 13 [1966]: 57-66) artificially construes a parallelism between the Christ hymn in 2:5-11 and the biographical section in 3:4-11 which would guarantee the unity of the epistle. R. Jewett ("The Epistolary Thanksgiving and Philippians," *Nov. Test.* 12 [1970]: 40-53, esp. pp. 49 ff.) regards the unity of the epistle as probable, on the basis of traditional arguments.

III

A glance at the introductions and commentaries shows how difficult it is to determine the nature of the heretics in Philippi. To one investigator they are Jews, since "the opponents can in no wise have a connection with the primitive Christian faith." [60] Others just as definitely see in them Judaizers.[61] A. Jülicher[62] speaks of "fresh-baked proselytes" of the Jewish community. W. M. L. de Wette[63] ventures no clear judgment. Schinz[64] comes after careful exegesis to the conclusion that what was involved in Philippi was after all not so much controversies over doctrine as rather social conflicts, and he has not failed to gain approval for this thesis.

The diversity of these theses itself is disconcerting. But in addition now there is the fact that hardly a single one of the exegetes comes out with a single battlefront in Phil. 3. One who in view of 3:2 ff. speaks of Judaizers or Jews usually sees himself compelled to have Paul in 3:17 ff. waging a polemic against Christians "who cannot free themselves from the old accustomed pagan sensuality," [65] "who take the doctrine of grace as an occasion for their libertinism." [66] E. Haupt thinks that Paul has in view the worst excesses of paganism.[67] E. Lohmeyer sees in the people opposed in 3:17 ff. *lapsi,* apostate Christians.[68] W. Lütgert[69] also thinks: "The fact that Paul was standing between two fronts may be observed most clearly in the debate with his opponents in the third chapter of the Philippian epistle." But it is always hazardous to propound this thesis of a double or even triple[70]

---

[60] E. Lohmeyer, [1], p. 125; cf. R. A. Lipsius, pp. 234, 240; M. Dibelius, HNT 11: 87; J. Weiss, *Earliest Christianity,* I (1959) : 386-87; A. F. J. Klijn, in *Nov. Test.* 7 (1964/65) : 278-84.

[61] E. Haupt, pp. 125-26; P. Ewald, p. 165; T. Zahn, I: 531-32; W. Lueken, p. 383; H. Appel, *Einleitung in das Neue Testament,* p. 57; P. Feine, *Die Abfassung des Philipperbriefes in Ephesus,* pp. 15 ff.

[62] A. Jülicher, p. 106.

[63] *Das Neue Testament,* II (Halle, 1885) : 341.

[64] *Die christliche Gemeinde zu Philippi* (Zürich, 1833) .

[65] W. Lueken, p. 386; cf. T. Zahn, I: 538.

[66] H. Appel, p. 57.

[67] E. Haupt, pp. 163-64.

[68] E. Lohmeyer, pp. 152 ff.; thus already F. Barth, *Einleitung in das Neue Testament,* p. 86.

[69] W. Lütgert, [2], p. 1.

[70] M. Albertz, pp. 320-21: Judaizers, enthusiasts, libertines.

battlefront when Paul himself within his polemic does not suggest with a single word that he now is thinking of a fight against other opponents. It is very easy then to trace this thesis back to the embarrassment of the exegetes. Only if it should be impossible to understand Phil. 3 in a unitary context will one be able to adopt, out of necessity, such a solution.

Of course even then it remains highly controversial as to where in Phil. 3 Paul passes over to the contest with the new opponents. W. Lütgert thinks that it is in 3:10.[71] H. Appel, on the contrary: "3:1-16 is directed against the Judaists .... 3:17–4:1 warns against other deceivers." Finally, others let the separated polemics 3:2 ff. and 3:17 ff. be separated by a nonpolemical intervening passage. In view of this state of things, it is no wonder that many expositors refrain from making any judgment about the nature of the people opposed by Paul in Phil. 3.[72]

The exegesis now following is to show that the thesis mentioned at the outset, that in his correspondence with Philippi Paul is debating with the same Gnostics who are active in the communities which he had founded in Galatia and Corinth, unequivocally clears up the question about the heretics in Philippi.[73]

Phil. 3:2a. Such name-calling has no parallel in Paul; nevertheless "dog" is a common term of abuse in antiquity in Judaism and in paganism,[74] and in fact it is one of the strongest expressions possible. Down to our own time wild dogs form a public nuisance in the Orient; they frequently feed on carrion.[75] To this point of comparison is to be traced back the use of the epithet "dog" above all for impure and immoral men,[76] as e.g. male hierodules (Deut. 23:19; Rev. 22:15). For this reason, for the Jews the Gentiles particularly were regarded as dogs.[77]

---

[71] Thus also K. Stürmer, *Auferstehung und Erwählung* (1953), p. 49.

[72] W. M. L. de Wette, pp. 341 ff.; H. J. Holtzmann, pp. 299-300: "The circumstances in Philippi presupposed here are by no means completely clear." W. Michaelis, [1], p. 203.

[73] Thus also J. Müller-Bardorff, pp. 592 ff.; G. Friedrich, p. 95, also now speaks properly of "Gnostic Jewish Christians."

[74] TDNT III: 1101 ff.; Billerbeck, I: 724-25; III: 621-22; M. Dibelius, *in loc.*

[75] A. Jeremias, *Das Alte Testament im Lichte des alten Orients* (1930, 4th ed.), p. 438. BQ 92B: "A dog when hungry devours excrement." (Quoted in Billerbeck, I: 724.)

[76] GnR 81 (52a): a rabbi says to a Samaritan: "Whom do you resemble? The dog, which is ravenous for carrion" (in Billerbeck, I: 725).

[77] Billerbeck, I: 724-25; III: 621-22; J. B. Lightfoot, [2], pp. 143-44.

Whom does Paul describe with this expression? The exegetes who see Paul fighting against Jews or Judaizers reproach one another with the impossibility of such a reference for τοὺς κύνας, and rightly so. Paul cannot possibly describe strict law-observing Jews with this epithet,[78] people who are doing what he too one time did in zeal for the law of his fathers, namely, persecuting the young Christian community (Gal. 1:14; I Cor. 15:9). He cannot revile his people all together as "dogs," the people to whom "sonship and the glory and the covenant and the law and the worship and the promises" belong (Rom. 9:4). Even when his judgment upon the Jews of Palestine is occasionally harsher than in the Roman epistle,[79] the epithet "dogs" in the mouth of Paul with respect to "his brothers, his fellow countrymen according to the flesh" (Rom. 9:3), is inconceivable.

But just as little can Paul denounce the so-called Judaists with this expression. These Judaists are indeed people of the circle around or near James, whose right to be called Christians Paul has never contested. He has divided the missionary territory with them amicably and has given them the right hand of fellowship (Gal. 2:9).[80] Before his last visit in Rome he diligently collects an offering for these brethren in Jerusalem. We are lacking any indication that the agreement of the so-called "apostolic council" ever in principle came to nought. Paul constantly speaks entirely naturally of James (I Cor. 9:5; 15:7; Gal. 1:19; 2:9, 12).[81] It is impossible that he should be reviling this Jewish Christian group of the one common church as "dogs." [82]

With Jews as well as Judaists, moreover, the common *tertium comparationis* of the derogatory comparison would be obviously inappropriate: I mean the impurity and immorality. If one holds, as it is obvious for Paul the Jew to do, to this usual specific of the

---

[78] E. Haupt, pp. 125-26.

[79] See I Thess. 2:14-16. Of course the genuineness of this passage is not uncontested (see P. Schmiedel, *in loc.;* below, p. 180).

[80] See Vol. 3, pp. 38 ff.

[81] Even in Gal. 2:11 ff. Paul does not utter a word against James, who throughout held to the framework of the agreements of Gal. 2:9, when he reproved the freedom which Peter had taken for himself; see Vol. 3, pp. 63 ff.

[82] Naturally one must free himself from Baur's image of the history, which everywhere in Paul's polemic saw just these Judaizers opposed. In Vol. 1 and above, pp. 13 ff., I have attempted to show how little justified this was for both Corinthian epistles and for the Galatian epistle.

comparison, then the very first word of polemic points to the fact that Paul is debating with immoral people within the community. But the only libertine movement within the Christian community of which we are informed from the primitive Christian era is the Gnostic movement.

Phil. 3:2b. A precise parallel to this in Paul is found in II Cor. 11:13: οἱ γὰρ τοιοῦτοι ψευδαπόστολοι, ἐργάται δόλιοι, μετασχηματιζόμενοι εἰς ἀποστόλους Χριστοῦ. Here, as there, primitive Christian missionaries are meant, workers in the kingdom of God, only of course bad workers, alleged apostles. "They are the very same," writes W. M. L. de Wette, correctly,[83] and E. Haupt also affirms "that the expression here cannot be understood otherwise than the ἐργάται δόλιοι in II Cor. 11:13."[84] This is the only uncontrived interpretation.[85] With it at least would be made clear the fact that Paul has in mind missionaries who are active in the Christian communities as "Christians."[86] When Paul calls them "evil workers" the radical rejection of their activity is expressed. What missionary movement of the primitive Christian era comes into consideration for such a judgment? If one has once freed himself from the false scholarly dogma that an anti-Pauline mission of Judaizers from Jerusalem was disturbing early Christianity,[87] there remains only the Gnostic movement.[88] But above all: if and while Gnostics are meant in II Cor. 11:13, in Phil. 3:2 no other people can be meant, if one does not, contrary to all probability, dismiss all the parallelism in the two passages.

Phil. 3:2c. κατατομή is paronomasia for περιτομή.[89] With this Paul identifies his opponents as those who place value in circumcision, are themselves circumcised and—possibly[90]—number the practice of circumcision among their "evil works." At the same

---

[83] W. M. L. de Wette, p. 341.

[84] E. Haupt, p. 127; cf. also P. Ewald, pp. 164-65; E. Lohmeyer, p. 125.

[85] Above all one would not have been able to refer the κακοὶ ἐργάται to "representatives of the 'works' of the law" (W. Lueken, p. 384).

[86] "The expression ἐργάται can be understood only of people who are active or wish to be active for the Christian cause" (D. Völter, p. 128).

[87] On this, see above, pp. 13 ff., 58 ff.

[88] Cf. also Rev. 2:2.

[89] Cf. Gal. 5:12.

[90] More cannot be said. For the understanding of the Pauline utterances in 3:2 ff., the assumption suffices that the evil workers in Philippi had gloried in their own circumcision or their Judaism. Cf. L. Goppelt, *Christentum und Judentum im ersten und zweiten Jahrhundert*, pp. 136-37.

time Paul gives biting expression with the designation κατατομή to his rejection of such an attitude. Therewith Paul can mean to pass a basic judgment on neither Jews nor Judaists. He, who himself was circumcised, never disputed to either of these the right of circumcision. His sharp judgment applies to the agitation emphasizing circumcision in his Gentile Christian communities. Once again, Jews do not come into the picture. Indeed Jews cannot strive within the Christian communities for circumcision or for Judaism; the making of proselytes among the Christians however is nowhere attested in the Christian era and is hardly conceivable in an organized form.

The circumcised ones can only have been Jewish (Christians). Thus for the student who rightly does not see Jews being opposed in Phil. 3:2, the conclusion appears compelling that κατατομή is a designation of Judaizers. But this also is impossible. The epithet κύων makes it likely, and the exegesis of 3:19 will make it certain, that Paul's opponents in Philippi are libertines. If one does not propose to see Paul fighting in a constant alternation against two entirely different fronts, then the circumcision people of 3:2 cannot be Judaizers; for there never was, and there cannot be, a libertine judaizing movement, since with circumcision the Judaizer puts himself precisely under the law. In addition, there is the fact that a Judaistic Gentile mission in truth is never attested for us. In other words, apart from the fact that such a mission constitutes a contradiction in itself, and apart from the fact that such a mission would represent a flagrant breach of the agreements of the so-called apostolic council, which in view of Paul's account in Gal. 2 may be altogether ruled out, the widespread thesis of the Judaistic agitation among the Gentile Christians is no compelling result of modern exegesis,[91] but a product of Baur's historical construction from the last century. F. C. Baur constructed his historical picture of primitive Christianity with the help of the Hegelian dialectic and on the basis of the historical knowledge of his time. Today neither of these presuppositions is any longer valid. After the abandonment of the strict method of the Hegelian system had already brought Baur's construction to the point of collapse at many passages, it completely collapses

---

[91] See above, pp. 32 ff.

when it is recognized that blame for the internal confusion of early Christianity was only in the slightest measure to be charged to Judaizers, and rather was above all due to Jewish Christian Gnosticism. This is particularly true since in the Gentile Christian mission territory of Paul, no competing judaizing mission can be proved, not even in Corinth and Galatia.[92] Then Philippi will have been no exception.[93] Rather, the Jewish Christians[94] in Philippi must have been Gnostics.

But Jewish Christian Gnostics are sufficiently attested to us from the early period of the church. First, it may be pointed out that the early judgment of T. Zahn[95] is turning out to be true, in increasing clarity: "The earlier the Gnosticism is, the more Jewish is it." In order to avoid misunderstandings,[96] to be sure, one will be obliged to formulate it more precisely: the older Christian Gnosticism is, the more it shows its Jewish character. This judgment contains first of all the acknowledgment that early Christianity must be explained from its Jewish roots. But this also says that the Judaism of the New Testament era is not simply to be equated with the Old Testament or with rabbinical orthodoxy, but among other things embraces a significant Gnostic heresy, of which direct testimonies are available to us only in meager quantity, but of whose influence and distribution there can be no doubt.[97] But if early Christian Gnosticism grew out of Jewish Gnosticism,[98] still it, like Hellenistic Christianity in its various forms and like the judaizing movement, belonged to the original forms of manifestation of Christianity.[99] Thus already on the basis of this general consideration it is only natural that

---

[92] See above, pp. 58 ff.

[93] The false teachers at Philippi "cannot, as was long assumed, have been nomistic Judaizers" (L. Goppelt, p. 136).

[94] In the following, this concept is used in the sense of Iren. I, 24.6, where Irenaeus quotes as the self-expression of the Basilidians, "Jews they are no longer, Christians not yet."

[95] According to W. Lütgert, *Freiheitspredigt und Schwarmgeister in Korinth* (1908), p. 47.

[96] T. Zahn hardly intends to say that Gnosticism in general is of Jewish origin.

[97] See Vol. 1, pp. 295 ff.

[98] The transition from Jewish to early Christian Gnosticism was easy because already *one* branch of the still pure Jewish Gnosticism proffered an explicit Christ Gnosticism. See Vol. 1, pp. 36 ff.

[99] See E. Käsemann in ZThK 54 (1957) : 18 ff.

a Christian Gnosticism of Jewish observance was conducting a mission simultaneously with Paul.

But now in the second place also sufficient individual documentation for the Jewish character of early Christian Gnosticism can be brought forward. I have already earlier assembled [100] the proofs which are of special interest to us here for the practice of circumcision among Christian Gnostics. From these proofs it emerges that on the side of Jewish Christian Gnosticism one could practice and demand circumcision. For this in fact the Galatian epistle, when properly interpreted, offers us the most immediate evidence. It is clear that this circumcision could not place one under the law in a Pharisaic sense, regardless of how far those who were circumcised may have gone in observing the law, e.g., of the Sabbath. Here I can also refer to what was said earlier about the meaning of Gnostic circumcision.[101] Thus among the Jewish Gnostics, libertine tendencies under the banner of circumcision, as they occur in Philippi, are by no means surprising to us. Naturally the Jewish Christian Gnostics also were not bound to the agreements of the apostolic council. Thus from that quarter nothing stood in the way of their mission in the Gentile world. It is all the more conceivable since the Gnostic missionary enthusiasm is well known.

Therewith the background of the βλέπετε τὴν κατατομήν would be disclosed. Paul can only have in mind Jewish Christian Gnostics. As we have said, it cannot be determined whether these people also still demanded the circumcision of the Gentiles. Circumcision understood as a symbol did not have fundamental significance for the Gnostic. He could refrain from the practice of it without great difficulty.[102]

Phil. 3:3. The "we" can only mean the Christians as a whole, who indeed "serve in the Spirit of God" and "glory in Christ Jesus." [103] They are in truth the circumcision, that is to say, the περιτομὴ καρδίας ἐν πνεύματι, as Paul says in Rom. 2:29, following Old Testament words. The activity of the circumcised false

---

[100] See above, p. 36, n. 63.

[101] See above, pp. 37 ff.

[102] See above, pp. 39 ff; Vol. 1, p. 297.

[103] T. Zahn (I: 539) disagrees; so also P. Ewald, p. 166, *et al.*, who think only of Paul and his coworkers.

teachers in Philippi thus signified an attack on the Pauline community as a whole. Paul sees its existence threatened if it were to honor the special wishes of the "evil workers." Again, it is not clear whether these wishes were the demand for circumcision, or whether people were only boasting of their own circumcision, i.e., of their Jewish origin. Nevertheless the latter is more probable. Paul seems to intend to say, "We Christians, not these Jews, are the true people of the circumcision," but not, "We Christians now already qualify, through our faith and without circumcision, as those who in truth are circumcised." But this verse contributes nothing further for our inquiry. We shall later recall the concept καυχώμενοι.

Phil. 3:4-6. First, it is clear that the false teachers in Philippi, whether they now demanded circumcision or not, themselves boasted of their circumcision or of their Jewish origin. Paul affirms that in this regard he could have still more πεποίθησις ἐν σαρκί than they,[104] but emphatically denies that such πεποίθησις is anything but refuse. The precise parallel of this section is found in II Cor. 11:18, 21 ff.; the agreement of the two passages is complete as to substance and extends even to the concepts.[105] The distinction, that in II Cor. 11:16 ff. Paul calls himself a fool before he enumerates his "fleshly" advantages, while in Phil. 3:7 ff. he subsequently calls these advantages "refuse," is only a formal distinction. In view of this state of affairs, it is not a normal solution to see different people opposed in the two passages.[106] If for Corinth only Jewish Christian Gnostics come into the picture, the same holds true for Philippi.

That Jewish Christian Gnostics glory in their Judaism is just as understandable as the same glorying among Jews or Judaists. The Old Testament was the Holy Scripture of Jewish and Jewish Christian Gnosticism and the source of their "knowledge." [107]

---

[104] We are by no means to think that his opponents also had the advantages of Pharisaism, of the persecution of the Christians, and of irreproachable righteousness before the law to point to. No more is conceded to them by Paul than the "advantages" of the flesh in the actual sense.

[105] Cf. Phil. 3:3-4: καυχώμενοι ἐν Χριστῷ 'Ιησοῦ καὶ οὐκ ἐν σαρκὶ πεποιθότες, καίπερ ἐγὼ ἔχων πεποίθησιν καὶ ἐν σαρκί. Εἴ τις δοκεῖ ἄλλος πεποιθέναι ἐν σαρκί, ἐγὼ μᾶλλον, with II Cor. 11:18, 21: ἐπεὶ πολλοὶ καυχῶνται κατὰ (τὴν) σάρκα, κἀγὼ καυχήσομαι . . . ἐν ᾧ δ' ἄν τις τολμᾷ, ἐν ἀφροσύνῃ λέγω, τολμῶ κἀγώ.

[106] E. Lohmeyer, p. 128.

[107] W. Schultz, Dokumente der Gnosis, pp. VIII ff., et passim; Vol. 1, p. 208.

The Gnostics were consistently skillful interpreters of Scripture[108] and thereby also stimulated the Great Church—for good and for ill. For them no less than for all the Jews, including Paul, it was an established fact that salvation is of the Jews (John 4:22).

In particular the mission may therein have been the motive for the missionaries to emphasize their Judaism. This holds true less for the pure Gentile mission, although even in the Gentile world Judaism often made a special impression and exerted not a little drawing power, as is shown by the numerous proselytes and God-fearers as well as by the frequently sharp—not racially based—anti-Semitism of antiquity.[109] One should note the influence which the Old Testament exerted far out into pagan Gnosticism! But within the young Gentile Christian communities, which indeed had acknowledged in principle that salvation comes from the Jews, the calling of the missionaries was in every case adjusted to their Judaism, especially since the Pauline communities may have consisted in large part of onetime σεβόμενοι of the synagogue. But this is the situation in Corinth as well as in Philippi. This holds true even more under the likely presupposition that the circumcision-faithful Gnostic Jewish Christians are making inroads into the Jewish communities with their mission at least just as strongly as into the Christian communities.

In vs. 4 Paul changes without warning from the ἡμεῖς of the preceding verse to ἐγώ. He too can exhibit all that by which the false teachers in Philippi are so highly recommended. This could be an insignificant rhetorical change. One might even ask how else Paul could have spoken of the advantages of his Jewish origin, in which indeed he could not combine himself with the Gentile Christian communities. Nevertheless it is to be noted that in the parallel passage in II Cor., as in the entire section II Cor. 10–13, Paul must be on the defensive against personal attacks which are directed against him as apostle. In Corinth as in Galatia the

---

[108] The early church could hardly make the fact that this skill consisted to a large extent in their reinterpreting the wording of the Old Testament to correspond to their own ideas into a complaint against the Gnostics. It is however characteristic that such interpretation was after all held to be necessary and that one did not venture to take the simple way of Marcion, the enemy of the Jews, who simply rejected the Old Testament.

[109] See, e.g., W. Foerster, *Das römische Weltreich zur Zeit des Neuen Testaments* (Hamburg, 1956), pp. 232-48.

Gnostics attempt to represent Paul as a mere man of flesh who lacks the Christ Pneuma and who therefore is at most an apostle from men, but never an authorized apostle of Christ.[110] The truth of the Pauline message is being disputed, in that the authority of the messenger is being doubted. It is hardly to be assumed that the Gnostics in Philippi would have refrained from using this tried and successful method. Thus in the twice emphasized ἐγώ of 3:4 there may be an indication of Paul's knowledge of the fact that the evil workers in Philippi also are striving to destroy his authority in favor of their own, although Paul, if conjecture is correct, has not heard anything more precise about the actual content of the charges against him.[111] Indeed the Jewish descent could not be used against him.

Phil. 3:8-11. Over against the false καύχησις and πεποίθησις, which are based upon the σάρξ, Paul now points to the true nature of Christian existence. This section does not contain any direct references to the adversaries being opposed. If one nevertheless bears in mind that Paul quite certainly has not lost sight of the "dogs," the question arises whether the section could not contain some allusions to the heretical teaching. It is acknowledged that also large parts especially of II Cor. are full of such allusions which are often difficult to recognize and not easy to understand. The scanty knowledge of his opponents' position, as it must have existed during the writing of Phil. 3, compels Paul to observe such caution in his argument.

Two concepts offer themselves for the possibility of such an allusion. First, the expression γνῶσις in vs. 8 or the corresponding γινώσκειν in vs. 10. R. Bultmann[112] correctly writes: "In the passage Phil. 3:8 ff., which also contains Gnostic expressions, Paul undoubtedly borrows from the Gnostics in describing the γνῶσις Χριστοῦ 'Ιησοῦ as a distinctive mark of the Christian," even though, as Bultmann further states, he defines the content and nature of this Gnosis in a totally non-Gnostic way. Now here

---

[110] E. Käsemann, [1], pp. 33-71; R. Bultmann, [1], pp. 20 ff.; Vol. 1, pp. 182 ff.; see above, pp. 19 ff.

[111] In Gal. also and even in II Cor. 10-13, Paul did not understand the actual Gnostic charges against his apostolate, which in fact hang together with the Gnostic anthropology which is incomprehensible to Paul, even where he has heard them and repeats them; see Vol. 1, pp. 182 ff.

[112] TDNT I: 710.

Paul naturally can speak utterly unreflectively in the Gnostic set of concepts which was to a large extent familiar to him. Of course, if one considers how in Paul's works, especially in the Corinthian epistles, in which he has recognized his opponents as γνωστικοί, the "Gnostic" use of the concept γνῶσις or of γινώσκειν is heaped up,[113] and if one considers further that in the Philippian epistle, γνῶσις and γινώσκειν occur in an appropriation of Gnostic terminology only in this section, then one will have to reckon seriously with the possibility that in 3:8 ff. Paul is making use of this concept in a conscious polemic, since he sets the true knowledge of Jesus Christ in opposition to the ἀντιθέσεις τῆς ψευδωνύμου γνώσεως.[114]

W. Lütgert placed the other concept in the center of his study: ἀνάστασις. He asserts that precisely the question of the resurrection was controverted between Paul and his opponents in Philippi. And indeed in 3:10-15 on the one hand Paul is said to set himself against the charge of his Jewish opponents that he is teaching the resurrection as having already happened, with which then II Tim. 2:18 should be compared. But on the other hand he is said to be opposing fanatical Christians in Philippi who deserve this charge.[115] The thesis of the twofold battlefront of Paul is certainly nowhere less needed and less credible than here. But the observation that the reference to the resurrection could spring from the polemical situation remains untouched by this criticism of Lütgert's exegesis.

The denial of the resurrection is a foundational dogma of the Gnostics, whether it occurs now in the form ἀνάστασις οὐκ ἔστιν[116] or in the other ἀνάστασιν ἤδη γεγονέναι.[117] The Gnostics in Corinth

---

[113] Ibid., pp. 709-10; Vol. I, pp. 141 ff.

[114] Of course if therein he had been of the opinion that his opponents are following the way of righteousness by the law, he would have been drawing a false conclusion from their praise of circumcision. Apparently, just as in Galatians, Paul cannot imagine a Jewish Christian theology which is not bound to the law righteousness, but wisely is careful not directly to impute this theology to his opponents, since it is simply irreconcilable with their other conduct. (On Galatians see above, pp. 37 ff.)

[115] W. Lütgert, [2], pp. 9 ff.; P. Ewald, p. 188.

[116] I Cor. 15:12; Iren. I, 24.5; apocryphal Epistle of the Corinthians to Paul, V, 12 (Hennecke-Schneemelcher-Wilson [1965, 3rd ed.], II: 374) ; Ep. Ap. 21-26; Justin Dial. 80.4; Clem. Alex. Strom. IV, 13.89; II Clem. 9.1; Eus. CH II, 23.9; Polyc. Phil. 7, et passim.

[117] II Tim. 2:18; Iren. I, 23.5; II, 31.2; Tert. de resurr. 19; John 5:24; 11:25;

represent this doctrine in the first form emphatically,[118] for the Galatian false teachers we can infer it from their rejection of the σάρξ,[119] and even in Thessalonica this problem is a current one.[120] Philippi then—assuming the correctness of our thesis— can have been no exception. Now in the Gnostic denial of the resurrection the contempt for corporeality in general is expressed. "But redemption extends only to the soul; for the body cannot do otherwise than decay, as is its nature" (Iren. I, 24.5). Thus if one wants to assume in Phil. 3:10-11 a concealed reference to the teachings of the Gnostics in Philippi, one will find this reference not only in the emphasis on the ἀνάστασις of Christ and of the believers but likewise in the simultaneous emphasizing of the Christians' fellowship with Christ in suffering and death. Denial of the bodily resurrection and contempt for the suffering body in general—in the case of Christ as well as with the Christians— are for the Gnostics just as inseparable[121] as for Paul the "suffer-ing and dying with Christ" and the "rising with him." [122] If one makes his interpretation out of this background, Paul would, in our passage, set the true Gnosis of the believer who recognizes Christ's cross and resurrection in their significance for man in opposition to the false Gnosis of the opponents, who play off the Pneuma-Christ against the crucified and resurrected One and the human pneuma-self against the submissive "suffering-with," the grateful "living-in-the-resurrection," and the hopeful "waiting-for-the-resurrection."

We must concede that vss. 10 and 11 are also completely under-standable without the assumption of a polemical intention. How-ever, one should note that nothing can be objected against such an assumption. The restraint in the polemic is explained by the incomplete information which Paul has and his deficient under-standing of the position of the opponents.[123] In vss. 12-15 also the

---

Eph. 5:14; Oxyrh. Pap. 654.5; Hipp. V, 8 (ed. Duncker-Schneidewin, p. 158), et passim.

[118] Cf. Vol. 1, pp. 155 ff., 259 ff.

[119] See above, pp. 49-50.

[120] I Thess. 4:13–5:11. Cf. below, pp. 160 ff.

[121] Cf. Vol. 1, pp. 155 ff., 160 ff., 259 ff.; see above, pp. 49-50.

[122] Rom. 6:1 ff.; II Cor. 4:7-15.

[123] I have received many a reproach for attributing deficient knowledge to the apostle in Paul's debate with his opponents in Corinth and Galatia. But do not these reproaches arise from entirely too modern presuppositions as to the trans-

indubitably polemical aim has often escaped the exegetes.

For that assumption, the following could be of some weight:

1. That the polemic is unmistakable before this and immediately afterward in the text of Philippians.

2. That nowhere else in Paul do we find so personally felt a prospect of the anticipated resurrection.[124] In the closest parallel —Rom. 6:5—the ethical aim of the thought is evident.

3. That in the Corinthian and Galatian epistles also the corresponding polemic is found.

4. That the basic ideas of vss. 10 and 11 are right away taken up in obvious polemic. That is to say, the δύναμις τῆς ἀναστάσεως means "the power of the resurrection that transforms the life of the Christian"[125] and therefore is to be seen together with the attack on the immoral conduct of the "many" in 3:17 ff. With "to know him and the power of his resurrection and the fellowship of his sufferings" (3:10) Paul stresses the saving significance of the cross—in opposition to the "enemies of the cross" in 3:18! The wish to attain "the resurrection of the dead" (3:11) corresponds entirely to the following polemical affirmation that he has not yet attained all.

5. That in the following verses also Paul does not conduct the debate in a fundamental discussion, but in such a way that he presents himself as the example of proper Christian existence.

Anyone who is ready to concede that in the formulation of Phil. 3:10-11 Paul is conscious of the denial of the resurrection

---

mission of news? It is a fact that this deficiency in information occasionally led to conspicuous misunderstandings, as, e.g., in the question of eschatology in I Cor. 15, where Paul concludes from the Gnostics' denial of the resurrection that he is dealing with radical skeptics! If such misunderstandings are possible, then Paul must have been imperfectly informed *in general*. Besides, with successive letters Paul shows himself to be better informed, both in his correspondence with Philippi and especially in that with Corinth, a state of affairs which can unmistakably be demonstrated. But then the earlier it was, the *more poorly informed* he was. It is not surprising that upon the very first reports, which appear in part to be based on hearsay (ἀκούω, Phil. 1:27; I Cor. 11:18; II Thess. 3:11), Paul opens his correspondence in anxiety about his communities. Cf. further Vol. 1, pp. 101-2; below, pp. 211-12; W. Marxsen, pp. 62-63. Ch. Dietzfelbinger, "Was ist Irrlehre," *Theologische Existenz heute* 143 (1967): 46.

[124] P. Ewald, p. 182, expects, not wholly without justification, instead of the wording of vs. 11 which we have, something like "εἴπως καταντήσω καὶ εἰς τὴν ζωὴν αὐτοῦ." He also remarks that the intensified form ἐξανάστασις as well as the ἐκ νεκρῶν instead of the usual simple νεκρῶν is unique in Paul's writings. In both cases the unusual would be well explained in terms of an anti-Gnostic polemic.

[125] W. Michaelis, [4], p. 57.

by his opponents will be obliged to judge vs. 21 in the same perspective. With this verse then Paul would be taking a stand against the same Gnostic opinion, according to which the "body cannot do otherwise than decay, as is its nature," which in fact also forced him to make the statement in I Cor. 15; cf. I Cor. 15:35-57.

Cf. also J. Gnilka ([1], p. 197): "The unique formulation ἡ ἐξανάστασις ἡ ἐκ νεκρῶν with the doubled ἐκ is intended unmistakably to express the realism of the resurrection from among the physically dead, but it makes sense only if it is distinguished from another interpretation. Paul also is acquainted with this other interpretation, which involves a participation in the resurrection already in this life," but sees "the fulfillment of meaning of the one given only in the other. The doubtful-sounding formulation, 'if haply I might attain . . .', indicates that in this interpretation he sees himself distinguished from his opponents, and thus that they think differently about the resurrection. Only if one perceives the polemical note of the sentence does one avoid a mistaken interpretation."

Phil. 3:12-14. The theme of this section is clear. Paul is emphasizing that his status as a Christian is not "perfect," complete, but consists in the fact that he is untiringly hastening toward the goal, that is, the heavenly calling of God in Christ Jesus. Verse 13 makes it clear that with these expressions he is dissociating himself from those who are of a different opinion: ἀδελφοί, ἐγὼ ἐμαυτὸν οὔπω λογίζομαι κατειληφέναι. "Paul wishes . . . to distinguish himself from others." [126] "He is in fact protesting against the false security." [127] "The stressing of the subject of the main clause points first of all to an opposition to others who think this of themselves." [128] W. Lueken[129] asks, "Were there perhaps in Philippi those who believed themselves already to have reached the goal?" and answers the question, along with the majority of exegetes, in the affirmative.[130] Anyone who answers the question

---

[126] *Ibid.*, p. 59.
[127] J. B. Lightfoot, [2], p. 152.
[128] P. Ewald, p. 188.
[129] W. Lueken, p. 385.
[130] Cf. further W. M. L. de Wette, p. 344; W. Lütgert, [2], p. 14; E. Haupt, p. 148. Of course vs. 12 is already spoken in the same direction, but not to those who in return accused Paul of holding himself to be τέλειος, as, e.g., W. Lütgert thinks.

in the negative always does so because "perfect people" in Philippi do not fit into the picture which is formed of the false teachers there.

But nothing fits better to the Gnostics of the early period than an exaggerated consciousness of perfection. The most obvious examples of this are afforded by the corresponding passages of the Corinthian epistles, especially I Cor. 4:7 ff.: "You are already filled; you are already rich; without us you have become kings," and further I Cor. 4:10; 5:2; II Cor. 3:4 ff.; 4:2-5; 5:11-15; 10:4-5; 10:12 ff.; 12:11; 13:9, etc.;[131] then those of Galatians, that is, Gal. 5:26; 6:3; also probably 6:13-14.[132] In addition there is an abundance of evidence from the other Gnostic, gnosticizing, and anti-Gnostic literature, which I have adduced in selection in the places mentioned in footnotes 131 and 132. From the passages not given there, reference may be made to Iren. III, 15.2: "But if anyone like a meek lamb yields to them (scil., the Gnostics) completely and by following them also achieves their 'redemption,' he is then so puffed up that he thinks that he is no longer living in heaven nor on earth, but has already entered into the Pleroma and has already embraced his angel; he turns up his nose and walks around proud as a cock. . . . Most, however, as those already perfect, have neither modesty nor heed, call themselves 'the spiritual ones,' and claim that they have already become acquainted with their place of refreshing in the Pleroma." Cf. further Tert. de praescr. haer. 41.4: "Omnes tument, omnes scientiam pollicentur; ante sunt perfecti catechumeni quam edocti." Ev. Ver. 42.27: ". . . the Father is in them, and they are in the Father, (they) being complete. . . ." Here also belongs Ep. Ap. 50:[133] "There will come another teaching and a conflict; and in that they seek their own glory and produce worthless teaching, an offence of death (of fornication?) will come thereby." Ep. Ap. 38: "But woe to those who walk in pride and boasting; for their end is destruction" (Hennecke-Schneemelcher-Wilson, I: 217). Rev. 3:17 will also have to be classified here, in view of the fact that the letters are constantly polemical against the

---

[131] On the exposition of these passages, see Vol. 1, pp. 179 ff.

[132] On this, see above, p. 48.

[133] Ed. H. Duensing, Kleine Texte, 152; Hennecke-Schneemelcher-Wilson, I: 227.

Gnosticism which has invaded the churches in Asia Minor; the church at Laodicea asserts concerning itself: πλούσιός εἰμι καὶ πεπλούτηκα[134] καὶ οὐδὲν χρείαν ἔχω. The remark of Irenaeus quoted above[135] makes it clear that the ultimate reason for the arrogance of the Gnostic is the fact that in ecstatic experience he can already anticipate the soul's journey to heaven and therewith the future perfection.[136] Indeed he lacks nothing of the ultimate perfection. That answers the question of what object is to be supplied to complete vss. 12-13. W. Lütgert thinks that it is ἀνάστασιν, in view of vs. 11 and II Tim. 2:18.[137] M. Dibelius[138] supplies Χριστόν because of the antiphon in vs. 12b. W. M. L. de Wette[139] thinks of what "is mentioned in vss. 10-11, the appropriating, imitative, and emulating knowledge of Christ." But no object at all needs to be supplied, as E. Haupt, K. v. Hofmann, P. Ewald, and others have already recognized from a sober consideration of the text. This fact is confirmed when one considers the anti-Gnostic thrust of vss. 12-14. The distinguishing mark of the Gnostic τέλειος is precisely not to have attained *something,* but *everything,* the ineffable blessedness, beyond which there is nothing more to attain. He has simply reached the goal. So then there is also lacking in the numerous Gnostic parallels to Phil. 3:12 ff. a clear object which could formally have been called the "goal" or "perfection" but was hardly to be defined as to content. They speak of "to be rich," "to have achieved lordship," "to be fulfilled," "to be perfect," "to have entered into the Pleroma," "to be satisfied," "to be in the heights," "to be free," "to have come to rest," "to have become God," and so on. Thus in 3:12-14, by omitting any object, Paul makes a direct hit on the boundless consciousness of perfection of his opponents.

On this point now we may also refer to epistle B. The paraenetic sections of this epistle, which are concerned with the situation in Philippi, are shaped to a large extent by the warning

---

[134] Cf. I Cor. 4:8.
[135] Cf., *inter alia,* Iren. I, 6.4; 13.6; 23.5; 25.3.
[136] Cf. II Cor. 12:1-12; on this, Vol. 1, pp. 209 ff.
[137] [2], pp. 9 ff.; thus also R. A. Lipsius, p. 238.
[138] M. Dibelius, p. 70.
[139] W. M. L. de Wette, p. 344; thus also E. Lohmeyer, p. 144; W. Michaelis, [4], p. 58.

against spiritual arrogance. W. Lueken[140] has already pointed to 2:3-4, "Do nothing from selfishness or conceit, but in humility count others better than yourselves. Let each of you look not only to his own interests, but also to the interests of others" (RSV), a principle beside which of course must be placed the entire Christ hymn in 2:5-11, which indeed Paul quotes here precisely because of the ταπείνωσις of Christ, and thus in a paraenetic interest, not with the aim of dogmatic exposition.[141] In vss. 12-13 the thought is carried further. The admonition to work out one's salvation with fear and trembling is nothing but the warning against the security of the one who knows himself to be perfect; and the reference to the fact that God effects the willing and the doing according to his own good pleasure is directed against the self-perfection of those who think that they have already laid hold of everything. Thus the entire section 2:1-13 is already shaped by the same theme which Paul takes up more concretely in epistle C in 3:12-14 and which there in principle dominates the entire section 3:4-15: the rejection of human boasting before God. But just this theme is the central theme of Pauline theology. Faith is the end of all καύχησις (Rom. 3:27) by which the Jew who glories in the law (Rom. 2:17, 23) wishes to live precisely as does the Greek who boasts of his wisdom (I Cor. 1:18-31). On this point therefore Paul is especially sensitive. In the discussion with the Corinthians he never tires of speaking of this problem.[142] Thus it is no wonder that with respect to this question already in epistle B he reacts intensely to the Philippians and then in epistle C, on the basis of fuller information, explicitly rejects the καυχᾶσθαι of the τέλειοι.

Here, moreover, we must refer to the expression καυχώμενοι ἐν Χριστῷ Ἰησοῦ in 3:3, which, in comparison with I Cor. 4:7; II Cor. 5:12; 10:13-17; 11:12–12:9, and other passages, and seen in retrospect from 3:12-14, is disclosed to be formulated deliberately against the self-praise of the Gnostic adversaries.

---

[140] W. Lueken, p. 385; cf. now also G. Friedrich, p. 107.

[141] The fact that the hymn is in no way ethically but mythologically doctrinally oriented (E. Käsemann, "Kritische Analyse von Phil. 2, 5-11," ZThK 47 [1950]: 313-60) does not prevent Paul from the ethically aimed quotation.

[142] See above, p. 96.

Phil. 3:15. E. Haupt [143] and W. Lütgert [144] appear to me to be correct in saying that in τέλειοι Paul is taking up a catchword circulating in Philippi, so that the expression in vs. 15 should be set in quotation marks. This thesis is demanded because in vs. 12 Paul had just declared that he was no τέλειος. When he then in vs. 15 suddenly speaks affirmatively of a group of τέλειοι whose "perfection" is said to consist in their very imperfection, and associates himself with this group, such a paradoxical way of speaking is understandable only if the circle of the τέλειοι already exists and is known to the readers. That these τέλειοι form a schismatic group within the community is shown clearly by the ὅσοι οὖν τέλειοι,[145] which does not mean the entire community, but—a thought which for Paul is impossible[146]—naturally also cannot mean a spiritually especially distinguished circle in the community. It must have to do with a group which sets itself apart as a flock of perfect ones within the community,[147] that is to say, precisely a group from which in vs. 13 Paul deliberately dissociates himself, because he is not and may not just yet be perfect. Because vs. 13 with certainty allows the deducing of a group of τέλειοι against whom Paul sets himself, at the beginning of vs. 15 the apostle can speak affirmatively of τέλειοι only in paradoxical regard to them: let us seek perfection in the humble confession of our imperfection. But precisely this connection of vs. 13 and vs. 15 renders necessary for vs. 13 as well as for vs. 15 the assumption of a group of τέλειοι existing in Philippi.

When M. Dibelius rejects such a concrete reference for vs. 15 because the epistolary situation "is now unknown" to us, one must ask how then the epistolary situation is supposed to be-

---

[143] E. Haupt, p. 152.

[144] [2], p. 19.

[145] It should not be translated, "All we who are perfect are to be thus minded." The ὅσοι οὖν τέλειοι may rather be aimed at a continuation in the second person plural (as in vs. 15b): τοῦτο φρονῆτε. To be sure, in the concluding clause then, in order to associate himself dialectically with those who think thus, Paul uses the first person plural, which may not, however, be immediately imputed to the ὅσοι: thus, "Whoever (of you) is 'perfect': we intend to be thus minded (we who precisely thereby prove our perfection) ."

[146] On I Cor. 3:1 ff., see Vol. 1, pp. 151 ff.

[147] M. Dibelius, in loc.: "τέλειος seems to have been a motto in the community or its environs."

come known to us if we do not observe the indications of the situation which the epistle itself puts in our hands.

In view of the close connection of vss. 12-14 to vs. 15a which is presupposed in our interpretation, the content of the τελειότης and the nature of the τέλειοι of vs. 15 is defined by what is said above on vss. 12-14. The τέλειοι are Gnostic pneumatics who through Gnosis and in their ecstasies attain the perfection of their eschatological existence. In their circles the concept τέλειοι, with the cognate words, is disseminated as *terminus technicus*.[148] Corp. Herm. IV, 4 is frequently quoted: ὅσοι μὲν οὖν συνῆκαν τοῦ κηρύγματος καὶ ἐβαπτίσαντο τοῦ νοός, οὗτοι μετέσχον τῆς γνώσεως καὶ τέλειοι ἐγένοντο ἄνθρωποι, τὸν νοῦν δεξάμενοι. Abundant documentation is found in Irenaeus:[149] in I, 6.4 we read: ἑαυτοὺς δὲ ὑπερυψοῦσι, τελείους ἀποκαλοῦντες καὶ σπέρματα ἐκλογῆς. Clem. Alex. Paid. I, 6 frequently, e.g., τελείους τινὲς τολμῶσι καλεῖν καὶ γνωστικοὺς . . . φυσιούμενοι . . . (I, 6.52.2). Often in Hipp. V, 8 and 9, *et passim*, e.g.: οὐδεὶς τούτων τῶν μυστηρίων ἀκροατὴς γέγονεν εἰ μὴ μόνοι οἱ γνωστικοὶ τέλειοι,[150] and: χαρακτηρίζει τὸν πνευματικὸν τέλειον ἄνθρωπον.[151] Ps. Cl. Hom. III, 29: τελείως ἐκφαίνειν τὸν μυστικὸν λόγον . . . τοῖς ἤδη τελείοις ἔφη. Passages from the mystery literature where the concept, in exact correspondence to the Gnostic usage, is brought into connection with the vision of God are found in Reitzenstein, *Die hellenistischen Mysterienreligionen*.[152] Τέλειοι, γνωστικοί, and πνευματικοί are interchangeable concepts, as is shown by the passages cited above and by a comparison of I Cor. 2:6 with 3:1, for in I Cor. 2:6 Paul is speaking, as is generally recognized, in Gnostic terminology.[153]

---

[148] R. Reitzenstein, pp. 338-39; H. Lietzmann, [1], p. 12; J. B. Lightfoot, [2], p. 153; E. Käsemann, *Das wandernde Gottesvolk* (2nd ed.), pp. 85 ff.; U. Wilckens, *Weisheit und Torheit*, BHT 26 (1959): 53 ff.; P. J. du Plessis, *Teleios* (1959), pp. 20-32. K. Deissner, *Paulus und die Mystik seiner Zeit* (1918), pp. 38 ff., *passim*. Cf. also the frequent occurrence of τέλειος in the recently discovered texts from Nag-Hammadi. There it is not by chance and quite certainly not puzzling that there is talk of consummation and perfection, sometimes with respect to the primal man, and again with respect to the individual Gnostic: the individual pneumatic finds his own fulfillment only in the perfect Christ-primal man—and conversely.

[149] E.g., I, 6.3-4; 13.6; 18.1.

[150] Ed. Duncker-Schneidewin, p. 160.6-7.

[151] *Ibid.*, p. 172.2-3. Cf. also Tert., de praescr. haer. 41.4.

[152] See also H. Jonas, [2], pp. 57 ff.

[153] The concept τέλειος, etc., in the New Testament further is to be understood from the perspective of Gnosticism in I Cor. 14:20; Eph. 4:13; Col. 1·28;

46051

It is true, the sacral concept τέλειος, τελετή, etc., is found disseminated beyond the narrower range of the actual Gnostic movement, but even apart from the fact that it is found most distinctively in Gnosticism, for the context of Phil. 3 naturally only Gnostics, who as τέλειοι boast of their perfection, come into question.

Thus vs. 15 contains a clear allusion[154] to Paul's opponents in Philippi, who are identified by the catchword τέλειος as Gnostic, and indeed in such a way that "there is the same reproachful irony[155] as in I Cor. VIII.1 οἴδαμεν ὅτι πάντες γνῶσιν ἔχομεν, in Rom. XV.1 ἡμεῖς οἱ δύνατοι, and possibly also in Gal. VI.1 ὑμεῖς οἱ πνευματικοί." [156]

Both the fact of the allusion and the ironical form of it may provide a guide for understanding the second half of the verse also. W. Michaelis translates it:[157] "If in anything you are of a different mind, God will surely reveal that to you." This translation is understandable in itself. If the "perfect" are thinking with respect to Christian existence otherwise than Paul had just set forth in vss. 12-14, then God will—the apostle hopes—reveal to them the correctness of the manner of perfection which Paul has presented. Whether one connects the τοῦτο in vs. 15b with the τοῦτο in 15a and thus to what has been set forth in vss. 12-14, or to the τι in 15b is immaterial, for the τι about which the τέλειοι perhaps have an opinion different from Paul's is indeed precisely what is designated in 15a with τοῦτο.

The translation quoted above, however, overlooks the second καί in vs. 15b. Paul says emphatically: this *too* will God reveal to you. Michaelis has indeed sensed the difficulty which lies in the fact that up to this point nothing has been said about God's having revealed anything to those who are of a different mind. How

---

4:12. E. Käsemann (*Das wandernde Gottesvolk*, esp. pp. 82 ff.) has shown that also in the numerous passages in Hebrews τελειοῦν, etc., is to be seen against a Gnostic background.

[154] A similar allusion possibly is found also in Barn. 4.10-11: μισήσωμεν τελείως τὰ ἔργα τῆς πονηρᾶς ὁδοῦ. μὴ καθ' ἑαυτοὺς ἐνδύνοντες μονάζετε ὡς ἤδη δεδικαιωμένοι, ἀλλ' ἐπὶ τὸ αὐτὸ συνερχόμενοι συνζητεῖτε περὶ τοῦ κοινῇ συμφέροντος . . . γενώμεθα πνευματικοί, γενώμεθα ναὸς τέλειος τῷ θεῷ.

[155] The "perfect" are, with Paul, to see in imperfection their perfection!

[156] J. B. Lightfoot, [2], *in loc.*

[157] [4], p. 60.

101

could such have been said, since Paul had found only things worthy of reproof! In view of the sharp polemic in Phil. 3 it is impossible to assume that Paul is of the opinion that everything else is already revealed to his opponents, that their knowledge is yet imperfect only in this one point. And yet the καὶ τοῦτο does clearly refer to something already revealed, which must also already have been known to the readers as such. But then the opponents can only have been boasting themselves of their "revelations," and Paul is making ironical reference to such boasting: If so much has been "revealed" to you, then no doubt God will reveal this to you also. Only thus does the καὶ τοῦτο become understandable without forcing; only thus can the whole of vs. 15 be understood in a unit as an allusion permeated with irony; only thus is cleared away the justifiable reservation which E. Haupt holds against the usual exegesis:[158] In view of the exhortation to humility "Paul would never have uttered a judgment with such indifference, since the presumption of being perfect already could plainly be a peril to their salvation." Irony is anything but a sign of indifference. It is also, especially in vs. 15, far removed from contempt and is coupled with that substantial seriousness which is the mark of true irony: May it yet become true that you become perfect and receive unlimited revelation from God.

The terminology ἀποκαλύπτειν-ἀποκάλυψις, presupposed with such an interpretation as was being used by the false teachers in Philippi, had already, before the rise of Christianity, won a definite technical significance which is defined by Origen[159] as follows: ὅταν ὁ νοῦς ἔξω γίνεται τῶν γηΐνων καὶ ἀποθῆται πᾶσαν πρᾶξιν σαρκικὴν δυνάμει θεοῦ. Thus ἀποκάλυψις denotes the reception of hidden knowledge in supernatural ways during ecstasy, through visions, by means of the mediation of angels, and so on.

In this sense the concept is at home in late Jewish literaure,[160] in the magical papyri, in Gnosticism, particularly in the vicinity of Judaism, and in the early Christian writings influenced from

---

[158] E. Haupt, p. 153.

[159] Fragment on I Cor. 14:6; according to TDNT III: 592. Cf. further O. Lührmann, pp. 40 ff.

[160] Here of course with respect to the distant past, which was the time of revelation, and with respect to the time of salvation, which will bring perfect revelation; cf. D. Rössler, *Gesetz und Geschichte* (1960), pp. 65 ff. Gnosticism emphasizes the *present* revelation through the pneumatics.

that quarter.[161] It always occurs in connection with *termini* which, like ὀπτασία, ὅρασις, μυστήριον, βάθυς, γνῶσις, σύνεσις, σοφία, παλιγγεννησία, προφητεία, φανεροῦν, etc., are widespread in the mystical-Gnostic religious practice of oriental-Hellenistic syncretism.

It is not necessary to investigate the concept in detail here, particularly in its connections with Jewish and Jewish Christian Gnosticism. For that in just that stream of Jewish Christian Gnosticism with which Paul has to debate in Philippi, among other places, great value was put upon ἀποκαλύψεις is shown with sufficient clarity in II Cor. 12:1 ff.; ἐλεύσομαι δὲ εἰς ὀπτασίας καί ἀποκαλύψεις κυρίου . . . . The section thus introduced stands within those statements of the apostle in which he unwillingly, in forced self-praise, sets the καγώ over against the ἐγώ of his opponents; it is marked by catchwords like γνῶσις (11:6), δωρεὰν εὐαγγελίζεσθαι (11:7 ff.), ἀπόστολος (11:5, 13 ff.), Ἑβραῖοι (11:22), and now precisely ὀπτασίαι and ἀποκαλύψεις (12:1, 7). There should never have been any dispute[162] that here Paul boasts *also* of *his* revelations because his opponents play off their own against him. But if this is so, then not only does the portrayal given by Paul in 12:1 ff. of the rapture give the impression of the ἀποκαλύψεις of which the opponents are boasting, but also the concept ἀποκάλυψις may then have been used by Paul in an acceptance of the Gnostic *terminus* of the Corinthians. How else should the Gnostic heretics have labeled those ecstatic experiences which were so supremely important for them than by the terms which were traditional in all late Judaism, ὀπτασία and ἀποκάλυψις?

In Galatia also the opponents emphasize that they have received their gospel by way of ἀποκάλυψις. Against their charge that he is dependent on men, Paul replies with the comment: "For *I too*

---

[161] Dan. 2:19, 22; 10:1 (Theod.), *et passim*; Jes. Sir. 4:18; 42:19; Test. Reub. 3:15; Test. Levi 1.2; Test. Jos. 6.5; IV Ezra 6.33; 10.38; Syr. Bar. 20.6; 48.3; 54.4, 7; 56.1; 76.1; 81.4; Corp. Herm. XIII, 1; Iambl. Myst. III, 17; on the magical texts, see TDNT III: 570-71; Rom. 16.25; I Cor. 2:10; 14:6, 26, 30; Gal. 1:12, 16; 2:2; Eph. 1:17; 3:3, 5; Rev. 1:1; Matt. 11:25, 27; Just. Dial. 78.2, 4, 7; Mart. Pol. 22.3; Herm. Vis. II, 2.4; 4:1; III, 1.2; 3.2 ff.; 4.3; 8.10, 10.2, 6 ff.; 12.2; 13.4; IV, 1.3; Act. Thom. 10; 15; 27; 47; 50; 145, *et passim*; Act. Phil. 45; Act. Joh. 106; Eus. CH III, 28; V, 3; VI, 11; Cl. Al. Strom. VII, 17.106.

[162] Thus H. Windisch, *Der zweite Korintherbrief*, Meyer's *Kommentar* VI (9th ed.) : 368; *contra*, rightly, R. Bultmann, [1], p. 25.

have not received the gospel from men . . . but through a revelation . . ." (Gal. 1:12). The *"I too"* can only refer to the opponents who accordingly are boasting of their revelations against Paul, the "apostle from men"; naturally not primeval or eschatological revelations, but personal, present-day visions, hence the Gnostic character of the alleged ἀποκάλυψις is evident.

In short: it is certain that that group of Jewish Christian Gnostics with whom Paul has to debate in his Asia Minor-Greek missionary territory is boasting of its gnostically understood ἀποκαλύψεις. Our conjecture that in Phil. 3:15 Paul alludes to the "revelations" of the Gnostic τέλειοι is supported by this fact.

Phil. 3:16. The commentaries and editions of the text usually make a division after vs. 16 and thus separate the preceding from the ethical admonitions and warnings that follow in vs. 17. But the division is to be made before vs. 16, for vs. 16 itself announces this new topic, even if πλήν first looks back at what has been said. πλήν occurs in Paul's writings four times (and in Eph. 5:33) and always restricts what has been said previously in its significance or leaves it to the judgment of the reader, insofar as now a new (I Cor. 11:11; Phil. 1:18; 4:14) or repeated (Eph. 5:33) utterance follows whose validity is unconditioned. Thus here: "But however you stand in that regard, the main thing is that in that which we have attained we should also walk," or, more briefly: "Only this: what we are ought to govern how we live."

Certainly the verse is attached to the preceding insofar as the τέλειοι are once more addressed with reference to what they pretend to be: if we are perfect, then we must also live as perfect ones. But the theme of this sentence is that of the following: live as you have me for an example, live as citizens of heaven. Thus Paul emphasizes that there can be no existence as a perfect one which is not manifested as such in conduct.

The closest substantive parallel to the verse is offered by Gal. 5:25 (cf. Gal. 5:16): εἰ ζῶμεν πνεύματι, πνεύματι καὶ στοιχῶμεν. As in Phil. 3:16 the τέλειοι, here the same people as πνευματικοί are reminded that it is meaningless to claim to possess the Spirit if one denies that possession with his manner of life. In the Corinthian epistles the same dialectic comes to expression, for example, in I Cor. 6:12, when alongside the πάντα μοι ἔξεστιν of the pneumatics Paul places the ἀλλ᾽ οὐ πάντα συμφέρει, or when in I Cor. 3:1 ff. he curtly disputes the pneumatic character of the pneumatics because their conduct gives evidence of none of the effects of the Spirit. This charge indeed then runs through the whole of the correspondence with the Corinthians.

This comparison already shows that the admonition expressed in Phil. 3:16 is typical of the anti-Gnostic battle. No wonder! It is precisely the perfection itself which makes possible for the Gnostic a manner of life which in the eyes of the church is so imperfect; it is the possession of the Spirit which allows or even demands the conduct according to the flesh. "In other words, as the gold does not lose its beauty in the muck and mire, but preserves its nature regardless of the dirt, so they too are not damaged, nor do they lose their spiritual nature, since material actions cannot do them any harm. Hence even the most perfect of them do everything that is forbidden without embarrassment. . . ."[163] Over against such an attitude the consequently very concrete admonition is given: the perfect also have to lead a moral life corresponding to their perfection. In the following now this conduct is spoken of in detail:

Phil. 3:17. The community is to follow the conduct of Paul and to take for an example those whose conduct corresponds to that of the apostle. The ἡμᾶς is placed at the end for emphasis. Thus there are also men who are leading a different, evil life, and these men must be known to the Philippians to the extent that they are in danger of following them. Of course the people in question are people within the community;[164] in no case are they pagans or even Jews, against whose evil manner of life it was not necessary for Paul to give warning in the form in which he does it in 3:17-18. The Philippians certainly are not in danger as Christians of taking as an example the heathen conduct. Therefore, however, the question with the τέλειοι is not one of apostasy to paganism or Judaism. It should not be assumed that these people with the evil manner of life are other than those against whom constant warning was earlier given and whose following

---

[163] Iren. I, 6.2-3. Further documentation for this in Vol. 1, pp. 218 ff.; above, p. 53.

[164] W. Michaelis, [4], p. 61-62.

apparently was addressed in 3:15-16 in particular, and this surmise is confirmed by what follows: they are the Gnostic libertinists (see below). Again that makes it clear that these people must be active in Philippi itself, if the community is in danger of becoming their followers.

A precise substantive and in part verbal parallel to Phil. 3:17 is offered by Rom. 16:17, a warning against the Gnostics who have appeared in Ephesus: "But I exhort you, brethren, to note those who create dissensions and stumbling blocks against the doctrine which you learned, and avoid them." Here too Christians are clearly meant, and indeed those are active in the community; cf. below, pp. 220 ff.

Phil. 3:18-19a. The "many," against whom Paul already earlier has warned,[165] are characterized as "enemies of the cross of Christ." How is this characterization to be understood? Pagans and Jews who reject the cross of Christ and oppose the word of the cross cannot be meant if the dangerousness of the opponents consists precisely in the fact that they as Christians give a bad example. But now just the unspiritual conduct charged against the false teachers could have been a practical demonstration of enmity against the cross even though the theology of these people did not reject the cross. Indeed Paul grounds the new manner of life of the Christian, which he actualizes as an example, in the cross and resurrection of Christ. If the corrupt conduct of the "evil workers" not only revealed the general inadequacy of the "new obedience" but, as indeed was actually the case with the Gnostics, was based upon libertinism in principle, from this perspective the judgment "enemies of the cross of Christ" is easily understandable, and quite certainly the reference to the enmity to the cross of Christ is also meant thus by Paul, since the whole narrower context deals only with problems of moral conduct. But the question is whether still more is to be said.

Phil. 3:18 is the only passage in the Pauline literature in which Paul explicitly accuses members of the community who are walking disorderly of enmity to the cross of Christ. This form of the

---

[165] It is not said that Paul had already warned especially against *these* enemies of the cross of Christ, that is, against Jewish Christian Gnostics. The warning could—and must—also have been issued, e.g., against Jews. Paul does say, not by chance, that there are many who walk thus, not one single group.

charge is thus unusual, in view of the frequent rebukes which Paul has to deliver. Only I Cor. 1:17–2:5, where Paul is debating with the Corinthian Gnostics who through their doctrine of wisdom "empty the cross of Christ," offers itself for comparison.[166] If the enemies of the cross of Christ according to Phil. 3:19 have incurred ἀπώλεια, according to I Cor. 1:18, in a precisely corresponding way, it is the ἀπολλύμενοι to whom the cross is foolishness. Now after all that has been said there can no longer be any doubt that the false teachers in Corinth and Philippi belong to the same group of Jewish-Christian missionaries. Thus the rejection of the saving significance of the cross, as it is to be asserted for the Corinthian Gnostics and moreover for Gnosticism in general,[167] is also to be assumed for the false teachers in Philippi. From this fact the expression "enemies of the cross of Christ" takes on its special meaning. Paul describes the libertinists thus, hardly by chance, but deliberately, because he knows that not only through their manner of life but also through the content of their proclamation they show themselves to be enemies of the cross of Christ. Of course he is not so extensively informed about this enmity toward the cross of Christ that he could, as in I Cor. 1:18 ff., in principle conduct a polemic against it.

On this interpretation now, conversely, the characterization of the opponents in Philippi as enemies of the cross of Christ can support the thesis that in them we have to do with Gnostics who, as in Corinth, put "knowledge" in place of the "folly of the cross."

Further, 3:19a, since it stands in close connection with other polemically pointed remarks, may not have been formulated without reference to the convictions of the false teachers in Philippi. The τέλος of the Gnostic is eternal rest after the return into the Pleroma. To be sure, it does not seem very likely to me that Paul is pointedly referring, with τέλος, to Gnostic doctrinal opinions. As in II Cor. 11:15, he introduces the concept τέλος itself, yet in our passage apparently with the intention of taking

---

[166] Cf. U. Wilckens, "Kreuz und Weisheit," in *Kerygma und Dogma,* 3 (1957), esp. p. 84; Vol. 1, pp. 135 ff.

[167] For the Docetists what happened at the cross could only be an illusion. But wherever in Gnosticism the actuality of the fleshly Jesus was asserted, the cross merited the same contempt which the flesh in general and thus also the Χριστὸς κατὰ σάρκα merited; cf. Iren. I, 26.1; Hipp. X, 21; I John 4:2; 5:6; Pol. Phil. 7:1; Ign. Trall. 10-11.

up the Gnostic concept τέλειος in the form of a play on words: the τέλος of the τέλειος will be corruption.

Phil. 3:19*b*. In this passage at the latest, all the exegetes who up to this point saw Paul conducting a polemic against Jews or Judaizers rightly become embarrassed. They now are confronted with the dilemma of assuming a sudden shifting of battlefronts by Paul, either with vs. 19, in the middle of the sentence, or with vs. 17, in the middle of a closed train of thought[168]—and the majority of exegetes decide in favor of the latter way[169]—or of making vs. 19*b* comprehensible in terms of the anti-Jewish or anti-judaizing front,[170] which does not succeed without exegetical violence. In fact an objective exegesis can refer vs. 19 only to libertinists, and just such exposition, which indeed is rightly the predominant kind, integrates vs. 19 also into the total picture which we have gained of the false teachers in Philippi.[171]

Now Gnostic libertinism of course is not a sign of a lack of religious ties, but on the contrary is an emphatic expression of Gnostic religiousness.[172] Libertinism can be understood as part of the process of redemption.[173] Hence it by no means dissolves all the bonds of honor, morality, and ethical behavior, but is related only to the commerce with the substance of the flesh which is at enmity with God. The ordinances which respect the fleshliness of man serve the demonic rulers of the world in keeping men imprisoned in the flesh. Therefore for the Gnostics it is necessary for salvation to escape these ordinances by means of asceticism or through libertinism. But this means that in principle there are only two kinds of conduct by which libertinism caused offense: sexual promiscuity and disregard for all regulations concerning foods. The polemic of all the church's warriors against Gnosticism, including Paul, is constantly directed against

---

[168] Thus most recently G. Delling in RGG V (3rd ed.), col. 334.

[169] W. Michaelis; J. B. Lightfoot; M. Dibelius; W. Lueken; E. Haupt; E. Lohmeyer.

[170] P. Ewald; R. A. Lipsius; P. Feine, *Die Abfassung des Philipperbriefes in Ephesus*, pp. 26 ff.

[171] Of course it does not make sense to speak, with B. Reicke, of *Judaistic Gnostics* ([1], pp. 298 ff.) or of Judaists who "were partially Gnostics" (! p. 302). There are no Judaistic Gnostics; cf. Vol. 1, pp. 294-95.

[172] On this and the following, cf. Vol. 1, pp. 218 ff.

[173] Hipp. VI, 19.5, 8; Iren. I, 6.4, *et passim*.

these two kinds of conduct.[174] Precisely these two problems are also addressed in vs. 19, a clear indication that Paul is in an anti-Gnostic battlefront.

In the phrase ὧν ὁ θεὸς ἡ κοιλία the issue is the disregard for rules concerning food. It is clear that the Jewish Christian Gnostic, who regarded his body as a prison, created by the demons for the pneuma-self, could not have such concern for the purity of the body as would be expressed in the observance of the Jewish dietary laws. The body is indeed itself impure in principle. Of course on this point still no conflict broke out with Pauline Christianity, since Paul disapproves precisely these dietary rules for other reasons. But even in the Pauline communities the eating of meat sacrificed to idols remained problematical, as did the participation, often bound up therewith, in the pagan sacrificial meals. The Gnostic emphasized his freedom to eat the sacrificed meats without hesitation, since in his opinion God was not concerned with this as a problem of the σάρξ.[175] Just this problematic leads, in the debate with the Gnostics in Corinth, to the discussion contained in I Cor. 6:12-13 and 8:1–11:1. I have earlier attempted to show that therein Paul in I Cor. 6:13 adopts the Gnostic line of argument and—in contrast with the later correspondence—affirms it, since he is still lacking the more exact insight into the backgrounds of such a train of thought:[176] "food for the belly and the belly for food, and God will bring both one and the other to nought." Because of the perishability of the κοιλία, so it asserted in Corinth, one can without scruple eat anything. This judgment, at first affirmed, is later limited by Paul:[177] love has a higher standing than liberty to eat all kinds of food including meats sacrificed to idols (I Cor. 8:1–9:23 and 10:23–11:1). To put freedom to eat above love for one's brother is sin against Christ (I Cor. 8:12) and, practically speaking, means nothing less than making the belly into God, as Paul very harshly formulates it in Phil. 3:19.

---

[174] Iren. I, 6.3; 26.3; Gal. 5:19-20; II Cor. 12:21; Rev. 2:14, 20: πορνεῦσαι καὶ φαγεῖν εἰδωλόθυτα.

[175] Iren. I, 6.2-3; 13.6; 23.3; 28.2; Hipp. VI, 19.7; Just. Dial. 35.1-6.

[176] Vol. 1, pp. 224 ff., esp. pp. 231-32.

[177] I Cor. 8:1 ff. This section belongs to a later epistle to Corinth than the passage I Cor. 6:12 ff.; see Vol. 1, pp. 92-93; 230 ff.

The closest parallel to this formulation is afforded by the equally anti-Gnostic verse Rom. 16:18. As in Phil. 3:17-18, first Paul calls for σκοπεῖν and warns against the Christians who set a bad example (Rom. 16:17). Then these false teachers are characterized as in Phil. 3:19: "For these people do not serve our Lord Christ, but their own bellies." By serving their bellies and not Christ, they make their bellies to be God and Lord. Thus the judgment in Rom. 16:18 is in principle of the same sharpness as that in Phil. 3:19.[178] In the Galatian epistle also Paul must warn against similar conduct.[179]

It is unnecessary alongside these closest parallels from Paul's struggle against his Gnostic opponents to point to profane parallels[180] or to adduce corresponding passages from other Gnosticism more than has been done in the notes above.[181] Above all, it should also be unnecessary to refute that exposition which has Paul accusing Jews or Judaizers that they made their bellies their god because they still observed the dietary laws. Such a judgment on his own past not only would be unique for Paul; it is even unthinkable for him: Rom. 9:3-5; 10:1-2; Gal. 1:13-14; Phil. 3:6 ff.[182] He places indeed much value in the fellowship with the Christians who still regard the dietary laws as valid for themselves (Gal. 2:7-9; Rom. 15:27 ff.) .[183]

Phil. 3:19c. This clause strikes at the other expression of Gnostic libertinism: sexual promiscuity, of which Paul may also be thinking in II Cor. 4:2, where the concept αἰσχύνη occurs a second time in his writings, and which quite certainly is also meant in Jude 13, when the Gnostics are charged with foaming out their own αἰσχύνη. Following after some church fathers and Bengel, of

---

[178] See below, pp. 229 ff.

[179] Gal. 5:19 ff.; see above, pp. 51 ff.

[180] E.g., M. Dibelius, [1], *in loc.*; J. B. Lightfoot, [2], *in loc.*; TDNT III: 786 ff.

[181] Cf. p. 109, notes 174-75. We quote only Iren. I, 6.3, since this passage expressly forms the bridge from 3:12-15 to 3:19b: "Hence even the most perfect of them do everything that is forbidden without hesitation . . . . They unhesitatingly eat idol sacrifices."

[182] Cf., e.g., G. Wohlenberg in P. Ewald, p. 207.

[183] "Even in the sharpest polemic Paul never let himself be lured into belittling the observance of commandments which for him too were and are God's commandments, even if they are no longer valid for Christianity" (W. Lütgert, [1], pp. 25-26) .

course P. Ewald and R. A. Lipsius translate αἰσχύνη in Phil. 3:19 as "shameful parts," in order thus to maintain the sense: "they seek their honor in their shameful parts" (that is, in having themselves circumcised) .[184] But besides the fact that they do not cite any parallel for this translation, such a judgment upon circumcision and the circumcised is unthinkable for Paul. Even he in fact had not in his Jewish period sought "his honor in his shameful parts"! [185]

Again it is not necessary to assemble in detail the abundant documentation[186] for the sexual libertinism of Gnosticism.[187] It is sufficient to point out that the Gnostics in Corinth also, with the catchword πάντα μοι ἔξεστιν, allowed themselves every sexual excess (I Cor. 6:12-20; 5:1-13; 7:1-40; II Cor. 4:2; 12:21) ,[188] and it must have come to Paul's ears that in Galatia also similar tendencies existed (Gal. 5:19-20) .[189]

But Paul's formulation is worthy of note. He not only charges his opponents with sexual libertinism as such, but also asserts that they even boast of such immoral conduct. This is no wrathful exaggeration by Paul, but an objective exposition of the Gnostic conduct. Whoever in Corinth demonstrated his freedom in sexual matters with the slogan πάντα μοι ἔξεστιν (I Cor. 6:12) likewise found his honor in "offering the sarkical to the sarkical" (Iren. I, 6.3), so that it was not surprising if someone were even puffed up because of his immorality (I Cor. 5:1-2). We also have testimony elsewhere of the corresponding behavior in libertine Gnosticism. Irenaeus tells, for example (I, 13.6), concerning the Marcosians that they claimed "to stand in the heights above all power; on account of which they also did everything in freedom, without having any fear in anything," and Hippolytus says (VI, 19.5) of the Simonians that they not only practiced sexual intercourse without restraint, ἀλλὰ καὶ μακαρίζουσιν ἑαυτοὺς ἐπὶ τῇ κοινῇ μίξει, ταύτην εἶναι λέγοντες τὴν τελείαν ἀγάπην.

---

[184] Most recently B. Reicke, [1], pp. 299-300.

[185] Paul "never forgets in the criticism of Judaism that he himself was once proud of being a Jew" (W. Lütgert, [1], p. 26) .

[186] Even in the rabbinical literature the polemic against the sexual libertinism of Jewish Gnostics is to be found; on this, cf. H. J. Schoeps, [4], pp. 243 ff., 255 ff.

[187] See Vol. 1, pp. 218 ff.

[188] See ibid., pp. 230 ff.

[189] See above, pp. 51 ff.

Phil. 3:19*d:* Οἱ τὰ ἐπίγεια φρονοῦντες. Thus reads Paul's concluding moral judgment on the Gnostic immorality. Of course the Gnostics will have denied this. Their libertinism, they would say, is precisely not an expression of an earthly frame of mind, but a sign that they are not just on the way to the πολίτευμα ἐν οὐρανοῖς but have long since gained it as a firm possession and therefore in libertine fashion can hold in contempt τὰ ἐπίγεια; to Paul, this represented precisely a "striving after what is earthly."

Phil. 3:20–4:1. What can be said on these verses from the perspective of our investigation has already been set forth above.[190]

Paul now comes to the conclusion of his admonitory and warning writing and pleads in particular for the preservation of the unity of the community.

Phil. 4:2, 3, 8, 9. It is unlikely that now at the end of the epistle, without a transition, a new subject is set forth, after the entire epistle up to this point has been concerned solely with the situation which had developed in Philippi because of the Gnostic agitation. Thus when Euodia and Syntyche are exhorted "to be of the same mind in the Lord," and the "true yoke fellow" is admonished to receive them; when, further, the Philippians are urged to think on all kinds of good things (4:8) and thereby to remain with what Paul had taught them, and thus not to do what others are teaching them, then certainly the threatened unity is endangered by nothing other than the very false teachers against whom the polemic of the whole epistle is directed.

So then the closest parallel to 4:8 and 9 is in fact found in 3:17 and 18, where Paul had already once set himself forth as an example, and indeed with specific reference to the false teachers who as enemies of the cross of Christ walk with their mind on earthly things and hence do not think on "what is true, honorable, just, pure, lovely, praiseworthy." For an example one should not take them but Paul (3:17-18), one should not follow after their words and their conduct, but that which one sees and hears in Paul.[191]

---

[190] See p. 94.

[191] In II Cor. 12:6-7 also, in debate with the Gnostic opponents, Paul refers

But if vss. 4:8-9 toward the end of the epistle are still shaped by the one theme of the whole writing, then it cannot be otherwise with the preceding vss. 4:2-3. Thus in fact also the exhortation, τὸ αὐτὸ φρονεῖν ἐν κυρίῳ, has already been expressed frequently with a view to the opponents. We already encounter it in epistle C, in 3:15: "Whoever now is perfect: we intend to be thus minded; and if in anything you are of a different mind, God will also reveal this to you," as well as in the warning against "those who mind earthly things" (3:19). But precisely this admonition already pervades epistle B, though there the specific background had not yet become clear. Perhaps one may even point to the proem: "I am confident that the one who has begun the good work in you will perfect it into the day of Christ Jesus; it is fitting for me to feel this way about you all, because I bear you in my heart" (1:6-7). Behind the emphasized confidence in God's further action there must be the special consciousness that the community is still a long way from perfection.[192] The same holds true for the following verses down to vs. 11. Verse 1:27 then plainly urges unity: ". . . that you stand in one spirit, in one mind striving for the faith of the gospel." Further, 2:2 ff.: "Enlarge my joy, in that you τὸ αὐτὸ φρονῆτε, having the same love, being of one mind, τὸ ἓν φρονοῦντες. Do nothing out of contentiousness or conceit, but with obliging humility give preference one to another; let each one look not to his own things, but to those of others. Conduct yourselves with one another in keeping with what you receive from Christ . . . ." Verse 2:14 also should be mentioned: "Do all things without grumbling or bad thoughts."

It is only too understandable that from the first reports about the appearance of difficulties in the community at Philippi, Paul could indeed deduce little that was concrete about the origin and the actual nature of the unrest in Philippi, but he did clearly

---

the community to that which one "sees in him and hears from him." Therewith, however, he places this which is to be seen and heard in him in opposition to the ecstatic ἀποκαλύψεις to which the Gnostics point and in terms of which Paul does not wish to be judged. It is not entirely excluded that in Phil. 4:9 also there is an echo of the unspoken thought: Do not trouble yourselves about the ecstasies which I have not exhibited before you.

[192] Thus R. A. Lipsius, p. 209. Striking is the fourfold πάντες in 1:4. 7, 8, more than in all the other proems of Paul's epistles taken together! I am indebted to G. Klein for this interesting point.

see the unity of the community endangered. Thus in fact the same exhortation to unity is found already in Paul's first epistle to Corinth, in which, moreover, he sees the community still standing under newly awakened influences of the old heathenism:[193] "I do not at all praise you, because you come together not for the better but for the worse. For in the first place, when you gather as a community, I hear that there are divisions among you, and I partly believe it. There must be divisions among you, that it may become evident who among you is genuine" (I Cor. 11:17-19). This exhortation then is frequently repeated in the later correspondence, e.g., in I Cor. 1:10 (= epistle B): "I admonish you, brethren, by the name of our Lord Jesus Christ, that you all say the same thing and that there be no factions among you; instead, stand fast in one mind and one judgment"; II Cor. 13:11 (= epistle D): "τὸ αὐτὸ φρονεῖτε, εἰρηνεύετε." In every case they are the Gnostics who are destroying the unity of the community. Numerous also are the exhortations to unity in Gal. 5:19–6:6, although Paul sees the community in Galatia not so much divided but in apostasy. The eloquent lament of the church fathers about the Gnostics who disrupt the unity of the church is in any case nothing new, but was already completely present in Paul.

It is and will remain a disputed question whether the two women mentioned in 4:2 have had a dispute with one another (as a result of the Gnostic agitation?), or whether the two of them in common denied the unity of the community by opening their assemblies—perhaps as leaders of house churches—to the Gnostics. Either is possible. The latter appears to me more probable, since the τὸ αὐτὸ φρονεῖν ἐν κυρίῳ is apparently only a variation on the preceding στήκετε ἐν κυρίῳ, and since the σύζυγος is to be concerned with one as well as the other.[194]

That concludes the exegesis of epistle C, together with the occasional glances at epistle B. Even one who does not agree

---

[193] I am convinced that this first epistle included II Cor. 6:14–7:1; I Cor. 9:24–10:22; 6:12-20; 11:2-34; 15; 16:13-24; see Vol. 1, pp. 90 ff.

[194] J. Müller-Bardorff, pp. 594 ff. (see above, n. 59) thinks that 4:1-3 must be assigned to epistle B, since the tone of the reproof in these verses stands in total contrast with the "philippic" in 3:2 ff. But one could argue thus only if it were established that the two women themselves belonged to the false teachers. Naturally that is out of the question.

with the proposed exposition in every particular and would add a "perhaps" or "possibly" more frequently than has been done will admit that the extant correspondence of Paul with the community in Philippi may be understood in the passages that come into consideration uniformly as a debate with the Jewish Christian Gnosticism which Paul also is opposing in the Corinthian epistles and, in my opinion, also in the Galatian epistle. That the correspondence may be understood only in this way if one does not wish artificially to create difficulties is my personal conviction, which however I should not want to force on anyone.[195]

IV

Some concluding remarks and views are now necessary.

1. The proposed exegesis has vindicated and confirmed in all points the attempt at the literary-critical division of the canonical Philippian epistle. With a consideration of the parallels in Paul's correspondence with Corinth and Galatia, a clear picture of Paul's opponents in Philippi may be gained from epistle C. It showed that epistle C was wholly shaped by Paul's dispute with his opponents. In contrast therewith, we now see that any reference to the disorder in the community at Philippi is (still) lacking in epistle A, which for altogether different reasons we placed at the beginning of the correspondence. We could and can nowhere adduce epistle A for the supplementing of the picture of the Gnostics in Philippi which we gained from epistle C. With epistle B it is a different story. It is true that we were not able even to supplement from it the information gained from epistle C. This information, however, did occasionally find confirmation in epistle B. Remarks of Paul in epistle B such as the warnings against pride and disunity, which even there more than remotely hinted at their concrete occasion, although we were obliged to surmise such occasion, suddenly become understandable against the background of epistle C, out of the situation in Philippi. But

---

[195] The fact that no later than the first half of the second century there was in Philippi a Gnostic community which was larger than the ecclesiastical community (W. Bauer, [1], pp. 72 ff.) is certainly worthy of note at this point in our investigation.

that reveals not only the unity of the motivation for epistle B and epistle C, but also the different times of their composition.

2. If the results of this investigation are correct, then Rome and Caesarea are excluded as the place of composition of the Philippian epistle. More precisely, we must now say the Philippian *epistles*.[196] A correspondence as lively as this one and the frequent and speedy news connections presupposed therein are inconceivable if Paul was sojourning in Rome or Caesarea, several months' travel removed from Philippi. Above all, however, the common occasion for the correspondence with Galatia, Philippi, and Corinth presupposes that the time and place of composition of the Philippian epistles coincides with the corresponding data for the epistles to Galatia and Corinth.[197] What should long since have been regarded as assured for other reasons is therefore hardly to be disputed any more: The Philippian epistle or epistles were written in Ephesus,[198] though epistle C, which was not necessarily written still in prison, can also have been written in the vicinity of Ephesus.[199] Against the epistle's having been written in Ephesus, a serious objection has not yet been brought forward.[200]

The question of how the epistles to Galatia, Philippi, and

---

[196] It is certain that we are actually dealing with three *Philippian* epistles. For epistles A and B are so connected by the collection which Epaphras delivered, and epistles B and C by the same polemical battlefront, that the address in Phil. 1:1 (epistle B) must also be appropriate for epistles A and C.

[197] Thus also argues P. Feine, pp. 37 ff. to be sure under the presupposition of judaizing opposition.

[198] Literature on this question and a good summary of the studies most recently in W. Michaelis, [1], pp. 204-11. Cf. also C. H. Dodd, *New Testament Studies* (1954, 2nd ed.), pp. 83 ff.: "The Chronological Order of the Pauline Epistles." Here he explicitly but not very convincingly defends the writing of Philippians in Rome, against S. Duncan, *St. Paul's Ephesian Ministry* (1929), in order then on pp. 108 ff. to reconstruct the "development in the thought of Paul." Whatever one thinks about the place and time of the writing of Philippians, for such reconstructions the thesis of Rome as the place of the writing of the Philippian epistle is just as much too uncertain as is the placing of the Thessalonian epistles in the first so-called missionary journey. Cf. now also W. Marxsen, p. 65; P. Hoffmann, pp. 326-27.

[199] See I Cor. 15:32; Acts 19:22; II Cor. 1:8. J. Gnilka ([1], p. 25) concludes—in my judgment incorrectly—from 3:16, 18, that in the meantime Paul has made another visit to Philippi. Therefore he proposes Corinth as the place of the composition of epistle C.

[200] Cf. further P. Dacquino, "Date e provenienza della lettera ai Fillipesi," in *Rivista Biblica*, 6 (1958): 224-34; see the review in NTA 3 (1959): 270-71. Further, G. Bornkamm, [3], pp. 199-200.

Corinth are related in point of time to one another and possibly overlap will be examined later.[201]

3. The image of the history of primitive Christianity is, down to our own days, dominated by the conclusions of F. C. Baur's studies to such an extent that people hold Paulinism and the Judaistic tendency to be the moving forces of this history, and indeed in such a way that these two forms of early Christianity stood in constant tension with each other. The alleged agitation of the Judaizers in the Pauline mission fields, which is inferred from the primitive Christian writings, formed and forms the foundation for this picture of the history. This foundation has long been shaken and damaged in many respects, and the buildings erected upon it are already for many no longer inhabitable. But if it is true that even in Corinth, Philippi, and Galatia no Judaizers emerged on the scene against Paul, it disappears completely. Therewith Baur's construction of the history is dissolved.[202]

We shall guard against putting in its place a new system of the history of primitive Christianity. We shall, however, have to describe this history anew in many respects.

Thus the relationship between Paul and James, between Antioch and Jerusalem, between Gentile Christians and Jewish Christians and their respective missionary efforts must and can be newly defined.[203] That will show not only how insignificant Palestinian Jewish Christianity was already in the time of Paul, but also that the fundamental tensions, up to the present regarded as so self-evident, and open disputes between the two tendencies were greatly exaggerated and the (certainly not tension-free) κοινωνία, as Paul bears witness to it in Gal. 2:9, in truth determined this relationship.[204]

Further, the significance of (Jewish) Christian Gnosticism in

---

[201] Cf. below, pp. 245 ff.

[202] Nothing is thereby taken away from the significance of this great historian. F. C. Baur's particular achievement was that he applied the idea of development even in the investigation of primitive Christianity. Our entire work on primitive Christianity down to the present time draws its very life therefrom.

[203] Cf. below, pp. 221 ff.; Vol. 3, *passim*.

[204] To arrive at this awareness, of course one may not take the often quite adventurous route which J. Munck proposes in his studies (*Paul and the Salvation of Mankind; Christus und Israel*). Moreover, the relationship between Paul and Jerusalem was hardly as harmonious as J. Munck imagines it.

early Christianity must be noted more than has previously been done. It is true that this Gnosticism can in no case occupy the position which Judaism held in Baur's picture of the history. But one must see that Gnosticism belongs in the very beginnings of Christianity, that the real intra-ecclesiastical struggles from the beginning onward were struggles with Gnosticism, and that an important part of even the "ecclesiastical" Christianity, primarily the branch stemming from the Syrian-Antiochian region, is not to be understood without reference to Gnostic influences.

Finally, more value is to be placed on the investigation of Hellenistic Christianity before and parallel with Paul, which, in contrast with the supposedly all-dominant great currents of Judaism and Paulinism, is usually treated as a stepchild, although it is the actual root of the early Catholic Church. It appears to me that we must make much more comprehensive use of the many-layered Synoptic tradition for the investigation of this branch of early Christianity.[205] Only when that has been done, in my opinion, can it be explained whether and what remnants of genuine Jesus tradition have been preserved in this tradition.

Addendum

In discussion with the foregoing essay, H. Koester has written on "The Purpose of the Polemic of a Pauline Fragment (Philippians III)" (in NTS 8 [1962]: 317-32).

Koester too is convinced that Phil. 3 is a piece of an originally independent epistle. From this he concludes that one must answer the question as to the heretical group being combated in Phil. 3 independently of the other parts of the Philippian epistle. Now a different epistle does not necessarily presuppose a different situation, but it certainly is methodologically permissible to explain Phil. 3 *first* in its own terms.

Further, it is methodologically correct when Koester proposes deliberately to interrogate Phil. 3 under the presupposition of a unitary

---

[205] Redaction-critical study, which is being pursued today in great breadth, affords for this an important preliminary work when it distinguishes between redaction and tradition. Occupying themselves with the actual work are, e.g., E. Grässer, *Das Problem der Parusieverzögerung in den synoptischen Evangelien und in der Apostelgeschichte* (1957); H. Koester, *Synoptische Überlieferung bei den apostolischen Vätern* (1957), idem, "Die ausserkanonischen Herrenworte als Produkte der christlichen Gemeinde" (ZNW 48 [1957]: 220 ff.).

battlefront. Of course he regards it as an erroneous interpretation to see in Paul's opponents in this part of the epistle Jewish Gnostics; in them we have rather to do, according to him, with strict legalist Jewish Christians of Gnostic observance.

Verses 2-6 are the point of departure for this interpretation. Because in vs. 2 a reference to "circumcision" is made with the "concision" and in vs. 6 Paul emphasizes that he lives according to the law without reproach, Koester thinks that the main point of contention must have been the Jewish law, whose *perfect fulfilling* the heretics in Philippi demanded and achieved. It is obvious, when one observes the context of vss. 2-11, that the verses mentioned afford no basis for *this* interpretation of the opponents' position. In this context Paul is concerned with unmasking the boasting of the opponents as a false, fleshly boasting (vss. 3-4). He does this by affirming that he too *could* glory in a fleshly way, but he has refrained from doing so for the sake of Christ, who is his true glory. The false, fleshly glorying, however, from which he refrains and which his opponents emphasize, is "to be of the circumcision," as both vs. 2 and vss. 5-6 show. *How* the opponents gloried in "being of the circumcision," however, simply is not to be deduced from Paul's words. That *Paul* according to vs. 6 lived according to the law without reproach tells just as little about the self-understanding of the opponents as Jews as does Paul's other assertion in vs. 6 that he had been a persecutor of the community with great zeal, an assertion which naturally does not purport to describe the opponents also; both comments pertain only to Paul's Jewish existence. Since Jews as well as Judaizers and, as we have seen, libertine Jewish Gnostics could boast of their Jewish origin, in vss. 2-6 we learn only that Paul's opponents in Phil. 3 were of Jewish origin and that these emphasized their origin; nothing more.

Then from vss. 7-16 Koester rightly infers that Paul's opponents call themselves "perfect" and that they proclaim the resurrection as their present possession (and thus deny the apocalyptic conception of the resurrection at the end of time). By this they are shown to be Gnostics, who nevertheless find their "perfection" not in the Gnostic manner in their pneumatic being but in the perfect fulfillment of the Jewish law. For Koester this latter point arises not out of vss. 7-16 but out of the connection of vss. 7-16 with his unjustified interpretation vss. 2-6. Now there is, as we have seen, abundant evidence for the connection between Gnostic perfection and Gnostic spiritualizing of the resurrection hope; but that the latter

ever was connected with Pharisaic legal rigorism is undocumented
and, in view of the distance in principle of Gnosticism's thought in
terms of being from Judaism's historical thought, is hardly even conceivable. Gnostic Judaism is a product of modern scholars, developed
out of a quite short-sighted erroneous interpretation of early Christian texts. As a historical phenomenon there never was any such
thing. At this point in his study at the latest, H. Koester would have
to revise his thesis of the legal rigorism of the heretics in Philippi,
especially in view of the other indications in vss. 7-16, unnoticed by
Koester, which underscore the Gnostic attitude of the heretics.

Since he omits such a revision, he must now undertake the insolu-
ble task of explaining in terms of anti-judaizing polemic vss. 17-21,
which have long been recognized as antilibertine; for he correctly
does not wish to dissolve the unitary character of the battlefront in
Phil. 3. His solution is as original as it is untenable: in vss. 7-16
Paul is setting himself partly against the Judaistic legal righteousness, partly against the Gnostic self-consciousness of the false teachers
in Philippi. Now the ambiguous charge that the opponents are
"enemies of the cross of Christ" (vs. 18) in itself naturally may also
be interpreted to mean that the heretics in Philippi (in fact) empty
the cross of Christ because they seek their righteousness in the fulfilling of the law. But in such an interpretation the fact is disregarded
that from vs. 16 onward Paul is criticizing the *ethical* conduct of
the opponents. Verse 16 in fact says: if a person claims to be perfect,
he must also live accordingly. But according to vss. 17-18 their conduct proves the opponents to be enemies of the cross of Christ. This
conduct is also addressed in vs. 19*b*: "whose god is their belly."
Already for this reason one cannot with Koester render this passage
in a paraphrase thus: your claim to be of a divine nature is transient
and evil like the belly—an interpretation, which otherwise also is
misleading, of this passage in which Paul bitingly accuses his opponents of having made the belly their god. It is no less misleading
when Koester interprets vs. 19*c* ("they seek their honor in their
shame"), with K. Barth's *Erklärung des Philipperbriefes* ([1928], p.
111), in the following way: Anyone who, while calling for holiness
and purity, seeks his salvation bypassing the cross of Christ is seeking
his honor in his shame. This interpretation too, apart from everything else, wholly disregards the topic of vss. 16-21, Christian *conduct*.
It is consistent then when vs. 19*d* ("who mind earthly things") also
according to Koester "can by no means be understood as a description
of the opponents, and every attempt to interpret it in such a way is

bound to fail completely"; instead, according to Koester, with this comment also Paul is reacting polemically to the lofty *religious* claims of his opponents, which he rejects and interprets as "minding earthly things." Nevertheless the two closest parallels, to which Koester emphatically refers with vs. 19*d*, namely Col. 3:2 and Ign. Smyrn. 11.3, are unequivocally ethically oriented.

It has become clear why I cannot regard Koester's essay as a fruitful contribution to the solution of our problem, no matter how good it is in its many observations of details and how useful in focusing on the problem as such in its various aspects. One of these aspects consists of the question whether during the third missionary journey Paul is confronted in his mission territory with a unitary heretical missionary movement or whether "the heresies in Paul's time are nothing but various and often *ad hoc* attempts, arising within the Christian movement, to solve the unavoidable internal problems of a syncretistic group (Early Christianity!), which emerged in the Hellenistic-Roman world," as Koester (p. 332) thinks. The foregoing studies are an attempt to establish the former of these opinions (on the problem itself, cf. further pp. 239 ff.). At this point it need only be remarked that the correct description of Pauline Christianity as a syncretistic religion may not be equated with the assertion that this Christianity contained clearly unsolved problems out of which heretical speculations unavoidably had to develop. A worse distortion of Pauline theology, Paul the theologian, and the phenomenon of syncretism cannot be made!

J. Gnilka ([1], pp. 211 ff.; [2], *passim*) describes the adversaries of Phil. 3 uniformly as adherents to a *theios aner* Christology, who document with their impressive appearance the *dynamis* of Christ and, as themselves perfect, with the help of a tradition-connected allegorical exposition of the Scripture communicate the true knowledge. I am unable to see that this picture can be gained from Phil. 3; it is characteristic, for example, that Gnilka must divest vs. 19 of its specific reference and hold it to be a "polemic against heretics of a general kind" ([1], p. 206). Further, it is an error in method to adduce in detail II Cor.—and this in a questionable exposition— but not other letters of Paul for the illumination of Phil. 3; I Cor. offers just as many parallels to Phil. 3 as does II Cor., parallels which, of course, if they were observed, would have to modify Gnilka's presentation significantly.

H. D. Betz (*Nachfolge und Nachahmung Jesu Christi im Neuen Testament*, BHT 37 [1967]: 145 ff.) again recently suggests a dual battlefront for Phil. 3: in 3:2-16 Paul is opposing law-observing gnosticizing Jewish Christians, but in 3:17 ff., people of a libertine, fleshly way of life. I do not understand why Betz does not attribute libertinism to gnosticizing Jewish Christians. It is true that the Jewish or Jewish Christian Gnostics mentioned earlier (p. 36, n. 63 above) do not connect a libertinism with their circumcision. Yet this observation can all the less prejudge the interpretation of Phil. 3, since we have testimony of libertines in Corinth and Galatia who emphasize their Judaism. But in Phil. 3 Paul in no way indicates a shift in battlefronts, and even Betz does not venture to assert that in 3:17-19 it *could* not be Gnostic libertines that are involved.

Robert Jewett ("The Epistolary Thanksgiving and Philippians," *Nov. Test.* 12 [1970]: 40-53) also argues for a dual battlefront in Phil. 3, to be sure otherwise than does H. D. Betz: vss. 3:2 ff. are directed against nomists, 3:18 ff. against gnosticizing libertines. In his essay "Conflicting Movements in the Early Church as Reflected in Philippians" (*Nov. Test.* 12 [1970]: 363-90), he works out this thesis further and (with the unity of the epistle!) reckons in 1:15 ff. and 2:21 with a third front, namely with missionaries of the type of the divine miracle-men (*theios aner*) whom Gnilka sees opposed in Phil. 3 but who, according to Jewett, appear against Paul in Ephesus. Once again, Paul, at least, in no way indicates such a differentiation among his opponents.

III

The Historical Situation
of the Thessalonian Epistles

I

The undoubtedly genuine Pauline epistles which are preserved for us all appear to have been written out of a specific occasion. The Roman epistle prepares the way for Paul's visit to Rome. The correspondence with Corinth, Philippi, and Galatia arose out of the threat, which had become evident, to these communities by outside preachers. The tone of these writings of Paul alternates, according to the immediate situation, between the sharp philippic in Phil. 3:2–4:3+4:8-9 and the calm address of the "epistle of joy" in II Cor. 1:1–2:13+7:5–8:24. Rom. 16—probably a letter of recommendation for Phoebe to Ephesus[1]—and the Epistle to Philemon clearly reveal their occasion which, to be sure, is less dramatic.

But what prompted Paul to write the epistle to Thessalonica which found acceptance in our canon as I Thess. and upon whose evaluation the judgment about II Thess. also in large measure depends? F. C. Baur[2] found fault with this writing for the lack of significance of its contents and the "lack of any special interest and of a definitely motivated occasion." What is only appended to the other epistles, he says, is made the main thing here: general instructions, admonitions, wishes.[3] This judgment is not wholly unfounded. I Thess. undoubtedly reveals its concrete occasion to the ordinary reader less than any of the apostle's other letters.

---

[1] See the commentaries; see below, pp. 236-37.

[2] *Paulus* (1845), p. 481.

[3] This judgment was his strongest argument against the genuineness of the epistle, an argument which of course could be employed just as forcefully against its having been forged.

But this does not mean that any such occasion was lacking.

F. C. Baur at the same time pointed to the striking and thoroughgoing points of contact between I Thess. and the other Pauline epistles, in particular the Corinthian epistles.[4] These points of contact are indisputable. They have been used with fundamental correctness in order to clarify the historical background of I Thess.[5] W. Lütgert,[6] in a careful study, inferred a close connection between the anti-Pauline movements in Corinth and Thessalonica. W. Hadorn in *Die Abfassung der Thessalonicherbriefe* went a step further and consistently has I Thess. appear during Paul's third missionary journey.

In fact W. Lütgert and W. Hadorn have correctly seen that the apparently so general statements of Paul in I Thess. have a very definite background and that this background corresponds to that situation which Paul's writings to Corinth, Philippi, and Galatia presuppose for these communities. In this way not only do the detailed statements in I Thess. become understandable, but the epistle also thus shows above all its concrete occasion, which in the apostle's other epistles lies more clearly on the surface. Without *this* concrete occasion, everything that is stated in our introductions and commentaries under the heading of "Occasion and Aim of the Epistle" remains unsatisfying,[7] and Baur's judgment about the lack of a "definitely motivated occasion" would remain unrefuted.

Naturally the special character of I Thess. within the related correspondence is not to be overlooked. To the community as

---

[4] "The first epistle only repeats what was already long known." ". . . with more or less clear reminiscences of other Pauline epistles, particularly the Corinthian epistles." (*Paulus* [1845], pp. 481, 488.) From this Baur inferred the use of the Corinthian epistles by the pseudo-Pauline author of I Thess.

[5] In the school of F. C. Baur this was already done by R. A. Lipsius, who in 1854, in the *Studien und Kritiken*, pp. 905 ff., fitted I Thess. also into the Tübingen historical picture by demonstrating an anti-judaizing tendency of the epistle on the basis of its polemical and apologetic passages and thus made possible even for Baur's school the recognition of the genuineness of the epistle.

[6] [2], pp. 55 ff. Of his numerous studies on primitive Christian enthusiasm, the work on the Thessalonian epistles appears to me to be the most successful.

[7] M. Dibelius [1] still thinks that the only occasion of the writing is the situation pictured in 2:17–3:6 and incidentally the community's unrest over cases of deaths. But if Paul writes the extensive I Thess. out of this occasion, then this writing would be unique within the Pauline corpus, and the epistle itself would remain a psychological enigma. Or would we imagine ourselves capable of writing such an epistle thus unmotivated?

a whole Paul can allow unrestrained praise to be given. He has reason to thank God for the Thessalonians (1:2 ff.; 2:13-14). With the communities in Macedonia and Achaia they are in the best repute (1:7 ff.). Timotheus has just brought to Paul, who is concerned about the community, a cheering report (3: 6 ff.). Even the still necessary admonitions do not lack interspersed praise (4:1, 9-10; 5:4 ff.). Thus the situation in Thessalonica is not comparable to that disorder which II Cor. 10–13 attests for Corinth and the Galatian epistle for Galatia. Distinctive also is the fact that Paul never speaks, as he does for example in II Cor. 10–13 or in Galatians, of special people who are bringing unrest upon the community. Now this has its parallels. In I Cor. Paul speaks so little of the alien intruders that down to the present time some still speak of a fanaticism that arose in Corinth itself, and likewise in Phil. 1:1–3:1+4:4-7, a separate epistle to Philippi,[8] no alien teachers are mentioned, but a warning is clearly given against the results of their agitation (1:27–2:18). At the time of these epistles Paul apparently still is less well informed than later. But can this have been the case at the time of I Thess.? Timotheus had indeed visited the community in Thessalonica at the apostle's behest and had reported to him. Thus I Thess. rather reminds one of the "joyful epistle," [9] which Paul writes after the end of the Corinthian confusion on the basis of the cheering news which Titus brings him from Corinth (II Cor. 7:5 ff.). This little letter hardly shows any of the sharpness of the preceding discussions. The community is praised much as in I Thess. (II Cor. 7:13-16). The lying apostles are no longer mentioned. The apology follows without sharpness (II Cor. 1:12 ff.). Warnings are almost completely lacking.

It is true that this latter cannot be said of I Thess., which is rather filled with admonitions and instructions and moreover contains a clear apology for the Pauline apostolate, even though all this is done with such reserve that the specific reference of many of Paul's statements has often escaped the exegetes. Why this frequently indefinite argument, if Timotheus had just in-

---

[8] See above, pp. 67 ff.

[9] II Cor. 1:1–2:13+7:5–8:24. Cf. J. Weiss, ThLZ (1894), pp. 512 ff.; Vol. 1, pp. 96 ff.

formed Paul about the situation in Thessalonica? Why the apology in 1:4–2:12, if 3:6 is correct? Why the admonitions that fill the epistle, if 3:8 is true? Is there not a discernible tension between 1:7-8 and 4:10 on the one hand, where faith and love of the Thessalonians apparently are presupposed as generally well known, and 3:6 on the other hand, where Paul strongly emphasizes how pleased he is over the unexpected message of the newly arrived Timotheus, that people in Thessalonica are holding fast to faith and love? And is not the position of the strongly personal part of the epistle, 2:17–3:10, in the *middle* of the corpus of the epistle quite extraordinary for Paul's epistles?

Is it possible that I Thess. is not a literary unity?

II

Those who maintain that I Thess. is not genuine have appealed on behalf of their view not only to the content of the epistle in general, but also to individual sections which appear to make the composition of the epistle by Paul impossible. Anyone who thought less critically about the epistle as a whole did still occasionally detach individual sections or verses as non-Pauline glosses from I Thess., which was held to be Pauline.[10] Verses 2:15-16 have always aroused the greatest suspicion in that respect.

Now in recent times—for the first time, so far as I can see— the attempt has been made to make our I Thess. understandable as a literary composition of two genuine letters of Paul. Even though we must regard this attempt as in essence abortive,[11] still K. G. Eckart with his essay, "Der zweite echte Brief des Apostels Paulus an die Thessalonicher," [12] has the merit that for the first time in the investigation of I Thess. a methodological route has been taken which with most other Pauline epistles has long been followed with some success and which in spite of the abortive beginning with Eckart is unavoidable with I Thess. also.

---

[10] See in C. Clemen, *Die Einheitlichkeit der paulinischen Briefe* . . . , pp. 13 ff.; W. G. Kümmel, *Das literarische und geschichtliche Problem des ersten Thessalonicherbriefes*, p. 214, n. 3.

[11] Cf. G. Bornkamm, [1], p. 35, n. 131; W. G. Kümmel, *Das literarische und geschichtliche Problem*. . . .

[12] ZThK 58 (1961) : 30 ff.

Eckart first excises from I Thess. as non-Pauline additions the following: 2:13-16; 3:5; 4:1-8, 10b-12; 5:12-22; 5:27.

He regards 3:5 as an editorial gloss which owes its origin to the fitting together of two originally independent epistles ("Der zweite echte Brief . . . ," p. 34). The justification of this excision collapses along with the correctness of Eckart's literary-critical operation in general (see below). For the removal of 2:13-16 Eckart can appeal to the long doubtful vss. 15 and 16. But even if one strikes out these two verses as glosses,[13] 2:13-14 still do not drop out. It is true that Eckart does not appeal to the difficulties in *content* presented by 2:15-16, but to the formal parallelism in clauses in this passage, which he then finds again in 2:13. But 2:14 is said to be "only apparently concrete," "but in essence altogether generally oriented" (p. 33), i.e., the verse lacks any reference to the situation in Thessalonica.

That defines the two standards which also justify the excision of the other sections just named, all of them paraeneses: the general, nonspecific content of the admonitions and the lofty form of expression. But these standards are not convincing. The claimed parallelism of the excised passages is not distinguished from linguistic formulations also occurring elsewhere in Paul, especially since the rhythmic pattern asserted by Eckart often appears quite artificially construed and moreover is said occasionally to be "disrupted by editing" (p. 56). On this, cf. W. G. Kümmel, pp. 216 ff., who rightly sets forth the Pauline character of the language and style of the sections disputed by Eckart. Eckart can assert that the excised sections are lacking in any concreteness only because he does not adequately clarify the situation of the epistles. Only for this reason, moreover, can he describe the contents of 1:2–2:12 in essence as "expression of thanks" and "recollection of the time of the missionary preaching" (p. 32). The exegesis of the epistle which follows below will demonstrate the specific reference of all these passages.

The most amazing thing in all this is that Eckart also asserts of 2:13: "In any case, under no circumstances is it an epistolary text" (p. 33); for just before this (p. 32) he had very correctly seen that this verse is a doublet to the thanksgiving in 1:2 ff., and

---

[13] On this, see p. 180.

thus the beginning of a second proem in I Thess.! [14] Certainly "a doublet in an epistle is very unusual" (p. 32), but for this very reason this doublet remains an *epistolary* text like 1:2 ff., even though hardly a text of the *same* epistle. Evidently a new epistle begins in 2:13.

K. G. Eckart divides the remnant of the epistle, after eliminating the sections mentioned, into two epistles:

The first epistle: 1:1–2:12+2:17–3:4+3:11-13.

The second epistle: 3:6-10+4:13–5:11+4:9-10a+5:23-26, 28.

The first reconstructed epistle is said to have been given to Timotheus to take with him on that journey whose happy ending is said to have provided the occasion for the second reconstructed epistle to Thessalonica.

The justification for this literary-critical operation is very scanty (p. 34). Eckart takes offense at the parallelism of 3:1 and 3:5 and at the fact that 3:1 ff. speaks of the aim of sending Timotheus, who according to 3:6 has already returned from the journey. I can find nothing to cause offense in either case. As we shall see, there are good reasons for Paul, after the return of Timotheus, once again to speak of the occasion for his journey. In his thesis, Eckart must not only presuppose the very rare

---

[14] P. Schubert, *Form and Function of the Pauline Thanksgiving*, pp. 17 ff., has already made this observation, without drawing the proper conclusions from it. In many respects I Thess. 3:9-10 also is formally reminiscent of the Pauline proem, but cannot be an original proem because the verses represent an interrogatory clause. In view of the series of thanksgivings in I Thess. 1:2; 2:13; 3:9, Schubert speaks (pp. 21 ff.) of a proem which extends into the corpus and determines the literary character of the epistle. He overlooks the fact that 3:9 cannot be compared formally with the introductions to the proems; further, he fails to note that the first proem finds a formal conclusion in 1:10 and therefore is not allowed to extend into the corpus. "I Thess. thus draws to a close at 2:12 and begins again at 2:13" (J. T. Sanders, "The Transition from Opening Epistolary Thanksgivings to Body in the Letters of the Pauline Corpus," JBL 81 [1962]: 356). That the introduction to the epistle is completed only with 4:1 is an assertion of W. G. Kümmel (p. 219) which is strange, not only in view of the Pauline epistolary style. This assertion is repeated by Karl J. Bjerkelund, *Parakalo*, pp. 125 ff. The difficulty of the proem which is repeated in 2:13 certainly is properly recognized in this assertion. But one cannot resolve this difficulty as E. v. Dobschütz (*Die Thessalonicherbriefe, in loc.*) does, by arbitrarily extending the introduction to the epistle into the latter half, with the assertion that Paul deliberately made a new start on the proem several times. The expression of thanks after the prescript is in itself just as formal and also a part of the epistolary formula which is just as firmly bound to the form of the letter as are the letter's other fixed parts—and thus is no more repeatable than these. On "thanksgiving" in the Pauline epistles, cf. B. Rigaux, *Paulus und seine Briefe* (1964), pp. 171-72.

epistolary aorist in 3:1-2 and excise 3:5 as a redactional, moreover superfluous and uncalled-for, gloss; in addition, he destroys an epistolary unity, as we shall see below in the exegesis.

In the further course of Eckart's essay, the assignment of the other parts of I Thess. to the two epistles which allegedly meet in 3:5 then follows quite arbitrarily (pp. 42 ff.). Nevertheless, Eckart rightly sees that in 3:11 begins the conclusion of an epistle, which to be sure does not end with 3:13, as he thinks, but at least includes 4:1 also (see below). Of course this observation is not new (see n. 250), but Eckart is the first rightly to recognize it and evaluate it in its literary significance.

Strangely enough, W. G. Kümmel, who (pp. 221 ff.) fully convincingly rejects Eckart's division of the epistle and demonstrates the untenability of most of Eckart's arguments, does not at all enter into this observation that an epistolary conclusion begins in 3:11, although on p. 214 he rightly states that this observation forms one of the foundations of Eckart's analysis. But on p. 221, under 3), this observation is no longer mentioned, and moreover there is no attempt to refute it. That can hardly be an oversight. In fact, that observation is rather indisputable and irrefutable. It will not do for Kümmel, without further ado, to expand his successful refutation of Eckart's analysis of I Thess. into the assertion that there are "no serious reasons" *at all* "for opposing the assumption that I Thess. in the form in which it has come down to us stems from Paul" (p. 225).

It is rewarding in this connection to take a brief comprehensive look at the "eschatocol" of Paul's epistles.[15] It is never wholly symmetrically constructed, but is always adapted to the individual writing. Still the schema which underlies all the eschatocols may be clearly recognized, although one must reckon with the fact that the editing of the Pauline epistles has not preserved all the epistle endings for us intact.

Usually *personal remarks* concerning the apostle's situation form the transition to the actual conclusion of the epistle.

The latter is often introduced with a passage which unites *intercession and doxology*. Karl J. Bjerkelund (*Parakalo*, p. 27) proposes,

---

[15] The comprehensive, in many particulars also instructive but on the whole unsatisfying study by O. Roller, *Das Formular der paulinischen Briefe* (1933), in essence fails the reader on this question.

with reason, to call this piece the benediction or simply the climax. This piece in fact does compete with the concluding (christological) benediction.

Then there regularly follows a *closing exhortation* which, even where it is given in general terms, is also related to the concrete situation of the recipients. This exhortation begins with ὥστε, παρα-καλῶ, or something similar, or with τὸ λοιπόν or something of the sort, and the use of one formula does not exclude the other.

This is followed by the personal *greetings*, which occasionally are enriched with brief remarks related to the situation.

A *benediction* concludes the eschatocol.

An examination of the individual conclusions of the epistles in terms of this fivefold schema yields the following picture:[16]

Epistle	Personal Notes	Intercession, Doxology	Paraenesis	Salutations	Benediction
Rom.[17]	15:14-29	15:5-6; 13	15:30-32	16:21-23	15:33
Rom.–Eph.[17]	16:1-2	16:20a	16:17-19	16:3-16	16:20b
Cor. A[18]	lacking	(I, 15:57)	I, 15:58 + 16:15-18	I, 16:19-21	I, 16:22-24
Cor. D[19]	II, 13:1 ff., 10	II, 13:11b	II, 13:11a	II, 13:12	II, 13:13
Gal.	lacking	(6:16)	6:17	lacking	6:18
Phil. A[20]	4:18	4:19-20	lacking	4:21-22	4:23
Phil. B[20]	2:19-30	4:7	3:1 + 4:4-6	lacking	lacking
Phil. C[20]	lacking	4:9b	4:2-3, 8-9a	lacking	lacking
Col.	4:7-9	lacking	4:2-6	4:10-18a	4:18b
I Thess.	lacking	5:23-24	5:25	5:26-27	5:28
II Thess.[21]	lacking	3:16	3:13-15	3:17	3:18
II Tim.	4:9-17	4:18	lacking	4:19-21	4:22
Titus	3:12-13	lacking	3:14	3:15a	3:15b
Philemon	22	lacking	lacking	23-24	25
I Peter	lacking	5:10-11	5:12	5:13-14a	5:14b
Hebrews	13:18-19	13:20-21	13:22-23	13:24	13:25

[16] Col. is included with reservations concerning its authenticity. II Tim. and Titus are included, because I regard the close of these epistles as Pauline; cf. RGG V (3rd ed.), art. "Pastoralbriefe." Heb. and I Peter are cited for the sake of comparison, since their eschatocols are typically Pauline. The pseudo-Pauline Laodicean epistle, already named by the Muratorian Canon, also contains a good example of the Pauline eschatocol.

[17] See pp. 236 ff.
[18] See pp. 245-46; Vol. 1, pp. 93-94.
[19] See p. 246; Vol. 1, p. 96.
[20] See pp. 67 ff.
[21] But cf. n. 259.

The survey shows that the schema is more consistently applied in the latter parts than in the earlier ones.

The benediction is not missing in any writing in which the conclusion of the epistle is extant.

The salutations are missing in Phil. B and C, because these epistles now stand in the middle of the text of the canonical Epistle to the Philippians; they may have been eliminated by the editor. Thus they were originally lacking only in Gal.; this is presumably just as intentional as the omission, to be noted only in Gal., of the proem and therewith of all personal remarks presently connecting sender and recipients of the epistle, in the entire epistle. This has often been observed and has been sufficiently reported and explained.

The *closing paraenesis* is significantly lacking in the writings to individuals. The fact that in Titus 3:14 nevertheless there is found an admonition confirms this judgment; for this admonition is addressed to the community, not to the recipient of the epistle. It would also have been extremely inappropriate if Paul had concluded Phil. A, the brief note of thanks for the love gift received from the Philippians, with an admonition; hence it is missing in this epistle. Otherwise it is always found, even if in Rom.-Eph., Col., and II Thess.[22] for obvious reasons, which however need not concern us here, it is fitted into the eschatocol other than in the usual way.

In the first two parts of the schema the exceptions are more frequent, yet with respect to the *personal remarks* this picture may be deceiving: in Gal. they were always lacking, for the reasons already given; in the other epistles the absence may in every case be traced back to editorial omissions, since a composite epistle could not contain self-contradictory allusions to the situation. Thus only the second position is even less firmly anchored in the schema; and indeed above all with respect to its location. Moreover, a comparison with Rom. 15:33 raises the question whether in Phil. 4:7 and 4:9b we do not have to do with the concluding benediction of Phil. B and Phil. C.

It would take us too far afield at this point to compare and to sketch the individual formulations and expressions of the eschatocol. Nevertheless I refer to some formulations which are typical of the epistolary conclusions in Paul:

ὁ θεὸς (ὁ κύριος) τῆς εἰρήνης is found only in the eschatocols: Rom. 15:33; 16:20b; II Cor. 13:11; Phil. 4:9; I Thess. 5:23; II Thess. 3:16; cf. Heb. 13:20; I Thess. 3:11; II Thess. 2:16; Rom. 15:5, 13.

---

[22] But cf. n. 259.

The same is true of (τὸ) λοιπόν or τοῦ λοιποῦ (ἀδελφοί) in the sense of "finally," "lastly"; II Cor. 13:11; Phil. 3:1; 4:8; Gal. 6:17.

The announcement that Paul will soon come to the recipients of the epistle is found as a rule in the personal remarks which lead to the *clausula epistolae:* Rom. 15:28-29; I Cor. 16:5 ff.; II Cor. 13:1 ff., 10; Philemon 22; cf. Heb. 13:18-19.

Specific requests for intercession for the apostle are found in Paul only in the closing parts of his epistles:[23] Rom. 15:30; Phil. 4:6; Col. 4:2; I Thess. 5:25; Philemon 22; cf. Heb. 13:18; II Thess. 3:1-2; Eph. 6:18 ff.

All observations made here apply in the same way to the eschatocols of Paul's letters which are preserved intact as well as to those reconstructed out of composite epistles. Thereby the literary-critical analyses undertaken previously in Vol. 1 and in the present investigation are confirmed.

But at the same time and above all, these observations have their weight for the literary-critical analysis of the Thessalonian epistles. For now there can be no serious doubt that Eckart made a correct observation when he suspected the conclusion of an epistle in I Thess. 3:11 ff.

The personal remarks which are usual before the *clausula epistolae* are found in abundance in the verses preceding 3:11. They end with the expression, typical at this point (see above) before the actual close of the epistle, of the expectation to be able soon to visit the recipients of the epistle.

Then with αὐτὸς δὲ ὁ θεός, precisely as in[24] I Thess. 5:23; II Thess. 3:16; Phil. 4:19, with a formula reserved in Paul for epistolary conclusions, there begins the intercession which approaches a doxology, ending, as in I Thess. 5:23, with a glance at the Parousia. W. Bousset has observed, not altogether incorrectly: "Actually he had already intended to conclude the epistle with 3:13, as the blessing which is found there indicates" (RGG IV [1st ed.], col. 1318).

This is followed by the paraenesis, which begins in 4:1 with

---

[23] Apart from the general and brief requests in Rom. 12:12 and I Thess. 5:17, which occur within more extensive paraeneses; for here we have to do with general exhortations to prayer, not the request for supplication for the apostle.

[24] Cf. the conclusions in Heb. 13:20; I Peter 5:10; I Cor. 15:57; Phil. 2:27; II Tim. 4:18.

λοιπὸν οὖν, ἀδελφοί, that is, with a formula which Paul employs exclusively to introduce the closing paraenesis (see above). In this paraenesis is found the recollection, also elsewhere popular in epistolary conclusions, of the warnings earlier given orally (cf. Phil. 4:8, see pp. 112-13; II Thess. 2:15, see pp. 194-95).

The ἀσπασμός, which must not have been missing from what follows, has been eliminated by the editor, as was done in Phil. B and C (cf. Rom.; see below, pp. 237-38), because it would have been out of place in the middle of the body of the epistle formed by the editor. In the elimination of the ἀσπασμός the concluding benediction has also been erased.

It is difficult to determine where the concluding paraenesis ends. One could assign to it the entire section 4:1-12, since no break is to be detected in this section. But this would be extraordinarily long for a concluding paraenesis. Besides, one then would have to assume that the admonitions occurring in 4:1-12 were appended to an epistle which, full of gratitude for the state of the Thessalonians' faith, does not lead us to expect these admonitions which throughout are very specific. Hence I should rather have the closing paraenesis and with it the extant conclusion of the epistle end already with 4:1 (or 4:2), fully aware that the skill with which the editor has constructed this seam makes a sure judgment impossible.

But if, as we have already seen, we have preserved for us in 2:13 ff. a doublet to the proem in 1:2 ff., and in 3:11–4:1 the close of an epistle, then it is obvious to regard the entire section 2:13–4:1 as an independent epistle, with which Paul is reacting to Timotheus' return from Thessalonica. The reasons adduced by Eckart for dividing up this section are, as we have already said, insufficient; the unity of the epistle which covers 2:13–4:1 will rather be confirmed in the following interpretation.

Then there would remain for the other epistle 1:1–2:12+4:2–5:28. It will be seen at once that 4:2 (or even 4:3) follows nicely after 2:12. Not so good, on the other hand, is the present connection of 2:13 with 2:12. It is not quite clear to what the καὶ διὰ τοῦτο καὶ ἡμεῖς refers, as admonitions after all follow 2:12 better than does an expression of thanksgiving. Since the second proem (like the first and like, in diverse variations, the proems in Paul generally) will have begun with the εὐχαριστοῦμεν, the καὶ διὰ τοῦτο καὶ ἡμεῖς may be an editorial parenthesis. This would also explain the logic which in view of the context is faulty and which has always caught the attention of the commentators. No one has yet been able to make it clear to what the διὰ τοῦτο actually refers. Whether one connects it with the preceding vss. 10-12 or an individual expression from them, or whether one lets it refer to the (causally understood) ὅτι clause in vs. 13: in any case it disrupts any conceivable logical sequence, although it must have served logical clarity. Even less sensible in the context is the emphatic καὶ ἡμεῖς, "which is only half explained by most exegetes and is not evaluated in its peculiarly emphatic position" (W. Bornemann, *Die Thessalonicherbriefe*, pp. 98-99). Where is anything said before this or afterward of others, beside whom "we too" thank God? Only as an editorial remark does the "and for this reason we too" fulfill its (in this case, modest) aim: the abrupt beginning, typical of a proem, is covered up.

The simple kind of editing, which skillfully inserts one epistle into the other, corresponds exactly to the way the redactor works which can be observed in the other epistolary composites of the Corpus Paulinum.[25]

The formal analysis proposed here will be confirmed in the following investigation of the contents of the two epistles that are united in I Thess. This much is already clear: in this way we find an easy explanation of the position of 4:13–5:11 in the epistle *as a whole* (already rightly sensed by E. Fuchs, "Hermeneutik?" p. 46, as peculiar) and of the insertion, unprecedented in Pauline epistolary style and unexpected in I Thess., of detailed personal remarks (2:13–4:1) into the apostle's theological statements. Moreover, the discrepancy noted above in section I of this chapter between Paul's good news about conditions in Thessalonica, to be assumed because of Timotheus' visit there, and the actually very cautious argument, as also the other mentioned tensions within I Thess., come to nothing if I Thess. em-

---

[25] It is a methodological error of Eckart's literary-critical analysis that he has not noted the parallel epistolary composites in the Corpus Paulinum, which render his complicated analysis of I Thess. not even probable.

braces two originally independent writings from evidently different situations.

In other words, then, Paul does not write the epistle composed of 1:1–2:12+4:2 (3)–5:28 on the basis of news received from Timotheus, but possibly on the basis of far less dependable information. This would account for the fact that Paul often is content only to mention what has happened, without any sharpness, so that for us the actual situation would remain to a large extent unclear if we were limited to I Thess. for its illumination. Yet we may in fact see I Thess. in close historical connection with Paul's epistles to Corinth, Philippi, and Galatia—*if W. Lütgert and W. Hadorn are correct.*

But the investigations by these two have gained little approval,[26] too little, as it appears to me. Too little approval, even if the weaknesses of these studies are not covered up. It is necessary and is high time again to ask, as they did, about the occasion of "I Thess.'

III

I Thess. 1:1. The absence of Paul's apostolic title in the prescript is striking. Should one conclude from this that no one in Thessalonica has attacked Paul's apostleship? [27] But Paul's use of the title is not solely for apologetic reasons, as the beginning to the Roman epistle shows. And in I Thess. 2:7 Paul obviously places value on the title, as then after all his authority was not undisputed in Thessalonica (see below). Hence one will have to be cautious about too far-reaching conclusions.[28] If Silvanus also could claim the title of apostle for himself, as appears to me very likely,[29] with the use of the title Paul would not only have been

---

[26] As recently as 1922, H. Appel, *Einleitung in das Neue Testament,* does not even mention Lütgert's work in his bibliography. P. Feine in his negative attitude toward Hadorn's and Lütgert's theses nevertheless shows himself to be impressed by their line of argument (*Einleitung in das NT* [1930, 5th ed.], pp. 107 ff.). W. Michaelis adopts Hadorn's thesis with his own proof for it, but at the same time curiously rejects Hadorn's most important proof and, along with it, Lütgert's thesis that the situations in Corinth and Thessalonica were similar ([1], pp. 223 ff.). On the other hand, K. Stürmer (*Auferstehung und Erwählung* [1953], p. 48) rightly acknowledges Lütgert's observations, but without affirming Hadorn's conclusions.

[27] P. W. Schmiedel, *in loc.*

[28] W. Bornemann, p. 51.

[29] Cf. I Thess. 2:7 and the commentaries on this passage; *The Office of Apostle,* pp. 65 ff.

distinguishing Silvanus with the same authority as himself, but would have placed him above Timotheus,[30] who certainly was no apostle. The former,[31] like the latter,[32] cannot have been a congenial idea to Paul. This could be sufficient explanation for Paul's refraining from the use of the apostolic title in the prescript to I Thess. But be that as it may, one may by no means infer from the absence of the title that its bearer was not under attack.

I Thess. 1:2–2:2. The thanksgiving now following is found in all of Paul's epistles except Gal. (and I Tim., Titus) as a typical part of epistles[33] which goes back to Jewish Hellenistic models. Thus, just as its absence in Gal. is determined by the situation, so also is it shaped in the other epistles according to the respective concrete situation: The repeatedly expressed joy over the state of the Thessalonians' faith must be seen in connection with the admonitions which follow shortly thereafter, and the references to Paul's successful preaching in Thessalonica (1:5-6, 9) prepare the way for the apology which follows in 2:1-12. Interesting to us for our inquiry above all is vs. 1:5, which forms a connection in content with 1:9 and 2:1-2.

Paul alludes to his εἴσοδος in Thessalonica, that is, to his first appearance there. M. Dibelius ([1], *in loc.*) would like to translate εἴσοδος in 1:9 as "acceptance," but such a meaning of the word has no documentation.[34] The subject in 1:9 and 2:1, as already in 1:5*b* ("οἷοι ἐγενήθημεν ἐν ὑμῖν") is not the conduct of the Thessalonians but the behavior of Paul and his friends; there are reports περὶ ἡμῶν everywhere! This εἴσοδος was not κενή, Paul emphasizes (2:1), and the preaching of the gospel had not been ἐν λόγῳ μόνον (1:5). As the Thessalonians know, Paul rather had come ἐν δυνάμει καὶ πνεύματι ἁγίῳ καὶ πληροφορίᾳ πολλῇ (1:5). Indeed, throughout Macedonia and Achaia one can hear what prosperity had attended Paul's missionary work in Thessalonica

---

[30] Cf. I Cor. 15:8.

[31] Cf. I Cor. 15:10; besides, during the third missionary journey Silvanus can no longer have played a significant role.

[32] Timotheus had just been in Thessalonica as Paul's authorized emissary.

[33] P. Schubert, *Form and Function of the Pauline Thanksgivings*, BZNW 20 (1939).

[34] See W. Michaelis in TDNT V: 107, n. 12.

(1:9). How then could the Thessalonians themselves fail to remember that in spite of much opposition, Paul had preached the gospel to them with vigorous boldness ("ἐπαρρησιασάμεθα")?

It is interesting how Paul three times transforms his praise of the Thessalonians into an apology for his activity in Thessalonica—from 1:4 to 1:5; from 1:8 to 1:9a; from 1:9b-10 to 2:1— then to dwell on this apology from 2:1 on. Thus the special interest already in the proem is directed toward this apology.[35] Now there can be no doubt that in 2:3 ff. Paul is defending himself against charges which were made against him in Thessalonica.[36] But if Paul's apology in 2:3 ff. goes back to specific charges against him, the same is true of the apology in 1:5, 9, and 2:1-2. The section 1:2–2:12 forms an indissoluble unity. But then also with the statement that his gospel did not come in word alone (1:5), his appearing in Thessalonica was effective (1:9) and by no means κενός (2:1), Paul is refuting corresponding charges. Of what kind are these charges?

When the word is used figuratively, as it is here, κενός can mean either "unsuccessful" [37] or "powerless." [38] The majority of exegetes rightly prefer in our passage the meaning "powerless, feeble." [39] Only thus does the contrast to ἐπαρρησιασάμεθα demanded by the ἀλλά at the beginning of 2:2 become evident; the emphasis in 2:2 is on this ἐπαρρησιασάμεθα, and it does not mean to speak "successfully," but "openly," "boldly." At the same time the bridge is built to 1:5, where the contrasting of λόγος and δύναμις or πνεῦμα is also meant to indicate the contrast "powerless" and "effectual," and to 1:9, where Paul's appearance in Thessalonica, which is not more precisely defined (ὁποίαν εἴσοδον), is identified by the reference to the evident success precisely as "powerful."

---

[35] Of course this is frequently overlooked by the exegetes.

[36] As much as the opinions diverge about *who* in Thessalonica had personally cast suspicion on the apostle, that divergence is matched by the extensive unanimity among exegetes since the time of the church fathers *that* the charges mentioned in 2:3 ff. actually were lodged against Paul. (It is true that this unanimity no longer exists at present; on this, see further below.)

[37] Thus in Paul, e.g., in I Cor. 15:10.

[38] Thus, e.g., in I Cor. 15:14.

[39] "Our appearance among you was not miserable, weak, powerless" (W. Bornemann, p. 74; cf. TDNT III: 660; P. W. Schmiedel, *in loc.*; G. Wohlenberg, *Erster und Zweiter Thessalonicherbrief, in loc.*; E. v. Dobschütz, [1], p. 83; M. Dibelius, [1], *in loc.*).

Thus Paul is defending himself against the charge that his preaching is powerless, miserable, and weak.

What does this charge mean? Obviously it cannot mean that Paul's preaching was *unsuccessful*. Even if with a reference to the success of his labor Paul guards himself against that charge,[40] still he is not thereby refuting a charge against the lack of success of his presence, but against the weak nature of his preaching. And since this success of his missionary activity in Thessalonica would have been indisputable even if in 1:7 ff., Paul may have somewhat exaggerated, the charge of unsuccessful labor would moreover have been manifestly false and hence simply nonsensical. It is no accident that this charge was not made, so far as we know, against Paul anywhere else.

Naturally the charge also is not directed against Paul's physical weakness, as appears to have been the case in Galatia, according to Gal. 4:12 ff.[41] His *preaching* was poor. Is this supposed to mean that Paul was somewhat lacking in desired rhetorical ability? Apparently Paul occasionally had to defend himself against this charge too.[42] But an inartistic discourse still is not κενός. And according to 1:5, people were not reproaching the wretched form of Paul's word, but the word as such in its wretchedness.

Now this likewise is not without parallels. According to II Cor. 10:1, Paul is supposed to have come to Corinth ταπεινός. His παρουσία (= εἴσοδος, I Thess. 1:9) in Corinth was, according to II Cor. 10:10, ἀσθενής καὶ ὁ λόγος ἐξουθενημένος. Also according to I Cor. 4:10 (cf. II Cor. 13:9) he and his fellow apostles are regarded as ἀσθενεῖς and as μωροὶ ἐν Χριστῷ. He is "nothing" in comparison with the super-apostles (II Cor. 12:11). It is alleged that Christ does not really speak in him (II Cor. 13:3). These passages leave no room for doubt that here it is not Paul's physical weakness but the weakness of his preaching that is criticized.[43] In this sense the false teachers set in opposition to Paul's weakness (II Cor. 10:9 ff.) their own Χριστοῦ εἶναι (II Cor. 10:7-8), and

---

[40] With the same argument Paul also defends his apostolic office (I Cor. 9:1-2; II Cor. 10:12 ff.), even though the success of his preaching had not been disputed; cf. *The Office of Apostle*, pp. 34-35.

[41] See above, pp. 49-50.

[42] Cf. I Cor. 1:17; 2:1, 4; II Cor. 10:10; 11:6; Rom. 16:18; and the commentaries on these passages.

[43] On details, cf. the commentaries and Vol. 1, pp. 182 ff.

they characterize Paul as ταπεινός (II Cor. 10:1), because they themselves are πνευματικοί (II Cor. 10:2).[44] The ἰσχυροί call Paul ἀσθενής (I Cor. 4:10), in comparison with the *super-apostles* Paul becomes nothing (II Cor. 12:11), and one no longer hears Christ speaking in him (II Cor. 13:3).

Wherein does the strength of the proclamation of the opponents in Corinth consist? It consists in the very fact that the proclamation occurs not in word alone but also in demonstrations of the Spirit! Paul, on the other hand, "is said to be no proper pneumatic";[45] he can only "talk." This concrete background of the Corinthian charges against Paul becomes clearest in II Cor. 5:11-15, where Paul sets over against each other the concepts, apparently used in Corinth, of ἀνθρώπους πείθειν or σωφρονεῖν and φανεροῦν or ἐκστῆναι. For the sake of the edification of the community the apostle abstains from the ecstatic productivity which the false teachers in Corinth regard as proof of the Spirit, and contents himself with "rational" discourse, which the opponents spitefully label as a "persuading." [46] Even when in the further course of the correspondence he allows himself to be compelled to tell of the ὀπτασίαι and ἀποκαλύψεις which have come to him too, he still emphasizes that he does not wish to be judged according to the ὑπερβολὴ τῶν ἀποκαλύψεων but according to the ὃ βλέπει με ἢ ἀκούει ἐξ ἐμοῦ (II Cor. 12:6-7),[47] i.e., once again according to sober preaching. Thus he maintains without reservation the original judgment, that he would rather speak five understandable words before the community than innumerable words in a tongue (I Cor. 14:19). He is well aware of his "weakness," but means to hold firm to it because it is not ecstasy but only sober discourse which edifies the community (I Cor. 14:3, 12, 17, 22 ff.).

Gal. 1:10 shows that a campaign was mounted against him in Galatia from the same side in similar fashion.[48]

How could one avoid recognizing that the charges against which Paul is defending himself in I Thess. 1:5, 9; 2:1-2 have

---

[44] Cf. Vol. 1, pp. 193 ff.

[45] E. Käsemann, [1], pp. 34 ff.; cf. Vol. 1, pp. 182 ff.

[46] Cf. R. Bultmann, [1], pp. 12 ff.: Vol. 1, pp. 187 ff.

[47] The text may be disarranged, but the sense of what Paul wants to say cannot be in doubt.

[48] Cf. above, pp. 56 ff.

the same background? "He is no pneumatic. . . . These are the very same charges which were made against the apostle in Corinth," writes W. Lütgert,[49] correctly. One could escape this conclusion if one regarded the verses mentioned as written without aim or purpose. But this is precisely what the parallels make utterly impossible. Thus some have made the charge against Paul that he only "talked" (ἐν λόγῳ μόνον) and that there is a total lack of ecstatic demonstrations of power, of speaking in tongues, and revelations. Hence his appearance was "empty," for a gospel without Pneuma is *devoid of content* in precisely the way in which an apostle without pneumatic deeds of might is *nothing* (II Cor. 12:11-12). These are the typical Gnostic charges which are in harmony with the fact that the Gnostic apostle, in the decisive performance of his mission, enlightens the hearer about himself: The real man is Pneuma, but he undertakes such enlightenment not only theoretically, but above all by the practical demonstration of his possession of the Pneuma in ecstasy, glossolalia, visions, revelations, etc.

Paul refutes the opponents' charges. No, he has not proclaimed the gospel only ἐν λόγῳ, but also ἐν δυνάμει καὶ ἐν πνεύματι ἁγίῳ καὶ πληροφορίᾳ πολλῇ. With this he satisfies, at any rate in wording, in I Thess. 1:5 the Gnostic demand just as he does in II Cor. 12: 12: "τὰ μὲν σημεῖα τοῦ ἀποστόλου κατειργάσθη ἐν ὑμῖν ἐν πάσῃ ὑπομονῇ, σημείοις τε καὶ τέρασιν καὶ δυνάμεσιν." If one further compares with these two passages Rom. 15:19; Heb. 2:4; I Cor. 2:4, and II Thess. 2:9, it becomes evident that in all these places we have variations of a formula which is obviously of Gnostic origin.[50] Thus the Gnostics in Corinth also demand of the true apostle that he identify himself by producing the signs mentioned in the formula (II Cor. 12:11 ff.). Such a demand is not concerned with miracles of healing, as for example the book of Acts relates them of Peter and John—such miracles play a role nowhere in the Pauline literature—but with φανέρωσις τοῦ πνεύματος,[51] in other words, with miraculous evidences of the pneuma-self of man, understood as substance. Thus the δύναμις

---

[49] [2], p. 64.
[50] Cf. above, p. 29.
[51] Vol. 1, pp. 189 ff.

of I Thess. 1:5 is equivalent to the δύναμις πνεύματος of Rom. 15:19, and this power of the Pneuma is expressed in the manifold ecstatic processes.[52] The same is meant in the Gnostic original sense of the formula also by the ambiguous "ἐν πνεύματι ἁγίῳ." On this one need only recall I Cor. 14:2, where Paul describes the glossolalia which no one understands: "He utters mysteries in the Spirit" (RSV) ; or still more clearly, I Cor. 14:14: "If I pray in a tongue, my spirit prays but my mind is unfruitful" (RSV). Finally, the "πληροφορία πολλῆ" here does not mean "certainty," but, in unison with δύναμις and πνεῦμα ἅγιον, "fullness."[53] The generality of this meaning points to the formula-like character of the concept in our passage. In our context as in I Clem. 42.3, what is meant, of course, is the πληροφορία τοῦ πνεύματος ἁγίου,[54] and a comparison with Heb. 2:4, where the same formula is varied, closes the circle: God confirms the apostle's preaching by means of "σημείοις τε καὶ τέρασιν καὶ ποικίλαις δυνάμεσιν καὶ πνεύματος ἁγίου μερισμοῖς κατὰ τὴν αὐτοῦ θέλησιν."

Does Paul mean to say that he has confirmed to the Thessalonians the word of preaching by pneumatic-ecstatic performances? By no means! It is true that one time he lets himself be constrained, with the greatest reluctance, in relation to the Corinthians, to present proof that he too has command of the ecstatic phenomena (II Cor. 12:1-10), but only while emphasizing that one should *not* judge his work and himself according to these phenomena (II Cor. 12:6-7, 11). Verses 6-7 show what Paul wishes to be understood by the saying that his gospel was preached not only ἐν λόγῳ but also "in power": the Thessalonians have received the Word with joy, a firm faith, and serious discipleship. The success of the preaching thus demonstrates its and the preached gospel's, i.e., the Word's own, miraculous power.[55] This line of argument, moreover, is characteristic of the dispute with

---

[52] Thus, e.g., at the end of the introduction of the famous so-called Mithras Liturgy there is mention of the δύναμις which the initiate received so that he might stride through the heavens "καὶ κατοπτεύω πάντα."

[53] G. Delling in TDNT VI: 311; W. Hadorn, p. 37.

[54] In Col. 2:2 also "πληροφορία" occurs in the sense of "fullness" within a terminologically strongly gnosticizing context.

[55] Paul is thinking "of the power of his preaching over the heart: it produces faith and a new moral life" (E. v. Dobschütz, [1], p. 71). Cf. also 2:13, where the thought of 1:5 ff. is briefly summarized with the conclusion: καὶ ἐνεργεῖται (*sc.* ὁ λόγος) ἐν ὑμῖν.

the Corinthian false teachers, as is shown by such passages as I Cor. 9:1 ff.; II Cor. 3:1 ff.; 5:11-15; 10:12-18. In this comparison once again the close connection between the situation in Corinth and that in Thessalonica becomes evident.

The same is true of the fact that in I Thess. 1:5 Paul meets the charge about his powerless preaching, as in II Cor. 12:12 he answers the contesting of his apostleship, by citing that formula which the Gnostics in Corinth combine with the demand that they be shown the "signs of the apostle." In that Corinthian passage also Paul certainly is thinking when he cites the formula, as he is in I Thess. 1:5, of the marvelous effect of the Word. Here, as there, it may be questioned whether he understood the original meaning of the formula. In any case it appears to me to be no accident when Paul refutes the charge made against his preaching of powerlessness by using a formula which according to II Cor. 12:12 the Corinthian false teachers are constantly talking about in making a similar charge and which he also uses against them there. The situation is the same here and there. Paul was aware of this. The only difference is that Paul is agitated when he writes II Cor. 10–13, but can argue calmly and reservedly with the Thessalonians; the situation in Thessalonica appears to him less threatening than that in Corinth at the time of the sorrowful epistle D.

With vs. 1:5, vss. 1:9 and 2:1-2 are also explained. What had been the apostle's performance in Thessalonica? Now the people in Macedonia and Achaia themselves proclaim that it had been successful and hence powerful, so that the complaint against the wretchedness of the preaching of the missionaries reveals itself to be slander (1:9). And the Thessalonians themselves know that in spite of all the distresses, by God's grace Paul had earlier proclaimed the gospel with much "boldness" in Philippi and then also in Thessalonica. What then was the charge that his performance was powerless supposed to mean? It is just as maliciously false as the Gnostic charge in Corinth that his gospel was hidden (II Cor. 4:3) and his παρουσία ἀσθενής (II Cor. 10:10) because he was no pneumatic (I Cor. 7:40b). It is the *same* malicious accusation.

I Thess. 2:3-12. From 2:3 onward the theme, within the apology, is changed, to be sure unobtrusively, but unmistakably. Up to this point Paul was refuting charges against the inner *authority* of his preaching. Hence the constant reference to the success of this preaching! His gospel was not empty, but full of the Holy Spirit. Now he answers the insinuations about the *intention* of his preaching and therefore he must refer to the personal integrity of the preachers. That the two charges do not accidentally coincide but are interrelated is shown by II Cor. 3–4, a similarly apologetic part of II Corinthians. In II Cor. 3, especially vss. 1-6, Paul uses the same arguments as in I Thess. 1:4–2:2 to defend himself against the charge of defective personal and substantive suitability for the preaching ministry. Following this, in II Cor. 4:1 ff. he refutes the assertion that he preaches with fraudulent intention.

The entire section I Thess. 2:3-12 is continuously shaped by this special apologetic tendency. This calls for an effort to find the specific charge which apparently stands behind all these verses.

We begin with 2:3. Paul rejects the charge of πλάνη, of ἀκαθαρσία, and of δόλος. The most definite of these false charges is that of δόλος. Paul's preaching is alleged to have been done with artifice. It is true that he preached the gospel, not, however, for the sake of the gospel, but with a wholly different intention. There is no need to *guess* what intention is supposed to be involved. The following verses show this clearly. But first and above all, II Cor. 12:16 offers a precise and at the same time clear parallel: ἀλλὰ ὑπάρχων πανοῦργος δόλῳ ὑμᾶς ἔλαβον. The background of this charge from Corinth has long been recognized by the exegetes. People were falsely accusing Paul that indeed during his missionary activity he had renounced support, but only in order all the better to be able to exploit the community through the collection now requested.[56] This is how deceitful he

---

[56] Cf. H. Preisker, ThBl 5 (1926): 154 ff.; H. Lietzmann, [1], *in loc.;* Vol. 1, pp. 108-9. This charge may also stand behind I Cor. 9. Paul then insured himself against similar charges by having the collection made and delivered by chosen representatives of the communities (II Cor. 8:16 ff.). Cf. G. Delling in TDNT VI: 273. Also in II Cor. 2:17 and 4:1-2 ("μὴ περιπατοῦντες ἐν πανουργίᾳ μηδὲ δολοῦντος τὸν λόγον τοῦ θεοῦ") Paul defends himself against this charge. One sees how much he concerned himself with the fact that some in Corinth were already saying that Paul now saw himself severely forced into a defense (II Cor. 12:19).

is![57] This insinuation apparently had come also to the ears of the Thessalonians—earlier or later than to the Corinthians—so that Paul must defend himself against it.[58] This he does continuously in the following verses, as is evident at once from the "οὔτε ἐν προφάσει πλεονεξίας" in vs. 5 and the reference in vs. 9 to the work with his own hands πρὸς τὸ μὴ ἐπιβαρῆσαί τινα. Thus it is to be presumed that the entire section 2:3-12, which defends the personal integrity of the missionaries, is to be understood in terms of this specific false charge.

In fact vs. 3 already suggests that the broader meaning of the concepts πλάνη and ἀκαθαρσία is more sharply defined by the precisely outlined δόλος. Accordingly, πλάνη here means "fraud," "deception."[59] This active meaning of the word is indeed less common than the widespread passive one, "error," "delusion,"[60] but not at all unique in New Testament Greek,[61] especially not if one counts the cases where the concept is ambiguous as to its meaning.[62] With this understanding also once again a parallel is found in II Cor., where Paul conceives of the apostles as "πλάνοι καὶ ἀληθεῖς" (II Cor. 6:8). That the antitheses in this Corinthian passage are after all strongly shaped by the dispute which was being conducted in the Corinthian epistles is especially evident in the concept πλάνος = deceiver. Thus in I Thess. 2:3, the accusation that Paul has been preaching with the intention of deceit may be the point of the refutation "οὐκ ἐκ πλάνης."[63]

---

[57] In contrast to the opinion dominant in contemporary exegesis, I believe that Paul's opponents in Corinth themselves also renounced any help in maintenance by the community. Still, I do not need here to justify this conviction, since this problem has no bearing on the accusations as such, which alone are of interest to us—though of course it does for the first time make these accusations understandable in all their sharpness; cf. *The Office of Apostle*, pp. 219 ff.

[58] Cf. W. Hadorn, pp. 44 ff.

[59] W. Lütgert, p. 61. Thus above all the exegesis of many Fathers. K. Stürmer, p. 48, n. 26, translates it as "Irreführung" [misleading statements]; this is probably correct. Cf. also R. Schnackenburg, *Die Johannesbriefe*, 2nd ed. (1963), pp. 226-27.

[60] Cf. H. Braun's splendid article "πλανάω," etc., in TDNT VI: 230 ff.; esp. 234, 238, 239, 250-51.

[61] Matt. 27:64; II Peter 3:17; I John 4:6; II Thess. 2:11; Diognetus 8.4; in 10:7, alongside ἀπάτη; 12.3.

[62] Cf. e.g., the frequent formula "τὰ πνεύματα τῆς πλάνης"; see TDNT IV: 238 ff.; τῆς πλάνης τὰ διδάγματα, Iren. I, 15.6.

[63] As an example of such a use of the concept, cf. Pap. Berol. 8502, 19.17 ff. = C. W. Till, p. 79, where after Jesus' death a Pharisee says to John: "With deceit (πλάνη) he has deceived (πλανᾶν) you, this Nazarene (Ναζωραῖος)"; further, Ev. Ver. 17.14-15 and the other passages cited in H.-M. Schenke, *Die Herkunft des*

Of course it is not necessary to assume that this charge was meant by Paul's opponents in just the same way as he understood it. The word group "πλάνος," etc., as is well known, attained a technical meaning in Gnosticism and thus in many late Jewish writings. The powers of darkness live in *error* concerning the power of light; the sparks of light know *nothing* of their heavenly origin; the demons as the deceivers hold them fast in their *error;* the redeemer liberates from entanglement in such delusion.[64] Thus from this the charge of πλάνη against Paul, like the other one that he is a πλάνος (II Cor. 6:8), is shown to be typically Gnostic, though of course it does not become clear in which precise sense it is intended. People could have described Paul therewith, for example, in the sense of the Gnostic myth or, as is more likely in II Cor. 6:8, as a demonic deceiver. But the apostle himself doubtless connects this charge with the intention to deceive imputed to his preaching with reference to the Jerusalem collection. Perhaps he is right, but, being unfamiliar with Gnostic mythology, he may, as he frequently does, misunderstand them.

The concept "ἐξ ἀκαθαρσίας" is then to be understood similarly. It is preferably employed to denote sexual immorality. But in this sense it does not fit into the context of I Thess. 2, and that anyone ever should have seriously charged Paul with sexual license is also incredible.[65] One would have to assume, with W. Lütgert,[66] that the community had lumped Paul together with his libertine opponents. But it is consistently clear that Paul is not setting himself against charges of his community but against charges of his opponents. Thus in our passage one will have to translate "ἀκαθαρσία," with many exegetes,[67] more generally as "lack of integrity" and connect the impure attitude thus described with the deceitful avarice of which Paul is accused. This more general meaning of the word is also common, and, particularly in conjunction with the "πλεονεξία" which also occurs in

---

sogenannten Evangelium Veritatis (1959), p. 34.

[64] H. Braun, TDNT VI: 252-53, 238 ff.; H. Jonas, [1], pp. 109 ff.; also frequently in the Gnostic texts from Nag Hammadi; cf. ThLZ 1958, cols. 498, 499, 668; 1959, cols. 6 ff.; ZNW 50 (1959): 169 ff.; Iren. I, 15.6; II John 7.

[65] Cf. Vol. 1, pp. 164-66.

[66] [2], p. 63.

[67] Cf. W. Bauer, [2], col. 57; TDNT III: 428; W. Bornemann, p. 78; G. Wohlenberg, p. 45; W. Lueken, *in loc.;* P. W. Schmiedel, *in loc.;* W. Hadorn, p. 43; E. v. Dobschütz, [1], p. 88; M. Dibelius, [1], *in loc.*

I Thess. 2:5, it is found, e.g., in Eph. 5:3, 5; Col. 3:5 and—apparently = πλεονεξία—Eph. 4:19. It is possible that in Paul's choice of this ambiguous word there is a thrust against the opponents whom Paul on his part accuses of sexual ἀκαθαρσία.[68]

In sharp contrast to the distrustful insinuations to which Paul is exposed stands the confidence that God bestows on him, since he has commissioned him to proclaim the gospel. Paul appropriately refers to this in 2:4. We first pass over the remark, also occurring in this verse and obviously apologetic, that Paul is not preaching to please men, and turn to the charges against which the apostle sets himself in defense in vss. 5-6. Again Paul enumerates three such charges. He is said to have come ἐν λόγῳ κολακείας, ἐν προφάσει πλεονεξίας, and ζητοῦντες ἐξ ἀνθρώπων δόξαν.

Clearest is the assertion that Paul has preached ἐν προφάσει πλεονεξίας. This means, literally, under the cloak of avarice, and is an abbreviation for "with a pretended occasion for the satisfaction of avarice." [69] Naturally we are to think in this connection that Paul, under the guise of wishing to gather an offering, wants to satisfy his personal avarice.[70] Thus also, indeed, it is not accidental that πλεονεκτεῖν appears in the instructive parallel passage in II Cor. 12:16 ff. Here Paul emphasizes that he has not enriched himself at the Corinthians' expense (ἐπλεονέκτησα), not even through others: μήτι ἐπλεονέκτησεν ὑμᾶς Τίτος. Also in II Cor. 7:2 the "οὐδένα ἐπλεονεκτήσαμεν" may have this background, and the allusion "καὶ μὴ ὡς πλεονεξίαν" within the recommendation of the collection in II Cor. 9:5 is best explained as a reminiscence of the past charges.[71] Finally, the curious "ἵνα μὴ πλεονεκτηθῶμεν ὑπὸ τοῦ σατανᾶ" (II Cor. 2:11) is also well explained as a play on words if the evildoers for whom Paul asks pardon had made against Paul the very charge of πλεονεξία in an offensive form, as is to be assumed with near certainty.[72] In any case the meaning of the assertion that Paul was preaching ἐν προφάσει πλεονεξίας cannot be in doubt.

But then it is beyond question that we are to connect with

[68] II Cor. 12:21; Gal. 5:19; see above, pp. 52-53; cf. I Thess. 4:7.
[69] See W. Bauer, [2], col. 1433.
[70] G. Wohlenberg, p. 48.
[71] K. Stürmer, p. 48.
[72] Vol. 1, pp. 108-9.

this the charge that Paul is dealing in words of flattery. Under-handed deceit and friendly flattery condition each other. Indeed, a friendly speech craftily made with unfriendly ulterior motives is already in itself to be regarded as a flattering speech.[73] espe-cially since ἐν λόγῳ κολακείας can simply be equivalent to ἐν κολακείᾳ. Naturally the charge may have been meant in a more pronounced sense. In what sense, it is difficult to say. Perhaps people were accusing Paul of having only curried favor with the community with his words, in contrast to the persuasive power of the ecstatic displays of the pneumatics, with which then we should compare the similar accusation of the same people that Paul was *persuading* the community (II Cor. 5:11; Gal. 1:10). It would also be possible that some had identified a recommenda-tion concerning the collection which had come to Thessalonica as λόγος κολακείας. Such a recommendation in somewhat the form of II Cor. 8:7-8 and 9:1-2 makes a spiteful accusation of this kind appear altogether conceivable.

Now there may be a close connection between the charge of flattering speech in vs. 5 and that of pleasing men in vs. 4. When Paul places κολακεία at the head of the three insinuations of vss. 5-6, this presumably is done because it logically follows the οὐχ ὡς ἀνθρώποις ἀρέσκοντες. That with this remark Paul is defending himself against a corresponding accusation is suggested by the wording of the remark itself and is assured by Gal. 1:10, where the "ἢ ζητῶ ἀνθρώποις ἀρέσκειν "without question is an answer to a specific insinuation.[74] According to the Galatian epistle, this charge is coupled with the other one, that Paul is *persuading* men, by which the bridge to II Cor. 5:11[75] is formed. The two charges are related. The preaching of the "man" Paul, which is done only τῷ νοΐ (I Cor. 14:15) or ἐν λόγῳ (I Thess. 1:5) be-comes, when compared with the convincing power of the pseudo-apostolic pneumatics, mere persuasion. If this "persuasion" more-over serves the πρόφασις πλεονεξίας, then it becomes a deceitful

---

[73] I refer to E. v. Dobschütz's good observation on I Thess. 2:5 in [1], p. 90: "δόλος and κολακία however are intrinsically akin: the LXX prefers to translate *hlk*, to flatter, and its derivatives with δολοῦν, δολιοῦν, δόλιος, δολιότης; this, along with πρὸς χάριν, replaces for the LXX the word group κόλαξ, κολακία, κολακεύω (only this three times in the LXX)...."

[74] Thus most recently J. Jeremias in ZNW 55 (1958) : 152-53.

[75] Cf. above, pp. 30-31.

attempt to please men. Indeed this must also be the sense of the malicious taunt concerning Paul that he was constantly commending himself. In II Cor. 3:1 and 5:12 Paul defends himself against this charge, and in II Cor. 10:12 ff. he repays his opponents in the same coin. Of course these complementary accusations of flattering speech, of pleasing men, and of self-commendation need not have had in mind only the gathering of the collection through which Paul as πανουργός craftily ensnares the community (II Cor. 12:16). They also give concrete form to the "ἀνθρώπους πείθομεν" (II Cor. 5:11; Gal. 1:10).[76] But when Paul in I Thess. 2:4 emphasizes the "οὐχ ὡς ἀνθρώποις ἀρέσκοντες" and the "οὔτε ἐν λόγῳ κολακείας," he does so precisely *here* because he knows that according to the charges of his opponents, there is concealed behind his pleasing men and his words of flattery that πλεονεξία, the avarice which is disguised as a recommendation of an offering.

Now some light may also be shed on the last charge in vs. 6, that Paul is seeking ἐξ ἀνθρώπων δόξαν. At first this is said as generally as the "ἀνθρώποις ἀρέσκειν." But the expansion of it, "οὔτε ἀφ᾽ ὑμῶν οὔτε ἀπ᾽ ἄλλων," shows that Paul is thinking of a quite definite honor; for the unconditional or unspecific statement "οὔτε ἐξ ἀνθρώπων δόξαν" as such did not require in addition the indication "οὔτε ἀφ᾽ ὑμῶν οὔτε ἀπ᾽ ἄλλων." What is he thinking of? "One has the impression that the subject of money is not suggested again here," writes G. Schrenk.[77] Now let us take a further look. Paul continues by saying that he has sought no honor δυνάμενοι ἐν βάρει εἶναι ὡς Χριστοῦ ἀπόστολοι. There can be no doubt that "βάρος" here has the sense of "weight," "esteem," "influence," "power."[78] As Christ's *apostles,* thus Paul emphasizes, he (and Silvanus) would have been able to appear with a claim to power. This is surprising. Elsewhere it is not Paul's custom to stress the rights of the apostle to regard and influence which are due to him *from the community.*[79] On the contrary! God has placed the

[76] In other words: Paul replaces the objective proof of the Spirit with the attempt to secure by flattery, by means of fine words, the confidence of the community on the basis of his personality.

[77] TDNT I: 556, n. 11.

[78] In the New Testament the word appears in this sense only here.

[79] *Hence* in our passage the issue is not the ἐξουσία which marks the apostle, which he possesses *with respect to the community* εἰς οἰκοδομήν (II Cor. 10:8;

apostles as ἐσχάτους, as a spectacle and refuse for the whole world (I Cor. 4:9 ff.) ; only the proclaimed word is important (II Cor. 3:4 ff.) ; the apostles are constantly given over to death for the sake of their ministry (II Cor. 4:7 ff.) ; their βάρος δόξης is heavenly (II Cor. 4:17) ; in all lowliness they are disclosed as God's servants (II Cor. 6:4 ff.) ; their strength is made perfect in their weakness (II Cor. 12:9). Only in *one* respect can the apostle claim a βάρος from the side of the community: he has the right to be supported by the community. In his discussion with the Corinthians Paul explicitly establishes this right (I Cor. 9:4-23) by referring to analogies, the Old Testament, and a saying of the Lord, in order to affirm: "ἐγὼ δὲ οὐ κέχρημα οὐδενὶ τούτων" (I Cor. 9:15). So then also the power which according to I Thess. 2:7 the apostle can claim and which Paul renounces must be the right of support,[80] and "ἐν βάρει εἶναι" with rhetorical aptness combines both meanings of the word into a single sense: "to claim importance"—with which the δόξα of vs. 6 is taken up—and "to be a burden."

That in fact the honor claimed in principle for the apostles is concretized in the right to support is shown by the following verses,[81] especially vs. 9, in which the "βάρος" is again taken up by "ἐπιβαρῆσαι," and indeed here in the unambiguous sense of "to be a burden." But first Paul says that he has come among the Thessalonians "friendly" (ἤπιος),[82] in that he has not burdened them—a theologically well-grounded friendliness, as I Cor. 9:18 ff. shows. His friendliness resembled the attitude of a mother to her child: in her relationship to the child the mother is only the giving one, not the receiving one. That this image used by Paul is meant in such a sense is best shown by the exact parallel from

---

13:10) or with the authority of his apostolic word. This is not noted by most of the exegetes.

[80] Otherwise one would have to join G. Schrenk (TDNT I: 556) in the opinion that one may speak of the apostles' "conscious self-assertion."

[81] The exegetes misunderstand the context when they connect: "βάρος" *either* with "δόξα" (vs. 6: thus G. Schrenk, TDNT I: 556; P. W. Schmiedel, *in loc.*; W. Bornemann, pp. 82-83) *or* with the following verses (see M. Dibelius [1], pp. 9-10; G. Wohlenberg, pp. 48-49). In truth vs. 7a connects vs. 6 with what follows. Thus, correctly, E. v. Dobschütz, [1], p. 93.

[82] "ἤπιος" would be no contrast at all with "βάρος" in the pure sense of "honor received." This causes difficulties for the exegetes who make the simple equation "βάρος"="δόξα."

the corresponding apology in II Cor. 12:14 ff.: "For it is not the children who ought to lay up treasures for the parents, but the parents for the children." Hence, so Paul concludes in this passage also, I have claimed no support, not even in the roundabout way of the collection. Strange that the exegetes always overlook this parallel and instead refer to Gal. 4:19! [83] This latter passage is of no interest here,[84] while the section II Cor. 12:12 ff. with its repeated parallels to the verses we are now investigating discloses the common concrete background.

But vs. 8 which now follows also shows that Paul means for his "family image" [85] to be understood in the sense of II Cor. 12:14 ff. The "μεταδοῦναι" stands in contrast to the "receiving," which would mean the "ἐν βάρει εἶναι" if Paul had not refrained from it. Instead of letting himself be supported, he had worked— the Thessalonians will recall—with his own hands day and night, with labor and toil, "in order not to burden any of you" (2:9). It is not to be overlooked that here he takes up the "βάρος" of vs. 7, which therefore must be understood *concretely* in the sense of "to be a burden." [86] Thus Paul's coming does not give occasion for any reproach (ἀμέμπτως); rather, like a father he has taught and admonished the Thessalonians as his children: a pastoral word concludes the apology (2:10-12).

From vs. 8 or even from vs. 7*b*, but often only from vs. 9 onward (W. Bornemann) the exegetes perforce see the theme of vss. 3-5, the πλεονεξία, again taken up. But this theme is not abandoned in vs. 6! Certainly the charge that Paul is seeking honor from men, like the charge of men-pleasing and of flattery, in itself includes more than the reference to the avarice that is craftily concealed behind the gathering of the offering; in the mouth of the opponents also—to be sure the formulation perhaps stems from Paul—it may not have been aimed solely at this. But in our passage Paul understands it, like these related accusations, without question in such specific terms and defends himself against the charge that with flattery and men-pleasing he zealously con-

---

[83] Thus M. Dibelius; E. v. Dobschütz; P. W. Schmiedel.

[84] In Gal. 4:19 the image clearly stems from the environment and the conceptual world of the mystery cults.

[85] On this, see now W. Grundmann in NTS 5 (1958/59) : 200.

[86] Cf. W. Hadorn, p. 47.

cerns himself with recognition and honor among the Thessalonians, in order then to profit financially from such recognition. Paul declares that he as an apostle may indeed seek this special honor and claim it, but refrains from doing so.

Thus also the remark, "neither from you nor from others" (2:6), gets the necessary color. Naturally it was being told in Thessalonica that Paul was following the same fraudulent course in all the communities, in order to enrich himself as a charlatan. It is a fact that indeed he was collecting the offering in his *entire* missionary territory (Rom. 15:26-27; I Cor. 16:1 ff.; II Cor. 8-9). Perhaps people also knew that at about the same time Paul had received a gift from Philippi (Phil. 4:10-20; 2:25), but in any case they must have remembered that during his stay in Thessalonica the apostle had several times[87] received and accepted a financial contribution from Philippi, apparently for himself personally (Phil. 4:16).[88] How could they have left unused the knowledge of this fact for the support of their calumny! Paul has already succeeded in insinuating himself into the confidence of others! Paul counters by saying that neither among the Thessalonians nor among others has he sought honor for the sake of money, although he could be a burden to the communities.

Thus the section 2:3-12, not unlike vss. 1:5–2:2, has a background as concrete as it is unequivocal and, moreover, clearly recognizable. It is impossible to explain these verses with their abundant, in part word-for-word, parallels in the Corinthian epistles and Galatians without regard to the situation in Thessalonica. Not only is the apology in I Thess. 1:5–2:12, considered by itself, incomprehensible if it were not determined by events in Thessalonica: The corresponding passages in the epistles to Corinth and Galatia leave no doubt that the charges appearing there were raised against Paul in the communities. For Thessalonica, then, it cannot have been otherwise. On this point the exegetes from the time of the Fathers down to the last century have never been in doubt.

In modern times this doubt has been aroused. It is disputed

---

[87] Thus is καὶ ἅπαξ καὶ δίς to be understood; see W. Bauer, [2], col. 160.

[88] Cf. also II Cor. 11:9. The messengers bringing money mentioned here may have touched Thessalonica, if they did not come from Thessalonica itself. Cf. p. 80, n. 59.

that Paul is referring to any events in Thessalonica. F. C. Baur may be responsible in part for this development. From the parallels between I Thess. and I and II Cor. and Gal., he inferred an anti-judaizing battlefront for I Thess. and thus its inauthenticity, since for the so-called second missionary journey an anti-judaizing agitation does not come into question. Besides, anyone who does not draw Baur's conclusion still finds himself confronted by the difficulty which Baur identified, so that one must either minimize the connections between the epistles named or place I Thess. in the time of the third missionary journey.[89] In the former case, one then can consistently deny any connection of I Thess. to the situation in Thessalonica.

This was already done early by Olshausen,[90] who regarded 1:5-2:12 as a preventive precaution against Judaizers who might possibly appear. This "psychological monstrosity" [91] was immediately and generally rejected. But then K. Bornemann[92] asserted that one must not assume any special charges or attacks against the person of Paul at the time of I Thess., neither in Thessalonica nor elsewhere, least of all by Judaistic false teachers.[93] He is followed—with some indecision[94]—by W. Lueken[95] and very surely by E. v. Dobschütz.[96] One must explain the apology at the beginning of I Thess. in terms of the attitude of the author, who was still discouraged from his stay in Athens and feared that

---

[89] A. Loisy opts for a third way: he excises 2:1-16 as a later insertion into a genuine epistle (*The Birth of the Christian Religion*, p. 20 and p. 362, n. 2). He will hardly find any agreement with this.

In the effort to hold to the traditional early dating of I Thess., W. Kümmel (p. 226) rejects the attempt set forth here (and in the following) to place the situation in Thessalonica in parallel with that in Corinth, Philippi, etc., because of "violent over-interpretation of individual texts." The reader may decide about the correctness of this judgment, but of course he should keep in mind that in the paralleling of the situations mentioned, our investigation is not based on individual texts but on the epistle as a whole. But when Kümmel continues that it is "by no means certain that in I Thess. Paul is at all combating accusations which have been made against him in Thessalonica," such a judgment of course seems to me to be utterly insupportable.

[90] *Biblischer Kommentar über sämtliche Schriften des NT*, IV (1840).

[91] E. v. Dobschütz, [1], p. 106.

[92] W. Bornemann, pp. 265 ff.; otherwise, to be sure, on p. 304.

[93] Here the battlefront against F. C. Baur becomes evident.

[94] Wavering also is C. Masson, *Les deux épîtres de Saint Paul aux Thessaloniciens* (1957); cf. p. 8 with p. 32.

[95] W. Lueken, pp. 9-10.

[96] [1], p. 107.

people in Thessalonica wherever possible held him to be a charlatan. When he hears from Timotheus that this has never been the case, he still must express in writing his heartfelt concern. E. v. Dobschütz calls this explanation "psychologically fine." [97] M. Dibelius also follows it.[98] Of course he rightly objects to letting one's fantasy play too freely. Paul certainly must not have been greatly agitated when he wrote I Thess. Rather what is involved in the apology is a "pet theme" which one handles without special urgency: the theme of the contrast between dishonest sorcerers and serious missionaries. Thus what we have in the apology is in fact a "meditation." [99]

But this interpretation itself as a psychological one leads *ad absurdum*.[100] Of course it is correct that the serious itinerant preachers were obliged to distinguish themselves from the charlatans. The charge which Paul is refuting may therefore very well have parallels in extra-biblical literature.[101] But one cannot say on the basis of I Thess. 1–2 alone that here we are dealing with a pet theme of Paul, especially since the occasion of this passage is the very thing that is under discussion. But above all: even though this theme may "be in the air" and though one may interpret it psychologically that even without specific occasion such fears arise within Paul or that he reflects on such ideas, it is psychologically absurd then to clothe all this in the form of the present apology. One cannot express such ideas in this form in a letter without imagining the surprised recipients of the letter, who now must necessarily assume that Paul, without reason, was seeing in their hearts active ideas of the accusation and calumny and bitter charges against him. The apostle must have appeared to the readers of such an epistle as worse than ridiculous, especially if—as the exegetes heretofore have unanimously assumed—the epistle was written on the strength of the report of Timotheus, who moreover can hardly have been sent to Thessalonica on the basis of a meditative mood of Paul. "His

---

[97] [1], p. 107.

[98] [1], pp. 10-11. The whole is "instinctive, prompted only by the recollection of the time of the mission."

[99] [1], pp. 4, 7.

[100] Cf. W. Hadorn, pp. 41-42.

[101] Although fairly literal parallels are not found in the material cited by M. Dibelius.

sensitive disposition saw specters," writes A. Oepke.[102] Well enough, but one no longer conjures them up when they have long since been dissolved into nothingness. It is true that here lies an undeniable difficulty. For if one affirms the current relevance of the statements in 1:2–2:12, then insofar as one proceeds on the assumption of the unity of the epistle, one must say of Paul's self-justification "that in the moment in which he writes it down, it is no longer currently relevant," [103] for in 3:6 ff. Paul expressly attests concerning the Thessalonians, on the basis of the report given by Timotheus from personal observation, that they stand without reservation on his side. But with this presupposition, the apology in 1:2–2:12 appears all the more as a psychological monstrosity which makes easily understandable the attempts of many scholars to replace it with another, indeed no less vulnerable, psychological combination. But from this it follows only that the section of I Thess. which we considered earlier belongs to another situation than the obviously later statements in 2:13–4:1, which were written in connection with the visit of Timotheus in Thessalonica. Thus our literary-critical analysis is confirmed by the contents of the epistle.

Some minimize the connections between I Thess. on the one side and I+II Cor. and Gal. on the other, even when, as it has frequently happened, the charges against which Paul takes his position in 1:2–2:12 are treated as coming from Jews or pagans.[104] Even then the composition of I Thess. on the so-called second missionary journey remains understandable. But one may not in this way overlook the parallels between the epistles, especially since they first disclose the background and specific content of the charges from Thessalonica. Such parallels indeed do not at all concern only the indictments made against Paul which we have investigated, but refer to numerous other questions bound up with them, as the investigation will further show. They require us to assume *the same* anti-Pauline agitators for Corinth

---

[102] NTD 8 (1955, 7th ed.) : 133.

[103] E. v. Dobschütz, [1], p. 107. ". . . the apology still would presuppose that some in the community had given a hearing to such opponents—and 3:6 ff. contradicts that!" (M. Dibelius, [1], p. 10).

[104] On this, see E. v. Dobschütz, [1], pp. 106-7; W. Lütgert, [2], pp. 57 ff.; M. Dibelius, [1], p. 10.

as for Thessalonica,[105] whatever the consequences for the historical circumstances of I Thess., especially for its integrity and the time of its composition. If one holds the Corinthian false teachers to be Judaizers, then one must also presuppose for I Thess. a judaizing opposition, "although not the slightest trace of anti-Judaistic polemic is shown in the epistle." [106] Thus this is no solution. But as in Corinth, so also in Thessalonica the charges come from Jewish or Jewish Christian Gnostics. This was already to be deduced from the apology in 1:5–2:12 and will become still clearer in what follows.

Like a father among his children, so had he dwelt among the Thessalonians, said the apostle in 2:11. In view of what precedes it, this means: without burdening the community. But in view of what follows, it also means: with paternal admonition. Verse 2:12, syntactically still belonging entirely to the preceding apology, thus prepares the way for the following admonitions. The actual transition to the admonitions is formed by vs. 4:2, which according to our foregoing literary-critical analysis may originally have been connected with 2:12: "For you know what admonitions we gave you for the sake of the Lord Jesus"; that is, Paul does not mean to say anything new to the Thessalonians, but to remind them of the rules, well known to them, of the Christian faith and life.

The arguments of the epistle now following are commonly divided into four larger sections.[107] This is too schematic. We shall have to make a more exact division.

I Thess. 4:3-8. Paul is concretely concerned first of all with πορνεία. Verse 3 suggests this subject in a general formulation. The following verses develop it. The unsolved controversial question whether σκεῦος in vs. 4 means "wife" or "body" we cannot and need not decide here. The context suggests that it means: each one of you should know how to acquire his own wife in

---

[105] Cf. E. Güttgemanns, p. 300. That these agitators were *Jews*, not Jewish Christians as in Corinth, is asserted, following the precedent set by others (cf. W. Lütgert, [2], pp. 58 ff.) , by P. Feine (*Einleitung in das NT* [1930, 5th ed.], p. 109) , in order to avoid the conclusion that I Thess. belongs to the time of the third missionary journey. But there are no points of support for this assertion in the text of the epistle itself.

[106] E. v. Dobschütz, [1], p. 106.

[107] E. v. Dobschütz, [1], p. 154.

holiness and modesty and not take the wife of another. Verse 5 sets this in opposition to the heathen πάθος ἐπιθυμίας. In my judgment in vs. 6 also the subject is unchastity: that no one go astray and in this matter "defraud" his brother. Thus the older exegetes since the time of the Fathers have understood it. Today the verse is usually connected with avarice: to wrong a brother in a dispute. But "ἐν τῷ πράγματι" is just not, as Grotius conjectured, = "ἔν τινι πράγματι," but as in II Cor. 7:11: in the matter *referred to*, namely, of πορνεία. In such an interpretation, of course, the πλεονεκτεῖν is unusual but, as we shall soon see, by no means inexplicable. In vs. 7 also, ἀκαθαρσία can have the meaning, as it frequently does, of πορνεία, so that vss. 4:3-8 all warn against unchastity.

One cannot very well deny that this warning is aimed at the "defects in the faith" of the Thessalonians. Even the position of this exhortation within the epistle, and even more its execution, forbids our speaking of an unmotivated, general paraenesis. Are we to think that among the Thessalonians "ethical views were still immature in several respects, the renunciation of earlier practices was not decided enough"? [108] This widely held explanation is possible, but is not suggested by the epistle itself. Besides, one should be careful with the equation, presupposed therein, of heathenism = immorality. Thus it is more probable to see the exhortation as motivated in those special circumstances which I Thess. also discloses elsewhere: the appearance of the false teachers. According to the evidence of the other epistles, the proclamation of an ethical libertinism was so central to their message [109] that it is easy to understand why at the beginning of his exhortations Paul takes a position against the possibility of πορνεία in Christian communities.

Moreover, these verses themselves point in this direction. Paul twice expressly emphasizes that the warning against πορνεία belonged to the gospel which had been declared to the Thessa-

---

[108] E. v. Dobschütz, [1], pp. 168-69; cf. P. W. Schmiedel, p. 5; W. Lueken, p. 14.

[109] Here too of course some have preferred to speak of remnants of heathen sensuality, which is demonstrably wrong. On the Corinthian epistles, see Vol. 1, pp. 218 ff.; on Phil. 3:19, above, pp. 107 ff.; on Gal., above, pp. 51 ff.; cf. also Rom. 16:18; see below, pp. 229 ff.

lonians (4:2, 6). Apparently it has been said to the Thessalonians in the meantime that the gospel was compatible with unchastity.[110] But this is the message of Gnostic libertinism. I should interpret from this perspective also the πλεονεκτεῖν in vs. 6, whose sexual reference in fact is "striking." [111] With it Paul may have taken the charge of πλεονεξία (2:5) which had been made against him and which he had just refuted, and returned it in a pointedly ironic way:[112] no one is to "enrich" himself in this matter at his brother's expense, by taking his wife away from him. This very thing in fact happens in libertine Gnosticism on principle, as I Cor. 5:1 ff. shows for Corinth[113] and as is often denounced by the anti-heretical literature: Iren. I, 6.3; Eus. CH IV, 7.11; V, 1.14. Epiphanius reports about the Gnostics: "They have their women in common . . . . When they have banqueted and satisfied themselves, then they give themselves over to lust. The man walks away from his wife and says to her, 'Stand up and make love to your *brother.*'" [114] This is a not very loving but objective description of a libertine practice which still breaks out in certain Christian circles down to our own day.

Verse 8 appears to me most clearly to point in the direction suspected here: "τοιγαροῦν ὁ ἀθετῶν οὐκ ἄνθρωπον ἀθετεῖ ἀλλὰ τὸν θεόν." This passage is correctly paraphrased by P. W. Schmiedel,[115] in agreement with the majority of exegetes, thus: "Therefore whoever rejects the above admonitions is not rejecting a man who urges them upon him, especially me, but God." Such a comment, however, is motivated only if the release of unchastity had been represented as a transgression of the Pauline command-

---

[110] W. Lütgert, [2], pp. 67 ff.; W. Hadorn, pp. 54 ff.

[111] M. Dibelius, [1], p. 22. H. Baltensweiler, "Erwägungen zu 1. Thess. 4, 3-8" (ThZ 19 [1963]: 1 ff.), has recently shown again, correctly, that the vss. I Thess. 4:3-8 clearly deal with the problem of unchastity. His interesting interpretation of the entire section with the help of the Greek custom of the law concerning an heiress, in the context of which the heiress was awarded to a man in a judicial proceeding, appears to me rightly construed. It collapses at the point that ἐν τῷ πράγματι can only mean "in the situation *described,*" not "in a proceeding (concerning an heiress)."

[112] Paul likes to make use of such allusive irony in the dispute with his opponents; e.g., II Cor. 5:3 (cf. Vol. 1, pp. 263 ff.); Phil. 3:15 (see above, pp. 101-2).

[113] Cf. Vol. 1, pp. 236-37. On this point it is striking that in I Cor. 5:9-10 the concepts πορνεία and πλεονεξία are immediately adjacent.

[114] Cf. W. Schultz, *Dokumente der Gnosis*, p. 162.

[115] P. W. Schmiedel, p. 27.

ment but not of the divine ordinance.[116] This cannot have been done by heathen, but points unmistakably to the religiously grounded libertinism with which Paul must contend also in Corinth, Galatia, Philippi, and Ephesus (Rom. 16).

On the other hand, I do not believe that "the stressing of the Spirit (vs. 8) can be taken as a reference to the pneumatic claims of the opponents." [117] Indeed this cannot be the case even in the parallel passage I Cor. 6:19, as much as this parallel again points to the same kind of situation in the two passages. It is correct, however—and this confirms our exegesis of 1:5–2:12—that in 4:8 we have "a reference to an attack mounted against Paul's apostolic authority in Thessalonica." [118]

I Thess. 4:9-12 is a new section, which begins with unrestrained praise of brotherly love, but then discloses a ὑστέρημα in Thessalonica which could easily lead to the point that some lay claim to the brotherly love of others unbecomingly (. . . καὶ μηδενὸς χρείαν ἔχητε).[119] This "lack" is not concretely enough described with "laziness." That is to say, the Thessalonians are to strive "ἡσυχάζειν καὶ πράσσειν τὰ ἴδια καὶ ἐργάζεσθαι ταῖς χερσὶν ὑμῶν." In 5:14 the people are identified as ἄτακτοι. One must speak of a religious excitement, of pious agitation which stirs some people in the community so that they are disquieted, leave their work, and are troubled with alien concerns. Church history offers many examples of a religious excitement expressing itself in this manner,[120] particularly in times of apocalyptic expectation of the end, but above all in circles of inspired people. Traditional exegesis usually thinks of the eschatological attitude as the cause of the unsettled behavior. The Christians were led astray "to speak much of God and his imminent mighty acts, and even to venture forth into public with such eschatological speculations and here to engage in active propaganda. Why slave for earthly possessions and the sustenance of life when the end of the world,

---

[116] Cf. W. Hadorn, p. 59.

[117] W. Hadorn, pp. 59-60.

[118] K. Stürmer, p. 48.

[119] This connection is somewhat contrived (E. v. Dobschütz, [1], p. 175; P. W. Schmiedel, p. 27). One notices that even here Paul would like to subordinate the admonition to a word of praise. His interest, however, concerns the admonition.

[120] See J. B. Lightfoot in his commentary, *in loc.*

and with it also the end of all need, was imminent? Was there not more important work to do?" [121] But nothing in our epistle —and moreover, nothing in II Thess. 3:6 ff.—points to *this* background of the unrest. This is generally acknowledged today.[122] Besides, Paul's preaching could hardly have been the occasion of such attitudes. One can only argue: "If this attitude of individuals in Thessalonica must have had a religious basis, I would not know what else it might have been." [123] But W. M. L. de Wette[124] rightly pointed out that Paul then would not have been able to support the eschatological tension with the following statements in 4:13 ff. Thus Paul himself in any case is not aware of a connection of these two themes.

Hence it is more obvious to explain the pious agitation from the same background which I Thess. has heretofore steadily disclosed to us: the enthusiastic movement of Gnosticism. W. Lütgert[125] has done this in convincing fashion.[126] For this, church history offers not only the most abundant parallels, but also the oldest and most direct, namely in the Pastoral Epistles: according to I Tim. 5:15 some of the younger widows are already being led astray by Satan, that is to say, to the Gnostic heresy, and the apostasy of these women is described in 5:13 as follows: "On their going into the houses they learn idleness, and not idleness alone, but also gossip and useless activity, in order to speak what is not becoming." One may also compare II Tim. 3:1 ff.; Titus 1:10-11.[127] Since one may also adduce II Thess. 3:6 ff.[128] for the case for authenticity as well as for inauthenticity, the picture takes on further clarity. Thus it is shown that the enthusiasm of the Gnostic missionaries has also stirred to pneumatic excitement

---

[121] E. v. Dobschütz, [1], p. 182.

[122] See in W. Lütgert, [2], pp. 72 ff., and M. Dibelius [1], p. 23.

[123] E. v. Dobschütz, [1], p. 183.

[124] *Kurzgefasstes exegetisches Handbuch zum Neuen Testament* (1841), p. 116.

[125] [2], pp. 71 ff. Cf. also B. Reicke, [1], pp. 243 ff.

[126] "The idlers at Thessalonica do give . . . altogether the impression of being more than ordinary vagabonds, rather agents of a heresy" (A. Hilgenfeld, *Einleitung in das NT* [1875], p. 651.

[127] W. Foerster (in NTS 5 [1958/59]: 216) correctly compares with I Thess. 4:11 and II Thess. 3:12 also the passages I Tim. 2:2 and 4:7-8, where we have to do, as in the Thessalonian epistles (!), with a "fanatical-gnosticizing movement," whose representatives are exhorted to εὐσέβεια, i.e. (in the original sense of the word), to an orderly civil manner of life.

[128] See below, pp. 197 ff.

some Thessalonians, who now in religious zeal conduct a missionary endeavor, obtrude themselves upon others with their knowledge and revelations, instead of being concerned with τὰ ἴδια, and neglect the work of their hands. How much more important are the lofty revelations which are granted to the pneumatic than despised manual labor.[129] Paul, who on his missionary journeys first sought work and then an opportunity to preach, rightly fears that these pneumatics will bring discredit on the entire community and ultimately even live at the expense of the heathen. Naturally then there must at least have been such people in Thessalonica earlier, and probably there were still such.

In 4:13-18 Paul goes into another ὑστέρημα of the belief of the Christians at Thessalonica: the uncertainty about the fate of those who had died. That the issue here concerns departed *Christians* I may assume as assured, with a reference to the *consensus omnium*. It is also beyond question today that it is useless and unnecessary to establish a closer connection of 4:13 ff. with the subject of the preceding verses.[130] But further, in the exegetes one often misses the desired consistency in thinking through the occasion which prompted Paul to make the eschatological statements in 4:13-18.

Paul clearly indicates in vs. 13 what the problem is. He does not wish to leave the community in ignorance about the fate of the dead, for with respect to their death or that of their fellow Christians they are not to be without hope as are others. There is no reason for mourning, for *the dead will arise*. Verse 14 says this, referring to Christ's death and resurrection. The succinct argument of vs. 14 corresponds precisely as to substance with the broader statements in I Cor. 15:12-28. The verse could be an excerpt from that passage. In vs. 15, in conclusion Paul affirms that the Christians who are living at the time of the Parousia will not have even a *temporary* advantage over those who have fallen asleep; for only *after* the resurrection of the dead comes the *common* ἀπάντησις τοῦ κυρίου εἰς ἀέρα (14:16-17). H. Grass indeed thinks that the πρῶτον and the ἔπειτα in 4:16-17 are not to be understood in a temporal sense but as an expression of the

---

[129] E. v. Dobschütz, [1], pp. 180 ff.

[130] E. v. Dobschütz, [1], p. 184; W. G. Kümmel, p. 223.

preeminence "which the dead have in the love of the Lord" (*Ostergeschehen und Osterberichte*, p. 151). This seems hardly tenable to me, but either way the intent of Paul is unmistakable: there is no reason to mourn death before the Parousia.

Accordingly, it is not to be concluded from Paul's argument in vss. 15-17 that people in Thessalonica were afraid only that the dead would not share *immediately* in Christ's kingdom.[131] That such fears are in themselves conceivable is of course presupposed by Paul's words; for the οὐ μὴ φθάσωμεν cannot mean, "only we who are alive shall reach the goal," but means, "we who are alive shall not reach the goal before the others." [132] But from vss. 13-14 it becomes evident with sufficient clarity that Paul must concern himself with doubts of the Thessalonians about the resurrection as such, not about a delayed resurrection. Indeed one cannot compare anxieties about a delayed resurrection with the hopelessness of the heathen.[133] Accordingly, as W. Lueken (p. 16) has already rightly recognized, vss. 15-17 serve Paul "to strengthen his confidence." [134] They are not anchored in the situation in Thessalonica, but in the apocalyptic tradition (IV Ezra 5:41-42; cf. 6:25; 7:27-28; 13:16-24; sBar. 30.1-2; 50.1 ff.[135] and may have long belonged to Paul's pastoral equipment in view of the beginning delay in the Parousia.[136]

The properly understood οὐ μὴ φθάσωμεν, however, also rules out Paul's intending deliberately in vss. 13-17 to set himself against an ultraconservative doctrine of the resurrection in Thessalonica, such as A. Schweitzer[137] assumes for Corinth also and

---

[131] Thus K. v. Hoffmann, p. 236; T. Zahn, [1], I: 157; G. Wohlenberg, pp. 102 ff.; W. Michaelis, [1], p. 220.

[132] See P. W. Schmiedel, pp. 28-29. Cf. P. Hoffmann, pp. 231 ff.

[133] See W. Lütgert, [2], pp. 77-78; P. W. Schmiedel, p. 29. Cf. also P. Hoffmann, pp. 231 ff.

[134] Paul's reference in 4:15 to the "word of the Lord" must not be allowed to lead to the false conclusion that the essential point of the whole argument must lie in this word; for how little the "word of the Lord" has a prime quality among Paul's other authorities is shown not only by the fact that Paul only most rarely cites a saying of the Lord at all, but also by the observation of how utterly without emphasis the authority of the Lord appears in I Cor. 9:14 alongside and after the authority of general considerations (9:7), of the Old Testament (9:8 ff.), and of Jewish practice (9:13). The λόγος κυρίου may have been: οἱ ζῶντες οὐ μὴ φθάσωσιν τοὺς κοιμηθέντας.

[135] Cf. M. Dibelius, [1], p. 25; IV Ezra 13:24.

[136] Cf. H. Koester in ZNW 48 (1957) : 233.

[137] A. Schweitzer, p. 93.

according to which only those who are living at the Parousia have anything to hope for at all.[138] Perhaps someone in Thessalonica held this opinion. But this cannot be concluded from Paul's argument, particularly in vs. 14. This argument acquaints us only with the simple fact that some in Thessalonica doubted or had doubted the resurrection of the dead.

Now to be sure it is not accidental that K. v. Hofmann and others wish to emend vss. 13-14 on the basis of vs. 15 and see as current in Thessalonica only certain questions about the relation of the (resurrected) dead to those who are living at the Parousia. For they regard it as inconceivable that Paul would have left the community in the dark about his doctrine of the resurrection during his preaching in Thessalonica. This is in fact inconceivable.[139] The doctrine of the resurrection of the dead belonged to his Jewish heritage and could not simply be dissolved by the intense anticipation. The proclamation of the resurrection of Jesus (I Thess. 1:10) cannot have disregarded the fact that he was the "firstfruits of them that sleep" (I Cor. 15:20); the proclamation of his Parousia cannot have omitted the fact that it was bound up with the resurrection. It is true that outside I Cor. 15 and I Thess. 4:13 ff. Paul does not very frequently speak of the general resurrection of the dead, but in the few passages he presupposes for his readers an acquaintance with the doctrine of the resurrection as self-evident: Rom. 6:8; 8:11; 14:8-9; Phil. 3:10-11. Moreover, the resurrection must have belonged *in essence* to Paul's preaching of the future, because in I Cor. 15 he immediately concludes from the denial of the *resurrection* by the Corinthians that they were denying *any* hope of the future. But most of all we must remember that Paul had more than twenty years of missionary experience behind him when he first preached in Thessalonica, and he knew from experience that the death of Christians had long before this become a problem and in Thessalonica also at least could become a problem. What

---

[138] Cf. W. Hadorn, pp. 53-54; IV Ezra 13:17-18: "Those who do not remain are sorrowful." A. Oepke, p. 142: "They hoped for the living, nevertheless cases of death disconcerted them." But in 4:15 ff. Paul is in fact no longer arguing for the resurrection in itself, but for the particular idea that those who have died will in no respect be worse off than the living.

[139] Cf. W. Bornemann, p. 195.

M. Dibelius writes ([1], p. 23) [140] is thus simply inconceivable: "The apostle's missionary preaching apparently had not spoken of the possibility that Christians would die before the Parousia . . . ; now he makes up for the omission." How then should one have been able to understand I Thess. 4:13 ff. as a first explanation of the fact that there is a resurrection of the dead in addition to the resurrection of Jesus from the dead!? No, Paul's preaching must have made the resurrection of the dead certain to the Thessalonians. Cf. also H. A. Wilcke, *Das Problem eines messianischen Zwischenreiches bei Paulus*, AThANT 51 (1967) : 119-20.

But then in the meantime the doctrine of the resurrection has been made doubtful to the Thessalonians. Paul does not tell us who or what aroused this doubt. It could, for example, have been the widespread skepticism of the Hellenists with respect to any hope at all of the beyond, which Paul attests in I Cor. 15:32 ff. and takes up in the rhetorical questions in I Cor. 15:35. But with this skepticism one could no longer live *within* the community. It is also in itself conceivable that the ancient Jewish doctrine of the earthly reign of peace, in which only the living participate, has been proclaimed. In this passage,[141] in fact, Paul appears not to be afraid that the Thessalonians are denying the Parousia also and therefore have abandoned the hope for the living. But

---

[140] Cf. E. v. Dobschütz, [1], p. 184. U. Wilckens also crudely represents this opinion, which in my judgment is inconceivable: "In the setting of the first missionary tradition . . . apparently not anything was said at first explicitly of the eschatological resurrection of the dead . . . . In I Thess. Paul goes into this question (4:13 ff.), and one sees here quite clearly how he . . . begins *ad hoc* to sketch a doctrine of the resurrection of those who have fallen asleep before the events of the end . . ." (in *Dogma und Denkstrukturen*, ed. by W. Joest and W. Pannenberg [1963], pp. 58-59). In this connection one should also consider that Paul's congregations were composed predominantly of people who—most of all as "God-fearers"—long before their conversion were followers of Judaism and thus had always been familiar with the hope of the resurrection. W. Marxsen, in his "Auslegung von 1. Thess. 4,13-18" (ZThK 66 [1969]: 27-29) also fails to take this into account. He considers it to be ruled out that the resurrection of the dead had been a "subject of teaching" of Paul in Thessalonica; for even in 4:14 the resurrection is not mentioned, but the argument is made with the parousia. This is correct, yet it says nothing for our problem; for how will the returning Jesus bring with him "those who have fallen asleep" except by means of the resurrection? Paul certainly did not get the idea that anyone could play off the parousia and the resurrection of the dead against each other. Cf. E. Grässer in *Bibelarbeiten, gehalten auf der Rheinischen Landessynode 1967*, pp. 16-17.

[141] Otherwise in 5:1-11; on this, see the statements below.

this doctrine is never attested elsewhere for primitive Christianity. Hence within the community the denial of the resurrection could appear only in connection with a spiritualistic hope of the hereafter, and this suggests acknowledging that W. Lütgert is right and recognizing also behind the denial of the resurrection in Thessalonica[142] that Gnostic agitation which is known to us above all from I Cor. 15,[143] but can be inferred with some probability also for Philippi[144] and Galatia.[145] Thus I Thess. 4:13-18 fits easily into the exposition of the entire epistle attempted here and, conversely, can lend support to this exposition. For the well-known Gnostic denial of the resurrection I refer to the works mentioned in the foregoing footnotes and the documentation adduced in them.[146]

In 5:1-11 Paul comes to speak to a second eschatological problem, the question of the time of the Parousia. What prompted him to make these statements? Some surmise that without any specific occasion the community had made inquiry through Timotheus about this time.[147] Since one is already invited to make conjectures, it is of course more logical to assume that it is not an inquiry of the Thessalonians—we never hear anything of such questions[148]—but the situation in Thessalonica that

---

[142] This Gnostic denial of the resurrection by no means signified for the Gnostic a hopelessness, yet in I Cor. 15 Paul understands the denial of the resurrection by his opponents in this sense. Hence it may have struck the members of the community in Thessalonica in the same way, especially those who could not compensate for the vanishing hope of the resurrection with an ecstatic display of their pneuma-self. Even according to the Gnostic view there is no hope for the non-pneumatics.

[143] Vol. 1, pp. 155 ff.

[144] See above, pp. 92 ff.

[145] See above, pp. 49-50.

[146] Naturally there are characteristic differences in the treatment of the same theme in I Cor. 15. There Paul must set himself against the current argument of the false teachers, while here he is comforting troubled members of the community. There Paul mistakenly takes the denial of the resurrection as an expression of utter hopelessness; here, as in II Cor. 5:1 ff., he no longer makes this assumption, at any rate not *expressis verbis*. Thus at the time of I Thess. 4:13 ff. he may have been somewhat better informed than at the time of I Cor. 15; see below, pp. 248-49.

[147] A. Oepke, p. 143; P. W. Schmiedel, p. 30; W. Lueken, p. 17; G. Wohlenberg, p. 107.

[148] In all of Paul's references to the situation in Thessalonica nothing is ever said of the sending of Timotheus and of questions communicated by him, or the like; in my judgment this is an indication of the correctness of our literary-critical analysis.

prompts Paul's statements in 5:1-11 as was the case down to 4:18 and from 5:12 on.[149] Besides, a comparison of 4:18 with 5:11 argues in favor of this view. The παρακαλεῖν apparently is needed in Thessalonica here as it is there. Moreover, 5:2 (cf. 5:11) offers the picture, typical of the *whole* epistle, of the apostle's statements. Paul does not say what follows vs. 2 without first having affirmed that the Thessalonians indeed already know it— and then he says it anyway.[150] The situation in Thessalonica is not very serious. Paul must not and does not wish to injure the community; nevertheless he considers his admonitions necessary. Finally, the tone of the entire passage is not keyed to communication and instruction but just to an exhortation to watchfulness and a warning against thoughtless security in prospect of the Parousia.

"The occasion for this statement, which must be sought in a report of Timotheus about the community,[151] does not therewith become fully clear."[152] Really? E. v. Dobschütz himself makes the discovery of this occasion more difficult when he has Paul speaking in two directions: against negligent unreadiness and against extravagant expectations.[153] The assumption of a double, mutually hostile and interwoven battlefront within a compact train of thought is extremely improbable. And where does Paul set himself against an exaggerated expectation of the end? The "drunken"[154] are the same as the "sleeping": both are inattentive and indifferent. But drunkenness here is not a figure for eschatological agitation, as curiously is often thought. The inaptness of such an understanding is shown by a look at I Peter 5:8a. Paul has in mind Christians who give little or no thought to the Parousia which is to be expected, are indifferent toward it, or even are doubtful about it at all.

Anyone who sees in 4:11-12 a fanatical eschatological expectation dealt with must then indeed be surprised at the contradic-

---

[149] Thus, correctly, E. v. Dobschütz, [1], p. 203.

[150] Cf. 1:5; 2:1, 11; 4:1, 9 *et passim;* one does not respond thus to a direct inquiry, even to one in a letter (thus Ch. Masson, *Les deux épîtres* . . .).

[151] But why does Paul not at least suggest this?

[152] E. v. Dobschütz, [1], p. 203.

[153] E. v. Dobschütz, [1], pp. 203, 209.

[154] That by the "drunken" in 5:7 are meant people who are intoxicated with alcohol is a curious notion of B. Reicke, [1], p. 242.

tion between those verses and these. But we have seen that in 4:
11-12 a warning is given against the religious officiousness of the
pneumatics. *This* officiousness, however, goes hand in hand with
the sovereign rejection of all earthly expectation of the end,
whether one calls it Parousia, resurrection, or judgment. We
have the best example of this in the Pastoral Epistles, when we
compare the Gnostics' denial of the resurrection, of which II
Tim. 2:18 tells, with their pneumatic officiousness, which is
portrayed in I Tim. 5:13. The τέλος of the individual Gnostic is
attained with his soul's ascent to heaven; the consummation of the
universe has occurred "when we all attain to the unity of the
faith and of the knowledge of the Son of God, to the perfect man,
to the measure of the stature of the Pleroma of Christ" (Eph.
4:13), i.e., in the Gnostic sense,[155] when all the members of the
primal man have been liberated from the world. Any sort of
eschatological happening on earth lies outside the Gnostic pos-
sibilities of conception. Thus either the church's eschatology is
directly denied [156] or its concepts and conceptions are reinterpreted, when, e.g., the attained knowledge is called the resurrection[157] or the resurrection is said to have occurred in the begetting
of children.[158] The absence of the promise of the Parousia in the
Gospel of John is based upon such a Gnostic inheritance.[159]

Most obvious for comparison with our passage is of course II
Thess. 2:2, where the assertion of some people, "ὅτι ἐνέστηκεν ἡ
ἡμέρα τοῦ κυρίου," can only mean, "The day of the Lord is
already here." [160] This assertion, which is to be understood in the
sense of II Tim. 2:18, is the clearest evidence for the Gnostic

---

[155] On the understanding of this passage in the sense of the author of On the
Ephesian epistle, one may now best consult H. Schlier, *Der Brief an die Epheser*
(1958, 2nd ed.), pp. 199 ff.

[156] Cf., e.g., Iren. I, 24.5; V, 31.1, *et passim;* Justin, Dial. 80.4; I Clem. 23-27;
Polyc. 7. 1; II Clem. 9.1; Ep. Ap. 21 ff.; apocryphal epistle of Paul to the
Corinthians 24-33; apocryphal epistle of the Corinthians to Paul 12; Clem. Alex.,
Strom. IV, 13.89; Eus., CH II, 23.9.

[157] II Tim. 2:18; Eph. 2:5; 5:14; Od. Sol. 22.8; Oxyrh. Pap. 654.5; Iren. I, 23.5;
II, 31.2; Act. Joh. 98; Tert., de res. 19; John 5:24; 11:25; Hipp. V.8=ed. Duncker-
Schn. 158.66 ff.; Letter to Rheginos in the Jung Codex; often in the Coptic
"Gospel of Philip," see ThLZ (1959), cols. 6 ff.; Saying 21; 63; 67; 76; 90; 92; 95;
Ep. Ap. 12 (23).

[158] Acta Pauli et Theclae 14.

[159] Cf. R. Bultmann, [2], II: 85.

[160] Cf. W. Lütgert, [2], pp. 82 ff.

spiritualizing of the idea of the Parousia. With the γινώσκειν, the Eschaton, the day of the Lord, is already given.[161] In the Gnostic terminology preserved by John the same idea is formulated somewhat differently: "This is the [eschatological!] judgment, that the light has come into the world" (John 3:19). We cannot decide here whether II Thess. is Pauline or not.[162] If so, then one would have no other possibility than to interpret I Thess. 5:1-11 from II Thess. 2:2. But even without the direct evidence of II Thess. 2:2, the indifference toward the Parousia, against which Paul must take a stand in 5:1-11, can only have its origin in that Gnostic agitation with whose influences Paul must also concern himself everywhere in our epistle.[163] Thus is the admonition of Paul himself explained; thus does the passage 5:1-11 fit harmoniously into the whole of the epistle; thus again the parallels in the other epistles also become valid. These are available in adequate number, for it is nothing other than the Gnostic assertion of the already achieved perfection against which Paul takes a stand in passages like I Cor. 4:8: "Have you already become satisfied? Are you already rich? Without us have you already become kings? Oh that you had become kings, so that we might also rule with you!" [164] (Cf. Clem. Alex., Strom. IV, 23.149; V, 14.96; Iren. I, 25.3, or Phil. 3:12-15: "Not that I have already attained or were already made perfect . . . ," [165] or even Gal. 6:3).

I Thess. 5:12-13 contains the exhortation to hold the leading and ministering brethren in the community in especially high regard and—if we follow the text of most of the witnesses[166]—to

---

[161] The Gnostics say that "the resurrection of the dead is the knowledge of their so-called truth" (Iren. II, 31.2). "But when anyone . . . has attained their 'redemption,' he is so puffed up that he believes that he is no longer living in heaven or on earth, but that he has entered into the Pleroma and has already embraced his angel" (Iren. III, 15.2).

[162] On this question and on II Thess. 2:2, see below, pp. 191 ff.

[163] If the passage 5:1-11 should have been prompted by specific questions of the Thessalonians—which I would dispute—even these questions have been evoked in connection with the Gnostic disputing of the Parousia.

[164] With this, cf. all those passages which take a position against the "φυσιοῦσθαι" of the Gnostics: I Cor. 4:6, 18-19; 5:2; 8:1; 13:4; II Cor. 12:20; see Vol. 1, p. 179.

[165] See above, pp. 95 ff.

[166] I should prefer this text. The admonition "εἰρηνεύετε ἐν ἑαυτοῖς" would stand in too isolated a position before the "παρακαλοῦμεν," which as also elsewhere (Rom. 15:30; Rom. 16:17; I Cor. 16:15) introduces the individual concluding

keep peace with them. Corresponding exhortations are found also in epistles to other communities: I Cor. 16:15-16; Phil. 2:29; Gal. 6:6. These passages make it more or less clear that Paul is anxious to stress the authority of the leaders of the community because of the threat to the community by the false teachers.[167] The same is to be assumed for our passage, which therewith fits well not only into the explanation given here of the historical situation of I Thess.,[168] but also into the corresponding admonitions of the anti-Gnostic struggle of the later church.

Such admonitions are typical of this struggle. Its characteristic mark in fact is not so much that one sets forth the true doctrine and the true teachers against the false doctrine and the false teachers (II Tim. 4:3), but that the church seeks to create authority for the traditional doctrine in itself and for the teacher in general—against the free sway of the pneumatic[169] and the unverifiable revelations of the Pneuma. At the beginning of this process stands the unfixed message of the apostles, prophets, and teachers, and a loose congregational order, as our two verses show;[170] at the end there is the fixed apostolic tradition and the sacramentally assured authoritative office of the church of the third century. This process is still visible to us in many details, and particularly for the prevailing of the tradition-bound office witness is borne by passages like I Tim. 1:3; 3:1, 12; 4:11 ff.; 5:1, 17; II Tim. 2:2; Heb. 13:7, 17;[171] I Clem. 1.3; 21.6; 44:3 ff.; 57:1;

---

exhortations, and would belong *after* this word. Cf. also I Clem. 63.4; G. Wohlenberg, p. 116; W. Bornemann, p. 235.

[167] See above, pp. 31-32.

[168] The interpreters who in 5:13 prefer the easier reading "ἐν ἑαυτοῖς" mostly find the "εἰρηνεύετε ἐν αὐτοῖς" too concrete for the picture which they presuppose for the situation in Thessalonica. But it is more proper methodologically to explain the stiuation from the text than to judge the text according to this situation.

[169] Tertullian gives a polemical portrayal (de praescr. haer. 41.6-8) of the pneumatic leadership of the Gnostic communities: "Their ordinations are heedless, casual, and without stability; now they install newly converted persons, now those who are entangled in the world, now those who have fallen away from us . . . . Nowhere can one become something more quickly than among the rebels . . . . Hence today this one is bishop, tomorrow that one; today someone is a deacon and tomorrow a lector; today one is a presbyter who tomorrow is a layman; for they entrust the sacred functions even to laymen."

[170] In this respect E. v. Dobschütz may have rightly interpreted the verses ([1], pp. 218-19).

[171] See O. Michel, *Der Brief an die Hebräer*, Meyer's *Kommentar*, XIII (1949, 8th ed.): 334, 356.

II Clem. 17.3, 5; Did. 15.1-2;[172] Ign. Eph. 2.2; 4.1; 5.3; 6.1; 20.2; Magn. 3.1-2; 6.1; 7.1-2; 13.2; Trall. 2.1; 7; 13.2; Philad. inscr.; 3.2; 8.1.

If the debate with Gnosticism already begins with Paul, it is only natural that he already uses the weapons which later brought victory to the church. The passages mentioned from his epistles including I Thess. 5:12-13 as also his and his co-workers' personal intervention in the leadership of the community are to be understood from this perspective. Everywhere, indeed, the Gnostic apostles set up their pneumatic authority against Paul, his helpers, and the local congregational leaders. Over against them Paul must constantly strengthen the standing of the guardians of the traditional doctrine.[173] Thus the admonition in I Thess. 5:12-13 also has its specific occasion in the anti-Pauline agitation in Thessalonica, though it is true that in the epistle discussed here we do not get any information on the question of how far this agitation has been successful.

I Thess. 5:14-18. The concluding exhortations which actually belong to the schema of the eschatocol are found in vs. 25. The scantiness of this integrating part of the epistle's conclusion is explained by the fact that the entire latter half of the epistle was paraenetically conceived. Hence one may regard vss. 14-18 as a preliminary concluding paraenesis. The scope of this paraenesis, as well as the fact that in Paul's writings the concluding paraeneses are always very concretely framed,[174] should warn us against regarding the exhortations as a whole as written "apparently without special occasion." [175] We must only keep in mind that traditional formulations can frame many exhortations quite generally, and we should indeed be cautious with the affirmation of the concrete reference in detail. But neither should we let ourselves be deceived by such tradition-bound formulations about their concrete usage.

---

[172] Cf. R. Knopf in HNT, *in loc.*

[173] I Cor. 4:17; 7:40; 9:1; 16:10-11, 15-16; II Cor. 10:7-8; 12:11-12; Gal. 1–2; 6:6; Phil. 2:19 ff., 29; 3:4 ff.

[174] Rom. 15:30-33; Rom. 16:17-20 (see below, pp. 219 ff.) ; I Cor. 15:58+16:13-18 (see Vol. 1, pp. 93-94) ; II Cor. 13:11-12; Gal. 6:17; Phil. 4:8-9; 3:1+4:4-7 (see above, p. 72) .

[175] M. Dibelius, [1], p. 31.

In vs. 14 [176] the community is first admonished to reprove the ἄτακτοι. "The ἄτακτοι are already described in 4:11." [177] This is correct. If II Thess. is genuine, this connection would be proved by II Thess. 3:6 ff., where the characterization of the fanatics of I Thess. 4:11-12 is repeated with the use of the term ἀτάκτως. If the epistle is not genuine, pseudo-Paul, with his equation of the ἄτακτοι of I Thess. 5:14 with the enthusiasts of 4:11, would have been making an observation with which one will readily agree. For Paul can speak of ἄτακτοι in 5:14 so generally only if he is referring to something already familiar. Thus they are members of the community who have gone astray on those pneumatic ways, for which, as we showed above, the Gnostics are responsible and to which also sexual libertinism and the fanatical disdain for the expectation of the Parousia belong. Paul asks that the members who are pursuing this course be called to order.

Then it says: "Comfort, encourage the fainthearted." E. v. Dobschütz thinks in this connection of those members of the community who had been disturbed by the contesting of the hope of the resurrection and whom Paul seeks to comfort in 4:13-18. This is possible. In that case the "comfort one another" of 4:18 is to be placed alongside the "comfort the fainthearted." Finally, the ἀσθενεῖς, whom the community is to care for, could be the morally weak ones of whom Paul is thinking in 4: (2) 3-8.[178] Then we should compare with this Rom. 5:6; Heb. 4:15; 7: 28, where ἀσθένεια at times approaches the meaning of "sin." [179] Or Paul is thinking of those members of the community who, as for example in Corinth, have not yet gained the right understanding of Christian liberty; cf. I Cor. 8:7 ff.; 9:22; II Cor. 11:29;

---

[176] If one wishes unconditionally to read in 5:13b, "εἰρηνεύετε ἐν ἑαυτοῖς," what is involved here is an exhortation to general peace in the community which, when it occurs in Paul's writings, always has its occasion in intra-congregational disputes, whether as a result of dietary laws (Rom. 14:17-19) or as a result of the Gnostic mission (e.g., I Cor. 1:10; II Cor. 13:11; Gal. 5:19–6:6, cf. above, pp. 51 ff.; Phil. 2:2; 4:2, cf. above, pp. 112 ff.). The same then would hold true for our passage, and it would again appear that the Gnostic effect did not pass by the community without leaving a trace.

[177] E. v. Dobschütz, [1], p. 220; cf. P. W. Schmiedel, p. 32; W. Lueken, p. 19; G. Wohlenberg, p. 117; C. Spicq, "Les Thessaloniciens 'inquiets' étaient-ils des paresseux?" Studia Theologica X: 1 ff., again rightly suggests that we see in the ἄτακτοι disorderly members of the community, not lazy ones.

[178] "Qui fornicatione deturpabantur," Theodore of Mopsuestia, in loc.

[179] Cf. TDNT I: 492.

Rom. 14:1; 15:1. At least in Corinth such weakness is revealed in the face of the Gnostic agitation. With this explanation therefore the bridge to the situation which we have assumed in Thessalonica would also be formed. A certain decision cannot be made; however, the latter explanation appears to me the more probable one, since elsewhere Paul himself apparently never equates ἀσθένεια and sin; that is to say, Rom. 5:6 may be a non-Pauline gloss. It suffices to say that the exhortations concerning the fainthearted and the weak may easily be explained under the presupposition that the situation in Thessalonica corresponds to that in Corinth.

The last clause of vs. 14 summarizes the other three: "Be patient with (them) all," though the admonition need not be thought of as limited to the people previously named.[180] Compared with II Cor. 12:19 ff., this concluding remark shows how little Paul regards the situation in Thessalonica as threatening. It corresponds, for example, to the situation in Corinth at the time of Cor. A and B. Cf. also II Thess. 3:15.

The principle "μακροθυμεῖτε πρὸς πάντας," which is still rooted in the concrete situation, is clothed in vs. 15 in the form of the well-known Christian requirement not to repay evil with evil, but always and toward all to have in mind only good. Specifically, this means: one should treat the false teachers with love; we are reminded of II Cor. 2:5 ff., where Paul asks forgiveness for the one who has wronged him. This is followed by a triad of traditional and, for Paul, characteristic exhortations: "πάντοτε χαίρετε" (II Cor. 6:10; 13:11; Rom. 12:12; Phil. 2:18, 28; 3:1; 4:4); "ἀδιαλείπτως προσεύχεσθε" (Phil. 4:6; I Thess. 5:25; Philemon 22; Rom. 15:30; "ἐν παντὶ εὐχαριστεῖτε" (II Cor. 1:11; 4:15; 9:12; Phil. 4:6; I Thess. 2:13). If one notes in the passages cited how particularly the summons to constant joy, but often also the exhortations to diligent prayer and thanksgiving, appear in the face of the imperiled situation of the apostle or of the readers of the epistle,[181] then in the light of passages such as 1:6; 2:14, and 3:3 ff. one will not hold it to be pure accident that precisely

---

[180] E. v. Dobschütz, [1], p. 221, correctly: "The last clause *initially* sums up the first three."

[181] E. v. Dobschütz, [1], p. 223.

these traditional admonitions appear in 5:17-18.[182]

In the vss. 5:19-22 "Paul speaks of the pneumatic manifestations. . . . One probably will not go astray if one ascribes to all five imperatives the aforementioned specific reference to the gifts of the Spirit." [183] "Most [184] seek the occasion for this admonition in the community which has in part taken a negative stance with respect to the charismata." [185] Rightly so! Accordingly, at the end of the epistle and of all his exhortations there stands the theme which Paul introduces in I Cor. in response to the community's letter with "περὶ δὲ τῶν πνευματικῶν" (12:1), and which occurs in varied form in the correspondence with the Corinthians,[186] and is of current interest also in Galatia (Gal. 3:2; 5:25; 6:1) [187] and—with different concepts—in Philippi (Phil. 3:15).[188] As in the entire I Thess., so here also Paul does not set himself against the pneumatics themselves, but against the effects of their agitation within the community. These now consist not only in a special high evaluation of the pneumatic charismata, as it is to be inferred from the behavior of the ἄτακτοι who are sympathetic toward the Gnostics, but apparently also in a disapproval, which goes too far for Paul,[189] of the pneumatic (in the narrow sense) manifestations, which—including prophecy—some wish to see banned from the community entirely.[190] This agrees with the particular situation in Thessalonica which we have repeatedly observed: the Gnostics have not been able to gain much ground in the community.

With the summons, "μακροθυμεῖτε πρὸς πάντας" (vs. 14), and vs. 15 which is bound up with it, the way is already prepared for the concrete admonition not to overshoot the goal in the defense against the pneumatics. It certainly is no accident that

---

[182] Cf. G. Wohlenberg, p. 118.
[183] Thus M. Dibelius, [1], p. 31, in justified agreement with most of the interpreters.
[184] Not, e.g., W. Bornemann, p. 243.
[185] E. v. Dobschütz, [1], p. 224.
[186] I Cor. 7:40*b;* 15:46; II Cor. 5:11-15; 11:4; 12:1-10; 13:3 ff.
[187] See above, pp. 46 ff.
[188] See above, pp. 99 ff.
[189] Cf. I Cor. 14:19; II Cor. 5:11 ff.; 12:6-7. Cf. E. v. Dobschütz, *Die Thessalonicherbriefe,* p. 226.
[190] The inquiry of the Corinthian community concerning the pneumatics (I Cor. 12:1) is *also* to be understood from this perspective.

this admonition stands at the very end of the epistle, after all the statements have set forth those effects of the Gnostic mission which betray a success, even though slight, of this mission. Those people who have especially firmly defended the Pauline position against the pneumatics are not to get the idea that Paul is writing against them.

Nevertheless, Paul does not wish to have the flame of the spiritual gifts, which in their diversity serve for the edification of the community (I Cor. 12:4-11), extinguished. In particular, one should not scorn free prophetic discourse. Paul holds this—in contrast to the ecstatic speaking in tongues—along with the related explanation or exposition of Scripture to be not unimportant (I Cor. 14). It is a discourse in understandable language, but on the basis of a sudden inspiration and heavenly "revelation," of course without the prophet's losing control over his Pneuma, as is the case in glossolalia (I Cor. 14:29-33). Naturally not every prophecy is good and right, i.e., the revelation of a *divine* secret. Therefore the prophetic utterances must be tested: "πάντα δὲ δοκιμάζετε" (5:21*a*). But the community in fact has the gift of such testing: I Cor. 12:10; 14:29, 37.[191] One should hold to that which in such testing is proved to be good (5:21*b*); on the other hand, one should keep away "ἀπὸ παντὸς εἴδους πονηροῦ" [192] (5:22). Still there is no reason for rejecting prophecies in principle.

The critical attitude, expressed in vss. 21-22, toward *uncontrolled* sway of the Pneuma therewith in fact already again bears anti-Gnostic features, without our being able to say definitely whether and to what extent in vss. 21-22 Paul consciously and deliberately employs the traditional expressions in this sense which elsewhere dominates the discussion. Gnosticism in any case knows only *one* Pneuma, the divine, and for the one who possesses this Pneuma it holds true that he can be judged by no one, as Paul says in I Cor. 2:15 in thoroughly Gnostic style. (On this, see Vol. 1, pp. 151 ff.)

If one leaves aside the fact that in comparison with the parallel

---

[191] Cf. I John 4:1.

[192] On "εἴδους πονηροῦ" see the commentaries and TDNT II: 375; nowadays this generally is translated, correctly, "every bad kind," namely, of προφητεία.

passages mentioned from the other epistles, the front has shifted and Paul is taking a stand primarily not against the pneumatics themselves or the preference for the ecstatic spiritual gifts, but against an exaggerated reaction to such pneumatic excesses,[193] the situation in Thessalonica is the same as in Galatia, Philippi, and Corinth.[194] Gnostic pneumatics have brought members of the community into their defensive position against any spiritual gifts at all. It may be doubted that these Gnostics separated speaking in tongues and prophetic discourse from one another as sharply as Paul did. The well-known portrayal of Gnostic prophets by Celsus (Orig. Cels. VII, 8 ff.) lets us see that prophetic discourse aimed at glossolalia as its climax.[195] But that would only make it all the more understandable that the Thessalonians in their parrying of the pneumatics also set themselves against the προφητεύειν which Paul highly esteemed. For the appearance of pneumatics in Thessalonica, one would also have to appeal to II Thess. 2:2, if the second epistle is genuine. But perhaps one may also—in retrospect—express the cautious conjecture that the repeated mention in I Thess. 1:5-6 (cf. 4:8) of the Holy Spirit who is bound up with Paul's preaching was not made without respect to the assertion of the Gnostics, known to us from the Corinthian epistles, that Paul was no pneumatic at all (I Cor. 7:40b;[196] II Cor. 10:1, 10;[197] 10:2 ff., et passim),[198] and thus has totally deprived the community of the Pneuma.[199]

Finally, we must also point out that the attitude of those members of the community who reject also the prophetic revelations of the Pneuma only corresponds to that attitude which the church soon, in spite of and against Paul, was obliged to take *officially*

---

[193] This shift could indicate that the epistle to Thessalonica in which the passage discussed here is located is earlier than that writing to Corinth in which Paul deals very critically with the πνευματικά; on this, see below, pp. 248 ff. Of course one can consider connecting 5:16-22 with 4: (1)2 (cf. 5:18 with 4:3!). Then this passage would belong to the "joyful epistle" to Thessalonica (see p. 179) which finally concludes the discussion, and the warning against too vigorous a reaction against the pneumatics would be especially easy to understand.

[194] "The fact is that we would not understand the exhortations in I Thess. 5:19-22 at all if we did not have I Cor." (W. Hadorn, p. 60).

[195] Cf. Vol. 1, pp. 276-77.

[196] See Vol. 1, pp. 170-71.

[197] *Ibid.*, pp. 176 ff.

[198] *Ibid.*, pp. 164 ff.

[199] Cf. II Cor. 11:4; 12:11 ff.

in the struggle with Gnosticism, when still in the first century she cut off all prophetism and not only persisted in this attitude in the face of the Montanist reaction, but also persists in it down to the present. Here too we see again how already at the time of Paul the weapons were forged with which the church finally conquered heresy (see pp. 167 ff.) .

I Thess. 5:23-28. The passage 5:23-24 announces the end of the epistle. Before the benediction, which as usual forms the conclusion of the epistle, we are surprised by a curious entreaty: "I adjure you by the Lord that this letter be read to *all* the brethren" (5:27 RSV). On this verse, even M. Dibelius must concede that it suggests "that the community does not form a closed, unified fellowship." [200] In any case, all the attempts of the exegetes to bypass this simple fact are without convincing force.[201] It is indeed true that Paul praises the community (1:3; 3:6) , but in fact he also praises the community in Corinth (I Cor. 1:4 ff.; 11:2; II Cor. 3:2; 7:7) , without anyone thinking therefore that everything was in order in Corinth. One should only compare I Cor. 11:2 with 11:17! Rather the next-to-last verse of our epistle once more discloses to us the situation in Thessalonica. The community stands on Paul's side; the rival Gnostic mission, however, has not remained without success. On the periphery of the community there are the ἄτακτοι, those pneumatics against whom the community is defending itself with anti-pneumatic rigorism; the charges against Paul's preaching and against its alleged deceitful intentions have been heard in the community; the message of libertinism signifies a temptation; many were wavering in the hope of the resurrection; the expectation of the Parousia is held in disdain by the "people on the periphery." Paul admonishes that one is to have patience with these doubtful brethren, not

---

[200] [1], p. 32; cf. G. Wohlenberg, p. 127; A. Oepke, p. 149.

[201] F. C. Baur and others had detected in this verse a sign of the inauthenticity of I Thess. E. v. Dobschütz thinks ([1], p. 233) that Paul has not sufficiently had experience with his epistles to the communities and is afraid that some member of the community could, out of negligence, leave it lying around. P. W. Schmiedel (p. 34) suggests that there were members of the community who were temporarily absent. According to K. v. Hofmann (pp. 273-74) , Paul was afraid that the community would disregard his epistle because they counted on his personal coming. K. G. Eckart avoids the problem of this verse when he writes, without any further justification: "5:27 certainly comes from the redactor" (p. 43, n. 5) .

repay them evil for evil, and admonish them, the ἄτακτοι, instead of creating a schism. Hence this epistle is to be given to *all,* even to them, to read. All this corresponds to the situation toward the end of the Corinthian confusion, not only because the Gnostics in Corinth also apparently usually read Paul's letters,[202] but above all because in Corinth also at the end the community stood on the apostle's side, yet with the exception of a minority who dissociated themselves from Paul (II Cor. 2:6).[203]

Let us summarize the results of our study. It may have become clear that it is possible to explain the epistle which has been exegeted in the foregoing, which forms the most important part as to contents of the epistolary composite known as I Thess., as a whole and in its individual expressions in terms of that situation which also forms the unified background of the Corinthian, Galatian, and Philippian epistles: the agitation by Gnostic missionaries of Jewish or Jewish Christian observance in the Pauline mission field. Moreover, I personally see no other possibility than to interpret the epistle in terms of this situation, if one does not wish to forgo a full explanation at all; still I am not so presumptuous as to hold the contesting of this explanation to be unscientific. Naturally the judgment as to the part of I Thess. already investigated depends in part on the information which is imparted by the other parts of Paul's correspondence with Thessalonica. Thus we must first investigate the separate epistle preserved in I Thess. 2:13–4:1 (2).

IV

There can be no doubt as to the external occasion of this writing. Timotheus has just returned from Thessalonica, has brought cheering news about the condition of the community, and in joy over this news Paul takes up his pen (3:6 ff.). Apparently the good news had not been expected as a foregone conclusion. Timotheus' return lightens Paul's anxious heart in the same way as at another time Paul was comforted by the arrival of Titus, who had come from Corinth to Macedonia to meet him (II Cor. 2:12-13+7:5 ff.). The parallelism of the situation here and there

---

[202] See Vol. 1, pp. 302 ff.
[203] See Vol. 1, p. 116.

is complete and pronounced, even to the very terms with which Paul expresses his relief. I Thess. 2:13–4:1 is the "joyful epistle" to Thessalonica.

Why had Paul been anxious? Why had he even several times formed the plan to travel to Thessalonica (2:17-18)? Why was he finally no longer able to bear it because of his anxiety, so that he sends his closest colleague from Athens to Thessalonica (3:1 ff.)? Twice, in 3:1 and in 3:5, Paul begins to tell the motive of his sending Timotheus. Here it is shown, in repeated expressions in 3:2b-3 and 5 ff., that Paul was concerned for the faith of the Thessalonians. He feared their apostasy; Satan had wanted to tempt them (3:5).

What prompts these fears? According to 3:3 they are based ἐν ταῖς θλίψεσιν ταύταις, i.e., in the current or well-known troubles. What is meant by these troubles is by no means troubles of the Thessalonians, so that, as the expositors regularly do, one could refer to 2:14. Instead, as E. v. Dobschütz ([1], p. 233) quite rightly has pointed out, these troubles refer to hardships into which *Paul* has come. Since 2:17, the "we" is the apostolic "we," and indeed, because of 3:1-2, clearly the apostolic "we" of Paul himself. Therefore it can only be this "we" in 3:3b also, where Paul comments on "these afflictions" with the remark: "for you yourselves know that 'we' are destined for this," especially since Paul continues immediately in vs. 4 with the undoubtedly apostolic "we": "for already when 'we' were with you, 'we' told you beforehand that 'we' must suffer affliction, just as it has also happened; and this you know."

These afflictions of the apostle can hardly have referred to outward hardships and persecutions; for Paul did not need to predict these to the Thessalonians: they were experiencing these themselves, along with him (Acts 17:1-9). Besides, Paul appears to have been completely free to travel when, filled with concern, he sends Timotheus. And finally, we cannot see why the apostle's sufferings would have made his message unworthy of being believed, and why it could have moved the Thessalonians to apostasy (cf. rather Phil. 1:14).

This insight is confirmed by 3:6-7. Timotheus brought the report that people thought of Paul personally in friendly and loving

177

fashion and longed for him just as much as he longed for them (3:6).[204] Thus Timotheus had gone to Thessalonica because the authority of the apostle appeared to be threatened.[205] This only confirms once more what we have already long known about the situation in Thessalonica.[206] Thus Paul had predicted to the Thessalonians that he as an apostle would be exposed to personal attacks which would cast suspicion on him as a charlatan and make his message untrustworthy. This prediction in the meantime has come true, and the Thessalonians know this (3:4) —apparently from their own observation and experience.

Behind his afflictions Paul sees Satan at work. Of course all evil comes from Satan, and thus possibly outward afflictions as well. In Paul, however, there are no parallels to this, but there are to the idea that Satan tempts the community by means of false teachings and teachers:[207] Rom. 16:20;[208] II Cor. 11:14-15. In both passages the same false teachers are involved who were were also at work in Thessalonica. Paul may also be thinking of them in I Thess. 3:5. Paul's joyful assurance, that he is greatly comforted by the report from Timotheus because "ὑμεῖς στήκετε ἐν κυρίῳ" (3:8, taking up 3:3), is reminiscent of the only word-for-word parallel in Phil. 4:1, which we have already mentioned in connection with 2:19-20: "οὕτως στήκετε ἐν κυρίῳ." This challenge concludes the sharp philippic against the Gnostic *false teachers* in Philippi. One is also most likely to speak of the "ὑστερήματα τῆς πίστεως" (3:10) in thinking of the danger from false doctrines. Thus in 3:3-4, 7, θλῖψις refers to the distresses into which Paul was brought by the accusations of his opponents in Thessalonica.

---

[204] One imagines hearing Paul sigh: if only it were similar in Galatia: Gal. 4:12 ff.

[205] Cf. the exact parallel in II Cor. 7:7, and on this, Vol. 1, pp. 108-9.

[206] Perhaps the threat to the community mentioned in 2:14 was causally connected with the peril from the false teachers who were attempting to undermine the authority of the apostle. It is reasonable to presume that the appearance of the Gnostic missionaries prompted the authorities in Thessalonica to take counteraction, similar to that which Paul experienced, according to Acts 17:1-9, on his first stay in Corinth, and that the community of Paul was not spared in this action. However, we cannot say for sure.

[207] The mention of Satan in I Thess. 2:18 may also be connnected with his activity as tempter and originator of heresy. For if I Thess. was written on the third missionary journey, then Paul has been hindered in the planned travels to Macedonia by the confusion in Corinth caused by Satan (II Cor. 11: 14-15) ! On this, see below, pp. 187 ff., and W. Hadorn, p. 79.

[208] See below, pp. 235-36.

Paul does frequently[209] use this concept in a broader sense.[210] In immediate connection with I Thess. 3:1 ff. in this respect stand the passages from Cor. C in which Paul speaks of his apostolic θλίψεις: II Cor. 2:4; 4:8; 6:4; 7:4; for 2:4 and 7:4 especially leave no doubt that what are involved here are those distresses into which Paul has come because of the attacks of his opponents who are disputing his apostolic authority in his communities. Indeed, in both cases the *same* distresses are involved; for Cor. C and I Thess. 3:1 ff. were written from Ephesus at about the same time (see pp. 187 ff.; 247 ff.

Thus it appears that in fact the epistle preserved in 2:13–4:1 (2) forms a conclusion to the discussion which was conducted in the other writing preserved within I Thess. In genuine anxiety about the living community in Thessalonica the apostle had sent Timotheus thither. The community was threatened from without by the pagan fellow citizens, and from within by the Jewish or Jewish Christian false teachers, who were undermining Paul's authority. The latter threat appeared to the apostle to be the more dangerous. It is only the successful rebuff to *them* that he mentions in 3:6 ff., where he tells of the return of Timotheus. His concern, to which he had previously given expression several times with regard to the Thessalonians (see below), thus had indeed been serious, but in essence unfounded. Hence the earlier discussion in his epistle is no more mentioned. This latter fact corresponds precisely to the "joyful epistle" which concludes the discussion with the Corinthians (see Vol. 1, p. 110), which likewise no longer makes the slightest mention of the false doctrines, the false teachers, and the vigorous controversies created by these, and mentions one of at least four earlier epistles only because Paul must dispel a misunderstanding connected with this epistle.

From this situation as a "joyful epistle" not only does the tension between 2:13–4:1 and the rest of I Thess. once more become evident—a tension confirmed by our literary-critical analysis— but also the section 2:13–4:1 itself becomes fully understandable.

The proem of this "joyful epistle" is reminiscent, even to de-

---

[209] Cf. Rom. 5:3; 8:35; I Cor. 7:28; II Cor. 8:2.

[210] E. v. Dobschütz's judgment that in Paul "θλῖψις always stands for external afflictions" ([1], p. 134) is refuted *expressis verbis* by II Cor. 7:4-5.

tails in formulation, of the proem in 1:2 ff., as also of other proems to Paul's epistles. In brief, Paul voices thanks for the fact that the Thessalonians have received his word as God's word, not as the word of man. This is also reminiscent of the apology in 1:5. The "οὐκ ἐν λόγῳ μόνον" appears here as "οὐ λόγον ἀνθρώπων," and the "ἀλλὰ καὶ ἐν δυνάμει καὶ ἐν πνεύματι ἁγίῳ καὶ πληροφορίᾳ πολλῇ" is taken up by "ἀλλὰ καθὼς ἀληθῶς ἐστιν λόγον θεοῦ, ὃς καὶ ἐνεργεῖται ἐν ὑμῖν τοῖς πιστεύουσιν." [211] Of course the distinctive difference is that these commendatory statements in 1:2 ff. are made with the founding visit in mind, to which Paul constantly refers in 1:2 ff., while in 2:13 the same statements are made with the *present* θλίψεις in mind, as vs. 14 shows. That is to say: while in the earlier epistle, with regard to the present state of the faith of the community, Paul considers necessary a number of admonitions and, in view of the attitude of the community to him, the apostle, the reminders of the "time of their first love," in 2:13-14 he confirms the adherence, unchanged even in the present, of the Thessalonians to the message which was preached to them at that time. Thus the situation presupposed in 2:13-14 is a different one from that to which Paul speaks in 1:2 ff.

If the interpretation given here is correct, vss. 15-16 create just as many or just as few difficulties as in any other situation presupposed for the epistle. I consider the difficulties to be considerable.[212] But in any case, these verses, whether they are from Paul or from a later hand, form a parenthetical remark which means nothing for the progression of the thought. Hence we can pass over them here.

If one excises vss. 15-16, then the ἡμεῖς δέ of vs. 17 connects with the ὑμεῖς γάρ of vs. 14, while in the present text a connection

---

[211] Cf. E. v. Dobschütz, [1], p. 105.

[212] "Why after all the invective against the Jews, when the persecution had come from the pagans?" (P. W. Schmiedel, *in loc.*). Can the former persecutor speak thus? The "anti-Semitism" of this passage contradicts all that Paul says elsewhere about his attitude to the nation of his fathers. Can Paul already say that the *Jews* have crucified Jesus, when the tradition correctly makes the Romans responsible for the crucifixion? Can vs. 16*b* be understood other than as *vaticinium ex eventu* of the catastrophe of the year 70? Cf. U. Wilckens, *Die Missionsreden der Apostelgeschichte*, pp. 119-20; W. G. Kümmel, pp. 220-21; V. Hasler, "Judenmission und Judenschuld," ThZ 24 (1968) : 173-90; O. Michel, in *Antijudaismus im Neuen Testament*, edited by W. P. Eckert, N. P. Levinson und M. Stöhr (1967), pp. 50-59.

of the ἡμεῖς δέ cannot be evident. Paul expresses his regret that his wish to see the community again has not yet been fulfilled (2:17-18). This regret is especially great because Paul can look upon the living community in Thessalonica with thanksgiving and joy (2:19-20). This fact makes it appear advisable for the apostle to speak of the motive for sending Timotheus. The commendatory addition to Timotheus' name in 3:2 suggests that Timotheus was not present during Paul's founding visit in Thessalonica. The book of Acts also does not mention Timotheus again after 16:3 until 17:14.

Only the new beginning in 3:5 makes it clear that Paul had genuine anxiety about the *faith* of the Thessalonians, and in 3:6 it becomes evident that this anxiety was not so much shaped by the fear that under persecution the Thessalonians would fall back again into paganism (or Judaism) as rather by the suspicion that they could be rejecting the apostle Paul in favor of other teachers, in other words, of false teachers. The arrival of Timotheus has destroyed these fears (3:6-8). Hence an expression of thanksgiving for the state of the faith of the Thessalonians toward the end of the epistle is altogether fitting (3:9), and Paul once again assures the community that he prays without ceasing that he might see them again soon. Then he can also set right their ὑστερήματα τῆς πίστεως (3:10-11). These defects of faith are apparently, according to the judgment of Timotheus, no longer of such a kind that he must now go into them in an epistle. So, apart from the traditional concluding paraenesis in 4:1, the entire epistle is free from any instruction and admonition: a genuine epistle of joy which, as we have seen, finds its end in 4:1 (or 4:2) and, not unlike the epistle of joy to Corinth, also ends the correspondence caused by the troubling situation in Thessalonica in general, and in a fashion satisfactory on all sides.

V

According to the interpretation set forth here, the two epistles combined in I Thess. are indeed somewhat separated from each other in point of time, but reflect the same discussion, and thus belong to the same situation. When were the two epistles written? Up until W. Hadorn's well-known study, there appears never to have been any doubt that Paul composed I Thess. on his so-called second missionary journey at the beginning of his stay in Corinth. Only Marcion—at any rate according to Hadorn's conjecture[213]—placed I Thess. in the time of the third missionary journey.

Even W. Lütgert apparently did not have the idea that with his interpretation I Thess. belongs together in time with the other major Pauline epistles and thus would have to be put in the time of the so-called third missionary journey. This is surprising, but is readily explained when one considers that for Lütgert, the gnosticizing current in the Pauline mission territory, which he pointed out with great perceptiveness, belonged to no organized missionary movement, but was a fanatical distortion of Pauline Christianity, fed from many unidentifiable sources, which made itself conspicuous everywhere independently and only slowly combined to form the great movement of Gnosticism which is known to us from the second century. Nowadays we may no longer think of Christian Gnosticism as having arisen in the Christian communities in this way. Gnosticism is pre-Christian and was introduced into the Christian communities.[214] In addition, there is the fact that already A. Schlatter[215] had to point out the obvious weakness of Lütgert's thesis: "This much is certain, that the opposition to Paul in Corinth did not arise out of Paulinism, does not represent a further development of the Pauline community, but has been introduced from without by those whose religious history ran a course independent of Paul . . ." ([1], pp. 35-36). This judgment is valid not only for Corinth,[216] but also for Philippi[217] and Galatia, where it was never disputed, and for Thessalonica, where, as Timotheus can relate, the agitation in fact is past, and thus had already been present. But then one can no longer date "I Thess." in the time of the second missionary journey. W. Hadorn was the first to draw this con-

---

[213] "Die Abfassung der Thessalonicherbriefe auf der dritten Missionsreise und der Kanon des Marcion," ZNW 19 (1919/20) : 67 ff.

[214] Instead of giving many references to literature, I refer only to R. Bultmann, [2], I: 164 ff., 362.

[215] [1], p. 36.

[216] Vol. 1, pp. 141 ff.

[217] See above, pp. 85 ff.

clusion. It is true that his study suffers from many an improbability in the picture of the opponents, but it sees that the "fanaticism" in Thessalonica cannot be explained apart from that movement which at the time of Paul's third journey was introduced into Corinth from without.[218]

For me this consideration would suffice to place both writings of "I Thess." in the time of the apostle's so-called third missionary journey. But now the attempt has recently been made in a completely new way to put "I Thess." *after* the second journey. W. Michaelis, in his *Einleitung in das Neue Testament* (p. 223),[219] thinks poorly of the attempts of W. Lütgert and W. Hadorn[220] to compare the situation in Corinth with that in Thessalonica. Nevertheless, for entirely different reasons he places I Thess. in the time of the third journey, wherein he adopts many of Hadorn's considerations, with which the latter had already attempted to support his thesis, even apart from the similarity of the discussions in Corinth and Thessalonica. I cite the most important of these reasons briefly and for the rest refer the reader to the works named.

1. The external situation during the composition of I Thess., as it is to be inferred from I Thess. 3:1 ff., is in no case to be harmonized with the account in the book of Acts of the second journey.[221]

2. According to I Thess. 2:17 ff., Paul had *several times* been

---

[218] W. Hadorn, pp. 63 ff. He considers it possible that this movement had reached out from Corinth to the other communities. This I do not believe. The Gnostic mission followed the tracks of Paul by way of Galatia, Philippi, and Thessalonica to Corinth, as is shown by an effort to arrange the individual epistles in chronological order; see below, pp. 245 ff.

[219] Cf. also W. Michaelis, *Die Gefangenschaft des Paulus in Ephesus* (1925), pp. 27 ff.

[220] W. Hadorn, pp. 32-33.

[221] This is generally recognized. According to Acts 17:14, Timotheus and Silas remain behind in Beroea upon Paul's departure and, in answer to his call, appear only in Corinth again with Paul (Acts 17:15; 18:5). According to I Thess. 3:1 Timotheus and *only* he was in Athens with Paul. Some solve the problem by explaining that the presentation in the book of Acts is untrustworthy, but in view of the nontendentious information in 17:14-15 and 18:5, one only reluctantly reaches this conclusion. Since the book of Acts tells nothing of a sending of Timotheus, and Paul tells nothing of his arrival in *Corinth*, there exist between the two accounts no demonstrable agreements, but only demonstrable discrepancies. In view of this fact, it is somewhat surprising that, of all things, the account in Acts appears to provoke in the mass of scholars the thesis of the composition of I Thess. at the beginning of Paul's first stay in Corinth.

about to visit the community without having been able to convert his intention into fact. *Therefore* he finally sent Timotheus from Athens to Thessalonica (I Thess. 3:1-2). Accordingly, his repeated intention falls in the time before this mission. What were involved here were specific travel plans! But how is Paul, at the beginning of his brief stay in Athens, a few weeks after his departure from Thessalonica, supposed to have thought seriously several times of wanting and being able to travel northward again instead of to Corinth? [222] How would his personal situation have been able to hinder him in the realization of such a resolution (Acts 18:1)? And further: Why, if in the first weeks after leaving Thessalonica he was several times hindered from making the planned trip, should Paul not have traveled to Thessalonica in the next five years? Did Satan also constantly frustrate his plans during the following one-and-a-half-year stay in Corinth, even though he longed day and night to make the trip (3:9-10)? That remark becomes understandable only in terms of the third journey: I Cor. 4:19; 16:5 ff.; II Cor. 1:15 ff.

3. According to I Thess. 1:8-9, the word of the Lord has sounded forth from Thessalonica "not only in Macedonia and Achaia, but everywhere your faith in God has become known." However broadly one may interpret these words, either clause is so little conceivable at the beginning of Paul's first stay in Corinth[223] that Paul's words are unexplainable even as "strong

---

[222] W. G. Kümmel, p. 226, completely overlooks this basic objection. Since Paul's stay in Athens was brief and his epistle to Thessalonica would have had to be written shortly after the return of Timotheus from there, its composition would fall in the first two or three months of his stay in Corinth, according to Acts 18:5 even before the time when he actually began his preaching in Corinth. Cf. also W. Hadorn, pp. 71-72.

[223] E. v. Dobschütz ([1], p. 17) calculates that I Thess. must have been written ten or twelve weeks after Paul's flight from Thessalonica and thinks that this figure still is rather high. If one takes a multiple of this period, then 1:8-9 remains still inconceivable. Unfortunately E. v. Dobschütz does not tell us how he manages with this verse in view of his chronological arrangement of the epistle. One would think, for example, that "in every place" embraces the whole territory of the Christian or at least of the Pauline mission. Jerusalem and Antioch cannot be excluded from it. Naturally Paul does not mean to say that precisely there people were speaking of the community at Thessalonica. But Paul's remark presupposes that since the time when the Christian community of Thessalonica through its missionary activity became a model for all the neighboring believers, up to the time of the composition of I Thess., the knowledge of the faith of the Thessalonians had reached even the remote Christian communities *and* Paul had been able to learn from these distant communities that people

exaggeration." Even this argument alone rules out the composition of "I Thess." on the second missionary journey.[224] In conjunction therewith stand the reservations toward an early time for the composition of "I Thess." which are suggested by I Thess. 4:10a.

4. "Even if the community should have consisted in the main of old people, it is doubtful that some four months after the founding (cf. Feine-Behm-Kümmel, p. 183) several deaths should already have occurred. Consequently 4:13 also presupposes that a longer time has elapsed since the founding." [225]

5. Less weighty is the judgment of W. Hadorn that I Thess. 2:14 can hardly be harmonized with the account in the book of Acts of the sufferings of the community (*Die Abfassung der Thessalonicherbriefe,* pp. 25 ff.) —although it is true that in I Thess. 2:14 the subject is persecution of the Thessalonians by the Gentiles, and in Acts 17:1-9 by the Jews—and W. Michaelis' casual suggestion ([1], p. 224) that I Thess. 2:14 sounds as though Paul has been in Palestine once since the founding of the community. Moreover, one may not argue, as W. Hadorn does (pp. 29 ff.), with I Thess. 5:12 for a later composition (which the Tübingen School did, for the sake of their thesis of inauthenticity), on the grounds that an official congregational leadership is already presupposed here. This is in fact not the case.[226]

---

there were talking about the Thessalonians. Actually the remark that the community at Thessalonica is the topic of conversation "in every place" may reflect an experience which Paul himself had had on his visit in the communities of the East following the second missionary journey; it is understandable thus without strain and without an abnormal exaggeration. Not least of all, Paul himself had reported in the East about the Thessalonians. Cf. II Thess. 1:4!

[224] Cf. W. Hadorn, pp. 21 ff. Curiously, M. Dibelius ([1]) completely passes over this problem in silence. P. Feine (p. 108) treats it in such a way as to suppress without hesitation the decisive vs. 1:8a! Similarly now also W. G. Kümmel, p. 226, who only remarks that the faith of the Thessalonians has become known even beyond Macedonia and Achaia. This alone is hardly conceivable within a scant quarter of a year. Nevertheless, in vss. 7 ff. Paul leaves no doubt at all that the πίστις of the Thessalonians has become known everywhere *because* the Macedonians have been successful in mission work in Macedonia and Achaia. In this regard vs. 8a is decisive for the understanding of I Thess. 1:7-9. That this section, "precisely considered," presupposes "no longer lapses of time" (p. 226) remains a mere assertion, since we learn nothing of the nature of this "precise consideration."

[225] W. Michaelis, [1], p. 223. Of course Paul's statements in 4:13 ff. are adequately accounted for even without the assumption of cases of death.

[226] See the commentaries.

These reasons, together with the thesis of W. Lütgert and W. Hadorn to which we have given renewed support, suffice to assure the composition of the writings combined in I Thess. during the third missionary journey.[227] Actually, of course, this dating has found little acceptance heretofore. It is commonly conceded that it promises "the solution of many difficulties," [228] but it is rejected "in spite of fine expositions in details." [229] The reason for this is, first, the staying power of an unassailed tradition which brings forward against the new interpretation more of an "unnecessary" than an "impossible." But in addition there are also individual reservations.

Of the many personal remarks in the first chapters, P. Feine thinks:[230] "All these appear to be quite fresh reminiscences." But this is read into Paul's words. What then will one infer from Phil. 4:15? [231] Further, one may not refer to 2:17: "πρὸς καιρὸν ὥρας." This expression says nothing about an absolute span of time, but, like the more common "πρὸς ὥραν" (II Cor. 7:8; Gal. 2:5; Philemon 15; John 5:35), only means "temporarily." [232]

Doubts may arise sooner from the prescript.[233] Paul, Silvanus, and Timotheus are introduced as the senders of the epistle. These are the companions on the second journey, as we learn from the book of Acts[234] and have confirmed by II Cor. 1:19. After Acts 18:5 Silas disappears from the account of the book of Acts, which thus does not mention him in connection with the third journey. But this does not mean that he must therefore have died or left the missionary service.[235] Paul had sought him out as companion for the second missionary journey, after he had separated from Barnabas (Acts 15:36 ff.). This corresponds to

---

[227] At least it is not justifiable on the basis of composition of I Thess. during the second so-called missionary journey, presupposed as a certainty, to construe important developments in the theological thought-world of Paul. Thus most recently C. H. Dodd, *New Testament Studies* (1954, 2nd ed.), pp. 83 ff., 108 ff.

[228] A. Oepke, p. 127.

[229] P. Feine, *Einleitung in das Neue Testament* (1930, 5th ed.), p. 107.

[230] *Ibid.*, p. 107.

[231] W. Michaelis, [1], p. 223.

[232] *Ibid.*, p. 224.

[233] A. Oepke, p. 128; on the following, cf. W. Hadorn, pp. 67 ff.

[234] Of course the book of Acts does not mention Timotheus from 16:4 to 17:13.

[235] Cf. I Peter 5:12.

the primitive Christian practice of doing mission work in pairs.[236] Silas may have been, like Barnabas, an apostle, and in that case —because of I Cor. 15:8—had been converted *before* Paul. According to Acts 16:1, at the beginning of this second journey Paul also takes with him (the Gentile Christian?) Timotheus, who in contrast to Silvanus becomes his personal pupil, at first was an ordinary assistant, but at the time of the third missionary journey occupies the place of Silvanus as Paul's chief companion (II Cor. 1:1; Phil. 1:1; Philemon 1), is assigned to independent work (I Cor. 4:17; 16:10; I Thess. 3:2 ff.) and is always thought of by Paul with special and heartfelt praise (I Cor. 4:17; 16:10; Phil. 2:19 ff.; I Thess. 3:2). He undoubtedly owes his position, in which he even surpasses Titus, to his special achievement, which moved Paul to prefer him to all other co-workers. We do not know what work Silvanus took over. We can hardly conceive how numerous were the independent filial missions in the Pauline mission territory.[237] From I Thess. 1:1 we learn that even at the time of the third journey Silvanus was with Paul at least part of the time, and in the composition of the epistle to the community in whose founding he had a part was included, certainly not without specific intention.[238] Neither of these facts is surprising; they signify a welcome enrichment of our knowledge of the fate of this missionary[239] and are not in the slightest degree suited for contesting the thesis that I Thess. was composed during the third missionary journey.

Thus there remains only one last reservation: Paul was hardly again in Athens at a later time.[240] But in view of the reasons which argue for the composition of "I Thess." on the third missionary journey, must we not rather say: By this we learn that during this journey Paul made a visit to Athens? But we know for sure that Paul had touched Athens once from Ephesus, and that

---

[236] Mark 6:7, *et passim.*

[237] Not inapt and not unfounded is the conjecture of W. Hartke (*Die Sammlung und die ältesten Ausgaben der Paulusbriefe* [Diss. Bonn, 1917], pp. 29 ff.) that Silas was resident in Ephesus, and in fact as leader of the "house of Onesiphorus" (II Tim. 1:16; 4:19) and as recipient of Rom. 16.

[238] The order, Silvanus first, then Timotheus, is chosen here, as in II Cor. 1:19, with a view in retrospect to the situation of the second journey.

[239] Cf. W. Michaelis, [2], pp. 34-35.

[240] A. Oepke, pp. 127-28.

before his second visit to Thessalonica, namely on that trip to Corinth which we usually call the "interim visit." [241] The ships which sailed from Ephesus to Achaia and back had to go by Athens and must have landed there frequently. One had a stop in Athens and then probably took another ship for the continuing voyage.[242] Now I Thess. 3:1 says no more than that Paul traveled on from Athens alone after he had sent Timotheus from there on the trip to Thessalonica. I had already earlier conjectured,[243] without knowing of W. Hadorn's study, that Paul's stay in Athens at the time of the "interim visit" is just the situation of which the apostle speaks in I Thess. 3:1. Now I see that Hadorn has justified this thesis so well [244] that nothing more of importance can be added to it.[245] It is true that the following observation needs to be supplemented. According to I Thess. 3:1-5, Paul sent Timotheus to Thessalonica because he feared that the θλίψεις which had struck *him* could move the Thessalonians to apostasy. Involved in these afflictions are the attacks against his apostolic authority to which Paul saw himself exposed in the community in Thessalonica (see pp. 177 ff.). But it was also just such dis-

---

[241] On this, see the introductions and the commentaries on the Corinthian epistles, as well as Vol. 1, pp. 103 ff.

[242] Cf. W. Michaelis, [2], p. 61.

[243] Vol. 1, p. 104, n. 35.

[244] W. Hadorn, pp. 83 ff.

[245] Still to be clarified would be only whether Paul sent Timotheus to Thessalonica *before* or *after* his visit in Corinth. Only the latter is likely. The "we decided to remain behind in Athens alone" is not very plausible if Paul had already made the decision in Ephesus to send Timotheus to Thessalonica. It would also be strange if the necessity for the sudden trips to Thessalonica had happened to come at the same time. Further, "to remain behind in Athens" makes good sense only if Paul was obliged to tarry in Athens. But in view of the short distance to Corinth, this is not very likely. Finally, it would be out of the way to go from Ephesus to Thessalonica by way of Athens. Thus we must assume that Paul took Timotheus as his companion to Corinth. There he must have received the disturbing news about the situation in Thessalonica. At the same time, in view of the situation in Corinth, he there changed his travel plans (Vol. 1, p. 103); the new plan once again postponed the long-promised visit with the Thessalonians (I Thess. 2:18!). This had to be communicated to the Thessalonians. Since I Thess. 2:13–4:1, written just after Timotheus' return, does not contain such a communication, Timotheus will already have conveyed it and, for the time being, substituted for Paul's visit. Now, moreover, the "we decided to remain behind in Athens alone" is quite in place, since this decision was a sudden one and Paul possibly had to wait in Athens for a sailing connection to Ephesus, and perhaps also wanted to spend a few days with the Christians there.

tresses that led Paul to make the interim visit to Corinth, namely, grave charges against him as apostle. The epistle Cor. C, which was written in connection with the interim visit, and the somewhat later sorrowful epistle make this evident (see Vol. 1, pp. 103). Such charges are in fact suited for making Paul's message unworthy of belief in the community. In other words: the motivation for the sending of Timotheus which Paul gives in I Thess. 3:1-5 is comprehensible only from the situation of the interim trip to Corinth, which took him by way of Athens, and not from the period of the second missionary journey.

Timotheus then after the completion of his trip met Paul again in Ephesus or its vicinity. Consequently, the joyful epistle preserved in I Thess. 2:13–4:1 (2) was written in Asia after Paul's interim visit in Corinth and falls, broadly speaking, in the period between I Cor. and II Cor.[246] The other writing contained in I Thess. is to be put in the same place, but before the interim visit.

W. Michaelis,[247] because of Acts 19:22, expresses doubt about this precise dating of the stay in Athens mentioned in I Thess. 3:1 ff. I do not understand this. For even if one holds the note in Acts to be historically assured, one still can have no objection to the idea that before his final departure from Ephesus, Paul once more sends Timotheus, who was with him again, together with Erastus to the Macedonian communities. One can even surmise the reason for this mission. It will have come at that time when Paul changed his travel plans for the last time and decided to travel, not, as previously anticipated (II Cor. 1:15 ff.), by way of Corinth to Macedonia, but by way of Macedonia to Corinth. The mission of the two co-workers thus probably was to prepare the way for Paul's visit which was connected with the gathering of the offering for Jerusalem and is to be compared with the corresponding mission of Titus and his co-workers to Achaia (II Cor. 8-9). To be sure, W. Michaelis appears to

---

[246] More precisely, it should be said: soon after epistle C, which according to my analysis (Vol. 1, pp. 98 ff.) includes II Cor. 2:14–6:13+7:2-4 and presumably was carried to Corinth by Titus, before Timotheus, coming from Thessalonica, reached Paul (cf. *ibid.*, p. 105).

[247] [1], p. 225. Otherwise in [2], p. 62.

assume—on what grounds? [248]—that the mission of Timotheus and Erastus occurred *before* the composition of I Thess., in fact, before the trip of Timotheus to Thessalonica mentioned in I Thess. 3:2. But that cannot be.

W. Hadorn (pp. 79 ff.) very sensitively calls attention to the fact that Paul's inner frame of mind before the return of Timotheus from Thessalonica, which he describes in I Thess. 3:7 with the words "ἐπὶ πάσῃ τῇ ἀνάγκῃ καὶ θλίψει ἡμῶν," fits in well with his attitude after the interim visit (cf. II Cor. 6:4) and that, as we have already stated,[249] it was in fact Satan standing behind the false teachers in Corinth (II Cor. 11:13 ff.) who according to I Thess. 2:18 canceled the apostle's travel plans during his stay in Ephesus. To this one could add in detail the evidence that the degree of acquaintance with the Gnostic doctrines and charges which Paul betrays in "I Thess." corresponds approximately to that state of things one can demonstrate for this time on the basis of the Corinthian epistles. But I shall not, in conclusion, burden this study with such questions, which hardly could significantly amplify the weight of the foregoing argument.

Recently W. G. Kümmel has given, in my opinion, a proof—to be sure, an unintended one—for the composition of I Thess. during the so-called third missionary journey. He would like decidedly to hold to the early dating of the epistle, which is "thus undoubtedly the earliest epistle of Paul preserved for us" (p. 227). The arguments against this dating are only very incompletely given and are abruptly dismissed (see above, notes 222, 224). The only argument, then, for the early dating, which accordingly must support the "undoubtedly," is: "However, arguing decisively against the dating of I Thess. in a time which lies several years from Paul's founding visit is the fact that Paul's account of his connections with the community since his departure (2:17–3:8) clearly shows that Paul has now heard from the community for the first time through Timotheus, and up till then had not even known whether the community still existed at all (3:5)."

That this is "not even conceivable after an interval of several years"

---

[248] Cf. W. Michaelis, [2], p. 54. Here, without sufficient reasons, he identifies the sending of Timotheus and Erastus mentioned in Acts 19:22 with that of Timotheus mentioned in I Cor. 4:17; 16:10.

[249] Cf. above, n. 207.

is undoubtedly correct, but that according to 2:17–3:8 Paul has heard through Timotheus anything at all about the community at Thessalonica for the first time since its founding not only is nowhere indicated in the passage cited, but is even excluded, because according to 3:2-3 Paul had sent Timotheus to Thessalonica when he *had heard* of distresses in the community, in which Timotheus was to strengthen and comfort the Thessalonians. Besides, in I Thess. 1:7 ff. Paul says clearly how many different reports he had received about the Thessalonians *constantly*. In view of the good reports mentioned in this passage, the *fears* aroused in Paul in contrast to these must all the more go back to other and different concrete communications.

Moreover, it is hardly possible to interpret 3:5 in such a way as to say that Paul was in doubt whether the community still existed at all; for he sends Timotheus to the existing community, whose faith is known everywhere (1:7 ff.), that he might strengthen this community in its difficulties (3:2-3) and guard it against apostasy to the false teachers, which according to 3:5 Paul obviously feared. Nevertheless even if one assumes that in the sending of Timotheus Paul was afraid that the community had been *dissolved*, this only says something *against* the early dating of the epistle. For that in about a quarter of a year both growth and extended missionary activity of the community in Thessalonica, as it was described in 1:7 ff., as well as the total dissolution of the same community, as W. G. Kümmel sees it suspected in 3:5, could have taken place is even more inconceivable than the already impossible fitting into such a brief span of time of the happenings presupposed in 1:7 ff. alone. The suspected "dissolution" of the community can have happened at any later time, thus even during the so-called third missionary journey, but not in the first quarter-year after the founding of the community. All the more it *must* not have happened in this quarter-year.

But if this argument, which consequently is untenable in all its parts, speaks as apparently the only reason, in any case "decisively," for the view that I Thess. "undoubtedly" was composed during the so-called second missionary journey, then such justification is in fact a proof, to be sure an unwilling but still a decisive one, that the early dating of the epistle is untenable.

VI

The question as to the genuineness of II Thess. is answered in various ways, now as always. We can hardly expect a unanimous answer in the foreseeable future. But on one point there is a dominant unity among those who deny it and those who defend it. If it is authentic, the second epistle is to be placed in immediate proximity in time to the first epistle and thus in the same historical situation. In the following, we first leave completely aside the question of genuineness and test to see whether II Thess. is understandable in terms of that situation which "I Thess." discloses for the circumstances in Thessalonica. If this is not possible, then one must, to be consistent, abandon the authenticity of II Thess. If it is possible, it would still not be irrefutable proof, but a strong argument for the genuineness would be gained. I refrain from giving a complete list of the manifold parallels and similarities in the two epistles, since these can be explained equally well: if the epistle is genuine, from the fact that it comes from the same time; if it is not genuine, from the author's method of copying. However, there are of course exceptions: see below, pp. 216-17.

Of course first of all, surprising as it may be, the literary unity of II Thess. is to be called in question.[250] In this epistle is repeated what was observed in I Thess., that within its corpus are found the proem and the eschatocol of another epistle, an observation which indeed has not yet been made in this specific

---

[250] Later un-Pauline insertions in a genuine epistle of Paul already have often been excised in order to rescue the authenticity of II Thess.; cf. C. Clemen, pp. 13 ff. In this, II Thess. 2:1-12 esp. was suspected. Up to now, however, to my knowledge II Thess. has not been explained as a composite of epistles. It is true that B. Rigaux has already rightly observed that an epistolary conclusion is found before II Thess. 3:6, and thus 3:6-16 appears to be appended to an epistle: "Cette péricope porte la trace d' une addition. La lettre semble finir par le souhait de III 5, qui suit un τὸ λοιπόν (III 1), souvent annonciateur d' une fin de lettre" (Les Epîtres aux Thessaloniciens, p. 73; cf. idem, Paulus und seine Briefe [1964], pp. 154-55). II Thess. 3:11 provides Rigaux with the possibility of explaining, not unskillfully, this striking and important observation with the conjecture that after finishing and before sending the epistle, Paul had received more new reports from Thessalonica (p. 710). The eschatocol character of II Thess. 2:16 ff., moreover, has often been recognized earlier. Cf. e.g., W. Wrede, pp. 78 ff.: "In the light of all this we shall assume that he (scil., the pseudonymous author of II Thess.!) actually intended originally to come to the conclusion with 3:1 (or 2:16-17)" (p. 79). "The author abandoned the idea of concluding already; in 3:6-15 he allows still another exhortation to follow" (p. 80). Cf. also K. v. Hofmann, in loc.; H. J. Holtzmann, p. 103; idem, Einleitung (1886, 2nd ed.), p. 236, and (1892, 3rd ed.), pp. 212-13; J. T. Sanders, p. 359. This observation necessarily leads to the same judgment for the parallel epistolary conclusion in I Thess. 3:11 ff.

form, but nevertheless has repeatedly served to describe the similarity between I Thess. and II Thess.

The doublet to the proem is found in 2:13-14.[251] There can be no doubt of the proem character of this passage, as a comparison with II Thess. 1:3 ff. and I Thess. 1:2 ff. shows, and a comparison also with the other proems of Paul's epistles will show even more clearly. Most commentators rightly note that the ἡμεῖς δέ in 2:13 has no sensible connection with the preceding verses.

Just as clearly, in 2:16 there begins with the formula αὐτὸς δὲ ὁ κύριος which is customary here (see pp. 131-32) an epistolary conclusion, to which 2:15 recognizably forms the transition. Verses 2:16-17 contain the intercession which approximates a doxology. With the formula τὸ λοιπόν, which, as we have seen (pp. 132-33), with Paul is used exclusively to introduce the concluding paraenesis, the stereotyped concluding admonitions begin (3:1 ff.). They contain above all the request for specific intercession which, as we also have seen (p. 132), is found in Paul only in eschatocols. The following ἀσπασμός, as with all the conclusions of letters which now stand in the corpus of a letter, has been eliminated by the editor; it could not well remain. With it the concluding benediction also has been omitted (but see below, n. 259).

II Thess. 2:13–3:1 ff.[252] thus represents the framework of an independent epistle, with prescript and ἀσπασμός omitted. The corpus of this epistle has dropped out between 2:14 and 2:15. Why? Unquestionably the fact is unique, that the editor omits the corpus of the epistle, only to keep the framework. Was the content of the epistle so unimportant and the framework so important? Or was the content of the epistle of such a kind that its acceptance into the composite and collection of epistles was

---

[251] Cf. P. Schubert, pp. 29 ff.

[252] For a more precise analysis of 3:1-5, cf. n. 259. Whether and to what extent the beginning of 2:13 was editorially tampered with can no longer be determined with certainty. One might assume that 2:13 originally began like II Thess. 1:3. It then would suffice to excise the ἡμεῖς δέ as an editorial parenthesis. It has often been stated (cf. W. Wrede, p. 21) that these words yield no sense that is directly illuminating in the context. Then the editor would have proceeeded in the composing of II Thess. precisely as in the assembling of I Thess. In I Thess. also, as we have seen, the second proem is artificially connected with the preceding verses by means of an editorial parenthesis in 2:13.

forbidden? But then why was the framework kept? It contains
nothing that would be unique within the Corpus Paulinum.
Therefore the conjecture is not unreasonable that the corpus of
this epistle actually has not been lost at all, but has only been
displaced. But if this is the case, it can only have consisted of
2:1-12. The placing of the proem after the corpus of its epistle
is easy to explain: Without this relocation both proems would
have followed immediately one after the other, and besides,
2:13-14, with respect to contents, would have adjoined 1:11-12
only with a quite harsh effect.

A glance at 2:15 shows that the suggested rearrangement is no
more conjecture, but an unavoidable procedure. This verse is
the only part of the corpus of the letter originally bracketed by
2:13-14 and 2:16–3:1 ff. that has remained in its proper place.
The commentaries rightly state that vs. 15 follows the thanksgiving in vss. 13-14 without any visible transition. If II Thess.
is only a later imitation of I Thess., one need not be surprised at
this break in style. But actually the ἄρα οὖν follows 2:12 and
shows that 2:15 concludes the argument of the epistle, and indeed the argument of the *entire* epistle; for vs. 15 itself hardly
leaves any doubt of the original connection of 2:15 and 2:16,
the beginning of the eschatocol. Moreover, the στήκετε leads into
the conclusion of the epistle also in I Cor. 16:13 (= Cor. A)
and in Phil. 4:1 (Phil. C).

Now 2:15 clearly refers back, as to content, to 2:1-2, and that
with characteristic variation and correction of the sources of
information named there (see p. 209). But then vs. 2:15 contains the conclusion drawn from vss. 2:1-12, and vss. 2:13-14 break
the logical connection in an intolerable way. Since we now have
already recognized 2:13-14 as the proem of an epistle, the relocation of these verses before 2:1 becomes unavoidable.

Thus our canonical II Thess. contains two writings, namely
1:1-12+3:6 ff.[253] and 2:1–3:5 (= 2:13-14+2:1-12+2:15–3:1 ff.).

---

[253] On the vss. 3:17-18, however, cf. below, n. 259. Karl J. Bjerkelund (p. 138)
opposes this literary reconstruction with the argument that after the "thanksgiving" Paul could not begin with παραγγέλλω, which "is a very harsh concept."
I do not see this, especially since neither in Paul (cf. II Thess. 3:4, 10, 12) nor
elsewhere in the New Testament does παραγγέλλω give the impression of any
special harshness.

As in I Thess., the one epistle is simple inserted into the other—which is the essential reason for the striking literary kinship of the two epistles—only that the inserted epistle for obvious reasons was rearranged as indicated. The proposal made here is, in my opinion, the only one suited for solving the literary problem of II Thess., namely the incontestable presence within the epistle of the framework of a second epistle. The solution offered will be verified and confirmed in the following exposition.

VII

The peculiar literary, stylistic, and theological character of the first chapter of II Thess. is abundantly described and discussed by the commentaries and introductions. Even more quickly than in the first epistle, the expression of thanks gains its concrete background in the peculiar situation in Thessalonica, only that now Paul does not come to speak in an apologetic tendency of his missionary activity in Thessalonica, but of the διωγμοί and θλίψεις of the Thessalonians. He refers explicitly to *all* persecutions; the occasion for mentioning them in this passage, however, can be sought only in the *present* sufferings, which are attested by the present tense in "ἀνέχεσθε" and "πάσχετε." The sufferings meant here can only be the "θλίψεις" which are also variously alluded to in I Thess. 2:14–3:7 ff. We learn nothing new in II Thess. 1 about these persecutions, whose connection with the appearance of the Gnostics we surmised (see pp. 176 ff.). Paul's primary interest in the composition of the second epistle does not concern them and the distresses which have arisen in Thessalonica because of them, although the statements in the first chapter almost altogether have the διωγμοί and θλίψεις as their background.

Paul writes the epistle out of anxiety over the threat to the community that comes from *within*, as we shall see presently. The occasion for the epistle is not praise or comfort, but admonition. It is understandable that Paul is anxious to offer such admonition only cautiously in the case of the community whom he had seen only during his founding visit and not again for years. For this purpose the theme of θλῖψις is well suited, for with it Paul can express to the community his heartfelt concern about their fate and thus gain a receptive ear for his apostolic admonitions. In similar fashion, the concern for the distresses in persecution of the Thessalonians in the "joyful epistle" to Thessalonica also serves after the event to take away anything that is offensive about the sending of Timotheus, although he had been sent in essence because of Paul's anxiety—apparently only partially justified—about the obedience of the Thessalonians to their apostle (see pp. 176 ff.).

Further, the praise and thanksgiving for the state of the Thessalonians' faith in II Thess. 1:3 ff. serves, just as it does in I Thess. 1:2 ff., obviously as preparation for the coming admonitions. Of course the detailed character of these preparations in 1:3-12 is striking. In I Thess. 1:2 ff. Paul comes much more quickly to the actual object of the epistle, as then the proem of II Thess. already distinguishes itself by its length from the proems of all the other epistles of Paul. This would be understandable if the epistle beginning in II Thess. 1:1 ff. were the first contact by letter between Paul and the Thessalonians, either at all or in the admonitions which form the subject of the following correspondence.

Strange also is the formal style of the proem in II Thess. 1:3-12. Verses 3-10 form a single sentence, an unusual construction for the genuine epistles of Paul. Some have wanted to see in this an indication of the inauthenticity of the epistle, and it is to be conceded in any case that the unique style in 1:3-12, which reveals a certain lack of familiarity between sender and addressee, can easily be explained if the epistle is not genuine. But it seems to me that we have just as good an explanation if one may regard the epistle which begins in II Thess. 1:1 as a first renewal of contact between Paul and the community at Thessalonica which had been separated from him for years.

A further problem is the extended reference to the Parousia in 1:7 ff. It is not explained, if one wants to see a problem in it at all, by saying that a Christian of the second or third generation proposes to reassure the communities because of the postponement of the Parousia. For the verses indeed attest precisely the imminent expectation of the Parousia at the time of Paul, and thus the very expectation which poses the problem of the delay in the Parousia for the following generations. But they do not solve this problem. On the other hand, the heightening of the hope of the Parousia becomes understandable against that background which we have also demonstrated for I Thess. 5:1-11: the Gnostic denial of the expectation of the Parousia at all. The fact that Paul does not explicate this problem in II Thess. 1:7 ff. as he does in I Thess. 5:1-11, but only appeals to the expectation of the Thessalonians, ὅτι ἐπιστεύθη τὸ μαρτύριον ἡμῶν ἐφ' ὑμᾶς (1: 10), again would be well explained if the epistle beginning in II Thess. 1:1 ff. comes before the one to which I Thess. 5:1-11 belongs; for in the former epistle Paul still is not discussing doctrinal questions at all but is only appealing to the Thessalonians, a procedure which apparently later appears to him inadequate. The writing to Thessalonica comprising I Thess. 1:1– 2:12 + 4:2–5:28 is dominated by argumentative discussion.

But what does the appeal say which Paul so abundantly prepares in II Thess. 1:1-12? We have seen that 3:6 follows just after 1:12. Then the admonishing appeal reads thus: "But we exhort you, brethren, in the name of the Lord Jesus Christ, that you keep away from any brother who walks disorderly and not according to the tradition which you have received from us" (3:6). The Thessalonians are to separate themselves from the disorderly brethren, the ἄτακτοι, who are also called this in I Thess. 5:14 and are briefly described in I Thess. 4:9 ff.

The treatment of this question in II Thess. 3:6-15 is more detailed than in the first epistle. It is beyond question, and is not seriously questioned by the exegetes, that the same group within the community is in mind in both cases, whether "II Thess." is genuine or not. Thus we can here reexamine our exegesis of I Thess. 4:9 ff.

In the second epistle also, it cannot be ordinary idleness against which Paul is taking a stand, for the ἄτακτοι are not yet adequately characterized with the "μηδὲν ἐργαζομένους," but are precisely described only by "περιεργαζομένους," in other words, as those who "do something unnecessary or useless" (W. Bauer, [2]). Moreover, they are not only urged to keep at their work, but (as in I Thess. 4:11) are also admonished to ἡσυχία. Further, the threat of church discipline would be, in the same form in

197

which it applies in I Cor. 5:9 ff. to adulterers, idol worshipers, etc., unnecessarily severe in the case of ordinary idleness: μὴ συναναμίγνυσθαι αὐτοῖς.[254]

Hence the passage II Thess. 3:6 ff. also is motivated by religious fanaticism (already known from I Thess.) which led to the abandonment of everyday labor. On this, unanimity prevails among the exegetes to a large extent.

Of course we learn nothing concrete from Paul's argument about the religious background of this fanaticism. It is to be deduced from the context. Anyone who in II Thess. 2 and in I Thess. 5:1 ff. sees a refutation of exaggerated speculations about the imminent end, consequently speaks of apocalyptic excitement. But we have already seen, and shall see still better, that people in Thessalonica by no means regarded the day of the Lord as immediately imminent. Even Paul himself apparently does not see the fanaticism of the "περιεργαζόμενοι" as grounded in exaggerated expectation of the end. Otherwise he would have had to make clear why in spite of the immediately imminent end one must still labor, or he would have had to point out the error of such expectation. Instead of this, he recalls his conduct of many years earlier, which however could naturally be no longer normative for the last days of the world, which people allegedly see dawning in Thessalonica.

Most suggestive is the reference to the example Paul gave during his stay in Thessalonica, which calls to order members of the community with a missionary activity similar to Paul's. The disorderliness of their activity consists in the fact that in their missionary busyness they neglect their existence in this world, thereby give a poor example to those "without" (I Thess. 4:12), and can easily acquire the bad name of a visionary or a charlatan.[255]

We have already seen, in our study of the first epistle, that such fanaticism is attested for the Gnostics of the Pastoral

---

[254] W. Lütgert, [2], p. 89.

[255] I Cor. 14:40 (cf. 14:33) also affords a certain parallel: "Let everything be done decently and in order." With this principle Paul takes a stand against the disturbance introduced into the congregation's worship by the Gnostic pneumatics as a particular case of the disorders evoked by the pneumatic ἄτακτοι. Cf. also C. Spicq, "Les Thessaloniciens 'inquiets' étaient-ils des paresseux?" (*Studia Theologica* X [1957]: 13).

Epistles.[256] It is also characteristic of the circles of "inspired peo-ple" of all periods of church history, here naturally often con-nected with apocalyptic speculations. As an illustration of this, I would like to cite a section from a presbytery protocol [257] of my home, in which the "inspired ones," who "have Jesus in the heart" (cf. II Cor. 13:3), are described as "secretly holding ex-ercises, departing from the Reformed religion, harboring errors, and speaking with contempt of the holy seal of the covenant (= the Supper). . . . Besides, they are very negligent of their business at home and through tribute paid to . . . (the Prophet) . . . and his kind seriously weaken their own resources, . . . give occasion to general nuisance, and strive to lead others astray." This parallel to the conditions in Thessalonica (and Corinth, the Pastoral Epistles, etc.), as unintentional and accidental as it is striking, speaks for itself.

One may also read, for example, the portrayal in Iren. I, 13 ff. of the missionary activity of the Gnostic Marcus and his pupils, who let themselves be supported by their hearers, or of the activ-ity of the Gnostic prophets in Orig. Cels. VII, 8-9, in either case, though, without the polemical slant of the reporters. Anyone who has to proclaim διὰ πνεύματος that the day of the Lord is al-ready here, that the kingdom of God represents an inner pos-session of man, and that Gnosis means the resurrection—him one will have to imagine in Thessalonica in that fanatical busyness against which Paul sets himself in II Thess. 3:6 ff.

Apparently Paul hopes to be able to render ineffective the poison of the new doctrine disseminated by the περιεργαζόμενοι, by forbidding the community to associate with these people who so completely fail to walk according to his example. In case any-one in the community is not ready to heed his admonition, he is to be excommunicated. The brief epistle reaches its climax in this demand: "If any one refuses to obey what we say in this letter, note that man, and have nothing to do with him" (vs. 14). μὴ συναναμίγνυσθαι in Paul's writings is a *terminus technicus* for the renunciation of church fellowship, as I Cor. 5:9, 11 shows (cf. W. Hadorn, *Die Abfassung der Thessalonicherbriefe*, pp. 123-24).

---

[256] In that connection, "περίεργοι" occurs in I Tim. 5:13.

[257] *Circa* 1770; reproduced in G. Hinsberg, *Sayn-Wittgenstein-Berleburg*, Band IV (Berleburg, 1925), privately printed.

That such an excommunication is to take place in the hope that the one expelled from the fellowship, ashamed, might repent (vss. 14b-15) does not undo the excommunication as such. Thus Paul hopes to be able to guard the community against apostasy and against infiltration by the poison of the false doctrine, by decreeing, without further discussion, that people should keep away from the heretics and their following and should withhold the church's fellowship from members of the community who do not obey this demand. Cf. Titus 3:10-11.

This presupposes either that Paul is not adequately informed to be able to argue in the presence of the community in view of the new situation, or that he regards the community as not yet seriously infected, in which case this latter judgment could, in consequence of scanty information, be based on an error. In any other case he would have had to name the false doctrines and to identify them as such. This he does not do, not *yet,* for in I Thess. 1:1–2:12 + 4:2–5:28 the picture has changed. Here Paul sets himself against the fruits which the seed sown by the ἄτακτοι in the community in spite of the apostle's warning to keep away from the evil brethren apparently is to bring to mind. It is clear: II Thess. 1:1-12 + 3:6-18 belong before I Thess. 1:1–2:12 + 4:2–5:28. It is impossible to reverse this relationship.

In this connection I should cite some noteworthy sentences from W. Hadorn (pp. 117, 123-24) which are meant to establish the priority of II Thess. over I Thess.: "The disorders appear in II Thess. 3:11 as something new, of which Paul has just heard. He appeals to his repeated earlier exhortations (imperfect tense) when they were with them, not to an epistle (II Thess. 3:10). On the other hand, in I Thess. 5:14 those who are unsettled are treated as already mentioned. The corresponding admonition in I Thess. 4:10, 12 is so brief that we understand it only because we are acquainted with II Thess. 3. The author of I Thess. appeals to a quite definite command (παρηγγείλαμεν, aorist, 4:11), which can easily be connected with an earlier epistle." Thus W. Hadorn. His comments, seen as a whole, appear to me convincing, indeed not for the priority of II Thess. over I Thess. simply, but for II Thess. 3:6-16 over I Thess. 4:2–5:28. Arguing for this also is the indefinite "by letter" in II Thess. 3:14, which refers to the letter in hand and makes it appear less probable that other epistles to Thessalonica had already preceded it. Arguing for it finally is the source of information which Paul indicates in the early epistle: "For we *hear* that some among you are walking disorderly, not working, but doing useless things" (3:11). Paul scrupulously says that his information is based on rumors. But these appear to him dependable enough to base his appeal on them. They apparently do not justify more, presumably because they are too scanty. For it is just this that the ἀκούομεν intends to express: I have *only* heard, as it is said explicitly in Gal. 1:23: μόνον δὲ ἀκούοντες. Also in the first epistle (A) to Corinth this ἀκούω occurs (I Cor. 11:18; see Vol. 1, p. 91), and likewise in the first epistle to Philippi which makes reference to the false teachers (B: Phil. 1:27; see p. 69). The scantiness of the information upon which Paul can base his respective first anti-Gnostic writings to Corinth and Philippi has been indicated in the places named.

These parallels may assure the sufficiently presented particular character of the epistle II Thess. 1:1-12 + 3:6-16: It involves that writing with which Paul reacts to the first reports to reach him about the appearance of the false teachers in Thessalonica.

The close of the epistle now in hand does not exactly follow the scheme described above on pp. 129 ff. It is true that it begins in 3:16 with αὐτὸς δὲ ὁ κύριος, precisely as in I Thess. 3:11; 5:23, and II Thess. 2:16. Thus the beginning is the same in all four epistles to Thessalonica.[258] Still, vs. 16*b* may be the concluding benediction, with whose brief form Rom. 15:33 is to be compared. But then vs. 18 is a doublet. In any case the concluding paraenesis is completely absent from its usual place. But above all, vs. 17, because of its contents, does not fit the end of the first epistle to Thessalonica: "I, Paul, am writing the greeting with my own hand, which is a mark in every one of my letters; this is the way I write." This verse is inconceivable without a specific occasion for it. The first epistle, which we have discussed, does not

---

[258] It is noteworthy that nowhere else in Paul does the same formula word for word introduce an epistolary conclusion, let alone a theme. Did Paul have in hand copies of the previous epistles when he was composing a new one? In any case this observation leaves no doubt that the two canonical Thessalonian epistles contain four original epistolary endings.

let us recognize such an occasion, but rather leads us to expect genuine greetings. Yet vs. 17 fits splendidly the end of that other writing to Thessalonica which II Thess. contains. This will presently be shown. Then the one epistle breaks off with 3:16, and the editor has replaced the broken-off conclusion with the ἀσπασμός and the benediction of the other epistle (3:17-18).[259] Accordingly, the other epistle, which is now to be investigated, contains 2:1–3:5, 17-18.

VIII

The proem of this epistle is found in 2:13-14. This is followed, as we have seen, by the corpus of the epistle, 2:1-12: "Now concerning the coming of our Lord Jesus Christ and our assembling to meet him, we beg you, brethren, not to be quickly shaken in mind or excited, either by spirit or by word, or by letter purporting to be from us, to the effect that the day of the Lord has come" (RSV). "The epistle was written probably for the sake of this passage." [260] In Thessalonica a false doctrine with respect to Christ's Parousia is being proclaimed. It is not ruled out from the outset that such views arose within the Pauline community. It is a more likely procedure, however, to reckon with alien influences. This is particularly true when one considers the peculiar content of this false doctrine.

The assertion contested by Paul undoubtedly has the meaning that the day of the Lord has already come.[261] "By no means 'is imminently at hand'; ἐνέστηκεν does not mean this." [262] "ἐνίστημι" means rather "to be present" and stands in explicit contrast to

---

[259] Did 3:4-5 first get its present place in this rearrangement? The eschatocol appears in 2:16–3:5 obviously overdone. The concluding greetings now contained in 3:17-18 could originally have followed after 3:3, while 3:4-5 find a good place after 3:16a. Verse 3:4 then would form the concluding admonition of the first epistle to Thessalonica which we have just noticed was missing. This admonition fits in well as the conclusion of an epistle which as its primary contents contains the demand that the community separate itself from the ἄτακτοι (cf. 3:6!), while it now ends an epistle which contains not so much admonition as instruction (see below). Thus the editor may have undertaken a simple rearrangement and exchanged places between 3:4-5 and 3:17-18. Still this question, which can hardly be decided with certainty, is without any great significance.

[260] A. Oepke, p. 152.

[261] Cf. B. Reicke, [1], p. 44.

[262] G. Wohlenberg, p. 144; cf. T. Zahn, [1], I: 235.

"μέλλειν": Rom. 8:38; I Cor. 3:22; Gal. 1:4.[263] "But the day of
the Lord has come' taken literally simply does not fit into the
situation of the readers. . . . That the day of the Lord in the
actual sense of the day of judgment and redemption has already
arrived cannot possibly have been the opinion of the Christians
languishing in grave tribulation." [264] Indeed! But one may not
draw from this fact the conclusion that therefore the ἐνέστηκεν
must mean "The day of the Lord is already about to arrive," as
it is customarily given by the exegetes in one variation or another.[265] We must rather seek for a meaning of the assertion, which
at first appears so meaningless, that the day of the Lord has already come.

This has been done long ago, and after already F. C. Baur[266]
and A. Hilgenfeld [267] attempted to interpret II Thess. 2:1-12 in
terms of an anti-Gnostic battlefront, Bahnsen[268] carried this interpretation through in a consistent fashion and, in the assertion
that the day of the Lord had come, recognized the Gnostic reinterpretation of the church's eschatology. That this interpretation is possible is not disputed by the later exegetes. It is the only
one that allows us to hold the plain wording of the "ἐνέστηκεν."

Such a reinterpretation of the church's conceptions of the end-
time was undertaken by Gnosticism, particularly with the doctrine
of the resurrection. The most obvious and best-known documentation of this is II Tim. 2:18: "ἀνάστασιν ἤδη γεγονέναι." With this
one may compare Iren. I, 23.5: "In other words, through his

---

[263] Occasionally "ἐνίστημι" also means "to be imminent." But in our passage, as
W. Bauer ([2]) correctly sees, the meaning of "to be imminent" by no means
comes into consideration; for the assertion that the day of the Lord is imminent
is a truism and is never a ground for criticism by Paul. Moreover, the two New
Testament passages cited by W. Bauer for "ἐνίστημι"="to be imminent" are
not relevant: in I Cor. 7:26 Paul is speaking of the *present* distress, and the future
tense in II Tim. 3:1 presupposes that the present tense means precisely "to be
present." The obscure passage in Barn. 17.2 also hardly belongs here.

[264] E. v. Dobschütz, [1], p. 267.

[265] Cf. most recently C. Masson, *in loc.*

[266] ThJ, 1855, pp. 141-68. T. Zahn ([1], p. 235) has recourse to the explanation that the day of the Lord that has come "of course is not conceived as
a day of twelve or twenty-four hours, but as an epoch during which one has
to expect the visible return of Christ at any moment—so to speak, hourly." But
the time in which one *awaits* the coming of the Lord is simply not, and nowhere,
the "day of the Lord."

[267] ZwTh, 1862, pp. 242-64.

[268] JpTh, 1880, pp. 681-705.

(Menander's) baptism his pupils receive the resurrection, thenceforward cannot die . . . ." Iren. III, 31.2: "The resurrection of the dead however is the knowledge of what they call the truth." Tert., de resurr. 19: "Woe to him who while he is in the flesh does not know the heretical secrets: for that is what they mean by the resurrection." Plotinus, Enn. III, 6.6.69 ff.: ". . . ἀπὸ σώματος, οὐ μετὰ σώματος, ἀνάστασις."

The assertion that the resurrection has already occurred through the reception of Gnosis radically eliminates the church's conceptions of the future. A "day of the Lord" as future is no longer conceivable.

Terminologically speaking, the assertion refuted by Paul in II Thess. 2:2 is very closely approximated by passages from the Gospel of John like John 5:24-25 and 11:25: "He who hears my word and believes him who sent me, has eternal life; he does not come into judgment, but has passed from death to life. Truly, truly, I say to you, the hour is coming, and *now is,* when the dead will hear the voice of the Son of God, and those who hear will live" (RSV). It does not matter whether John here appropriates a Gnostic source writing or is speaking in the Gnostic language of his environment: the underlying conception—which John to be sure "radically historicizes" [269]—is genuinely Gnostic and is the same one which is expressed in the assertion that the day of the Lord has already come.

The most exact parallel from Gnosticism which has come to my attention is afforded now by Saying 52 of the Coptic Gospel of Thomas (cf. Leipoldt-Schenke, p. 18): "His disciples said to him, 'When will the rest of the dead begin? and when will the new world come?' He said to them, 'The one which you await, *it has come;* but you do not recognize it.'" Cf. Saying 111: "His disciples said to him: 'When will the kingdom come?' (Jesus said): 'It will not come as one expects (it). They will not say, "Lo, (now it is) here or lo, (now it is) there." But the kingdom of the Father has spread over the world, and men do not see it.'" Thus the kingdom is already present. Interesting also is the Manichaean eschatology according to the portrayal of Sahrastani (Haarbrücker, pp. 191-92): "All the parts of the light unceasingly

----

[269] R. Bultmann, *The Gospel of John* (ET, 1971), p. 259, n. 2.

ascend and are raised into the heights, and the parts of darkness unceasingly descend and sink into the depths, until these parts are freed from those and the mixing is frustrated and the combinations are dissolved and each part attains to its whole and to its world. *And this is the resurrection and the parousia.*" [270]

Bahnsen's interpretation of II Thess. 2:2 has found little acceptance, even when people have had to admit that it is the only one that does justice to the natural understanding of the "ἐνέστηκεν." In the acceptance of this interpretation one had to give up the authenticity of II Thess., so long as one still regarded the Gnosticism as a post-Pauline product of the decay of Christianity; this fact may have contributed to the lack of acceptance of Bahnsen's interpretation. Today *this* inference is superfluous. Paul must constantly debate with Gnostics who reject the church's eschatology, deny the resurrection, boast of their perfection, and reckon on no Parousia. This holds true for the situation in Corinth,[271] Galatia,[272] and Philippi,[273] and equally so for the epistle to Thessalonica discussed above on pp. 135 ff., as we saw in the examination of it. The doubt as to resurrection and Parousia, against which Paul takes a stand in that epistle, and the assertion that the day of the Lord has already come, which he refutes in the epistle now under discussion, are identical. P. W. Schmiedel is correct when he says: "Since the Parousia had not occurred, no one could think that the day of the Lord had already come unless he interpreted it spiritually as a Gnostic." [274] Precisely this happened in Thessalonica.[275]

In harmony with this interpretation is the fact that this false teaching comes about διὰ πνεύματος, διὰ λόγου, and δι' ἐπιστολῆς ὡς δι' ἡμῶν.[276] There is dispute as to what the "ὡς δι' ἡμῶν" refers

---

[270] Cf. also in the Codex Brucianus (ed. C. Schmidt-W. Till, p. 306.40 ff.) : "And I say to you that they, since they have been on the earth, have already inherited the kingdom of God; they share in the light-treasure and are immortal gods." For other passages, see above, p. 166, n. 157.

[271] Vol. 1, pp. 155 ff., 179 ff., 259 ff.

[272] See above, pp. 47 ff.

[273] See above, pp. 92 ff., 95 ff.

[274] P. W. Schmiedel, p. 37.

[275] Thus also R. Schippers, *Mythologie en Eschatologie in 2. Thessalonicenzen 2, 1-17* (Assen, 1961) , pp. 7 ff.

[276] Cf. K. Stürmer, p. 49.

to. Along with most, I would prefer to relate it only to "δι' ἐπιστολῆς," but this question is not of decisive importance.

The false teachers first appeal to the Pneuma. The exegetes with great unanimity understand by this the immediate utterance of the divine Spirit through the Christian prophets. In I Cor. 14 Paul himself portrays the practice of the προφητεύειν which he too treasures and prefers to the speaking in tongues. I am convinced that this προφητεύειν, like the ecstatic speaking in tongues also, is a Gnostic inheritance of the Pauline missionary practice. It is unnecessary, however, more precisely to justify this judgment here. For it is certain anyway that the Gnostic opponents of Paul in Thessalonica as well as in Corinth, Galatia, and Philippi boasted of their possession of the Spirit with great emphasis and in an anti-Pauline tendency. For Corinth one may compare passages such as I Cor. 7:40; 12–14; 15:46; II Cor. 11:4; 12:1-10, 11-13; for Galatia, Gal. 3:2; 5:25; 6:1;[277] for Thessalonica, I Thess. 5:19-22 and the explanation of that passage already given on pp. 172 ff. With the appeal to revelations of the Spirit the Gnostics play their weightiest authority.

Along with this, they proclaim their false doctrine διὰ λόγου, that is, by means of sober discourse, perhaps exposition of Scripture, perhaps rational persuasive argument. Even Gnosticism never renounced the "word."

But finally, they also appeal to a purported letter of Paul, and Paul himself is at a loss how to explain such an appeal. It is incredible that his opponents would have circulated forged epistles of the apostle. Such a procedure could not have succeeded during the apostle's lifetime, and it is inconceivable that one would have taken such pains to gain for one's own argument the authority of the so sharply contested apostle. The only comprehensible explanation is that, referring to actual letters of the apostle, people were saying: See, in principle, on this question Paul cannot say anything other than what we say; or: If you only draw the correct implications from Paul's proclamation, then you will recognize that we are right. That Paul's opponents or, as is more likely, the members of the community who had gone over from him to the new teachers argued thus appears to me obvious from the fact

---

[277] On this, see above, pp. 46 ff.

that they occasionally provided glosses to the epistles of Paul in their own interpretation.[278] Also, E. v. Dobschütz ([1], p. 268) has already recognized that the Gnostic conception of the present character of the day of the Lord could be connected with Pauline expressions such as Rom. 6:4 ff.; II Cor. 5:17; Gal. 3:26, *et al.* Von Dobschütz even refers to I Thess. 5:5! In all these passages Paul speaks in gnosticizing terminology. Even without our attempting to determine whether a passage from Paul's letters which we have was used by the Gnostics in Thessalonica, and which passage, we can say that the use of Paul's epistolary utterances in the sense described above is completely understandable among people who proclaim through Spirit and word that the day of the Lord has already come. We know to what extent later Gnosticism on behalf of its teaching laid claim not only upon Paul but even upon the Synoptics.

Within the discussion in the community at Thessalonica, the appeal of the schismatics to I Thess. 5:5, as E. v. Dobschütz already recognized,[279] is most clearly suggested: "For you are all sons of light and sons of the *day;* we are not of the night nor of the darkness," as then also vss. 6-8 can be interpreted as a precise representation of the Gnostic certainty of salvation, although they are intended to be directed precisely against the "already now."

In view of the sensational new message Paul warns the community "not to be quickly shaken in mind or excited" (RSV).

The Christians are not to lose their composure and become agitated.[280] This may be a conscious reference to the ἄτακτοι of the other epistles.

Paul describes the Gnostic assertion as a deception (vs. 3) and refutes it by pointing out that the omens of the end in fact are not yet present. Thus all the more the end itself cannot yet be here. Indeed the mystery of lawlessness is already at work, but the lawless one himself, whom the returning Christ will destroy, is still concealed. One can see that Paul has not recognized the "spiritualistic" background of the Gnostic assertion that the day of the Lord has already come. One should not be surprised at this

---

[278] Cf. Vol. 1, pp. 302 ff.; see also above, p. 40, on Gal. 5:11.

[279] Thus also W. Wrede, pp. 46-47, 67, to be sure with the presupposition that II Thess. is not authentic.

[280] "θροεῖσθαι" can have both meanings. A decision is difficult.

in the apostle who at about the same time concludes from the denial of the resurrection of the Corinthian false teachers that they are radical skeptics! Above all, one may not infer from Paul's argument in 2:3-12 that with the assertion of vs. 2 his opponents could not have undertaken a reinterpretation of the expectation of the Parousia *because* Paul goes into it in such an "apocalyptic" manner.

We can pass over the apocalyptic passage 2:3-12.[281] Whatever of truth in content may be concealed in the conjectures of Baur, Hilgenfeld, Bahnsen, Pfleiderer, Lütgert, and others, that behind the ἀνομία and the ἄνομος stands the Gnostic heresy with its libertinism, for the situation in Thessalonica it yields no information. For the apostle does not indicate that his acquaintance with the already active mystery of lawlessness was communicated to him precisely in Thessalonica.[282]

Verse 15 is immediately connected with the somber prospect of the judgment in vs. 12, and it sums up the entire body of the letter and leads to its conclusion: "So now, brethren, stand firm and hold to the traditions which you have been taught, whether by word or by letter from us." Since the preceding theme of the epistle was eschatology, we are to understand the παραδόσεις *in concreto* to consist principally of the eschatological doctrinal traditions which were handed on by Paul to the Thessalonians either orally or by letter. "διὰ λόγου" refers to the missionary preaching; "δι' ἐπιστολῆς" can mean the present epistle as also an earlier one; it apparently is intentionally stated indefinitely.

Also when Paul elsewhere urges the holding fast to the παραδόσεις, this is always in an anti-Gnostic front. In I Cor. 11:2, praise for the maintaining of the tradition is given in view of the Gnostic agitation. This praise of course is expressly limited in 11:17, 23: Over against the disruptive practice of the Supper by his opponents, Paul must call back to memory the words of in-

---

[281] The assertion of K. G. Eckart, pp. 30-31, that this passage is "decidedly anti-Pauline in its contents," is not proved by Eckart himself and, in this form, is undoubtedly unfounded.

[282] Only a good observation of K. Stürmer (p. 49) should be related, since it warns against any anti*Judaistic* understanding of II Thess.: "Especially significant is the characterizing of the antichrist as ἄνθρωπος τῆς ἀνομίας: it is not in the nomists but in the antinomians that Paul sees the chief danger for the community."

stitution *that have been handed down*.[283] In I Cor. 15:1 ff., in view
of the Gnostics' denial of the resurrection, the community is reminded of the Easter *tradition* of the primitive community. We
know that the apostolic tradition, fixed in canon and symbol and
guaranteed by office, became the church's chief weapon against
pneumatic Gnosticism. Even in II Thess. 2:15 we see how Paul
already employs this weapon on the same battlefront.

The same is true of the group of concepts "διδάσκειν, διδαχή,"
etc., which increasingly acquired technical import in the church's
anti-Gnostic struggle. I have dealt with this in another place,[284]
and here I only point out that this language usage in Paul also already is paving the way within his anti-Gnostic polemic: I Cor.
4:17; (Rom. 6:17-18) ; Rom. 16:17. II Thess. 2:15 fits well into
this picture. Paul never refers to the traditional doctrine in any
context other than the anti-Gnostic battlefront.

Because people in Thessalonica are to hold fast to *the* traditions which they have received by word of mouth or in writing
by Paul's letter, in the command in 2:15 at the end of the argument, obviously a correction is distinctively made in the sources,
mentioned at the beginning of the argument in 2:2, of the doctrines being disseminated in Thessalonica. The source "διὰ
πνεύματος" is completely muted. Apparently the said matter of
the Spirit has not been sufficiently tested by the Thessalonians.
(It is not to be assumed that Paul writes I Thess. 5:19-20 *after*
this correction. But then II Thess. 2:1–3:3 (5), 17-18 comes later
than the epistle to which I Thess. 5:19-20 belongs.[285]) People
still should heed the "word," but according to 2:15 it must be
Paul's word: διὰ λόγου . . . ἡμῶν. Of course the apostle's letters also
continue to be binding—if they actually are *his* letters: δι'
ἐπιστολῆς ἡμῶν and not ὡς δι' ἡμῶν (2:2) .

Paul apparently is not clear as to how epistles from him served
to support the assertion that the day of the Lord has already come.
Since he had never made such an assertion, he had to assume that
people in Thessalonica were working with forgeries. Hence in
2:2 he chooses the indefinite expression "ὡς δι' ἡμῶν." But for

---

[283] Cf. Vol. 1, pp. 250 ff.
[284] Cf. below, pp. 226 ff.
[285] Cf. also R. Schippers, p. 9.

this reason also he closes his epistle in the context of the usual eschatocol in 2:16–3:3 (or 3:5) + 3:17-18 with the statement which in this connection is well explained and utterly unsuspected, and indeed even necessary: "I, Paul, am writing the greeting with my own hand, which is a mark in every one of my letters; this is the way I write" (3:17).

The assertion that the day of the Lord has already come could hardly be supported in Thessalonica by any letter of Paul other than one addressed to Thessalonica. Of the letters to Thessalonica known to us the first one offers no occasion for such a misinterpretation, but indeed, as we have seen, that letter containing I Thess. 5:1 ff. does. Hence we have confirmation of the conjecture just expressed, that the letter II Thess. 2:1–3:3 (or 5) + 3:17-18 is later than the one to which I Thess. 5:1 ff. belongs (see below).

It is not least of all the passage II Thess. 2:1-12 which has served and still serves to establish the inauthenticity of "II Thess." This is hardly correct. It has often been said that the treatment of the eschatological problematic significantly shifts between I Thess. and II Thess. Nevertheless, in the first epistle Paul found it necessary to take a stand against the denial of the resurrection and against the indifference with respect to the Parousia. In the second epistle we learn specifically of the background of such a heretical attitude: the day of the Lord has already come. Thus there can be no question of a shift in the handling of the eschatological theme. The situation of "II Thess." coincides precisely with that of "I Thess."

Of course it is conceivable that an ecclesiastical Christian around the turn of the century wanted to take a stand decisively under Paul's authority against the eschatological heresy of the Gnostics of his time and to this end composed II Thess. 2:1-12. But in such a forger it would simply be incomprehensible if he had taken the assertion that the day of the Lord has already come in the literal sense of the church, as the author of II Thess. does. That writer of the third generation would have known that this assertion was meant "spiritually" and therefore would not have been able to counter it with apocalyptic speculations about the still-lacking signs of the approaching end. The argument in II

Thess. 2:1-12 is conceivable only as unreflective reaction to an only half-understood report: this is the situation of Paul, which later is no longer conceivable in this form.[286]

I know that some will object that the matter would be significantly different if one reads in 2:2: "The day of the Lord is immediately imminent," and then has pseudo-Paul criticizing the expectation of the early end. But this is simply not what it says. And even if it did, the point of the forgery would still be a riddle. For II Thess. 2:3 ff.—as distinguished from II Peter—is by no means directed against a disappointed *imminent* expectation of the end. Of course the end has not yet come, for the man of lawlessness has not yet appeared. But the mystery of lawlessness is already at work; there yet remains only the κατέχων to be moved out of the way, and then the lawless one, whom the Lord will destroy, will be revealed. In II Thess. 2:3 ff., Paul sets himself against the assertion that the end has *already* come, but from vs. 6 onward, he is also parrying a possible misunderstanding of such a conclusion, to the effect that the day of the Lord is still far off; it is not yet here, but it stands at the doors.[287] This is the expression in 2:3 ff. which to that extent is completely in harmony with I Thess. 5:1 ff. With such words, in which Paul's imminent expectation cannot be overlooked, no forger is calming the second or even third generation,[288] concerned about the delay of the Parousia,[289] who, precisely as we do today, were obliged to give

---

[286] On this consideration the historical interpretation of II Thess. by W. Marxsen, *Introduction to the New Testament* (1969), pp. 38 ff., runs aground. He very properly recognizes the anti-Gnostic front of II Thess.—hence I refer with emphasis to his statements—which, however, he holds to be post-Pauline. For he overlooks the fact that in the second generation one cannot wage a polemic against the Gnostic assertion that the day of the Lord has already come with an "apocalyptic timetable" "which enumerates the events which are yet to occur before the end, in order to prove that the alleged consummation by no means could have already occurred"; for with this the Gnostic meaning is not touched at all, let alone refuted. This kind of apocalyptic argument against the Gnostic reinterpretation of the church's eschatology is possible only on the basis of a misunderstanding.

[287] Only from a biased perspective can one read from II Thess. 2:3 ff. "that the tendency to postponement of the Parousia passes into uncertainty" (P. W. Schmiedel, p. 9).

[288] A. Jülicher, p. 53.

[289] That this pseudo-Paul in the third generation wishes to refute an intense fanatical immediate expectation (cf. also H. Conzelmann in *Neutestamentliche Studien für R. Bultmann* [1954], p. 194, n. 1; A. Loisy; C. Masson) is moreover

a negative answer to the question whether a period of some generations could have been intended in 2:6-7. And that this pseudo-Paul had taken the ingenious pains so authentically to reconstruct the situation of II Thess. only for the purpose of getting rid of a couple of interesting apocalyptic pet ideas—one can regard this as motive for the forgery only if this forgery were established on other grounds.

IX

It is in order now briefly to summarize the outcome, which is of interest for the problems of introduction, of the analysis of the individual writings to Thessalonica incorporated in the two canonical Thessalonian epistles:

Thess. A = II Thess. 1:1-12 + 3:6-16.

Paul hears (3:11) that the agitation by alien preachers is going on in Thessalonica also. In a first writing he only warns the community to stay away from these preachers and their followers and to give no place in the community to Gnostic enthusiasm. Especially careful preparation is made in the proem, 1:1-12, for the admonitions of this first epistle, with which after a long period Paul resumes contact with the community in Thessalonica.

Thess. B = I Thess. 1:1–2:12 + 4:2–5:28.

Paul learns that the agitation by the new apostles has not remained without influence and impact upon the community. He writes a second epistle, in which he first explicitly defends his apostolate against the spiteful accusations of the Gnostics that he is no pneumatic and that he preaches for money (the collection). Then he admonishes and instructs the community with regard to the novelties proclaimed or practiced by the false teachers: unchastity; fanaticism; disregard for the teachers; denial of the resurrection and the Parousia. The cautious tone of this letter—unlike Cor. D and Phil. C—shows that he does not yet see the community as having slipped from his hands, but he does see

---

not very believable, for historical reasons. The problem of the third generation was the postponement of the Parousia, not its coming.

the arguments of the alien apostles as having some effect in the community.

Thess. C = II Thess. 2:13-14 + 2:1-12 + 2:15-3:3 (5), 17-18.

Paul hears that, in order to disseminate the Gnostic assertion that the day of the Lord has already come, some are appealing, among other things, to an epistle which he is supposed to have written. Apparently in doing this they are relying on epistle B (I Thess. 5:5 ff.). Therefore Paul writes a brief epistle in order to set straight the eschatological fanaticism, as he understands it, and to parry the misuse of his (genuine or forged) epistle.

Thess. D = I Thess. 2:13-4:1.

The continuing concern for the community leads Paul, at the same time in which he himself is making a brief interim visit to Corinth, to send Timotheus to Thessalonica. The latter comes back from Thessalonica with a good report. Out of joy over this, Paul writes his "joyful epistle" to Thessalonica, in which praise and thanksgiving appear in place of the apology and paraenesis which marked the preceding writings and in which the sending of Timotheus in retrospect is justified with a reference to the attacks which Paul is having to suffer at the hands of his opponents. At this time Paul is counting on visiting in Thessalonica soon (3:11).[290]

Only epistle D contains direct allusions to the situation. Such allusions hardly will have been lacking in the other writings originally; however, they have been excised by the editor, who kept the allusions of epistle D for his I Thess. and presumably for this reason also had to eliminate the genuine allusions in his later II Thess.

For the order of the four epistles given above, however, our analysis has yielded sufficient indications. One can ask whether the Thessalonian Aristarchus, who is first mentioned in Acts 19:29 toward the end of Paul's stay in Ephesus (cf. Acts 20:4; 27:2; Col.

---

[290] W. Bauer ([1], pp. 74-75) makes it appear likely that Gnosticism soon completely drove ecclesiastical Christianity out of Thessalonica. Cf. also II Tim. 4:10!

4:10; Philemon 24), has informed Paul about the situation in Thessalonica. In any case epistle B presupposes relatively detailed news from Thessalonica; cf. W. Michaelis, [2], pp. 51-52.

Epistle D was written soon after Paul's interim visit in Corinth (see pp. 187 ff.). Epistles A, B, and C then belong to the time before the interim visit.

On the placing of the correspondence to Thessalonica among the other epistles written during the third so-called missionary journey of Paul, see pp. 247 ff.

The often posed question about the order of the two epistles to Thessalonica,[291] for which the arrangement in our present collection of the epistles in fact is of no decisive importance, is answered by our analysis of itself. This analysis has tacitly utilized some arguments which the defenders of the priority of II Thess. customarily bring forth.[292]

X

The conclusions of the foregoing investigation cannot fail to have a bearing on the question of the genuineness of "II Thess." The arguments for or against the genuineness which are adduced from theological and philological considerations are so little convincing that the decision on this question will always be made in the investigation of the *situation* of II Thess., of its intention and destination, and hence of its substantive and literary relationship to the first epistle.

The situation, however, with the presupposition of the proposed literary-critical analysis, proves to be "authentic." It is impossible to assume that already before the editing of the collection one of the four epistles to Thessalonica was falsified.

In the course of the investigation we have already refuted those objections to the genuineness of "II Thess." which are raised on the basis of the eschatological passage 2:1-12, and we have seen that this passage becomes understandable at all only when seen in the light of Paul's situation.

---

[291] H. Appel's original solution may at least be mentioned because of its curious character: I Thess. was written first but not sent; then II Thess. is written and sent; finally I Thess. is sent (*Einleitung in das Neue Testament*, p. 18).

[292] On this, cf. in detail my essay on "Die Thessalonicherbriefe als Briefkomposition" in *Zeit und Geschichte, Dankesgabe zum 80. Geburtstag von Rudolf Bultmann*.

Further, we have seen that, given the situation which we have presupposed, the peculiar form of the proem in II Thess. 1:3 ff. = epistle A becomes easily understandable.

As in his correspondence with Corinth and Philippi, Paul takes a position by letter several times, at brief intervals, upon new reports, with respect to the developing situation in Thessalonica. This explains the (often exaggeratedly portrayed) close terminological affinity of the two writings as well as their topical affinity. Every letter has peculiarities of language; in the case of "II Thess." they remain altogether within the range of normal variety.[293] Just as little can one take offense at the individual variations of theological ideas.[294] The only thing suspicious here is the formulation in 1:12, where one expects a "τοῦ" before the "κυρίου." Now if this "τοῦ" actually is indispensable, it may sometime have been omitted through an oversight. One cannot deduce the inauthenticity of the entire epistle from this passage.

In view of the uncertainty as to whether and how the mythical figures of the second chapter are to be interpreted historically, it also will not do to make a certain historical interpretation of these figures the basis of a declaration of inauthenticity. II Thess. 3:17 is adequately accounted for by 2:2, 15, as we have seen.

In his lecture on the shorter epistles of Paul, R. Bultmann placed great weight upon the fact that in II Thess. 2:13, precisely as in I Thess. 2:13, the proem is again taken up, and he concluded from this that II Thess. is an imitation of I Thess. Therewith he took up an argument strongly emphasized by W. Wrede.[295] But the fact that in I Thess. 2:13 the proem is repeated is no less puzzling than the same phenomenon in the second epistle (2:13-

---

[293] On this, see E. v. Dobschütz, [1], pp. 39 ff.

[294] Cf. H. Braun, "Zur nachpaulinischen Herkunft des Zweiten Thessalonicherbriefes" (ZNW 44 [1952/53]: 152-56), who in my judgment overemphasizes such nuances. For example, when Paul explains in II Thess. 1:3 ff. that the sufferings of the community are a sign that the Christians would be made worthy of the kingdom of God, but their oppressors would be punished, such a thought indeed is not genuinely Pauline, but also not genuinely un-Pauline. Instead, the idea of judgment thus expressed stems from the late Jewish tradition familiar to Paul and his readers, and, in the form in which it is presented, is quite capable of being harmonized with Paul's theory of suffering; for why should a Christian not be allowed, or indeed obliged, to understand his "suffering with Christ" as a sign that he belongs to Christ?

[295] W. Wrede, pp. 20 ff., cf. also H. Holtzmann, "Zum 2. Thessalonicherbrief," ZNW 2 (1901) : 97 ff., and my essay mentioned in n. 292.

14 // 1:3 ff.). In both cases the problem can be solved only by literary-critical means, and it is satisfactorily solved in this way.

The same is true for the parallelism of the eschatocols found in the text of both epistles, namely I Thess. 3:11 ff. // II Thess. 2:16 ff. "A most striking parallelism!" writes W. Wrede, p. 21. Indeed! It appears in the same way in I Thess. 5:23 ff. // II Thess. 3:16 ff. and only proves the fact that both epistles represent a literary composite. If one is not willing to draw this conclusion, then of course one must concede that W. Wrede is right, and, on the basis of the literary parallels between the two epistles, must explain one of them as an imitation and deny it to Paul; for one cannot assume that Paul imitated his first epistle with a second one; in other words, if in this way we "save the epistle, we would wrong the apostle" (W. Wrede, p. 33). Wrede is correct in saying (p. 31) that "the singular congruence in details and particularly even in minor and external aspects, and moreover the peculiar location of the parallels" cannot be accidental.[296] Instead, Wrede has correctly seen in his impressive study that the literary affinity between the two epistles, as it is shown above all in the repetition of I Thess. 2:13-14 in II Thess. 2:13 ff., and of I Thess. 3:11 ff. in II Thess. 2:16 ff., represents the real and, for the question of genuineness, decisive problem, beside which all other arguments for inauthenticity have secondary importance. But even he has not seen that the thesis of the inauthenticity of the second epistle indeed explains the imitation of the first epistle apparently to be observed in it, but not the presence within I Thess. of the complete epistolary framework allegedly imitated by II Thess. Both observations are equally puzzling and demand a

---

[296] The strength of Wrede's argument is unwillingly attested by J. Wrzol, *Die Echtheit des zweiten Thessalonicherbriefes* (1916), (with a good survey of research on the subject), when, taking up a thesis of T. Zahn, he explains that Paul has retained a conception of the first epistle and, in composing II Thess., held to it, in order to raise the prestige of I Thess., which possibly was shaken. But this explanation, in itself quite unusual, fails precisely at the point of making understandable that purely formal repetition of the epistolary framework which is found within I Thess. and is already incomprehensible there. B. Reicke can write (RGG [3rd ed.], VI, col. 852) that the stylistic similarity of I Thess. and II Thess. appears "to an unprejudiced observer . . . rather to indicate authenticity" only because in fact he has not taken into account at all the problem of the literary affinity of the two epistles.

common explanation, namely the literary explanation given above, which also lets us see that Paul repeatedly corresponded with the Thessalonians at brief intervals.

W. Wrede especially stressed the following parallels between I Thess. and II Thess. (pp. 15 ff.) :

a) I Thess. 1:1	// II Thess. 1:1	cf. Wrede, p. 27
b) I Thess. 1:2-8	// II Thess. 1:1-2	cf. Wrede, pp. 18 ff.
c) I Thess. 2:13 ff.	// II Thess. 2:13 ff.	cf. Wrede, pp. 20-21
d) I Thess. 3: (8) 11–4:2	// II Thess. 2:15– 3:5	cf. Wrede, pp. 18 ff,. 21-22, 22-23
e) I Thess. 5:24-25	// II Thess. 3:1-3	cf. Wrede, pp. 18 ff.
f) I Thess. 2:9	// II Thess. 3:8	cf. Wrede, pp. 27-28
g) I Thess. 4:1-12	// II Thess. 3:6-12	cf. Wrede, pp. 17-18, 18 ff., 23.

When these are compared, the parallels a) through e) are explained from the fact that the Thessalonian epistles are epistolary composites, in which the relatively close but not unusual points of contact in a) and b) perhaps could indicate that epistles A and B to Thessalonica, to which these passages belong, came in close succession. The parallelism of g) is to be explained only as grounded in the situation, since I Thess. 4:11-12 (Thess. B) *follows* II Thess. 3:6-15 (Thess. A). On this, cf. above, pp. 200-201. Finally, the parallelism of f) simply shows that in both passages Paul is using a formula familiar to him, which is obvious anyway and in no case affects the question of the genuineness of II Thess.

From our solution of the question of genuineness it also follows that it is neither possible nor necessary to prefer some solution which mediates between the hypotheses of authenticity and inauthenticity: that II Thess. was directed to the Jewish Christian minority of the community along with or soon after I Thess.;[297] that Timotheus composed the epistle under commission from Paul, using a Jewish apocalypse;[298] that I Thess. was in fact ad-

---

[297] A. v. Harnack, *Das Problem des 2. Thess.* (SBA, phil.-hist. Kl. [1910], pp. 560-78) ; M. Dibelius, [1], pp. 57-58. This solution stands under the impact of W. Wrede's arguments.

[298] F. Spitta, "Der zweite Brief an die Thessalonicher" (1893), (*Zur Geschichte und Literatur des Urchristentums,* I: 109-54) .

dressed to Philippi;[299] that II Thess. represents the later reworking of a shorter draft;[300] and so forth.

Addendum

With the literary-critical analysis of the Thessalonian epistles presented in the foregoing essay, cf. now: William C. Robinson, Jr., "Word and Power," in *Soli Deo Gloria*, New Testament Studies in Honor of William C. Robinson (1968), pp. 78-79; W. Schenk, "Der 1. Korintherbrief als Briefsammlung," ZNW 60 (1969) : 242-43; Karl J. Bjerkelund, *Parakalo*, pp. 125 ff.

---

[299] E. Schweizer, "Der zweite Thessalonicherbrief ein Philipperbrief?" ThZ 1 (1945) : 90 ff., 286 ff.

[300] P. W. Schmidt in the excursus in his commentary on I Thess. (1885).

IV

The False Teachers of Romans 16:17-20[1]

The polemical concluding verses of the Epistle to the Romans have always stimulated the interest of the exegetes and have given rise to diverse conclusions. What interests us here above all is the question: Against what false teachers is Paul warning the community?

F. C. Baur thought that in these verses reference was made to Gnostic opinions.[2] I regard this as an insight as penetrating as it is correct, even though of course one must regard as outdated the conclusion which was necessary for Baur and his time from this insight, that these verses must therefore come from the post-apostolic period.[3]

To be sure, the correctness of Baur's insight is matched by its lack of consistency within his view of the history of primitive Christianity. There are many parallels to Rom. 16:17-20, some of them word for word, in other epistles of Paul, as in the Corinthian epistles, in Galatians, and in Phil. 3, which demand the conclusion that "they must be agitators hostile to Paul, as in Galatia, Philippi, and Corinth." [4] But according to Baur, these epistles are anti-Judaistic in their orientation. Hence it is not surprising that many of Baur's pupils saw the verses Rom. 16:17-

---

[1] First published in *Studia Theologica* XIII (1959) : 51-69. The version given here has been revised.

[2] Tübinger ThZ, 1836, pp. 114 ff.; ThJ, 1857, pp. 60 ff. Similarly Volkmar, *Paulus Römerbrief* (1875), pp. 69 ff.; W. Lütgert ([3], pp. 138-39) speaks of libertines.

[3] Thus still, with a reference to the Gnosticism addressed in these verses, H. J. Holtzmann in his *Einleitung in das Neue Testament* (1886, 2nd ed.), p. 273; cf. also O. Pfleiderer, *Urchristentum* (1887), p. 145.

[4] A. Jülicher in *Die Schriften des Neuen Testaments* (1908, 2nd ed.), II: 325.

20 also as written on an anti-Judaistic front.[5] Indeed, Baur himself apparently wavered in his view.[6]

The view which sees Judaizers being opposed in Rom. 16:17-20 has continued to be the dominant one down to the present. It can be repeated without discussion in a commentary like that of H. Lietzmann[7] and even that of P. Althaus.[8] H. Appel[9] of course thinks of "libertinist heretics." Even O. Michel[10] rightly says of the warning in Rom. 16:17-20: ". . . In no case can one treat it as directed exclusively against Judaizers." He suggests that it "could also have an anti-Gnostic thrust," but refrains from making a definite exposition.

Such restraint seems to me to be unnecessary. For Rom. 16:17-20 only an anti-Gnostic battlefront comes into question, and indeed precisely when one considers the parallels in the other epistles of Paul.

Verse 17.

The first words, "I exhort you, brethren," do not contribute anything for our question, precisely because of their numerous parallels in all the other Pauline epistles. The expression is stereotyped, particularly at the end of epistles (Rom. 15:30; I Cor. 16:15; I Thess. 5:14; II Thess. 3:12), and says nothing about the content of the following admonitions. Even the σκοπεῖν, which occurs only here in the NT in the context of the warning against false teachers, is quite generally put.[11]

But now, as the first and apparently the most general content of the exhortation, there follows the warning against τοὺς τὰς διχοστασίας ποιοῦντας. The expression διχοστασία occurs in Paul also in Gal. 5:20 (along with ἐριθεῖα and αἱρέσεις) and in a

---

[5] R. A. Lipsius, p. 203: "The reference to Gnostics is not made necessary by anything."

[6] In *Paulus* (1845), p. 415, he thinks of judaizing heretics.

[7] [2], p. 127.

[8] P. Althaus, p. 128.

[9] H. Appel, p. 47.

[10] O. Michel, p. 10; more cautiously on p. 339, n. 2; on p. 11 he can even say: "The explicit polemic in Rom. 16:17-20 proves that . . . the anti-judaizing tendency may not be minimized." B. Reicke ([1], p. 297) speaks of "Gnostic arrogance" *and* of a "judaizing kind."

[11] But one may compare from the anti-Gnostic discussion, e.g., Phil. 3:2, 17; Col. 2:8.

strongly attested reading in I Cor. 3:3 (along with ζῆλος and ἔρις). We translate it with "dissension" or "division." There are people there who are causing this division. A warning is given against such people. It is evident that Paul does not see the community itself as broken apart into two segments, so that he must exhort them to unity. Instead, certain people (οἱ τοιοῦτοι, vs. 18) are seeking to destroy the existing unity of the community over which Paul rejoices (vs. 19). What currents of the apostolic period can have sent rival missionaries into Paul's communities? We know of a Jewish Christian mission and of a Gnostic missionary movement.

The earliest and most reliable report on the Jewish Christian mission within the Pauline missionary territory is given to us by Paul in his epistle to the Galatians (2:7-10). According to this, Paul and the Jerusalemites mutually confirm to one another the special qualification for or even the call to the mission: the Gentile mission is entrusted to Paul, and the Jewish mission to Peter. It was decided to divide the missionary task accordingly (Gal. 2:9): the Jerusalemites organize the Jewish mission; Peter is the leading missionary (Gal. 2:7-8). Paul and his circle preach to the Gentiles. We need not explore here the reasons for this division within the common task.[12] It is enough to say that, according to all that we know, this arrangement was restricted to the lifetime of Paul.[13] The episode in Antioch (Gal. 2:11-21) testifies that as compared with Peter, James insisted on stricter observance of the Jerusalem agreement: the Jewish Christian community should preserve its own life under the law.[14] Thus we find Peter also, or at least his community, alongside the Pauline community in Corinth, and indeed in a common defense against the intruding "Christ party."[15] For Rome we may infer this side-by-side existence from the discussion on the question of foods (Rom. 14:1–15:13). The same set of circumstances perhaps is attested for Ephesus by Phil. 1:15 ff. Other places then will have

---

[12] See Vol. 3, pp. 38 ff.

[13] If the tendentious report of the book of Acts, which has Paul beginning his mission usually in the synagogues, were maintained, then the Paul of Gal. 2 of course would be unmasked as a hypocrite. Cf. Vol. 3, p. 56.

[14] See Vol. 3, pp. 63 ff.

[15] I Cor. 1:12; cf. Vol. 1, pp. 199 ff.; J. Jeremias in ZNW 49 (1958): 151; Eus. CH II, 25.8.

shown a similar picture. The struggle against Gnosticism of course very soon led the Gentile Christian end Jewish Christian communities together in a common defensive position, and indeed this happened during the apostolic era.[16] Even from the second century—if we except Palestine and its environs—we have no more certain reports of independent purely Jewish Christian communities within the Great Church.[17]

There is no question that this Jewish Christian mission, issuing from Jerusalem or from James and organized by Peter, cannot be held responsible for the divisions in the Pauline community against which Paul speaks in Rom. 16:17. The arrangement of which Paul tells in Gal. 2, in fact, was aimed precisely at an amicable coexistence of Jewish Christian and Gentile Christian communities. We have no report from which a violation of this agreement may be inferred. Quite the contrary! When Paul writes Gal. 2, it must still have been in force, just as it is later, when Paul gathers an offering for Jerusalem with great personal diligence. It is in Phil. 1:15—if the passage is not, as is likely, to be understood otherwise[18]—that Paul utters the most critical judgment on the collateral Jewish Christian mission. But even in this passage he testifies of the others that they are proclaiming Christ,[19] which he specifically denies of his adversaries in Rom. 16:18. He rejoices over *that* mission; but *this* one he regards as the work of the devil (Rom. 16:20). In Rom. 14–15 also he takes a stand for coexistence, and the so-called apostolic decree— if it has any place at all in the life of primitive Christianity[20]— opens up the possibility of such amicable fellowship. There is never a critical word about James. Paul cannot possibly attribute

---

[16] Vol. 1, pp. 199 ff.

[17] Justin (Dial. 47), it is true, knows such Jewish Christians in the Great Church. But he comes from Palestine, whose special circumstances are in his mind, and moreover, it is not even certain whether he does not transfer conditions of the apostolic era into his own present. The Palestinian Jewish Christian Hegesippus, on his travels in the West, visits no exclusive communities of his observance, but rather lives in such fellowship with the Gentile Christians that even for Palestine one can no longer assume a Christianity of the Great Church which holds unconditionally to the law. What Origen (Cels. V, 65) and Epiphanius (Haer. XXIX) report—moreover only from the Palestinian area—is capable of varied interpretations. Cf. incidentally Vol. 3, pp. 106 ff.

[18] See above, pp. 74-75.

[19] Cf. Mark 9:38-41.

[20] See Vol. 3, pp. 97 ff.

to the devil the missionary work of Peter which is supported by Jerusalem in the way he does with the work of his opponents in Corinth, Galatia, and Philippi.[21]

Now the number of investigators who make James and Peter responsible for a Jewish Christian countermission in Paul's missionary field is no longer very large.[22] Therewith the veil of uncertainty descends over the origin of the alleged aggressive and anti-Pauline Judaism of the apostolic period. This could be tolerated if the existence of such a Judaism were evident. But what do we actually know about the existence of such a Judaism? It seems to me that we know nothing of it.

I have sought to show in Vol. 3, pp. 107 ff., that Gal. 2:4 (and Acts 15:5, 24 as well) cannot form the basis of such knowledge.

The ecclesiastical authors of the second and third century then of course know much to report of a heretical, apparently variously aligned, very disunited, and always anti-Pauline and Palestinian Jewish Christianity.[23] But is there not a scholarly consensus that this Jewish Christianity which was separated from the Great Church belongs, as a product of a sectarian development, to the period after 70, when the Jewish Christians had to leave Jerusalem?[24] This Jewish Christianity emphatically appeals to James. Thus its origins undoubtedly are to be sought in James' congregation in Jerusalem. The frequently fanatical opposition to Paul of these Jewish Christian circles, however, shows that it is no longer the James of Gal. 2 and of Acts 21:15-26 (= Rom. 15:25-33) to whom they appeal. The numerous peculiar doctrines of these groups, which H. J. Schoeps ([2]) has presented, do not belong to the original community in Jerusalem. This is all the more true of the later quite strong Gnostic touch of this Judaism or of a part of it.[25] The very fact that we must trace this later heretical judaizing tendency back to James's community in Jeru-

---

[21] See above, pp. 82 ff.

[22] Cf. the—to be sure frequently vulnerable—statements of J. Munck, pp. 238 ff.

[23] The sources are well collected by H. J. Schoeps, [2], pp. 14-70.

[24] Of course this sectarian development may have been started already before 70, in a tendency toward anti-Paulinism perhaps in Jerusalem itself, and in tendency toward Gnosticism in its Syrian-Samaritan centers or in the area of the baptist circles along the Jordan. Cf. Vol. 3, pp. 106 ff.

[25] On this, cf. now G. Strecker, *Das Judenchristentum in den Pseudo-Clementinen*, TU 70 (1958).

salem shows that in the apostolic period there cannot yet have been a judaizing movement comparable to that later one existing alongside James's community. Tendencies of this kind, which one need not deny, were not able to prevail, at any rate in Jerusalem. It is also to be noted that we find the later Jewish Christians almost exclusively in Palestine and the neighboring territories. Understandably, nothing is known to us of missionary tendencies of these heretical groups, particularly among the Gentiles.[26] How could such an exclusively Jewish Christian group have conducted a Gentile mission? [27]

The later anti-Pauline and anti-missionary judaizing movement, which appeals to James, thus simply rules out for the time of James a judaizing movement opposed to Paul and conducting a mission among the Gentiles. Actually the James-Peter community rather had a twofold issue—as Justin (Dial. 47) very correctly observes. The majority of the Jewish Christian communities in the Roman Empire, so far as they did not succumb to Gnosticism, very early joined the Great Church in the anti-Gnostic struggle and entered into that Great Church. In the environs of Palestine itself, on the other hand, there occurred a peculiar law-observing development which often could not escape alien influences and which in the eyes of the Great Church soon acquired a sectarian character.

Nevertheless: do we not know with unassailable certainty from Paul's epistles to Galatia, Philippi, and Corinth that a judaizing movement in the communities of Paul was agitating against him? Anyone who is captivated by Baur's picture of history of course has no doubt on this point. But does an interrogation of the epistles on their own historical background require the assumption of a judaizing opposition? By no means. Quite the contrary: already in Baur's own time resistance was raised against his representation of the historical backgrounds of the major Pauline epistles.[28] This resistance has steadily grown. Today, in fact, no one any longer sees with Baur an anti-judaizing polemical docu-

---

[26] In my opinion this judgment is confirmed in H. J. Schoep's comments ([2], pp. 296 ff.) on "Judenchristliche Missionstendenzen."

[27] Only the genuinely Gnostic Elchasaites are to be excepted from this judgment; cf. H. J. Schoeps, [2], pp. 325 ff.

[28] Schenkel, de Wette, and others.

ment in the Epistle to the Romans. Hardly anyone still ventures to give an adequate explanation of the Corinthian epistles in terms of an anti-judaizing stance. For Philippians as well as for Galatians, Baur's position is at least strongly shaken. It is my conviction, developed in Vol. 1 and in the present investigation, that Paul's opponents in Corinth, Galatia, and Philippi are not Judaizers, but that in them we have to do with Jewish or Jewish Christian Gnostics. But this means that we actually know nothing of the existence of a judaizing mission in competition with Paul.

This means, further, that the διχοστασίαι, against whose instigators Paul warns in Rom. 16:17, must also have been provoked by Jewish Christian Gnostics, at least if we wish to relate these instigators at all to any movement of primitive Christianity otherwise known to us.

Such a correlation with early Gnosticism, however, not only is necessary from these general historical considerations, but is compellingly demanded by the text as well.

The concept διχοστασία already announces such a demand. Wherever it occurs in primitive Christian literature to designate a schism within the church, the division is always caused by the Gnostics.[29] One may compare I Cor. 3:3;[30] Gal. 5:20;[31] I Clem. 46.5; 51.1;[32] Herm. Sim. VIII, 10.2. The same holds true for the related concepts which occur in the passages named along with διχοστασία, e.g. αἵρεσις (Gal. 5:20; I Cor. 11:19; Titus 3:10; II Peter 2:1; Ign. Eph. 6.2;[33] Trall. 6.1; Epil. Mosq. 1), σχίσμα (1 Cor. 1:10; 11:18; I Clem. 2.6; 46.5, 9; 49.5; 54.2; Herm. Sim. VIII, 9.4), ζῆλος (I Cor. 3.3; Gal. 5:20; II Cor. 12:20; I Clem. 3.2), ἔρις (I Cor. 1:11; 3:3; II Cor. 12:20; Gal. 5:20; I Tim. 6:4; Titus 3:9; Ign. Eph. 8.1; I Clem. 3.2; 9.1; 14.2; 46.5; 54.2), ἐριθεία (II Cor. 12:20; Gal. 5:20; Phil. 2:3; Ign. Philad. 8.2), θυμός, ἔχθραι, πόλεμος, and στάσις. On the other hand, these con-

---

[29] Cf. also the anti-Gnostic passage in Iren. IV, 33.7: "He will also judge those who cause divisions. Void of the love of God, they look to their own advantage and not to the unity of the church; for small and trifling reasons they rend the great and glorious body of Christ into pieces and, if it were within their power, would kill him."

[30] Cf. Vol. 1, pp. 90 ff.

[31] Cf. above, p. 52.

[32] Cf. W. Bauer, [1], pp. 95 ff.

[33] Today it no longer needs to be proved that the schismatics of the Ignatian epistles are Jewish Christian Gnostics.

cepts do not occur in early Christian literature in the debate over so-called judaizing. This debate stands rather under the express catchword "κοινωνία" (Gal. 2:9).[34]

Even clearer than the concept διχοστασία is the characterization of the opponents as "τοὺς τὰς διχοστασίας καὶ τὰ σκάνδαλα παρὰ τὴν διδαχὴν ἣν ὑμεῖς ἐμάθετε ποιοῦντας." Like the related διδασκαλία, the word διδαχή was not taken over into the language of early Christianity because of a definite technical meaning which was already given with the word. But it soon acquires such a meaning, and this in fact in the struggle with Gnosticism, and the substance denoted with the word διδαχή was the only decisive ecclesiastical weapon against the heretics. The concept was introduced in its technical significance in order to be able to suppress the free sway of the Pneuma and the uncontrollable proclamation of the Gnostic pneumatic, with a reference to the teaching that had been handed down. Later, even in the Gnostic movement, the pneumatic intensity slackened and made a place for a teaching function; the more this happened, the more narrowly constricted did the concept διδαχή become in the church and the more did it become a technical expression for rigidly formulated confessional principles,[35] which now are set in contrast to the false teaching of the Gnostics.

This process is clearly portrayed already in the New Testament. It should be noted that of the twenty-one New Testament passages in which διδασκαλία occurs, fifteen are found in the Pastoral Epistles, and thus are employed in the anti-Gnostic polemic,[36] and in Col. 2:22, and probably in Eph. 4:14 also, the false teaching of the Gnostics is refuted. In the New Testament writings, at the following places διδαχή is used positively or negatively in the debate with the Gnostics: II Tim. 4:2; Titus 1:9; Heb. 13:9; II John 9-10; Rev. 2:14-15, 24,[37] and among these, the technical

---

[34] Phil. 1:15 ff., where ἔρις and ἐριθεία occur, does not form an exception, even if this passage should be concerned with Jewish Christian missionaries. For in this passage these ambiguous expressions do not denote a division of the community.

[35] TDNT II: 164.

[36] On this, cf. H. Schlier, "Die Ordnung der Kirche nach den Pastoralbriefen," in the Gogarten *Festschrift* (1948), esp. pp. 45 ff.

[37] It is difficult to determine to what extent the passages in the book of Acts (esp. Acts 2:42) repeat the technical usage of the church.

usage in II John is especially striking. From the literature of the Apostolic Fathers, reference may be made, for example, to Did. 2.1; 6.1; 11.1-2, and to the descriptive title of this writing, to Barn. 9.9; 16.9; 18.1; Ign. Magn. 6.2; Eph. 17.1; 9.1; 16.2, and Herm. Sim. VIII, 6.5.[38] The same is true of the related concepts.[39]

Naturally Paul is not yet acquainted with a technical usage in this anti-Gnostic sense. Of course he does set his received message in substance over against the pneumatic teaching authority of the Gnostic adversaries: I Cor. 1:12-13;[40] 2:1-2; 4:7, 17; 7:10 ff., 40; 11:2, 23; 12:28 ff.;[41] 15:1 ff.; II Cor. 5:11 ff.;[42] Gal. 1:6-9; Phil. 2:12; 3:17; 4:9. In view of this state of things then a formulation like I Cor. 4:17 does not surprise us: καθὼς πανταχοῦ ἐν πάσῃ ἐκκλησίᾳ διδάσκω (cf. I Cor. 7:17); thus is Timotheus to familiarize the Corinthians with the true doctrine, so that they can persist in the struggle against the invading Gnostics. Some have regarded this passage as a later ecclesiastical interpolation.[43] This is not correct. It does not presuppose the doctrinal concept of the church of the second century, but prepares the way for it. For the same reason Rom. 16:17 is above the suspicion of non-Pauline origin. This passage also prepares the way for the technical use of διδαχή in the Great Church. The inference is suggested, then, that Rom. 16:17 also was written in an anti-Gnostic battlefront alignment.[44] Only important reasons could move us to reject this inference. Those reasons are not present, and indeed all the less since Paul never feels himself obliged to defend either doctrine in general or even the correct doctrine as over against the Jewish Christians.[45]

---

[38] Rom. 6.17b, which is suspected as a gloss, possibly also belongs here.

[39] H. Schlier, n. 36, counts no less than 13 different formulations for "teach" in the Pastoral Epistles.

[40] See Vol. 1, pp. 199 ff.

[41] As in chap. 14, Paul emphatically puts ecstatic gifts of the spirit in last place.

[42] Paul sets the proclamation of the word of God against the Gnostic demand for ecstasies; see Vol. 1, pp. 187 ff.

[43] See J. Weiss in Meyer's Kommentar, in loc.

[44] It is worthy of note in this context that the anti-Gnostic ecclesiastical concept of doctrine is developed in the Pauline and related literature. The Pastoral Epistles speak on its behalf an eloquent language, especially in comparison with the contemporary literature remote from Paul.

[45] In Gal. 2:1-10 Paul is obviously concerned not to allow the impression to

Since the concepts for "division" as well as those for "teaching" occur in early Christian literature pointedly in the debate with Gnosticism, it is only natural that the arrangement of the two concepts which we have in the verse we are examining is also found elsewhere in the same battlefront, e.g., in I Tim. 6:3-4; Titus 3:9 ff.; I Cor. 4:17-18; II Peter 2:1. Such passages are the most immediate parallels to Rom. 16:17. In the debates about judaizing such expressions are lacking.

In Rom. 16:17 the doctrine is more precisely characterized as that "ἣν ὑμεῖς ἐμάθετε." The history of the concept μανθάνειν and the related concepts within Christian usage runs parallel to that of διδαχή, etc. The concept μανθάνειν also was not adopted into ecclesiastical language because of a definite technical import. But it early acquired such import. If διδάσκειν denotes the communication of the authoritative doctrine as over against the ecstatic revelation of Gnosticism, sometimes particularly the tradition of the formulas of faith as over against the false Gnostic doctrine, with μανθάνειν the appropriation of this doctrinal tradition and ultimately of the fixed symbol as the only true doctrine is expressed, and therewith the obedience toward the tradition is affirmed. K. H. Rengstorf has assembled documents in adequate number (in TDNT IV: 412-13) for this technical usage that developed in the struggle with Gnosticism in the age of the church fathers.[46] Phil. 4:9 [47] clearly shows, as does II Tim. 3:14,[48] that this usage also begins already in the anti-Gnostic discussion in the New Testament writings. Perhaps one may also refer to Eph.

---

arise among his readers that there are doctrinal differences. Like Paul, Peter is entrusted with the one gospel, is granted the one grace. The fellowship asserted is preeminently fellowship in the one teaching. Only the "false brethren"—perhaps Jews (see above, p. 14)—offer refutation when Paul presents his gospel to the Jerusalemites (Gal. 2:1 ff.). Similarly, in Gal. 2:11 ff. no doctrinal difference is affirmed—there is not a word of reproof for James—but Peter's personal conduct, his hypocrisy, is criticized; cf. Vol. 3, pp. 63 ff.

[46] In this documentation one should note the juxtaposition of διδάσκειν and μανθάνειν to which Rengstorf calls attention. By way of supplement I cite only one characteristic quotation: "οὗτος γὰρ ὁ Εἰρηναῖος . . . πολλοὺς ἐδίδαξεν· οὗ καὶ πολλὰ συγγράμματα κάλλιστα καὶ ὀρθότατα φέρεται· ἐν οἷς μέμνηται Πολυκάρπου, ὅτι παρ' αὐτοῦ ἔμαθεν" (Epil. Mosq. 1).

[47] Cf. above, pp. 112 ff.

[48] One should note the association of διδασκαλία in 3:16 with the reference to the heretics in 3:13.

4:20 and Col. 1:7.⁴⁹ Rom. 16:17 undoubtedly belongs in this context. I do not know of any place where the primitive Christian community is admonished to cling to the doctrine that has been learned as over against judaizing agitators.

On the other hand, the fact that Paul calls the work of the false teachers a σκάνδαλον is of no importance for our inquiry. In fact the concept is also found elsewhere in the debate with the Gnostics (not with the Judaizers!), e.g., in Rev. 2:14; Polyc. 6.3. However, it never became a *terminus technicus* in this sense.

More interesting are the concluding words of the first verse of our text: ἐκκλίνετε ἀπ' αὐτῶν. The Gnostics have constantly made the claim that they are Christians, members of the one church, and brothers of all.⁵⁰ The Great Church has stubbornly rejected this claim from the beginning on. To her the Gnostics are false brethren, schismatics, and apostates.⁵¹ The church willed the *schisma*, the separation from the Gnostics. Hence the exhortation, ἐκκλίνετε ἀπ' αὐτῶν, in whatever form, is stereotyped in the anti-Gnostic struggle, particularly in the Pauline tradition: εἰώθασι γάρ τινες δόλῳ πονηρῷ τὸ ὄνομα περιφέρειν, ἄλλα τινὰ πράσσοντες ἀνάξια θεοῦ· οὓς δεῖ ὑμᾶς ὡς θηρία ἐκκλίνειν" (Ign. Eph. 7.1). Cf. also, e.g., I Cor. 5:11 ff.; II Thess. 3:6 ff.; I Tim. 6:5; II Tim. 2:21; 3:5; Titus 3:10; II John 10-11; Ign. Smyrn. 4.1. In the intra-ecclesiastical debate about the law such a demand is totally lacking, if we except the late period in which the judaizing movement in Palestine had developed into a (partly strongly gnosticizing) sect. Quite the contrary! The κοινωνία of the Gentile Christian and Jewish Christian communities in the Roman Empire is attested unanimously and without demur from Gal. 2:9 to Justin Dial. 47.2. Hence Rom. 16:17 also can be warning only against a Jewish Christian Gnosticism.

Verse 18.
Paul asserts that the heretics do not serve the Lord Christ.

---

⁴⁹ In substance, e.g., the passage Gal. 1:6-9 belongs in this connection; it cannot be aimed against Jerusalem Judaizers since in Gal. 2:1 ff. Paul attests the fellowship in the gospel with Jerusalemites.

⁵⁰ Eus. CH III, 26.3-4; IV, 7.2-3; II Cor. 10:7; 11:23.

⁵¹ Cf., e.g., Polyc. 6.3; Ign. Eph. 7.1; Herm. Sim. IX, 19.2-3; Rom. 16:18; II Tim. 3:5; II Cor. 11:13 ff.; I John 2:18, 22; 4:1, 3-4. These and other passages presuppose the Gnostics' *claim* to the name "Christian."

Such a statement would be unnecessary if these people themselves did not purport to be Christians. But they apparently claim to be διάκονοι Χριστοῦ. It is just this claim that Paul refuses them. Claim and the disputing of a claim in this form are typical of the anti-Gnostic struggle, as the passages cited in note 51 show. The closest parallels are found in Paul himself. The Corinthian Gnostics assert concerning themselves that they are διάκονοι Χριστοῦ (II Cor. 11:23).[52] Paul vigorously contests this: οἱ διάκονοι (τοῦ σατανᾶ) μετασχηματίζονται ὡς διάκονοι δικαιοσύνης (II Cor. 11:15). They wish to be apostles of Christ (II Cor. 10:7), but Paul calls them μετασχηματιζόμενοι εἰς ἀποστόλους Χριστοῦ (II Cor. 11:13). The Galatian Gnostics also intend to proclaim Christ, but in truth they are perverting the gospel of Christ (Gal. 1:6-7). The Gnostics in Philippi purport even already to be "perfect" in Christ (Phil. 3:12-15). But Paul calls them enemies of the cross of Christ (Phil. 3:18).[53] These parallels adequately assure us that in Rom. 16:18 Paul has in mind the same Gnostic Jewish Christians as in the other epistles. On the other hand, he never had the idea of denying the Christian faith of Peter, James, or the Jewish Christian community in Jerusalem. When, at the time of the so-called apostolic council, he extends to them the hand of fellowship, they are for him servants of Christ, just as they still are at the end of his life, when he gathers an offering for them among the Gentile Christians.

Thus these false teachers are not, in Paul's opinion, serving Christ, but, he thinks, they are serving their bellies. Herewith for the first time a specific characteristic of the heretics is indicated. Of course it is ruled out that Paul describes law-observing Jewish Christians as "servants of the belly," because they observe the Jewish dietary laws. Paul certainly was not unhappy to see the Jewish Christians practicing table fellowship with the Gentile Christians. This is shown by Gal. 2:12. But if at the meeting in Jerusalem the Jerusalem Christians recognized Paul's non-law-observing mission, still Paul also recognized the law-observing mission of the Jerusalemites. As we have already seen,

---

[52] It is unimportant for our inquiry whether this *formulation* is to be attributed to Paul or reproduces the Gnostics' own expression; cf. Vol. 1, pp. 207-8.

[53] See above, pp. 106-7. L. Goppelt also sees (pp. 136-37) the substantive connection of Rom. 16:17-20 with Phil. 3.

this agreement was still in force at least at the time when Paul wrote Gal. 2:1-10, and thus probably also still when he wrote Rom. 16:18 and was gathering the offering for Jerusalem. It is not known at all whether the agreement had ever been canceled. The development of the post-apostolic period abolished it, and indeed Justin still apparently attests a remnant of the separation of the communities.

Thus here also there remains the option only of regarding the expression as directed against the Jewish Christian Gnostics, with whose libertinism Paul frequently, and in part with similar-sounding phraseology, debates. I have earlier presented my view of the origin and nature of Gnostic libertinism.[54] Here I only repeat that the religious libertinism of Gnosticism by no means breaks all the ties of morality and order—the presentation of the Church Fathers could sometimes arouse this impression—but only concerns the commerce with the perishable σάρξ, and thus is related in particular to the liberty of sexual intercourse and contempt for all cultic dietary laws.[55] The Gnostics in Corinth vigorously represent this libertinism.[56] It can also be demonstrated with certainty for Galatia,[57] as W. Lütgert has already seen.[58] Finally, the most precise parallel to our verse is found in the Philippian epistle, where it can only have an anti-libertine meaning:[59] πολλοὶ γὰρ περιπατοῦσιν οὓς πολλάκις ἔλεγον ὑμῖν, νῦν δὲ καὶ κλαίων λέγω, τοὺς ἐχθροὺς τοῦ σταυροῦ τοῦ Χριστοῦ, ὧν τὸ τέλος ἀπώλεια, ὧν ὁ θεὸς ἡ κοιλία καὶ ἡ δόξα ἐν τῇ αἰσχύνῃ αὐτῶν, οἱ τὰ ἐπίγεια φρονοῦντες (Phil. 3:18-19). In view of the perfect parallelism of the two utterances,[60] we can only see the same adversaries opposed in Rom. 16:18 as in Phil. 3:17 ff. Since the latter passage deals with libertine Gnostics, the same holds for the former.

The formulation in Rom. 16:18 is more concise than that of the passage quoted from the Philippian epistle. It is not to be

---

[54] Vol. 1, pp. 218 ff.; above, pp. 108 ff.

[55] Naturally libertinism was only *one* possible expression of contempt for the flesh. Asceticism, e.g., is another.

[56] Vol. 1, pp. 218 ff.; note, above all, I Cor. 6:13.

[57] See above, pp. 50 ff.

[58] [1], pp. 18 ff.

[59] Thus the majority of exegetes. Cf. above, pp. 106 ff.

[60] In Rom. 16:18 also, Paul says indirectly that the belly is the God of the heretics. They are serving it instead of Christ. Cf. W. Lütgert, [3], pp. 138-39.

inferred from this that in the reference to the κοιλία in our passage Paul is criticizing only the free practice with regard to food,[61] even though in I Cor. 6:13, in the debate about the eating of meat sacrificed to idols, and perhaps in Phil. 3:19, Paul uses the concept κοιλία in this narrow sense. Common Greek derogatory usage uses the word κοιλία to denote the stomach and the sexual organs as well, especially in the Septuagint.[62] One who serves his belly is thereby characterized as not only a glutton but also a sexually dissolute person. Paul must have both in mind in our passage. Gnosticism, however, is the only libertine movement within the early Christian church.[63] Thus it alone must be the target of Paul's opposition in Rom. 16:18.

Paul further asserts that the false brethren deceived the hearts of the simple διὰ τῆς χρηστολογίας καὶ εὐλογίας. The former word is rare and a *hapax legomenon* in the New Testament. Julius Capitolinus, Pertinax 13, defines the word: "χρηστολόγον *eum appellantes, qui bene loqueretur et male faceret.*" Thus "fine rhetoric" is a fitting translation. That also determines the meaning of the common εὐλογία, which likewise must have here the unusual meaning, again understood *sensu malo,* of "fine rhetoric." [64] Does Paul mean only to say that the false teachers wish to deceive the community with empty words? [65] Hardly, for according to their definition, χρηστολογία and εὐλογία must also be understood as a reference to a rhetorical elegance, to a formally perfect speech of the opponents who are addressed.[66] When we consider this, the parallels particularly from the Corinthian epistles come to mind. In I Cor. 1:17 Paul asserts that he (in

---

[61] Against this practice as such, Paul cannot raise any objection. Of course he wants the freedom of eating to be guided by love, while for the Gnostics this very freedom itself is the central religious concern (I Cor. 8 ff.).

[62] Thus also the rabbinical literature; cf. TDNT III: 786-87.

[63] Of course O. Michel (*in loc.*) recalls Assumptio Mos. 7.4-7, where there is said to be a polemic against dissolute teachers of the law. But to me the reference to the Pharisees in this obscure passage is by no means certain. Jewish Gnostics could at least just as well be meant. The scanty accounts from rabbinical sources concerning heretical Jewish Gnosticism make it appear outspokenly libertine (cf. K. Schubert, *Die Religion des nachbiblischen Judentums* [1955], pp. 94 ff.). But in no case does this passage allow us to infer a libertine judaizing tendency of early *Christianity.*

[64] Cf. the variant reading εὐγλωττία.

[65] Cf. Col. 2:4; I Tim. 1:6; Titus 1:10.

[66] Cf. O. Michel, p. 347.

contrast to his opponents) has proclaimed the gospel οὐκ ἐν σοφίᾳ λόγου. The same sense is found in the assertion that follows in 2:1, that he has not come to Corinth καθ' ὑπεροχὴν λόγου ἢ σοφίας, and his message was not in πειθοῖς σοφίας λόγοις (2:4). Finally, from II Cor. 10:10 and 11:6 it is to be inferred not only that Paul regarded his opponents' manner of uttering wisdom as worthy of note in contrast to his manner of speech, but also that they had the impression that in comparison with them, Paul was an ἰδιώτης τῷ λόγῳ, and made this a charge against him.[67]

One can hardly avoid seeing the same adversaries opposed in these passages against whose χρηστολογία and εὐλογία Paul warns in Rom. 16:18. The parallelism of the two passages extends even to the ἐξαπατᾶν τὰς καρδίας τῶν ἀκάκων. That is to say, in I Cor. 2:6 ff.; 3:1 ff., Paul explains, after he has made the charge of the utterance of wisdom against his opponents, that he has refrained from such speech because the Corinthians are still νήπιοι ἐν Χριστῷ. Therewith he expresses, in the form of an apology, precisely the same thing which in Rom. 16:18 he clothes in the form of an accusation against his opponents.[68]

It cannot be said with certainty what in detail were the peculiar identifying marks of the speech of wisdom of the Corinthian adversaries. Undoubtedly what was involved was in essence the contrast of the pneumatic-ecstatic speech of the Gnostics with the λαλῆσαι τῷ νοΐ of Paul, a contrast which, as is known, is frequently discussed in the Corinthian epistles: I Cor. 14;[69] II Cor. 5:11-15; 12:1-10; 13:3.[70] Moreover, the Gnostics unquestionably passed the content of their message off as the revelation of special and unprecedented wisdom, as they also called themselves σοφοί (I Cor. 3:18; even Paul speaks not seldom in Gnostic fashion of his or God's σοφία: Rom. 11:33; I Cor. 1:1:24, 30; 2:6-7; 12:8). Presumably in the passages cited above, however, the "speaking

---

[67] Less apt are the references, often given in the commentaries, to I Tim. 1:6; 6:20; Titus 1:10; Col. 2:4.

[68] One may also compare the following anti-Gnostic parallels in Irenaeus: "By means of pretences which they artfully assemble, they deceive the half-educated and take them captive . . . . As counselors, by means of artful words they lead the simple on the way of seeking and plunge them helpless into destruction" (Foreword to Book I). "The apostles foresaw in the Spirit those who would deceive the simple" (Foreword to Book IV, 3).

[69] Cf. Vol. 1, pp. 171 ff.

[70] Cf. Vol. 1, pp. 193 ff.

wisdom" is also characterized in view of its formally perfect rhetoric; in any case, no commentator to my knowledge rejects such an exegesis. Besides, this fits well with the picture which we must form of the Gnostics of the early period. The Gnostics were the poets of the early church. Not a few hymns of Gnostic origin are preserved for us already in the New Testament. The rhetoric of the Gnostics of later times also cannot be disputed.[71]

That, of all people, judaizing missionaries from Palestine, who could speak Greek only as a foreign language, could be described by Paul as rhetorically gifted, charming speakers is just as improbable as the assumption that they appeared as teachers of wisdom and ecstatics κατ' ἐξοχήν. For this reason we would have to conclude from Rom. 16:18b, even without the parallels in the Corinthian epistles, that Paul is accusing Jewish Christian Gnostics from the hellenized Syrian Mesopotamian region of deceiving the guileless community by means of rhetorical hocus-pocus.

Verse 19.

Paul begins with a commendation, by which he hopes to secure a better hearing for his admonitions. Then he gives expression to his wish that the readers might be σοφούς as to what is good, but guileless as to what is evil. Many exegetes presume[72] that with σοφούς Paul refers to a catchword of his opponents, who accordingly claim to bring wisdom and to be wise. This cannot be proved with certainty, but it appears to me to be likely. In view of the close parallel of our passage with the polemical passages of the other Pauline epistles, one naturally also suspects, upon the appearance of the term σοφός, that it is connected with the numerous passages in the Corinthian epistles in which σοφία or γνῶσις, with the same sense, occurs (I Cor. 1:17 ff.; 2:1 ff.; 3:18 ff.; 6:5; 8:1 ff.; 13:2, 8; II Cor. 1:12; 11:6). In the Philippian epistle also, Paul appears to allude to the γνῶσις claimed by the false teachers.[73] It is particularly noticeable that, as in Rom. 16:

---

[71] Cf. further, Vol. 1, p. 324.

[72] W. M. L. de Wette, *Das Neue Testament mit kurzem Commentar* (Halle, 1885), *in loc.;* cf. A. Jülicher, *Der Brief an die Römer* (*Die Schriften des Neuen Testaments* [1908, 2nd ed.], II), *in loc.*

[73] See above, pp. 91-92.

18+19, so also in the Corinthian epistles, Paul connects the concepts σοφία and λόγος with one another (I Cor. 1:17; 2:1, 4; II Cor. 11:6). Most obvious for comparison are the passages with a hidden allusion, like I Cor. 15:34 [74] and 6:5. If—as these considerations suggest—with his wish that the readers might be wise toward the good, Paul is adopting a catchword of his opponents, then by such a catchword these opponents would declare themselves to be Gnostics, even if we had to dispense with the parallels, particularly in the Corinthian epistles. For if one looks for a primitive Christian movement in which the term σοφία has a central significance, only Gnosticism comes into question, which in its Jewish or Jewish Christian form, according to all appearance, preferred the designation σοφία alongside the more Hellenistic γνῶσις. [75]

Verse 20.

This verse concludes the brief polemical passage: the God of peace will shortly trample Satan under your feet. "Verse 20 appears only to be the expression, clothed in apocalyptic form, of the certainty that the adversaries will soon be defeated; hardly a reference to the imminent Parousia." [76] This judgment appears to me to be correct. Nevertheless, even the person who wishes to see in vs. 20 a reference to the final consummation[77] must start out from the fact that this reference arises out of the concrete situation. That is to say, the expression "God of peace" stands in obviously intentional antithesis to "τοὺς τὰς διχοστασίας καὶ τὰ σκάνδαλα ποιοῦντας," [78] and Satan correspondingly is that antigodly power which is manifested in the "servants of the belly." This latter judgment is important for our inquiry. Thus the heretics against whom Paul warns are servants of Satan. This is a harsh judgment, to which however II Cor. 11:13-15 is an exact parallel: "They are false apostles, deceivers, disguising themselves as apostles of Christ. No wonder! Even Satan himself is disguised as an angel of light. Hence it is nothing strange if

---

[74] Cf. Evald Lövenstam, "Über die neutestamentliche Aufforderung zur Nüchternheit," *Studia Theologica* XII (1958) : 83-84.

[75] Cf. in the New Testament I Cor. 1:17 ff.; 3:18; Col. 2:23; (2:8).

[76] H. Lietzmann, [2], *in loc.*

[77] O. Michel, *in loc.*

[78] O. Michel, *in loc.*

his servants also disguise themselves as servants of righteousness. Their end will correspond to their deeds!" That Paul here addresses the so-called "original apostles" as servants of Satan is regarded today as impossible even by the exegetes who otherwise reckon with judaizing agitation in Corinth.[79] Impossible, of course! Paul can call neither the pillars in Jerusalem nor their emissaries apostles of the devil. On the other hand, this harsh judgment fits well with the Gnostic Christ apostles, against whose agitation, in my judgment, the whole of Paul's correspondence with Corinth is directed. The same holds true then for Rom. 16:20. In this passage also Paul cannot be describing any people around James as servants of Satan. But we know nothing of ultra-Jacobine and anti-Jacobine Judaizers. Hence as in II Cor. 11:13 ff., so also in Rom. 16:20, it can only be Gnostics to whom Paul is affixing the devil's name. This anti-Gnostic judgment, moreover, has numerous parallels in later ecclesiastical literature.[80]

As the result of this brief study it is to be maintained that the passage Rom. 16:17-20 fits well into the anti-Gnostic polemic known to us from Paul's other epistles and, for many reasons, rules out an anti-Judaistic battle line.[81]

Therewith also an important argument for Ephesus as the destination of Rom. 16 is gained.[82] Even without precisely defining the line of battle of Rom. 16:17-20, W. Michaelis,[83] for example, can cite this passage as argument against a Roman destination: "However, nothing is said in chapters 1-15 of such an imperiling of the Roman community." [84] In fact, for various reasons, which are adequately enumerated by the commentaries, it seems to me that Rome as the destination of Rom. 16 is most

---

[79] R. Reitzenstein; H. Lietzmann; W. G. Kümmel; H. Windisch, and others.

[80] Cf. I John 2:18; 4:3; I Tim. 4:1; 5:14; I Clem. 51.1; then, e.g., repeatedly in Eus. CH: II, 13.1; 14.1; III, 26.1; IV, 7.1 ff.; IV, 23.12; III, 27.1, *et passim;* Tert., de praescr. haer. 40, *et passim.*

[81] B. Reicke ([1], p. 297) speaks, with reference to Rom. 16: 17-20, of *Judaistic* Gnostics. The existence of such people, however, is in my judgment inconceivable. Cf. G. Friedrich, RGG (3rd ed.), V: 1138.

[82] A good survey of the study of this question in R. Schumacher, *Die beiden letzten Kapitel des Römerbriefes, Neutestamentliche Abhandlungen,* XIV, 4 (1929) : 3-28. Cf. G. Friedrich, RGG (3rd ed.) , V: 1138.

[83] [1], p. 161.

[84] Similarly R. A. Lipsius, *in loc. Contra* B. Reicke, [1], pp. 296-97.

inappropriate, nay, even impossible. If the verses Rom. 16:17-20 are directed against the same false teachers whose missionary course we can trace, through Paul's epistles, to Galatia, Philippi, Thessalonica, and Corinth, this judgment is confirmed; for in these verses also a community within the missionary territory defined by these places must have been the addressee. In other words, it is hardly to be assumed that these missionaries, with whom Paul had just been engaged in debate in Corinth, in the meantime had already reached Rome and had done their missionary work so successfully there in the Roman community that Paul has received news of it.

Of course that does not yet determine that Rom. 16 was directed specifically to Ephesus, although in my opinion there are sufficient reasons arguing for this conjecture. Further, our definition of the battlefront in vss. 17-20 says nothing about the place and exact time of composition of Rom. 16, although everything argues in favor of Paul's last stay in Achaia.[85] We shall still have to forgo an unobjectionably certain answer to these questions, particularly since there is no unanimity as to the delimitation of the "Ephesian epistle." [86]

---

[85] To be sure, W. Michaelis ([2], pp. 85 ff.) argues strongly for its composition in Philippi during the stay mentioned in Acts 20:6.

[86] Does this epistle begin as early as chap. 12 (J. Weiss) or in chap. 14? Does 16:1-2 still belong to the Roman epistle (W. Michaelis; P. Feine)? Or does 16:21-23 again belong to the Roman epistle (R. A. Lipsius)? I should assume the latter. In Paul's writings the concluding salutations always precede the benediction which definitively closes the epistle (see above, pp. 129 ff.). But in Rom. 16:21-23 they follow the benediction in vs. 20b, because of which some manuscripts move vs. 20b to a position after the salutations. The greetings in the brief writing to Ephesus also already appear in 16:3-16, where in vss. 3-15 the Ephesians who are greeted are named, and in vs. 16 the ones who send the greetings. (The "ἀσπάζονται ὑμᾶς αἱ ἐκκλησίαι πᾶσαι τοῦ Χριστοῦ" in 16:16 is not suspect, for of course it does not mean all Christian communities in general, but those house churches within Paul's reach, as is shown to some extent more precisely by II Cor. 13:12b; I Cor. 16:19a, 20a; Phil. 4:22; I Thess. 5:26; Titus 3:15.) In an epistle to Ephesus Paul would hardly expressly picture Timotheus as his fellow worker. But then 16:21-23 belongs in the genuine Roman epistle between 15:32 and 15:33. It is understandable that the benediction has remained in 15:33; otherwise it would have followed very close after 16:20b.

The verse Rom. 16:24, which is found in many manuscripts, represents an obviously corrective expansion by the editor of the Western text, who also excises 16:20b, and not a third benediction along with 15:33 and 16:20b, as W. Marxsen (p. 108) thinks. Of course under these circumstances the fact that the Textus Receptus (in this case tertiary) has 16:20b and 16:24, does not argue for the originality of 16:24. Hence there also is no occasion to suspect in chap. 16 fragments of other epistles not otherwise extant, as W. Marxsen does.

Nevertheless it is certain that the Roman epistle also betrays the hand of an editor; for however one delimits the "Ephesian epistle," since the conclusion of the Roman epistle either has been broken off or has been transposed to Rom. 16:21-23, an accidental conflation of the two epistles is not conceivable.[87] If Rom. 16 was a brief letter of recommendation for Phoebe, its isolated acceptance into the Corpus Paulinum did not make much sense. The place at the end of the Roman epistle, on the other hand, is fitting. At the same time, in this way the Roman epistle, addressed to a strange community, acquires the personal conclusion which the other epistles have made customary[88]—and this could also adequately account for the process of editing.[89]

---

[87] I cannot agree with W. Michaelis (ThZ 14 [1958]: 322-23) that it signifies an essential difference whether an editor *interweaves* several epistles or *appends* one to another. The former happens (according to my analysis) in I Cor. and in I and II Thess., the latter in Rom., while in II Cor. and Phil. both methods are employed indiscriminately. An essential distinction does exist between a deliberate editing and an accidental conflation of separate writings.

[88] T. W. Manson's thesis ("St. Paul's Letter to the Romans—and Others," *Bulletin of the John Rylands Library,* 31 [1948]: 224-40), according to which Paul *himself* is the editor of a Roman epistle and an Ephesian epistle, is unnecessarily complicated, particularly in view of the uncontestable fact of the post-Pauline editing of other letters of the apostle.

[89] On the reasons for the editorial reworking of the Roman epistle, cf. also below, p. 259, n.52; p. 262, n. 69; pp. 271 ff.

in memoriam Ferdinand Christian Baur, died December 2, 1860

V

On the Composition and Earliest Collection of the Major Epistles of Paul[1]

I

In the Epilogue to his *Theology of the New Testament*,[2] R. Bultmann, in concise, splendid sentences, evaluated the significance of F. C. Baur for New Testament theology and deplored the fact that Baur's most significant perception for a long time was not allowed to have a decisive impact, namely the insight that truth "can be grasped only in a particular historical form." On the other hand, thanks to Baur, it has become the common property of theological labors to affirm the law of development for the history of primitive Christianity, of the church in general and of its dogma. Of course the rigidity of the Hegelian scheme of thesis, antithesis, and synthesis, into which Baur forced the development of the primitive church,[3] was more and more abandoned by his pupils as time went on. Until well into our century, however, for the exegesis of the major Pauline epistles the fundamental judgment of the Baur school has been determinative, that it is a *single* front against which Paul sets himself in Gal., in I and II Cor., in Phil., in Rom. 16, and—if here we are to reckon with an intra-ecclesiastical polemic at all—in I and II Thess., and thus that a *single* rival mission was disturbing his community. *This* legacy of F. C. Baur deserves our attention.

Even in this question, present-day exegesis is no longer able to follow the traditional evaluation, coming to us from Baur, of the

---

[1] In the following, for reasons shortly to be seen, Rom., I and II Cor., Gal., Phil., and I and II Thess. are to be treated as the major epistles. The present essay was first published in ZNW 51 (1960): 225-45; the present version has been appreciably revised.

[2] ET by Kendrick Grobel, II (1955): 244.

[3] *Das Christentum und die christliche Kirche der drei ersten Jahrhunderte* (1853; 3rd ed., 1863).

Pauline polemic. Now Paul is seen in the various epistles fighting against diverse adversaries, and even in the same place various groups are seen as opposed; indeed, today's exegesis can examine individual chapters of a *single* epistle which "textually, apart from this [are] clearly demarcated" [4] for an opposition which by no means needs to be found in the other polemical chapters of the same epistle.

One can study this development, for example, in J. Munck's examination of *Paul and the Salvation of Mankind,* which in explicit and sharply polemical debate with F. C. Baur[5] attempts to adduce proof that the primitive community in Jerusalem and Paul performed their common work in remarkable agreement. "The immense simplification that Baur's theory brings with it by finding everywhere in all Pauline texts the same contrast between the apostle and Jewish Christianity . . . , has ever since lain like a load on the exposition of the Pauline letters." This burden is shaken off by the proof that, for example, in Galatia the judaizing tendency arose *ad hoc* from Pauline beginnings, but in Corinth at the time of the first epistle no parties at all existed, then at the time of II Cor. Jewish apostles whom it is difficult to characterize appeared, and so on.[6]

On the other hand, even an investigator so closely bound to F. C. Baur as H. J. Schoeps cannot avoid, in his book on Paul,[7] limiting the anti-judaizing battlefront to some parts of the Pauline correspondence, while in the others he reckons with a different opposition.

Most characteristic is H. Koester's article, "Häretiker im Urchristentum," in RGG (3rd ed., III; cf. the same author in ZThK 65 [1968]: 190 ff.) which is based in part on several recent Heidelberg dissertations: In Gal. Paul is opposing *Judaizers* with a syncretistic tendency, in I Cor. *non-Jewish Gnostics,* in II Cor. *Hellenistic Jewish Christians,* in Phil. *Jewish Christian Gnostics.* To be sure different people are involved in each case. If Koester had also included for consideration I and II Thess. and Rom.

---

[4] E. Käsemann, [1], p. 34.

[5] J. Munck, pp. 69 ff.

[6] For a criticism of these constructions, see R. Bultmann, ThLZ 84 (1959), cols. 481 ff.

[7] [1], pp. 74 ff.

16, presumably the number of these "crossings" of heretics would have been increased by two. Like Koester, his teacher G. Born-kamm, in RGG (3rd ed.), V, col. 173, makes the classification: "Judaizers in Galatia . . . , in Corinth Gentile Christian Gnostics (I Cor.), and later (II Cor.) Hellenistic itinerant teachers of Jewish Christian provenance (yet not actually Judaizers) . . . , also Jewish Christian Gnostics in Philippi." Cf. also Robert Jewett, "Conflicting Movements in the Early Church," *Nov. Test.* 12 (1970) : 362-90, esp. 387 ff.; James M. Robinson, "Basic Shifts in German Theology," *Interpretation* 16 (1962) : 79 ff.

Not that in this presentation the present state of exegetical work is precisely reflected in detail. The views on the various heretics in primitive Christanity are still widely divergent. But Koester's article splendidly illustrates the complete dissolution of the unitary character of Baur's portrayal of the line of battle in the Pauline epistles. Only a few scholars today would dare to protest against this dissolution as such. It is regarded as an ad-vance in scholarship: One can no longer uniformly tar the heresies fought by Paul with the same brush of judaizing tendencies; consequently, was not even that unitary character which was emphasized by Baur only a demand, as necessary as it was un-founded, of his historical scheme of thesis and antithesis?

Of course one can view the state of affairs in this way. Whether it is justified is the question. For as much as Baur worked accord-ing to his scheme, still he was and remained an exegete. He based his assertion of the unitary battlefront of the Pauline epistles which he recognized as genuine upon the *exegetical* judgment that the sketch of the opponents found in the one epistle ap-peared also in the other epistle. While it occasionally seems to present-day exegesis as expressly required to examine an epistle or part of an epistle without consideration of the parallels in the other epistles as to the adversaries being opposed therein, it was the method of Baur and his school carefully to compare the perti-nent utterances of the individual epistles. In this respect the commentaries and introductions by Baur's pupils are a model example of comparative exegesis. Who would deny the greater appropriateness of this method?

One should consider that W. M. L. de Wette, in his exegetical-historical work so unjustly forgotten, before Baur and independent of him, sought to describe Paul's opponents in just as unitary a fashion as Baur, though in a different way. And must we not here also refer to W. Lütgert? He profoundly shook Baur's thesis of the anti-judaizing battlefront of the epistles of Paul. Hence the collapse of Baur's position, described in H. Koester's article, in considerable measure also goes back to him. Still Lütgert in his studies, no less than Baur, insisted that the false teachers opposed in one epistle were also opposed in the others. In this he was not guided by any sort of systematic interest such as could be charged against F. C. Baur. Instead, as he explains, to his own surprise he was compelled by his exegetical work to discover in the other epistles also the opponents of Paul first described on the basis of I and II Cor.

Certainly! What appeared forgotten since F. C. Baur again became evident through W. Lütgert: how difficult it is on the basis of our modest knowledge of the history of primitive Christianity to identify the opponents of Paul during his so-called third missionary journey. Indeed this difficulty then also makes it understandable that a multiplicity of battlefronts can be discovered if one examines individual sections of the Pauline correspondence with express disregard for the parallels in the other sections. It is not comprehensible, however, how one can then regard the results achieved by such a method as an advance over earlier exegesis, which asserted a *similar* battlefront, of whatever kind it was, in *all* the epistles.

On this point Baur and Lütgert are to be refuted only if one, like them, investigates the major Pauline epistles *as a whole* or at least in the individual investigations keeps in mind the *entirety* of the contemporary epistles.[8] But if one does this, such

---

[8] The fact that this is not done is the *methodological* defect, not without significance for their conclusions, of studies like U. Wilckens, *Weisheit und Torheit* (Tübingen, 1959), in which there is an exploration of the battlefront of I Cor. 1–2; or D. Georgi, *Die Gegner des Paulus im Zweiten Korintherbrief* (Diss. Heidelberg, 1958), which is based on *parts* of II Cor.; or, as R. Bultmann ([1], pp. 20 ff.) has already shown, even E. Käsemann, "Die Legitimität des Apostels," ZNW 41 (1942), which is concerned only with the adversaries of II Cor. 10–13. It is true that U. Wilckens enlarges the conclusion of his study at least with respect to the Corinthian epistles: "But everything else that Paul indicates in *both Corinthian epistles* concerning the theology of the Corinthian opponents can be understood, from the results of our analysis, without further ado in the very same context" (p.

refutation can hardly be successful; for the parallels that are actually present have a weight that cannot be disregarded. For those who like the frequently very useful statistics, a series of such parallels is set forth in the following table:

Rom. 16	I Cor.	II Cor.	Gal.	Phil.	I Thess.	II Thess.
16:18a		11:15				
16:18b	8:1 ff.			3:19		
16:18c	1:17; 2:4					
16:20		11:13 ff.			3:5	
	9:1	12:11	1:1		4:8	
	16:15-16		6:6	2:29	5:12-13	
		11:18-22	6:12-13	3:2 ff.		
	7:40;	11:4	3:2; 5:25;		5:19	
	12:3		6:1			
	14:1				5:20	
	4:6-10;	10:17-18;	5:26; 6:3	2:3-4;		
	5:2	12:11		3:12 ff.		
		10:2	4:14			
	5:1 ff.;	12:21	5:19	3:19	4:3-8	
	6:12 ff.					
		5:11	1:10a			
		3:1; 5:12;	1:10b		2:4 ff.	
		10:12				
		11:13		3:2b		
		11:4c	1:11-12			
(16:19b)	8:1;	11:6		(3:8, 10)		
	13:8 ff.					
	15:12	5:1 ff.		(3:10-11)	4:13	
	4:8				5:1-11	2:2
	(6:12)		5:25	3:16		
16:17				3:17		

212). On the other hand, G. Bornkamm ([1], p. 16, n. 66) writes: "With strange passion W. Schmithals . . . maintains the identity of the battlefront in all of Paul's epistles." He regards the charge against the investigations mentioned as unjustified, since these works in fact "with important exegetical reasons" dispute the unity of the battlefront. Here he misunderstands me: my complaint is not even directed at all against the exegesis performed in these studies, which in any case is discussible and not seldom is even convincing, but against the method employed in them, not to consider in the exegesis of individual sections the parallels in other sections of the same correspondence or of other epistles of Paul. That this method is not discussible, of course, I think I must say and I do say—if you will— with "strange passion"; on the other hand, I maintain "the identity of the battle-front" with, I hope, exegetical reasons. I have attempted to show in Vol. 1, pp. 289 ff., using the example of D. Georgi's dissertation, what consequences the method criticized here can have in an essentially correct exegesis. Cf. *contra* Ch. Dietzfelbinger, "Was ist Irrlehre," *Theologische Existenz heute* 143 (1967): 46.

Rom. 16	I Cor.	II Cor.	Gal.	Phil.	I Thess.	II Thess.
	1:17–2:5			3:18		
16:17	1:10; 11:17-19	13:11	5:20 ff.	1:27; 2:2; 4:2	5:14	
	12:3	11:4				
	1:12	10:7; 13:3				
	4:10	10:1, 10; 13:3	1:11-12		1:5, 9; 2:1	
		12:16 ff.; 6:8; 7:2			2:3, 5	
	9:4 ff.; 15	12:14 ff.			2:7, 9	
					4:9 ff.; 5:14	3:6 ff.
16:17	11:2, 17		1:6-9	4:9		2:15

This selection is limited to those passages in which (with the exception of the references in parentheses) the polemical or apologetic reference as such *and* the concrete content of such reference are recognizable without further interpretation. The passages chosen with this point of view suffice to show that it was primarily exegetical and not systematic demands which caused the exegetes down to the most recent past to affirm a common battlefront throughout the major Pauline epistles. This judgment should be maintained until the opposite is proven.

Therewith nothing is said yet about the character of the heresy that was opposing Paul. That what was involved cannot have been a judaizing movement, as F. C. Baur and his school asserted, has been shown by the more recent studies since W. Lütgert in various ways. Lütgert's own solution to the problem suffers from his presupposition of a battlefront which though similar is nevertheless dual, against the pneumatics *and* against the Judaizers, in the epistles of Paul which he investigated. In the foregoing studies as well as in Vol. 1, I have attempted to produce the evidence that in his epistles composed during the so-called third missionary journey Paul was debating with missionary representatives of a pronounced Gnosticism of Jewish or Jewish Christian observance. Further discussion must show to what extent this attempt has been successful. Provisionally I may appeal to the results of these studies. Nevertheless they do not serve in detail as a foundation for the following reflections, but only in the basic judgment, which agrees with F. C. Baur and W. Lütgert, that in all the epistles the same battlefront is involved. In this it is not my intention in any way to question the pluriformity of primitive Christianity and its syncretistic as well as heretical peripheral phenomena. My investigations are concerned exclusively with those opponents who during the so-called third missionary journey of Paul are troubling his communities in Asia Minor and Greece. For their rival mission a multiformity is not from the outset likely. Therefore one should call in question the theological uniformity of these opponents only if the sources require it.

II

The seven major Pauline epistles which concern us (I and II Cor., Gal., Phil., I and II Thess., Rom.) were all written during the third so-called missionary journey of Paul. Thus they, together with the discussion conducted in them, belong within a very restricted span of time. No proof of this is required for I and II Cor. and Gal. On the other hand, it is by no means generally acknowledged that Phil. and I and II Thess. also belong to this time, but it has often and, for my conviction, adequately been substantiated.[9]

If one assumes this dating—its correctness will be confirmed in the following—then the question arises, which is not without importance even for the understanding of the individual epistles, in what sequence in time they were composed. Of course this question must be answered on the basis of a literary-critical analysis of the Pauline epistles, as I have attempted in the foregoing studies and in Vol. 1. This analysis has disclosed the existence of the following epistles or fragments of epistles:

Cor. A   = II Cor. 6:14–7:1; I Cor. 6:12-20; 9:24–10:22; 11:2-34; 15; 16:13-24.

Cor. B   = I Cor. 1:1–6:11; 7:1–9:23; 10:23–11:1; 12:1–14:40; 16:1-12.

Cor. C   = II Cor. 2:14–6:13; 7:2-4.

---

[9] On this, see W. Michaelis, [1], pp. 204 ff., 221 ff., and above, pp. 115 ff., 181 ff., 212 ff.

Cor. D   = II Cor. 10:1–13:13.
Cor. E   = II Cor. 9:1-15.
Cor. F   = II Cor. 1:1–2:13; 7:5–8:24.
Gal.   = Gal. 1:1–6:18.
Phil. A = Phil. 4:10-23.
Phil. B = Phil. 1:1–3:1; 4:4-7.
Phil. C = Phil. 3:2–4:3; 4:8-9.
Rom.   = Rom. 1–15; 16:21-23.
Rom.-Eph. = Rom. 16:1-20.
Thess. A = II Thess. 1:1-12; 3:6-16.
Thess. B = I Thess. 1:1–2:12; 4:2–5:28.
Thess. C = II Thess. 2:13-14; 2:1-12; 2:15–3:5; 3:17-18.
Thess. D = I Thess. 2:13–4:1.

I have earlier attempted to explain the circumstances of the composition of the six different letters to Corinth.[10] Cor. A-D—or, according to the customary view, I Cor.—were written during Paul's stay in Ephesus and its environs, and Cor. E-F—or, according to the customary view, II Cor.—during Paul's last journey from Ephesus to Corinth. Now we must investigate the question of how the other writings in this correspondence are to be fitted before, after, or into that journey.

The most important norms for this investigation are:
1. Indications about the personal circumstances of senders, bearers, or recipients of the writings, about travels or travel plans, and the like.
2. The status of the discussion with the opponents, particularly the changing form of the Pauline reaction to their agitation and the (growing) state of his knowledge of the heretical position.
3. The geographical situation of the communities addressed, since according to all appearance the heretical mission traversed Asia Minor and Greece on the same route which Paul traveled.
Rom. can most easily be fitted in. Its composition in Achaia and thus after Cor. F is generally assumed. Not much more difficulty is caused by Rom.-Eph., which was written in Achaia—to be sure, according to W. Michaelis only *after* the last stay in

_____
[10] Vol. 1, pp. 87 ff.

Corinth, about the time of Acts 20:6.[11] Thus it too is later than Cor. F; we cannot determine whether it was written before or after the Roman epistle.

The placing of Gal. also causes few difficulties if this epistle—under the presupposition of the North Galatian theory—was written on the so-called third missionary journey. This dating is rightly preferred today. It is necessary if and because in the Galatian epistle the same adversaries are opposed against whom Paul contends in Corinth. In other words, under the presupposition of the South Galatian theory, Paul had written the epistle on his second journey, but once again visited the communities addressed on his third journey. On this visit he must have become acquainted with the heretics or their views. The beginning of the debate during his stay in Ephesus (Cor. A), however, is lacking any such acquaintance. Thus the North Galatian theory is to be preferred for this reason also.

Galatians, then, was written in Ephesus or its environs. Since the heresy opposed moves from East to West, Gal. naturally belongs before Cor. A. Arguing for this view also is the fact that of all the epistles Gal. discloses the slightest knowledge on Paul's part of the opponents' position. Further, in Gal. the question of circumcision is *still* acute; cf. above, p. 41. On the other hand, no *decisive* weight for this dating may be placed on the fact that at the time of Cor. A (I Cor. 16:1 ff.) the gathering of the collection was already under way in Galatia, while it is not mentioned in Gal. This "not" need not be a "not yet," but could be a "no longer," explainable by the strained situation—in which case of course one would then have expected in Gal. 2:10 an indication: . . . καθὼς οἴδατε. Either way, Gal. presumably was written before Cor. A and hence during Paul's Ephesian sojourn.[12]

More difficult is the arranging in order of the other epistles, in which also the dating of Phil. and I and II Thess. on the third tour must be maintained. Thess. D is preceded by: Paul's brief interim visit from Ephesus in Corinth; the sending, bound up

---

[11] [1], p. 165; the reasons given for this dating are not compelling. There is much to argue against this later dating.

[12] C. E. Faw, "The Anomaly of Galatians," *Bibl. Res.*, 4 (1960): 25-38, with insufficient reasons dates Gal. after the end of the Ephesian sojourn and thus after the correspondence with Corinth.

with that visit, of Timotheus from Athens and to Thessalonica
(I Thess. 3:1-3) ; and the latter's return from Thessalonica to
Ephesus (I Thess. 3:6 ff.) .[13] Some time must lie between Paul's
arrival in Ephesus after his interim visit and the return of
Timotheus to Ephesus. Now Cor. C was written soon after Paul's
return from Corinth to Ephesus.[14] Therefore Thess. D was
written *after* Cor. C. But at the same time it belongs *before* Cor.
D. Arguing for this is not only the fact that Thess. D completely
lacks the harshness of the epistle Cor. D. More important is the
observation that the "sorrowful epistle," Cor. D, was written a
short time before Paul's departure for Macedonia (II Cor. 12:19–
13:2), while Thess. D still knows nothing of such an imminent
visit of Paul in Thessalonica. Therefore at the time of Thess. D
the travel plan still appears to have been in effect which Paul
describes in II Cor. 1:15-16 and which postponed the visit in
Thessalonica (I Thess. 2:17-18), which however had been abandoned at the time of the "sorrowful epistle" Cor. D (II Cor. 1:
17 ff.) .[15] Therefore Thess. D belongs *before* Cor. D. Arguing in
favor of this also is the fact that at the time of the composition of
Thess. D Timotheus was with Paul, which could no longer have
been the case at the time of Cor. D, if the note in Acts 19:21-22
is to be trusted. That is to say, then, the sending of Timotheus
and Erastus mentioned here served as preparation for Paul's visit
in Macedonia and the gathering of the offering connected with
it. Such a sending must in any case have preceded Paul's visit, because the Macedonians were still counting on the travel plan of
Paul set forth in II Cor. 1:15-16. Since in Macedonia Timotheus
is again staying with Paul (II Cor. 1:1), it is likely that Paul had
entrusted him with this task.

Thess. A-C belong before Paul's interim visit in Corinth and
thus before Cor. C. Since the three epistles contain no indications
of the situation (at least no longer), it is difficult to arrange
them. Of course, for Thess. A as for Phil. B and for Cor. A, the
"ἀκούω" (see p. 201) serves as a source of information. Moreover, Thess. A contains only the admonition to separate oneself
from the ἄτακτοι, but no debate with their false teachers, as then

---

[13] Cf. W. Hadorn, *Die Abfassung der Thessalonicherbriefe.* . . .
[14] Vol. 1, p. 105.
[15] Vol. 1, pp. 105-6.

from Thess. A one could not at all recognize the ἄτακτοι as false
teachers. Since Phil. B was written before Cor. A (see below), it
is most obvious, when one notes the route of the false teachers
from Macedonia to Achaia, to place Thess. A between Phil. B
and Cor. A.

Thess. B and Thess. C then in any case belong in the vicinity
of Cor. B. This also corresponds to the contents of these epistles,
which point to approximately the same stage of the discussion. It
is difficult to determine whether the order must be Thess. B—
Thess. C—Cor. B or Thess. B—Cor. B—Thess. C or Cor. B—
Thess. B—Thess. C. Since the unprejudiced attitude toward the
πνεῦμα and προφητεία in I Thess. 5:19-20 (= Thess. B) is more
understandable before I Cor. 12–14 (Cor. B) than after it, with
all reserve I place Thess. B before Cor. B. Arguing for this also
is the conjecture expressed on p. 212, that Thess. B was written
not long after Thess. A. I leave Thess. C with Thess. B and thus
before Cor. B because the two epistles are closely related to each
other, although in Thess. C., in contrast to Thess. B (but cf.
p. 174, n. 193) and as in Cor. B (I Cor. 12–14), the "πνεῦμα" is
characteristically supposed (see pp. 172 ff.), and from this
perspective one could just as well have Thess. C *follow* Cor. B.

There remains the task of fitting the writings to Philippi into
this correspondence. Phil. B contains, as its most important indication of the situation, the statement that Paul has written
the epistle during an imprisonment (Phil. 1:12 ff.) which he
hopes soon happily to have overcome (Phil. 1:25-26). None of the
Corinthian epistles indicates that it was written from an imprisonment. Besides none of them knows of such an imprisonment[16] with the expection of Cor. A. Thus Phil. B is to be dated
before the Corinthian epistles.

That is to say, I Cor. 15:32 presupposes a happily overcome
imprisonment of Paul in Ephesus which could possibly have
ended with a condemnation to the arena with the wild beasts.
This interpretation of the passage I Cor. 15:32, which had already
been represented by J. Weiss,[17] has been convincingly justified,

---

[16] θλῖψις in II Cor. 1:8 can hardly testify to an *imprisonment*, but to some
acute threat of death; see the commentaries *in loc. Contra* G. Bornkamm, [1],
p. 9, n. 13; J. Müller-Bardorff, p. 599.

[17] Meyer's *Kommentar*, V (1910, 9th ed.) : 365-66.

above all from the context, by W. Michaelis[18] and defended [19] against the objections of J. Schmid.[20] Thus Paul is saying, "If, humanly speaking, I had survived the fight with wild beasts in Ephesus—for which I was ready—what would I have gained from that?"

But even if one wishes to take the θηριομαχεῖν figuratively— it is impossible to assume that Paul *actually* had survived a bull- fight in Ephesus, for various reasons indicated by W. Michaelis and the commentaries—the expression must be speaking of a threat of death, which renders likely the assumption of an im- prisonment connected therewith. Under the presupposition of an Ephesian destination for Rom. 16, vss. 4 and 7 of that chapter also argue for such an imprisonment.[21]

Further, it is important to note that Paul proposes shortly— probably after his trial ends—to send Timotheus to Philippi (Phil. 2:19 ff.). We know of three trips to Macedonia by Timotheus during the time of Paul's sojourn in Ephesus. The last two trips have already been mentioned: from Athens by way of Macedonia to Thessalonica before the writing of Thess. D, and from Ephesus to Macedonia before Paul's final departure from Ephesus. In addition to these there is the first of the three trips, the one announced in Phil. 2:19 ff. The beginning of this trip of Timotheus lies *before* Cor. A, for in I Cor. 16:10-11 the departure apparently is already presupposed. At the time of Cor. B Timotheus has not yet returned (I Cor. 1:1), indeed Paul ap- parently does not even reckon on his having arrived in Corinth already at the time of Cor. B (I Cor. 4:17). But then Timotheus has traveled by way of Macedonia, as it was planned according to Phil. 2:19 ff.[22]

Thus Phil. B belongs in the time shortly before Cor. A. We must not put too much time between the two epistles, since Timotheus set out *after* Paul's release, which was already expected

---

[18] [2], pp. 117 ff.

[19] W. Michaelis, *Die Datierung des Philipperbriefes* (Gütersloh, 1933).

[20] J. Schmid, *Zeit und Ort der paulinischen Gefangenschaftsbriefe* (Freiburg, 1931).

[21] W. Michaelis, *Die Datierung des Philipperbriefes*, pp. 52 ff.

[22] W. Michaelis, pp. 49 ff., wrongly identifies the third trip of our enumeration with the first which we are now discussing. G. Friedrich, p. 94, also now holds the explanation given above.

soon at the time of Phil. B (Phil. 1:25), but at the time of Cor. B he had not yet arrived in Corinth (I Cor. 4:17).

This dating is confirmed by the fact that Phil. B and Cor. A both make the first reference to the unrest being suffered in the respective communities.[23] If one considers the direction of this mission which, like that of Paul, advances from Asia Minor by way of Macedonia to Achaia, it is completely natural that Paul feels compelled to the first intervention first in Philippi and only somewhat later in Corinth.

Phil. A is a letter of thanks for the Philippians' gift,[24] which apparently reached Paul when he was already in prison, and which was meant to reach him *there* (Phil. 4:14). In that case, at the time of Phil. A the imprisonment had already lasted some time. Hence a very long span of time is hardly to be placed between Phil. A and Phil B; this time span would have to suffice only for Epaphroditus' falling ill and recovery. Since Gal. was *not* written in prison, in any case it comes before Phil. A.

The absence of any allusion to the situation makes it very difficult to fit Phil. C into the whole of the correspondence. Naturally, because of the advanced stage of the debate, Phil. C must be later than Phil. B. The tone of the "philippic" which marks Phil. C is only to be compared with Cor. D. But in content also there exist between the two epistles especially close connections, in part limited to these writings.[25] One may compare, for example:

Phil. 3:2	with II Cor. 11:13 ff.
Phil. 3:3	with II Cor. 10:2-3
Phil. 3:4	with II Cor. 11:18
Phil. 3:5 ff.	with II Cor. 11:21 ff.
Phil. 3:12-14	with II Cor. 10:12, 17-18
Phil. 3:15	with II Cor. 12:1
Phil. 3:18-19	with II Cor. 11:13, 15.

---

[23] See Vol. 1, pp. 101 ff.; above, pp. 69 ff. S. Duncan, *St. Paul's Ephesian Ministry* (1929), also places Phil. before I Cor. in an Ephesian imprisonment.

[24] See above, pp. 77-78.

[25] J. H. Michael, *The Epistle of Paul to the Philippians* (1946, 4th ed.), p. XIX, has also noted this; cf. also G. Bornkamm, [3], p. 199.

Against the connection in point of time between Cor. D and Phil. C suggested by these observations, one could object that Paul could hardly at the same time in the same sharp fashion take a stand against the "evil workers," because these hardly would have been creating so much disturbance simultaneously in Philippi *and* Corinth. But over against this consideration, reference should be made to the discernible difference, with all the similarity, between Phil. 3 and II Cor. 10–13. While in Cor. D Paul is constantly arguing with the false apostles and their Corinthian following, in whose hands he sees the community already practically ensnared, he only warns the Philippians against these false teachers who are well known to them from their own experience. In this the situation in *Corinth* could have caused the sharp *tone* throughout, with which Paul takes his stand against the opponents who are engaged in further activity in Philippi—perhaps primarily through their newly won following.

If the suspicion should be correct that the recipient of Phil. C was Paul's γνήσιος σύζυγος Timotheus,[26] this would fit in with the assumption that at about the time of Cor. D—probably somewhat earlier, as soon as Paul had altered his travel plans on the basis of the news from Corinth, and this alteration may already be *presupposed* in II Cor. 13:1 (= Cor. D; cf. II Cor. 1:17)— Timotheus was on his way to Macedonia, where Paul again was already with him at the time of Cor. F (II Cor. 1:1). Then Phil. C would probably have been written somewhat after Cor. D.

It is to be conceded that this fitting into place of Phil. C is the least certain of all the epistles. The few available indications, however, make this dating only likely.

Hence there results the following order of the correspondence: Gal.—Phil. A—Phil. B—Thess. A—Cor. A—Thess. B—Thess. C—Cor. B—Cor. C—Thess. D—Cor. D—Phil. C—Cor. E—Cor. F—Rom.—Rom.-Eph.

I have calculated the span of time over which Paul's correspondence with *Corinth* extends at about eight months, say from February to October.

If one proceeds from the fact that Rom. and Rom.-Eph. were written in Achaia, but Paul celebrated the following Passover al-

---

[26] Phil. 4:3; cf. above, p. 76.

ready in Philippi (Acts 20:6), the time span of eight months is to be lengthened by some three to four months, if it is to include Rom. and Rom.-Eph.

Another two or three months earlier are to be assumed for Phil. A and B. We cannot say precisely how long the interim between Gal. and Phil. A is. Even if one includes in the calculation some intermediate mission stations of the heretics—for the Pauline mission they are explicitly denied in Acts 16:6 ff.—the way from Galatia to Philippi is to be made in six months to a year at the most. This period is further to be shortened by the time which one allows for the news about circumstances in Galatia to reach Ephesus. Thus the time from Gal. to Cor. A is to be assumed at the very most as one year, but it probably is considerably less.

We conclude that Paul's major epistles which we have examined were written within a span of less than two years during the so-called third missionary journey. According to the absolute chronology which is widely held today[27] but is wholly uncertain. this span of time would include the period from the summer of 54 to the spring of 56.

Anyone who recognizes this conclusion of our study in principle will be cautious in using arguments of style and word statistics in the question of the inauthenticity of individual ones of the other six epistles attributed to Paul. If I and II Thess. were written on the second missionary journey, but Phil. in the Roman imprisonment, then in fact the style and vocabulary of the major Pauline epistles would be an unconditional yardstick for Paul's style in general. But if these epistles belong within the narrowly limited span of less than two years, one will be able to measure epistles from an entirely different time by this yardstick only with caution. Cf. Hoffmann, pp. 234 ff.; 323 ff.

III

The question as to the form of the *earliest collection of Paul's epistles* has occupied the exegetes and historians so often and

---

[27] W. Michaelis, [1], pp. 153-54.

with so much ingenuity[28] that one takes up this question with only slight hope of new convincing results. Nevertheless this problem must be approached once more. In doing so, the point of beginning must be the oldest canonical lists or manuscripts.[29] Here they are placed side by side:

Muratorian Canon	Tertullian, adv. Marc. IV 5 and de praescr. haer. 36[30]	Marcion	P46[31]	List in Codex Claromontanus[32]	39th Festal Letter of Athanasius (367)
I, II Cor.	I, II Cor.	Gal.	Rom.	Rom.	Rom.
Eph.	Gal.	I, II Cor.	Hebr.	I, II Cor.	I, II Cor.
Phil.	Phil.	Rom.	I, II Cor.	Gal.	Gal.
Col.	I, II Thess.	I, II Thess.	Eph.	Eph.	Eph.
Gal.	Eph.	Eph.	Gal.	(Phil.)	Phil.
I, II Thess.	(Col.?)	Col.	Phil.	(I, II Thess.)	Col.
Rom.	Rom.	Phil.[33]	Col.	I, II Tim.	I, II Thess.
					Hebrews
Philemon	(Philemon?)	Philemon	I (II) Thess.	Titus	I, II Tim.
Titus			(Philemon)	Col.	Titus
I, II Tim.				Philemon	Philemon

[28] From the literature we may mention: T. Zahn, *Geschichte des neutestamentlichen Kanons*, I (1888-89), II (1890-92); A. Deissmann, *Bible Studies* (1909), pp. 3-59; *idem, Light from the Ancient East* (1927), pp. 227 ff.; J. Weiss, *Earliest Christianity* (1959), II: 684; W. Hartke, *Die Sammlung und die älteste Ausgabe der Paulusbriefe*, Diss. Bonn, 1917; A. v. Harnack, *Die Briefsammlung des Apostels Paulus* (Leipzig, 1926); P. L. Couchoud, "La première édition de St. Paul," RHR, 1926; E. J. Goodspeed, *The Formation of the New Testament* (1926); *idem, New Solutions of New Testament Problems* (1927); *idem, The Key to Ephesians* (1956); *idem, The Meaning of Ephesians* (1933); *idem, An Introduction to the New Testament* (1958, 14th ed.), pp. 210-39; H. Lietzmann, "Einführung in die Textgeschichte der Paulusbriefe," HNT 8 (1933, 4th ed.): 1 ff., and *Kleine Schriften* II, TU 68: 138 ff.; J. Knox, *Philemon Among the Letters of Paul* (1935, 1959, 2nd ed.); *idem, Marcion and the New Testament* (1942); *idem, "A Note on the Format of the Pauline Corpus," HTR 50 (1957): 311-14; C. L. Mitton, *The Formation of the Pauline Corpus of Letters* (1955); A. E. Barnett, *Paul Becomes a Literary Influence* (1941); K. Lake, *An Introduction to the NT* (1948, 2nd ed.), pp. 96 ff.; C. H. Buck, "The Early Order of the Pauline Corpus," JBL 68 (1949): 351-57; E. Kamlah, *Traditionsgeschichtliche Untersuchungen zur Schlussdoxologie des Römerbriefes*, Diss. Tübingen, 1955; J. Finegan, "The Original Form of the Pauline Collection," HTR 49 (1956): 85-103; E. Hennecke-Schneemelcher-Wilson, *New Testament Apocrypha*, I: 1 ff.; N. A. Dahl, "Welche Ordnung der Paulusbriefe wird vom Muratorischen Kanon vorausgesetzt," ZNW 52 (1961): 39 ff.; D. Guthrie, *New Testament Introduction*, "The Pauline Epistles" (1961), pp. 255-69. W. G. Kümmel, *Introduction to the New Testament* (1965), p. 337 (Lit.); L. Foster, "The Earliest Collection of Paul's Epistles," *Bull. Evang. Theol. Soc.* 10 (1967): 44-55; H. v. Campenhausen, *Die*

If one compares these lists, no justification should be required when Hebrews is eliminated as not belonging to the original collection.[34] Moreover, no objection should be raised when one judges the Pastoral Epistles similarly. Even if one may find reasons in a particular case why they could have been omitted by Tertullian, Marcion, and P[46], the fact that they are lacking precisely in three of the earliest lists, but not later, argues against their belonging to the earliest collection of epistles.[35] Hence their place too is still doubtful at first: in the Muratorian Canon they are appended to the other ten epistles;[36] the list in the Codex Claromontanus places them in the middle of the other epistles; the usual order arranges the personal epistles according to length and therefore places the Pastoral Epistles before Philemon. Finally, it is generally recognized that Marcion arranges his Pauline canon according to his own point of view; whether ac-

---

Entstehung der christlichen Bibel, BHT 39 (1968): 292-93 (Lit.).

[29] Even later the order of the epistles in the Corpus Paulinum varies quite significantly, especially among the Latins; cf. A. Jülicher, *Einleitung* (1906, 5th and 6th eds.), pp. 506-7; (1931, 7th ed.), p. 547. The variations however are all already present in the early period and are explained in terms of particular principles of order. Thus, e.g., the so-called Decretum Gelasianum (Preuschen, *Analecta* II: 54) arranges them according to length: Eph., I Thess., II Thess., Gal., Phil., Col. (cf. n. 85).

[30] On the basis of the order in which Tertullian, in the passage cited, enumerates the apostolic communities, to be sure not completely, but consistently. Cf. J. Knox, *Marcion,* p. 44; T. Zahn, II, 1: 344-45. N. A. Dahl (n. 28, above), pp. 41-42, incorrectly opposes this inference.

[31] The manuscript, a codex of 104 leaves altogether, 86 of which are preserved, breaks off in I Thess. On the missing pages II Thess. and Philemon were included; this leaves some four leaves to be accounted for. The space is far too little for the Pastoral Epistles. "The Pastoral Epistles apparently never belonged to it," writes the editor of P46, F. Kenyon, in *The Text of the Greek Bible* (1952), p. 45. Cf. also J. Finegan (n. 28, above), p. 93. It is not to be assumed that Philemon also could have been lacking, while Col. and Eph. are present; cf. K. Lake (n. 28, above), p. 98; W. Kümmel in ThRS, 1938, pp. 301 ff.

[32] See E. Preuschen, *Analecta,* II (1910, 2nd ed.): 40 ff.; Hennecke-Schneemelcher-Wilson, I: 21. Phil. and I and II Thess. are inadvertently omitted; of course it is not wholly certain whether precisely at this point.

[33] Thus Tertullian, adv. Marc. V; Epiph., Haer. XLII, 9, gives at the end the order of Philemon and then Philippians (see above).

[34] Cf. W. H. P. Hatch, "The Position of Hebrews in the Canon of the New Testament," HTR 29 (1936): 133 ff.

[35] A. v. Harnack, [1], p. 6; *idem, Marcion* (2nd ed.), pp. 170* ff.; W. Hartke (n. 28, above), pp. 61 ff.; J. Knox, *Marcion,* p. 175.

[36] Even from the *handling* of the Pastoral Epistles in the Muratorian Canon, W. Hartke, p. 63, infers "that for a long time they were unknown or were regarded as inauthentic." He also refers there to Tatian, who according to Jerome rejected the Pastoral Epistles, but possibly did not know them at all.

cording to length,[37] according to time of composition,[38] or according to other norms[39] is disputed. In any case his order in detail cannot tell us anything certain about the original ecclesiastical order;[40] therefore we may leave it aside for the moment.

If we take into account these considerations, the lists look as follows:

Muratorian Canon	Tertullian	P46	List in Codex Claromontanus	Athanasius
I, II Cor.	I, II Cor.	Rom.	Rom.	Rom.
Eph.	Gal.	I, II Cor.	I, II Cor.	I, II Cor.
Phil.	Phil.	Eph.	Gal.	Gal.
Col.	I, II Thess.	Gal.	Eph.	Eph.
Gal.	Eph.	Phil.	(Phil.)	Phil.
I, II Thess.	(Col.?)	Col.	(I, II) Thess.	Col.
Rom.	Rom.	I (II) Thess.	Col.	I, II Thess.
Philemon	(Philemon?)	(Philemon)	Philemon	Philemon

Particularly striking now is the change in the position of the Roman epistle. Undoubtedly the position of the Corinthian epistles at the head of the collection is the original one. This has been well established by A. v. Harnack,[41] following others. To his arguments we may add that a later downgrading of Rom. appears unthinkable, while the later placing of Rom. at the head in the interest of Rome[42] easily explains the change in the position of Rom. Even A. v. Harnack did not note that I Clem. already was acquainted with a collection of Paul's epistles at the head of which—in Rome!—stood the Corinthian epistles.[43] If one

---

[37] Thus A. v. Harnack, [1], p. 13; J. Finegan, p. 85.

[38] Thus W. Hartke, p. 73; W. Hadorn, "Die Abfassung der Thessalonicherbriefe auf der 3. Missionsreise und der Kanon des Marcion," ZNW 19 (1919): 67 ff.; T. Zahn, I: 623; II: 346-47; C. L. Mitton, pp. 38 ff.

[39] Cf. C. H. Buck, pp. 351-57.

[40] The same is true of the old Syriac canonical lists which follow Marcion.

[41] A. v. Harnack, [1], pp. 8 ff.; T. Zahn, II, 1: 346, also appeals to Marcion's canon for the original leading position of the Corinthian epistles and finds still other ancient traces of this order. See further n. 51.

[42] Cf. A. v. Harnack, [1], pp. 22-23.

[43] Cf. I Clem. 47.1-2, and on this, R. Knopf in the *Ergänzungsband* to HNT, *in loc.* Clement writes: Ἀναλάβετε τὴν ἐπιστολὴν τοῦ μακαρίου Παύλου τοῦ ἀποστόλου. τί πρῶτον ὑμῖν ἐν ἀρχῇ τοῦ εὐαγγελίου ἔγραψεν;—then follows the reference to I Cor. 1 ff. This text becomes comprehensible when one understands ἐπιστολή as a collection of epistles (as ἡ γραφή alongside αἱ γραφαί), whose first (πρῶτον) and therefore allegedly oldest (ἐν ἀρχῇ) writing was I Cor. W. Hartke

now places Rom. back in its old position, the following order emerges:

Muratorian Canon	Tertullian	P46	List in Codex Claro-montanus	Athanasius
I, II Cor.	I, II Cor.	I, II Cor.	I, II Cor.	I, II Cor.
Eph.	Gal.	Eph.	Gal.	Gal.
Phil.	Phil.	Gal.	Eph.	Eph.
Col.	I, II Thess.	Phil.	(Phil.)	Phil.
Gal.	Eph.	Col.	(I, II Thess.)	Col.
I, II Thess.	(Col.?)	I (II) Thess.	Col.	I, II Thess.
Rom.	Rom.	Rom.	Rom.	Rom.
Philemon	(Philemon?)	(Philemon)	Philemon	Philemon

It will be noted that the remaining differences concern the uncertain position of Eph. and Col.[44] All the other epistles have a fixed place.[45] Of course, as we shall see shortly, Rome originally closed the early collection. Philemon also cannot always have stood in its present place. But it appears never to have had another place. Now Eph., Col., and Philemon belong close together anyway. This invites us to make the attempt even to excise this group of three epistles. Then there remain the seven major epistles in a fixed order:

I Cor. II Cor. Gal. Phil. I Thess. II Thess. Rom.

In addition to the formal analysis attempted here, there are many substantive reasons arguing that herewith we have before us the earliest collection of the epistles of Paul.

(pp. 56 ff.) has made this interpretation likely: Irenaeus "says in III, 16.5: *propter quod et in epistula (Ioannes domini discipulus) sic testificatus est nobis:* then follows I John 2:18 ff. He continues in vs. 8: *Ioannes in praedicta epistula fugere eos praecepit dicens:* now follows II John 7 f. He says further: *Et rursus in epistula ait,* with I John 4:1 following; in I, 16.3 also II John is cited. Irenaeus had before him a collection of epistles of John including at least I and II John . . . with the superscription: ἐπιστολὴ ʼΙωάννου" (p. 56). For this understanding of ἐπιστολή as a collection of epistles one may also compare: Polycarp, Phil. 11.2-3; Eus. CH VI, 11.3; VII, 25 ff.

[44] According to A. Jülicher, *Einleitung* (1906, 5th and 6th eds.), p. 507; (1931, 7th ed.), p. 547, "in the West even far into the Middle Ages, Col. had not achieved a firm place." On this, cf. J. Finegan, p. 102; T. Zahn, II, 1: 349 ff.; C. R. Gregory in the Prolegomena to Tischendorf's *Novum Testamentum* (1884), III: 139-40; N. A. Dahl, p. 43; Augustine, De doct. christ. 2.13; P. Corssen, ZNW 10 (1909): 10; 36.

[45] Excepted is only the later position of Gal. in the Muratorian Canon. I have no explanation for this. It may be due to an oversight.

Important first of all is the fact that this—and only this—collection possesses an editorial beginning and conclusion. The *beginning* is found in I Cor. 1:2*b*, in that remark which introduced the entire collection and made it binding for the Christian community everywhere.[46] "Every effort of the exegetes to explain this ecumenical address of the so personal epistle is in my opinion futile; there remains no other choice but to see in these words an addition *which pertains to the entire collection of epistles.*" [47]

The *conclusion* is formed by the doxology in Rom. 16:25-27. It has long been established that it is non-Pauline. The complicated problem of its varied position at the end of the Roman epistle cannot be treated here.[48] If it had its original position after Rom. 16, then Rom. formed the conclusion of the collection; for otherwise it would be incomprehensible why in the middle of a collection such a doxology was attached to Rom. and only there. If it originally stood after 14:23,[49] then it replaced the conclusion of the epistle which had been lost in a manuscript. Even such a loss of the last pages presupposes that Rom. concluded the collection.[50] But this does not matter, nor does it

---

[46] Thus, correctly, J. Weiss in Meyer's *Kommentar* V (1910, 9th ed.), *in loc.* Cf. also J. Leipoldt in ZNW 44 (1953) : 143; A. v. Harnack, [1], p. 9; Vol. 1, p. 89; R. Knopf on I Clem. 47.1 ff. in the *Ergänzungsband* to HNT. When the Epistle to the Romans came to stand at the head of the collection, Codex G achieved a similar effect by omitting the ἐν Ῥώμῃ in Rom. 1:7, 15.

[47] A. v. Harnack, [1], p. 9. H. Lietzmann (*An die Korinther*, HNT 9 [1949, 4th ed.]: 5; cf. also p. 166) refers to two Jewish synagogue inscriptions: "Let peace be upon this place and upon all the places of Israel." This is a suggestive expansion of the salutation of peace. But the ecumenical address of a private epistle of Paul to Corinth is simply meaningless and is by no means to be accounted for by that salutation of peace. Even the complicated explanation of U. Wickert in ZNW 50 (1959) : 73 ff., will hardly find any acceptance. According to Wickert, Paul intended to say: "I am writing to you *in the fellowship of the faith with all* who call on the name of Christ in every place, whether theirs or ours." But *actually* Paul does not say this. What stands in I Cor. 1:1-2, according to all the rules of grammar, can only mean: "I am writing to you and to all who . . . ." Anyone who—rightly—does not credit Paul with such an address will be obliged to recognize in it the hand of an editor.

[48] On this, see H. Lietzmann, *An die Römer*, HNT 8 (1933, 4th ed.): 130-31.

[49] In P46 the doxology follows 15:33. This, like many another uncertainty about the end of Rom. 14, 15, and 16, could be explained if the Roman epistle was already circulating in the West in copies before it acquired its present form in the first collection.

[50] That the verses Rom. 16:24-27 are Marcionite, as is often asserted (see the introductions and commentaries), is unprovable and as good as ruled out by the fact that a Marcionite addition could hardly survive in the total ecclesiastical textual tradition. Besides, it cannot be demonstrated that Marcion's text included 16:24-27. On the entire problem, cf. E. Kamlah; K. Lake, pp. 97-98.

matter whether it was the editor of the collection or a later hand
that added the doxology; either way, the doxology presupposes
the collection of (seven) epistles running from I Cor. to Rom.[51]

Especially important are the observations which may be related to the number seven of these epistles. Of course this number is not accidental; how much it is a deliberately intended
thing becomes especially clear when one notes that it first emerged
through the editorial conflation of a larger number of original
writings.[52] The number seven is characteristic of the early Christian collections of epistles: the Apocalypse of John contains seven
letters;[53] the oldest and genuine collection of Ignatius' epistles
contains seven of his writings; the collection of Bishop Dionysius
of Corinth included seven epistles.[54] Then it certainly is no
accident that the "catholic" epistles of the New Testament were
canonized as a collection of seven, particularly since the Corpus
Paulinum also finally embraced, with the inclusion of Hebrews,
2 x 7 writings and even the author of the Muratorian Canon still
contrived the number seven out of the ten congregational epistles

---

[51] When the editor put the section Rom. 16:21-23, which originally stood after
Rom. 15:32 (see p. 237, n. 86), in its present place, he left the benediction, which
closed the genuine Roman epistle, standing in Rom. 15:33. Similarly, he left the
concluding benediction of Rom.-Eph. in Rom. 16:20b standing *before* the greetings in Rom. 16:21-23. Thus the Roman epistle is the only one in the Corpus
Paulinum to lack the concluding benediction, which led some manuscripts to re-
locate vs. 20b after vs. 23. The absence of the benediction at the end of the Roman
epistle wrought by the editing is understandable if the doxology in Rom. 16:25-27
were meant to mark the actual conclusion. But then the latter may come from the
editor of the entire collection.

On the problem of collection, cf. J. Weiss, *Earliest Christianity*, II: 684, n. 43:
"In the oldest collection (Muratorian Canon) Romans stood at the end; the editorial concluding doxology would be very appropriate here. We may have, thus, in
the additions in [I] Cor. 1:2 and Rom. 16:25 ff., traces of the earliest collection
before us."

[52] In Vol. 1 and in the foregoing studies I have enumerated reasons, so far as
necessary, which could account for the editorial conflating in individual cases. On
this, see W. Michaelis, "Teilungshypothesen bei Paulusbriefen," ThZ 1959, pp. 1 ff.
In all cases one will also have to take into account the influencing, imponderable
in details, by the number seven of the epistles to be achieved. Cf. further n. 69 and
pp. 271 ff.

[53] Cf. J. Knox, *Philemon*, p. 73.

[54] Cf. Eus. CH IV, 23; A. v. Harnack, [1], pp. 36 ff.; *idem, Geschichte der
altchristlichen Literatur*, I, 1: 235. The epistles go to Lacedaemonia, Athens,
Nicomedia, Gortyna and all Crete, Amastris and all Pontus, Knossos, and Rome.
Another epistle of Dionysius to a certain Chrysophora, also mentioned by
Eusebius, cannot have belonged to the collection of epistles to churches. But see
n. 78.

of the Corpus Paulinum:[55] "The first (epistle) to the Corinthians, the second to the Ephesians, the third to the Philippians, the fourth to the Colossians, the fifth to the Galatians, the sixth to the Thessalonians, the seventh to the Romans" (!!).[56] Jerome still reports (Ep. 53 [103] ad Paulinum) : "Paulus apostolus ad VII ecclesias scribit."

Why this number seven? It is because of that ecumenical address with which the editor of the oldest collection of the Pauline epistles introduced them (I Cor. 1:2)! E. Lohmeyer has clearly seen this for the seven letters in the Apocalypse: "It is indeed certain that the writings to these churches never . . . were intended to be delivered individually to the churches addressed; this appears not only from the similarity of form, but also, for example, from the occasional reference to 'all the churches' (2:23). As a whole they rather form parts of a book intended for the totality of primitive Christian communities, which is outwardly clothed in the form of an epistle 'to the seven churches' (1:4) . . . . They ultimately represent the totality of all primitive Christian communities." [57]

The Muratorian Canon says it still more clearly[58] in the continuation of the quotation cited above: "But even though another letter was written to the Corinthians and to the Thessalonians for their instruction, it is clearly evident that *one* community is scattered over the whole earth. For John in the Revelation also indeed writes to the seven churches, but he is speaking to all." Thus also the designation "catholic" epistles, which de-

---

[55] According to J. Knox, *Marcion*, p. 46, Marcion's collection also is supposed to have embraced seven epistles. Marcion is said to have counted I and II Cor., I and II Thess., and Col. and Philemon as one epistle each; on this, see pp. 267 ff. Amphilochius speaks of ἐπιστολὰς δὶς ἑπτά of Paul; cf. *Some Early Lists . . .* , ed. F. W. Grosheide, *Textus Minores*, I (1968) : 21.

[56] Lines 50-54. Counting the two epistles to the same address as *one* is also common elsewhere; see R. Knopf in the *Ergänzungsband* to HNT on I Clem. 47.1.

[57] *Die Offenbarung des Johannes*, HNT 16 (1953, 2nd ed.) : 42.

[58] Cf. further in N. A. Dahl, pp. 44-45; A. v. Harnack, "Über den Verfasser und den literarischen Charakter des muratorischen Fragments," ZNW 24 (1925) : 1-16, with reference to Victorinus of Pettau's (martyr under Diocletian) commentary on Rev. 1:20 (CSEL 49: 27-28) : ". . . *denique sive in Asia sive in toto orbe septem ecclesias omnes et septem nominatas unam esse catholicam Paulus docuit.*" On the relation of Victorinus to the Muratorian Canon, see in A. v. Harnack, pp. 11-12. Cf. further N. A. Dahl, "The Particularity of the Pauline Epistles," in *Neotestamentica et Patristica* (1962) , pp. 261 ff.

notes the ecumenical import of these epistles[59] and which Eusebius perhaps also uses for the collection of Dionysius' epistles,[60] may be related to the number seven, wherever the disputed *origin* of that designation may lie.

Thus the number seven of the epistles[61] makes them appear to be directed to the whole of Christendom.[62] This is not the place to look into the origin of this special symbolism of numbers.[63] But it is impossible to assume that precisely with the Pauline epistles this conception, which was so centrally dominant in the primitive Christian collections, should have been left out of consideration. On the contrary, the seven-epistle collection of Paul may have become the direct model for the other collec-

---

[59] Cf. W. Michaelis, [1], pp. 147-48; RGG (3rd ed.), III, cols. 1198-99.

[60] A. v. Harnack, [1], p. 79, n. 2.

[61] At first not of *communities*, as is shown by the Pauline collection, the Ignatian epistles with the epistle to Polycarp, and even the Muratorian Canon; for even the last-named in fact does not enumerate seven *communities* but rather seven *epistles*.

[62] On the "ecumenical" significance of the number seven, cf. Zech. 4:10 and Rev. 5:6; cf. also Matt. 18:21-22, where, as is frequently the case, seven appears as the number of completeness. The number seven of the leaders of the Hellenistic community in Jerusalem (Acts 6:1-7) could indicate that the Seven were understood from the very beginning as the representatives of the entire Hellenistic church. Philo (de opif. mundi 99-100) praises the number seven, because it is the only one among the first ten numbers which "neither produces other numbers nor can be produced by them," i.e., it is neither the result nor a factor of a multiplication within the numbers one to ten. Therefore he can describe the number seven as the very image of God. Thus the number seven is the expression of original and perfect unity. It appears thus already in the Indo-Iranian cosmology; cf. Bundahisn, *passim;* G. Widengren, *Iranische Geisteswelt* (1961), pp. 30, 33, 65-66. Cf. further Philo, Quis rer. div. haer. 170; spec. leg. II, 64; seven archangels, seven classes of angels: Bousset-Gressmann, *Die Religion des Judentums,* HNT 21 (1966, 4th ed.) : 325-26; seven disciples = all disciples: John 21:2; seven men: Mark 12:20 ff. par.; Tob. 3:8; 6:14; Apollonius of Tyana also had seven disciples: Philostratus I, 18; seven Jewish sects as the sum of heresy: Justin, Dial. 80.4; Eus. CH IV, 22.7; the *semeia* source of the Gospel of John contains seven miracles; seventy times seven means "always": Gen. 4:24; Test. Benj. 7; Matt. 18:22; Luke 17:4; Acts 20:4 names seven companions of Paul, who represent his communities; seven commandments of Noah apply to all men: Billerbeck III, 37 ff.; for further material, see article, ἑπτά, TDNT II, 627 ff. (Lit.) ; Billerbeck II, 641; J. Hehn, *Siebenzahl und Sabbat bei den Babyloniern und im Alten Testament* (1907) ; R. Reitzenstein, *Die Vorgeschichte der christlichen Taufe* (1929), pp. 343-44.

[63] I know of no example of a collection of seven writings before the primitive Christian collections. This makes the frequency of this number in the primitive Christian collections a special problem; see Leipoldt-Morenz, *Heilige Schriften* (Leipzig, 1953), pp. 40 ff. One should note that according to IV Ezra 14:37 ff., Ezra the scribe is said to have written down 94 books, namely the 24 canonical books of the Old Testament as well as 70 books which (as apocrypha) were to be given to the wise men of the people.

tions.[64] This has to be regarded as certain in the case of the Corinthian collection of Dionysius' letters, and as very likely in the case of the Ignatian epistles.[65] It is more difficult to say what the case is with the letters in the Apocalypse. Since I Clem. already uses this—the earliest—collection of Paul's letters, it must have emerged at the latest in the eighties[66] and thus must be earlier than the Apocalypse. If one compares the congregations addressed in the two collections—Paul's epistles to Greece and Galatia, the letters in the Apocalypse to western Asia Minor—the complementary parallelism of the two collections is striking, matched by a parallelism of the church's influence.[67] Thus the collection in the Apocalypse could also have been patterned after the Pauline collection,[68] particularly since it has the same tendency as the latter, namely the anti-Gnostic tendency.

We must also give attention to the contents of this collection of seven letters. All the letters come from the same period, from the same limited area, and out of a common occasion. Of course the latter is not true of the actual Roman epistle; but by the attachment of the little epistle of Rom. 16, which in Rom. 16:17-20 contains an anti-Gnostic polemic, Romans also is given the special polemical character. Thus now each of the seven epistles contains a more or less comprehensive debate of Paul with his (Gnostic) opponents, even if individual ones of the underlying writings (Rom., Phil. A) did not bear this character.[69] This is not

---

[64] "It is even very possible that this venture (scil., collecting writings to seven churches) at the very beginning played a role in the canonizing of Paul's epistles with their particular addresses" (A. v. Harnack [above, n. 58], p. 12, n. 2). "It may be taken therefore as highly probable that it was the Pauline Corpus which served as a model for the letter-collections in Revelation and Ignatius" (C. L. Mitton [above, n. 28], p. 33, with detailed justification of this opinion).

[65] Cf. W. G. Kümmel, "Notwendigkeit und Grenze des neutestamentlichen Kanons," ZThK 47 (1950): 283. Is it accidental that both collections also contain an epistle to the Romans, which moreover in Dionysius' collection, as in one branch of the Ignatian tradition, concludes the collection? Hardly! All the collections, moreover, are shaped by the same anti-Gnostic tendency!

[66] Cf. I Clem. 47.1 ff.; 35.5-6; 49.5; R. Knopf in the Ergänzungsband to HNT on I Clem. 47.1 ff.; P. Feine, Einleitung in das NT (1936), p. 288; J. Finegan, p. 85.

[67] At the time of these collections, it seems, Greece and Galatia—so far as they were orthodox—were under Pauline influence, while Asia Minor was rather under that of a more "synoptic" type of ecclesiastical piety (see E. Lohmeyer, Die Offenbarung des Johannes, HNT 16 [1953, 2nd ed.]: 42).

[68] Cf. E. J. Goodspeed, New Solutions, pp. 7, 21 ff.; J. Knox, Marcion, pp. 56-57.

[69] One will also have to take into account the tendency to show the same polemic in all seven epistles when one considers the question of the motives of

accidental, but is an indication of the intention with which this collection was instituted and one more proof of the original unitary character of this collection of seven epistles; for of the three other epistles appearing in the collection of ten, Ephesians and Philemon at any rate contain no corresponding polemic. This group of three is thereby clearly separated from the seven major epistles, even if one wishes to connect the former with the seven epistles with respect to their genuineness as well as the place and time of their origin.

In view of these facts, there can be no doubt as to the intention of this collection: it was to be used as a weapon in the struggle against the spreading Gnostic heresy. Indeed, this is already done by I Clement, which is the earliest witness for this collection.[70] In this aim, the original Corpus Paulinum became the model for almost all other primitive Christian collections of epistles, including the letters of the Apocalypse, and including also smaller collections like that of the epistles of John or the Pastoral Epistles.

A. v. Harnack has already shown[71]—convincingly, it seems to me—that Corinth[72] is the place of origin of this collection of the letters. In fact all the traces lead in this direction, and I Clem. tells us how seriously Corinth, as the center of Pauline Christianity, had to contend with Gnosticism even in the post-apostolic age.[73]

If one considers this homogeneity of the seven letters as to place, time, and contents, and the related aim in their being collected, this argues not only for the original independence of this collection, but also against the conclusion that the other six epistles attributed to Paul must not be genuine *because* they were later added to the earliest collection. Whoever collected them did not intend to make a complete collection of Paul's

---

the editor or editors; cf. n. 52.

[70] See n. 66.

[71] [1], pp. 8-9.

[72] *Contra* J. Knox, *Marcion*, pp. 174 ff.; C. L. Mitton, pp. 45 ff. Both argue for Ephesus as the place where Paul's epistles were first collected. The thesis is connected with their understanding of the Ephesian epistle and stands or falls with the correctness of this understanding; see n. 77. Ephesus appears incidentally very early to have been lost to the Pauline sphere of influence; see n. 67; Acts 20:16-17 and the commentaries *in loc.*; W. Bauer, [1], pp. 82 ff.

[73] Harnack, [1], pp. 36 ff., p. 73, n. 12; W. Bauer, [1], pp. 105 ff.

epistles, but to publish *seven* of the apostle's letters with an *anti-Gnostic* thrust.

In view of this state of affairs, the later edition of other—authentic or inauthentic—epistles of Paul created no difficulties.

Anyone who recognizes the editorial reworking of the seven epistles will also be obliged to see therein an argument that the collection of seven was the original one. That is to say, however one may evaluate Eph., Col., and Philemon, the very distinctive hand of the redactor of the seven epistles is not to be detected in these writings. This observation is only slightly limited by the fact that Gal. also has apparently been spared any editorial tampering; for its place in the collection of the seven epistles is well established anyway.

It is evident that the collection of ten epistles of Paul, which is still literarily preserved in P[46] and whose number is already explained by the author of the Muratorian Canon with the help of the number seven, cannot have been *originally* related to the scheme of seven. If one proceeds from the number of the *epistles,* there are just ten epistles, not seven. Even if one combines I and II Cor., and I and II Thess., into one epistle respectively, in spite of their complete independence, there still remain eight epistles; for counting Col. and Philemon as one epistle (see below, p. 265) is all the more a makeshift solution. If, as later became customary (see n. 61), one proceeds from the number of the *churches,* again Philemon falls completely out of the picture. Thus in any case the collection of the ten epistles has been connected with the schema of the seven only with difficulty.

What occasion was there for this artificial combination? It was hardly anything but the fact that with the earliest collection of Paul's epistles the number seven was bound up as a *constitutivum,* i.e., that this collection actually included seven epistles. When this collection was enlarged, the attempt was made to preserve the old schema, which ultimately was best accomplished by counting only the number of the churches addressed. In the collection of ten epistles as well as in that of thirteen, by ignoring Philemon and the Pastorals, this yielded the number seven. The fact that now the schema no longer embraced the entire collection, whose catholicity therefore also was no longer in principle demonstrated by the applied schema, shows again that a collection of seven epistles must have stood at the beginning of the Corpus Paulinum.

Since the ten-epistle canon served generally as a collection of seven units, and thus I-II Cor., I-II Thess., and Col.-Philemon were counted as *one* epistle each, J. Knox ("A Conjecture . . .") assumes that the editor of the ten-epistle collection excised the prescript from II Cor. and II Thess. Thus in each case two epistles appeared as one epistle. Only around 150, after the acceptance of the Pastoral Epistles, when the number seven completely disappeared, were II Cor. and II Thess. again furnished with prescripts which were newly formed and were patterned after the prescripts of I Cor. and I Thess. This would explain the especially close similarity between the prescripts of I and II Cor., and of I and II Thess.

This striking fact is very simply explained: In each case Paul is writing the later epistle to the same recipients in the same situation in the awareness of the preceding epistle. Besides, Knox's thesis has the problem that it cannot be carried through in the case of Col.-Philemon. Its importance lies in the correct impression that a canon of ten can hardly be connected with the number seven. Thus there was earlier a canon of seven!

Finally, a consideration of the other two groups of three epistles also argues for the originally independent existence of the seven major epistles. That is to say, these six epistles obviously consist of two originally independent collections of three epistles each. Every exegete knows that for several reasons of substance, Eph.-Col.-Philemon[74] and I Tim.-II Tim.-Titus belong together. It is obvious also that the two smaller collections are clearly distinguished from each other and from the seven major epistles. And the number three apparently is the other fixed number for collections of writings in primitive Christianity. One recalls the three epistles of John;[75] Clement of Alexandria quotes from three

---

[74] E. v. Dobschütz (*Die evangelische Theologie* [Halle, 1927], p. 9) already suspected, without giving more specific reason for it, a collection coming from Asia and consisting of Eph.-Col.-Philemon. In the Codex Claromontanus, with Marcion, and in other manuscripts, Col. follows Eph.

[75] Is it accidental that the Johannine collection of epistles, like the collection of Eph.-Col.-Philemon, contains in order a circular letter, a congregational letter, and a personal letter? E. J. Goodspeed (*New Solutions*, pp. 36, 44) thinks not.

epistles of Valentinus;[76] the three-gospel canon of Papias may also be recalled, which may well have been assembled as such around 130/150 in Asia Minor (A. v. Harnack, [3], pp. 48-49), as well as the Gnostic canon which is attested by Pistis Sophia 42 ff. A. v. Harnack ([3], p. 57) with good reason infers a Roman collection of three apocalypses: the Apocalypse of John; the Apocalypse of Peter; and the Shepherd of Hermas. P[72] contains, alongside extra-New Testament writings, the Epistle of Jude and I and II Peter. Clement of Alexandria composed a trilogy: Protrepticus, Paedogogus, and Stromateis. The number three, which has "beginning, middle, and end" (Philo, quis rer. div. haer. 126), symbolizes unity, the whole. It may well be of significance for the evaluation of these two groups of three epistles (i.e., Eph.-Col.-Philemon and I Tim.-II Tim.-Titus) to recognize that they were published as two originally independent collections.[77]

If what has been said is essentially correct, then at the beginning of the Corpus Paulinum stands that anti-Gnostic collection, published in Corinth, of seven epistles editorially constructed out of undoubtedly genuine writings. This collection is nowhere handed down to us in its original form. It was first expanded by a collection of three Pauline epistles (Eph.-Col.-Philemon) which at first circulated independently. For a long time the position of these three within the other epistles remained uncertain. The collection of ten epistles which arose thus is attested to us, for example, by P[46].[78] Later this corpus now embracing these ten

---

[76] Harnack, [1], p. 71, n. 11.

[77] J. Knox attempted to prove that the earliest collection of the Pauline epistles had begun with Eph., which the other epistles followed in order of length. On this, cf. his studies cited in n. 28. Nothing in our reflections has yielded even an indication in favor of this thesis. It has no basis in the tradition; cf. C. H. Buck, p. 357. Of course Knox's reflections might well have some value for the smaller collection Eph.-Col.-Philemon. The same is true of Goodspeed's studies cited in n. 28, in which Onesimus is supposed to be shown as the author of Eph., which he supposedly wrote for an introduction to the collection of (all) the epistles of Paul which he published. Certainly Eph. (without an addresss) introduced the *small* collection! To consider this is not wholly without significance for the understanding of the Ephesian epistle. Cf. further J. Weiss, *Earliest Christianity* (1959), I: 684; W. Hartke, pp. 51 ff.; A. Jülicher, *Einleitung* (1906, 5th and 6th eds.), pp. 123-24, 127; W. Michaelis, [1], pp. 195-96; H. Schlier, *Der Brief an die Epheser* (1958), p. 26; J. Weiss, RGG (1st ed.), III: 2209; C. L. Mitton attempts to publicize in England the thesis of Knox and Goodspeed. In addition, he gives it an independent revision and also provides some corrections.

[78] Besides the seven congregational epistles of Dionysius of Corinth, Eusebius

writings was enlarged with the Pastoral Epistles, which likewise may have been in circulation for a long time as an independent collection. With Hebrews then this collection was finally expanded to 2 x 7 epistles.

Incidentally, the Ignatian epistles also followed the expansion from seven to thirteen epistles. It may be taken as assured that the original Corpus Ignatianum contained the seven epistles which today we regard as genuine. But the longer recension of the Ignatiana, which reaches back at least into the fourth century, contains, in addition to these seven epistles, six more, and thus likewise thirteen epistles!

We also must take a look at Marcion's *Apostolicon*. It contained ten epistles, as Tertullian and Epiphanius agree in telling us. These are the same ten epistles which the church's collection contained before the addition of the Pastoral Epistles. With Marcion the canonical Ephesians bore the heading *ad Laodicenos*.[79]

The arrangement of the Marcionite *Apostolicon*, which may be deduced from Tertullian's running commentary on Marcion's collection in adv. Marc. V, is the following:

> Gal.
> I, II Cor.
> Rom.
> I, II Thess.
> Laod./Eph.
> Col.
> Phil.
> Philemon.

In Haer. XLII, 9.4 and 11.10, Epiphanius twice explicitly enumerates the epistles of Marcion's *Apostolicon* in order. They are the same epistles which were to be deduced from Tertullian,

---

also mentions a personal letter. If the latter belonged to the collection of epistles published by Dionysius himself, but Dionysius counted the nine congregational epistles of Paul as seven epistles as, e.g., the Muratorian Canon did, then he could have taken the second stage of the Corpus Paulinum as a model; for in such an enumeration the corpus of ten contains 7 + 1 epistles.

[79] Tertullian, adv. Marc. V, 17.1.

and the order is also the same except that at the end Philippians and Philemon are transposed.

Herein Epiphanius may well have given the original arrangement,[80] for Col. and Philemon *originally* belong together. It is understandable that the private letter to Philemon could later move to the end of the collection. It belongs there because of its brevity, once it was accepted as an independent unit. But presumably it did not at first represent such an independent unit in the Marcionite canon; for there is much to argue that Philemon originally did not have a Marcionite prologue,[81] but formed a unit with Col. The seven prologues of Gal., Cor., Rom., Thess., Laod.,[82] Col., and Phil. are arranged altogether alike. I and II Cor. and I and II Thess. served at first as units and possessed only *one* prologue for each pair. Separate prologues for II Cor. and II Thess. were added later. The prologue to Philemon matches them; for the structure of these three prologues is distinguished significantly from that of the earlier prologues. Moreover, the prologue to Philemon represents this epistle as having been written from Rome, while the prologue to Col. correctly has the Colossian epistle as written in Ephesus. Thus the original arrangement of the Marcionite Pauline canon is as follows:

> Gal.
> I, II Cor.
> Rom.
> I, II Thess.
> Laod./Eph.
> Col. and Philemon
> Phil.

If, as is to be presumed, I + II Cor., I + II Thess., and Col. + Philemon originally belonged together, then according to the opinion of the Marcionites Paul wrote seven letters to seven churches and, through them, to the whole church.[83] Thus the

---

[80] Cf. J. Knox, *Philemon*, pp. 84 ff.; T. Zahn, I: 623.

[81] J. Knox, *Marcion*, pp. 43-44.

[82] On this, cf. A. v. Harnack, [2], p. 129*. The prologue also in E. Preuschen, *Analecta*, II (1910, 2nd ed.): 85 ff. Cf. P. Corssen in ZNW 10 (1909): 37 ff.

[83] Cf. J. Knox, *Marcion*, pp. 42, 46.

way of numbering them corresponds to that of the anti-Marcionite Muratorian Canon.

It is striking also that in Marcion's canon, Eph., Col., and Philemon stand together.

> Gal.
> I, II Cor.
> Rom.
> I, II Thess.
> Eph., Col., and Philemon
> Phil.

This confirms our judgment that these epistles formed an originally independent collection. If one removes them from the larger collection, there remain the seven epistles of the earliest ecclesiastical collection, and these are—with the understandable pre-positioning of Galatians—apparently arranged according to length:[84] Gal., I Cor., II Cor., Rom., I Thess., II Thess., Phil.

It is certain that this order of the seven epistles is secondary as compared with the church's collection, if one does not wish to dispute the greater age of the ecclesiastical collection which presumably arose in Corinth. Eph. and Col. + Philemon were fitted into the collection of seven epistles in such a way that the order according to length was retained as far as possible. Actually Eph. would have had to stand before I and II Thess. According to Euthalius it contained 312 lines as against 299 for I and II Thess. The fact that Eph. nevertheless comes after I and II Thess. may be an indication of the original independence of the collection which consisted of Eph., Col., and Philemon, which was not entirely to be effaced by the insertion of the collection of three into the collection of seven epistles; for then the arrangement of the smaller collection after I and II Thess. was the most sensible one, if at the same time the order according to length was to be preserved insofar as feasible.[85]

---

[84] Cf. *ibid.*, p. 46; J. Finegan, p. 101.

[85] The Gelasian decree and Victorinus of Pettau (see his work cited in n. 58 above) show how a collection of Paul's epistles would look precisely arranged according to the number of lines: Rom., I Cor., II Cor., Eph., I Thess., II Thess., Gal., Phil., Col., I Tim., II Tim., Titus, Philemon. This arrangement, whereby the second epistle to the same address was understandably left with the first,

It is possible that Marcion's Apostolicon contained ten epistles from the very first. I should rather assume, however, that at first it contained only seven epistles, which later, corresponding to the church's collection, were expanded to include Eph., Col., and Philemon. On this occasion then the seven old Marcionite prologues may have arisen, by which even in the collection of ten epistles the symbolic enumeration of seven units could be preserved.

Either way, Marcion's Apostolicon confirms the judgments reached in the consideration of the church's collection of the letters of Paul.

If what has been said is correct, the earliest collection of Paul's epistles was published deliberately as a collection of *seven* epistles because the number seven underscored the catholicity of the collection. That the collector was interested in this significance of his collection is clearly shown by the catholicizing remark inserted into the beginning of the collection (I Cor. 1:2*b*), that in writing to individual communities Paul has written to all the believers in every place.[86]

Therewith, however, we also find the important motive which led to the editorial conflation of several of the apostle's letters into precisely seven writings: The number seven had to be achieved without incorporating into the collection only parts of the apostle's correspondence available to the collector.

To be sure, it is only the literary judgment concerning the epistles themselves that decides the question whether editorial composite epistles are to be found among the epistles of Paul. The affirmative answer to this question cannot be made dependent upon our being able, either conjecturally or with the force of proof, to discover the motives of the editor. For it would indeed be quite natural if we should be in a position to prove the work of the editors while their motives remained hidden from us.[87] Nevertheless, the question as to these motives naturally remains an interesting and consequential one, and an illuminating

---

of course means nothing for the question of an earlier order (*contra* N. A. Dahl, p. 17).

[86] Cf. Vol. 1, p. 89.

[87] *Contra* W. G. Kümmel, pp. 224-25, n. 2; W. Michaelis (n. 52, above); U. Luz, "Zum Aufbau von Röm. 1-8," ThZ 25 (1969): 161.

answer to this question undoubtedly would add to the convincing force of the foregoing literary analysis.

I have earlier set forth some conjectures about the motives for the individual epistolary composites;[88] at that time I had not yet become aware of the problem of the collection of the epistles. The same inquiry with respect to individual epistles also occupies the attention of G. Bornkamm in connection with II Cor.[89] and Phil.[90] These reflections on individual epistles in any case retain their importance for the question as to the special forms of the individual composite epistles. Yet they hardly explain the undertaking of the editors in general. This may well be true even if the one who published the first collection and the one who edited all the epistles were one and the same person, as J. Müller-Bardorff (p. 601) correctly assumes. This restriction is all the more true if the various composite epistles appeared independent of one another in various places, at various times, from various editors, and for various reasons, as G. Bornkamm attempts to prove. For this would have had to be a curious composition-psychosis, to which Rom., I Cor., II Cor., Phil., I Thess., and II Thess. owe their origin in their present form, independently of one another! Moreover, there are no parallels for such a process.[91] Only in our epistle of Polycarp do we possess, in all likelihood, a composite epistle, but even it may look back to the conflation of the Pauline epistles as a model.

Besides, the reasons which Bornkamm adduces for the composition of individual epistles are hardly adequate. With respect to II Cor., Bornkamm ([1], pp. 24 ff.) refers to a law governing forms of primitive Christian writings, according to which the warning against false teachers frequently occurs at the *end* of parts of writings or the like. Of course there are not fewer but rather more examples of the nonobservance of this law of form—the Philippian epistle is, as a composite epistle, the most obvious example of this—so that even in the other cases we must always ask whether a literary method actually is employed or whether the warning against the false teachers which occurs toward the

---

[88] Cf. above, pp. 77; 238; Vol. 1, pp. 88 ff.
[89] [1], pp. 24 ff.
[90] [3], pp. 192 ff.
[91] Cf. W. G. Kümmel, p. 225.

end is not rather based on substantive reasons in each case. So there remains only the *possibility* that the redactor of II Cor. has placed the "sorrowful epistle" which includes chapters 10–13 at the end of the epistle because he meant therewith to be following a widespread literary *topos*. But that says hardly anything about the reasons for the conflation of II Cor. *in the first place*, particularly since Bornkamm rightly counts four different writings out of which our II Cor. was formed. That the editor who composed II Cor. placed the "sorrowful epistle" at the end thus could easily be explained in the way suggested by Bornkamm. That he composed the epistle only in order to be able to place the "sorrowful epistle" at the end appears to me, on the other hand, not to be an adequate explanation.

According to Bornkamm ([3], pp. 200-201), the Philippian epistle was composed by a different editor. This opinion is a likely one, because in the constructing of Philippians the polemical part of the epistle was not put at the end. But is it true, as Bornkamm writes, that "the only question is why the compiler put epistle A at the end"? The more important question is rather why he undertook the composition *at all*. Bornkamm speaks of this only in a subordinate clause in which the subject is the time "when individual congregations made available to others in the immediate or wider vicinity the apostle's letters addressed to them and to that end combined them into a single letter according to a method that was also common elsewhere" ([3], p. 202). But was this method actually common elsewhere? I would not know where. Of course the method mentioned could have arisen within the communities and become common there. But why did it develop? And who, for example, joined the letter addressed to Ephesus, which is now the sixteenth chapter of Romans, to Rom. 1–15?

This much is clear: the existence of composite epistles in the Corpus Paulinum is adequately explained only if one sees in the editor also the publisher of the first collection who in essence was prompted to do the conflating as a whole by the demands of this his collection of seven epistles, so that these conflations all come from the same hand. Arguing for this conclusion also is the essentially similar method by which all the presently existing epistles were editorially composed.

Of course Bornkamm counters this with the argument that then all the epistles also would have had to be known in the communities and hence also have been used in equal measure. But this would not be true. I Clem., Ign., and Polyc., who know and use individual Pauline epistles, indeed occasionally cite I Cor., but possibly never[92] II Cor.[93] Thus, according to his argument, the two epistles were not published at the same time.

But one must first observe that the thesis that the editor of the epistles was also the publisher of the first Corpus Paulinum does not rule out the possibility that individual letters of the apostle were already in circulation earlier. In Bornkamm's opinion Polyc. 3.2 makes this possibility appear as quite likely for example for Paul's correspondence with Philippi.[94] But then one cannot argue as Bornkamm does, but first the question should be posed, which is hardly to be answered with certainty, whether the individual later writers had before them individual epistles or the collection of Paul's epistles. If it were the former, the preference for individual epistles would be quite natural.

But even if one leaves this point of view out of consideration, Bornkamm can hardly have correctly interpreted the general neglect of II Cor. The *certain* quotations from Paul's epistles in the apostolic fathers mentioned—uncertain ones are found even from II Cor. in abundance—are so scarce that they offer no adequate basis for a n y k i n d of *argumentum e silentio*. Even Phil., for example, is certainly attested only in Polycarp's Philippian epistle, and there it naturally had a favored position; other epistles are just as totally absent as II Cor. That Rom. and I Cor. apparently were used most frequently is understandable from the fact that they stood at the beginning and the end of the roll or of the codex which contained the first collection of the epistles of Paul. Besides, as far as content is concerned, they are the most significant and also the most readily usable writings, which even

---

[92] If—and this is now as always worth considering—the Epistle to Diognetus also belongs to the time of the Apostolic Fathers, II Cor. would also be used (in Diogn. 5) extensively quite early.

[93] [1], pp. 33 ff.; cf. W. Bauer, [1], pp. 216 ff.

[94] [3], p. 200; see above, p. 79, n. 58.

for this reason alone were presumably far more widely distributed in the communities in individual copies than were copies of the Corpus Paulinum as a whole. Conversely, the neglect of II Cor. (still in Irenaeus, who was acquainted with the Corpus Paulinum! See ed. Stieren I, 100.3) which the epistle shared at that time with other parts of the Corpus Paulinum and which marks it even today in the churches, is a consequence of its difficult and "unpractical" content, since it consists almost entirely of an apology on behalf of the Pauline apostolate, and hence also hardly could have been widely distributed, even in individual copies, as other epistles presumably were.

Thus presumably a churchman near the end of the first century, when he proposed for the reasons given and in the form indicated to establish a collection of Paul's epistles, asked the communities in the former missionary territory of the apostle for copies of the epistles still available and then combined these in the fashion described into his collection of seven.[95] Since the epistles of Paul at that time undoubtedly did not yet have canonical status, he was able to use his method without hesitation or contravention. His collection itself then of course had a kind of canonizing effect.[96]

---

[95] It is obvious that the reconstruction of the collection of seven epistles as it has been presented here represents a hypothesis. So long as none of the earliest manuscripts of the Corpus Paulinum is found, so long as one must therefore reconstruct the earliest form of this corpus, *every* attempt to arrive at an answer with respect to our inquiry leads to a hypothetical conclusion. That our conclusion was arrived at in an "arbitrary way," as W. G. Kümmel (p. 225) thinks, of course is convincing to me only if every hypothesis likewise is represented as an act of arbitrariness.

[96] J. Weiss, *Earliest Christianity*, I: 151, already correctly asserts the connection between collecting and editing of the epistles. Cf. also my essay mentioned on p. 214, n. 292.

Bibliography

The works listed here are cited in the text and footnotes only with the authors' names. If an author is represented by more than one work, these are indicated below as [1], [2], [3], and so on. Works used only infrequently are fully identified in the footnotes. My own studies are cited as follows:

The Office of Apostle = *The Office of Apostle in the Early Church;* ET 1969 by John E. Steely of *Das kirchliche Apostelamt,* FRLANT 79, 1961.

Vol. 1 = *Gnosticism in Corinth;* ET 1971 by John E. Steely of *Die Gnosis in Korinth,* 3rd ed., FRLANT 66, 1969.

Vol. 3 = *Paul and James,* SBT 46; ET 1965 by Dorothea M. Barton of *Paulus und Jakobus,* FRLANT 85, 1963.

P. Althaus, *Der Brief an die Römer,* NTD 6, 5th ed., 1946.

H. Appel, *Einleitung in das Neue Testament,* 1922.

F. Barth, *Einleitung in das Neue Testament,* 3rd ed., 1914.

G. Barth, "Matthew's Understanding of the Law," pp. 58-164 in *Tradition and Interpretation in Matthew;* ET 1960 by Percy Scott of *Überlieferung und Auslegung im Matthäusevangelium,* WMANT 1.

W. Bauer, [1], *Orthodoxy and Heresy in Earliest Christianity;* ET 1971, edited by Robert Kraft and Gerhard Krodel, of *Rechtgläubigkeit und Ketzerei im ältesten Christentum,* 2nd ed., 1964.

———— [2], *Wörterbuch zum Neuen Testament,* 5th ed., 1958.

O. Bauernfeind, *Die Apostelgeschichte,* ThHKNT V, 1939.

F. W. Beare, *The Epistle to the Philippians,* 1959.

H. W. Beyer, *Die Apostelgeschichte,* NTD 5, 4th ed., 1947.

Karl J. Bjerkelund, *Parakalo,* 1967.

W. Bornemann, *Die Thessalonicherbriefe,* Meyer's *Kommentar* X, 5th and 6th eds., 1894.

G. Bornkamm, [1], *Die Vorgeschichte des sogenannten zweiten Korintherbriefes,* SAH 1961, 2.

———— [2], "End-expectation and Church in Matthew," pp. 15-57 in *Tradition and Interpretation in Matthew.*

———— [3], "Der Philipperbrief als paulinische Briefsammlung," in

Neotestamentica et Patristica (Supplement to *Novum Testamentum* VI), 1962, pp. 192 ff.

W. Bousset, in *Die Schriften des Neuen Testaments* II, 2nd ed., 1908.

R. Bultmann, [1], *Exegetische Probleme des zweiten Korintherbriefes,* Uppsala, 1947.

——— [2], *Theology of the New Testament;* ET 1951, 1955 by Kendrick Grobel of *Theologie des Neuen Testaments.*

——— [3], *The History of the Synoptic Tradition;* ET 1968, rev. ed., by John Marsh of *Die Geschichte der synoptischen Tradition,* FRLANT 29.

——— [4], "Zur Auslegung von Gal. 2, 15-18," in *Ecclesia semper reformanda,* 1952, pp. 41 ff.

H. J. Cadbury, in *The Beginnings of Christianity* V, 1933.

C. Clemen, *Die Einheitlichkeit der paulinischen Briefe an Hand der bisher mit Bezug auf sie aufgestellten Interpolations- und Compilationshypothesen,* 1894.

H. Conzelmann, *Der Brief an die Kolosser,* NTD 8, 9th ed., 1962.

P. Dalbert, *Die Theologie der hellenistisch-jüdischen Missionsliteratur unter Ausschluss von Philo und Josephus,* 1954.

M. Dibelius, [1], *An die Thessalonicher* I, II; *An die Philipper,* HNT 11, 3rd ed., 1937.

——— [2], *Aufsätze zur Apostelgeschichte,* FRLANT 60, 1951.

E. v. Dobschütz, *Die Thessalonicherbriefe,* Meyer's *Kommentar* X, 7th ed., 1909.

K. G. Eckart, "Der zweite echte Brief des Apostels Paulus an die Thessalonicher," ZThK 58, 1961, pp. 30 ff.

P. Ewald, *Der Brief des Paulus an die Philipper,* 3rd ed., 1917.

P. Feine, *Die Abfassung des Philipperbriefes in Ephesus,* 1916.

W. Foerster, [1], "Die δοκοῦντες in Gal. 2," ZNW 37, 1938, pp. 286 ff.

——— [2], *Neutestamentliche Zeitgeschichte* I, 2nd ed., 1955; II, 1956.

G. Friedrich, *Der Brief an die Philipper,* NTD 8, 9th ed., 1962.

E. Fuchs, "Hermeneutik?" *Theologia Viatorum* 7, 1960, pp. 44 ff.

D. Georgi, *Die Geschichte der Kollekte des Paulus für Jerusalem,* 1965.

J. Gnilka, [1], *Der Philipperbrief,* 1968.

——— [2], "Die antipaulinische Mission in Philippi," *Biblische Zeitschrift* 9, 1965, pp. 258-76.

L. Goppelt, *Christentum und Judentum im ersten und zweiten Jahrhundert,* 1954.

H. Grass, *Ostergeschehen und Osterberichte,* 2nd ed., 1962.

E. Güttgemanns, *Der leidende Apostel und sein Herr,* FRLANT 90, 1966.

W. Hadorn, *Die Abfassung der Thessalonicherbriefe in der Zeit der dritten Missionsreise des Paulus,* 1919.

E. Haenchen, *Die Apostelgeschichte,* Meyer's *Kommentar* II, 10th ed., 1956; 13th ed., 1961.

A. v. Harnack, [1], *Die Briefsammlung des Apostels Paulus,* 1926.

———— [2], *Marcion,* 2nd ed., 1924; reprint 1960.

———— [3], *Beiträge zur Einleitung in das Neue Testament* VI, 1914.

W. Hartke, *Die Sammlung und die älteste Ausgabe der Paulusbriefe,* Diss. Bonn, 1917.

E. Haupt, *Der Brief an die Philipper,* Meyer's *Kommentar* IX, 7th ed., 1902.

E. Hennecke—W. Schneemelcher—R. M. Wilson, *New Testament Apocrypha* I, ET 1961.

P. Hoffmann, *Die Toten in Christus,* NtAbh NF 2, 1966.

K. v. Hofmann, *Der erste und zweite Brief an die Thessalonicher,* 2nd ed., 1869.

H. J. Holtzmann, *Die Apostelgeschichte, Handcommentar zum Neuen Testament* I, 2, 3rd ed., 1901.

O. Holtzmann, *Das Neue Testament* I, II, 1926.

H. Jonas, *Gnosis und spätantiker Geist* I, FRLANT 51, 2nd ed., 1954; II, 1, FRLANT 63, 1954.

A. Jülicher, *Einleitung in das Neue Testament,* 5th and 6th eds., 1906.

E. Käsemann, [1], "Die Legitimität des Apostels," ZNW 41, 1942, pp. 33 ff.

———— [2], *Das wandernde Gottesvolk,* FRLANT 55, 2nd ed., 1957.

G. Klein, [1], review of E. Haenchen, *Die Apostelgeschichte,* in ZKG 68, 1957, pp. 362 ff.

———— [2], *Die zwölf Apostel,* FRLANT 77, 1961.

———— [3], "Gal. 2, 6-9 und die Geschichte der Jerusalemer Urgemeinde," ZThK 57, 1960, pp. 275 ff.

———— [4], "Die Verleugnung des Petrus," ZThK 58, 1961, pp. 285-328.

J. Knox, "A Conjecture as to the Original Status of II Corinthians and II Thessalonians in the Pauline Corpus," JBL LV, 1936, pp. 145-53.

W. G. Kümmel, "Das literarische und geschichtliche Problem des ersten Thessalonicherbriefes," in *Neotestamentica et Patristica,* 1962, pp. 213 ff.

J. Leipoldt—H.-M. Schenke, *Koptisch-gnostische Schriften aus den Papyrus-Codices von Nag-Hamadi,* 1960.

M. Lidzbarski, *Ginza,* 1925.

H. Lietzmann, [1], *An die Korinther*, HNT 9, 4th ed., 1949, with supplements by W. G. Kümmel.

———— [2], *An die Römer*, HNT 8, 4th ed., 1933.

———— [3], *An die Galater*, HNT 10, 3rd ed., 1932.

J. B. Lightfoot, *Saint Paul's Epistle to the Galatians*, 10th ed., 1896.

R. A. Lipsius, in *Handcommentar zum Neuen Testament* II, 2, 2nd ed., 1892.

E. Lohmeyer, *Die Briefe an die Philipper, Kolosser und an Philemon*, Meyer's *Kommentar* IX, 9th ed., 1953.

W. Lueken, in *Die Schriften des Neuen Testaments* II, 2nd ed., 1908.

D. Lührmann, *Das Offenbarungsverständnis bei Paulus und in paulinischen Gemeinden*, WMANT 16, 1965.

W. Lütgert, [1], *Gesetz und Geist*, 1919.

———— [2], *Die Vollkommenen im Philipperbrief und die Enthusiasten in Thessalonich*, 1909.

———— [3], *Freiheitspredigt und Schwarmgeister in Korinth*, 1908.

W. Marxsen, *Introduction to the New Testament; An Approach to Its Problems*, ET 1968 by G. Buswell of *Einleitung in das Neue Testament*, 1963.

W. Michaelis, [1], *Einleitung in das Neue Testament*, 2nd ed., 1954.

———— [2], *Die Gefangenschaft des Paulus in Ephesus*, 1925.

———— [3], *Ergänzungsheft* to [1], 1961.

———— [4], *Der Brief des Paulus an die Philipper*, ThHKNT XI, 1935.

O. Michel, *Der Brief an die Römer*, Meyer's *Kommentar* IV, 10th ed., 1955.

J. Müller-Bardorff, "Zur Frage der literàrischen Einheit des Philipperbriefes," *Wissenschaftliche Zeitschrift der Universität Jena* 7, 1957/58, pp. 591-604.

J. Munck, *Paul and the Salvation of Mankind*, ET 1959 by Frank Clarke of *Paulus und die Heilsgeschichte*, 1954.

A. Oepke, *Der Brief des Paulus an die Galater*, ThHKNT 9, 2nd ed., 1957.

E. Preuschen, *Die Apostelgeschichte*, HNT 4, 1912.

B. Reicke, [1], *Diakonie, Festfreude und Zelos*, Uppsala, 1951.

———— [2], *Glaube und Leben der Urgemeinde*, 1957.

R. Reitzenstein, *Die hellenistichen Mysterienreligionen*, 3rd ed., 1927.

B. Rigaux, *Les Épîtres aux Thessaloniciens, Études bibliques*, 1956.

A. Schlatter, [1], *Die korinthische Theologie*, 1914.

———— [2], *Erläuterungen zum Neuen Testament* II, 4th ed., 1928.

H. Schlier, [1], *Der Brief an die Galater*, Meyer's *Kommentar* VII, 10th ed., 1949.

——— [2], *Der Brief an die Epheser,* 2nd ed., 1958.

P. W. Schmiedel, in *Handcommentar zum Neuen Testament* II, 1, 2nd ed., 1893.

H. J. Schoeps, [1], *Paul: The Theology of the Apostle in the Light of Jewish Religious History,* ET 1961 by Harold Knight of *Paulus,* 1959.

——— [2], *Theologie und Geschichte des Judenchristentums,* 1949.

——— [3], *Urgemeinde, Judenchristentum, Gnosis,* 1956.

——— [4], *Aus frühchristlicher Zeit,* 1950.

P. Schubert, *Form and Function of the Pauline Thanksgivings,* 1939.

W. Schultz, *Dokumente der Gnosis,* 1910.

A. Schweitzer, *The Mysticism of Paul the Apostle,* ET 1931, by William Montgomery of *Die Mystik des Apostels Paulus,* 1930.

F. Sieffert, *Der Brief an die Galater,* Meyer's *Kommentar* VII, 9th ed., 1899.

M. Simon, *St. Stephen and the Hellenists,* 1958.

G. Strecker, *Das Judenchristentum in den Pseudoclementinen,* 1958.

H. E. Tödt, *The Son of Man in the Synoptic Tradition,* ET 1963 by Dorothea M. Barton of *Der Menschensohn in der synoptischen Überlieferung,* 1959.

K. Wegenast, *Das Verständnis der Tradition bei Paulus und in den Deutero-Paulinen,* WMANT 8, 1962.

H. H. Wendt, *Die Apostelgeschichte,* Meyer's *Kommentar* III, 9th ed., 1899.

U. Wilckens, *Die Missionsreden der Apostelgeschichte,* 1961.

G. Wohlenberg, *Erster und zweiter Thessalonicherbrief,* 2nd ed., 1908.

W. Wrede, *Die Echtheit des zweiten Thessalonicherbriefes,* 1903.

T. Zahn, *Introduction to the New Testament,* ET 1909 by J. M. Trout and others of *Einleitung in das Neue Testament* I, 3rd ed., 1906; II, 3rd ed., 1907.